Lecture Notes in Computer Science 14036

Founding Editors

Gerhard Goos
Juris Hartmanis

The series Lecture Notes in Computer Science (LNCS), including its subseries Lecture Notes in Artificial Intelligence (LNAI) and Lecture Notes in Bioinformatics (LNBI), has established itself as a medium for the publication of new developments in computer science and information technology research, teaching, and education.

LNCS enjoys close cooperation with the computer science R & D community, the series counts many renowned academics among its volume editors and paper authors, and collaborates with prestigious societies. Its mission is to serve this international community by providing an invaluable service, mainly focused on the publication of conference and workshop proceedings and postproceedings. LNCS commenced publication in 1973.

Norbert A. Streitz · Shin'ichi Konomi
Editors

Distributed, Ambient and Pervasive Interactions

11th International Conference, DAPI 2023
Held as Part of the 25th HCI International Conference, HCII 2023
Copenhagen, Denmark, July 23–28, 2023
Proceedings, Part I

 Springer

Editors
Norbert A. Streitz
Smart Future Initiative
Frankfurt am Main, Germany

Shin'ichi Konomi
Kyushu University
Fukuoka, Japan

ISSN 0302-9743   ISSN 1611-3349 (electronic)
Lecture Notes in Computer Science
ISBN 978-3-031-34667-5   ISBN 978-3-031-34668-2 (eBook)
https://doi.org/10.1007/978-3-031-34668-2

This Springer imprint is published by the registered company Springer Nature Switzerland AG
The registered company address is: Gewerbestrasse 11, 6330 Cham, Switzerland

Foreword

Human-computer interaction (HCI) is acquiring an ever-increasing scientific and industrial importance, as well as having more impact on people's everyday lives, as an ever-growing number of human activities are progressively moving from the physical to the digital world. This process, which has been ongoing for some time now, was further accelerated during the acute period of the COVID-19 pandemic. The HCI International (HCII) conference series, held annually, aims to respond to the compelling need to advance the exchange of knowledge and research and development efforts on the human aspects of design and use of computing systems.

The 25th International Conference on Human-Computer Interaction, HCI International 2023 (HCII 2023), was held in the emerging post-pandemic era as a 'hybrid' event at the AC Bella Sky Hotel and Bella Center, Copenhagen, Denmark, during July 23–28, 2023. It incorporated the 21 thematic areas and affiliated conferences listed below.

A total of 7472 individuals from academia, research institutes, industry, and government agencies from 85 countries submitted contributions, and 1578 papers and 396 posters were included in the volumes of the proceedings that were published just before the start of the conference, these are listed below. The contributions thoroughly cover the entire field of human-computer interaction, addressing major advances in knowledge and effective use of computers in a variety of application areas. These papers provide academics, researchers, engineers, scientists, practitioners and students with state-of-the-art information on the most recent advances in HCI.

The HCI International (HCII) conference also offers the option of presenting 'Late Breaking Work', and this applies both for papers and posters, with corresponding volumes of proceedings that will be published after the conference. Full papers will be included in the 'HCII 2023 - Late Breaking Work - Papers' volumes of the proceedings to be published in the Springer LNCS series, while 'Poster Extended Abstracts' will be included as short research papers in the 'HCII 2023 - Late Breaking Work - Posters' volumes to be published in the Springer CCIS series.

I would like to thank the Program Board Chairs and the members of the Program Boards of all thematic areas and affiliated conferences for their contribution towards the high scientific quality and overall success of the HCI International 2023 conference. Their manifold support in terms of paper reviewing (single-blind review process, with a minimum of two reviews per submission), session organization and their willingness to act as goodwill ambassadors for the conference is most highly appreciated.

This conference would not have been possible without the continuous and unwavering support and advice of Gavriel Salvendy, founder, General Chair Emeritus, and Scientific Advisor. For his outstanding efforts, I would like to express my sincere appreciation to Abbas Moallem, Communications Chair and Editor of HCI International News.

July 2023   Constantine Stephanidis

HCI International 2023 Thematic Areas and Affiliated Conferences

Thematic Areas

- HCI: Human-Computer Interaction
- HIMI: Human Interface and the Management of Information

Affiliated Conferences

- EPCE: 20th International Conference on Engineering Psychology and Cognitive Ergonomics
- AC: 17th International Conference on Augmented Cognition
- UAHCI: 17th International Conference on Universal Access in Human-Computer Interaction
- CCD: 15th International Conference on Cross-Cultural Design
- SCSM: 15th International Conference on Social Computing and Social Media
- VAMR: 15th International Conference on Virtual, Augmented and Mixed Reality
- DHM: 14th International Conference on Digital Human Modeling and Applications in Health, Safety, Ergonomics and Risk Management
- DUXU: 12th International Conference on Design, User Experience and Usability
- C&C: 11th International Conference on Culture and Computing
- DAPI: 11th International Conference on Distributed, Ambient and Pervasive Interactions
- HCIBGO: 10th International Conference on HCI in Business, Government and Organizations
- LCT: 10th International Conference on Learning and Collaboration Technologies
- ITAP: 9th International Conference on Human Aspects of IT for the Aged Population
- AIS: 5th International Conference on Adaptive Instructional Systems
- HCI-CPT: 5th International Conference on HCI for Cybersecurity, Privacy and Trust
- HCI-Games: 5th International Conference on HCI in Games
- MobiTAS: 5th International Conference on HCI in Mobility, Transport and Automotive Systems
- AI-HCI: 4th International Conference on Artificial Intelligence in HCI
- MOBILE: 4th International Conference on Design, Operation and Evaluation of Mobile Communications

List of Conference Proceedings Volumes Appearing Before the Conference

1. LNCS 14011, Human-Computer Interaction: Part I, edited by Masaaki Kurosu and Ayako Hashizume
2. LNCS 14012, Human-Computer Interaction: Part II, edited by Masaaki Kurosu and Ayako Hashizume
3. LNCS 14013, Human-Computer Interaction: Part III, edited by Masaaki Kurosu and Ayako Hashizume
4. LNCS 14014, Human-Computer Interaction: Part IV, edited by Masaaki Kurosu and Ayako Hashizume
5. LNCS 14015, Human Interface and the Management of Information: Part I, edited by Hirohiko Mori and Yumi Asahi
6. LNCS 14016, Human Interface and the Management of Information: Part II, edited by Hirohiko Mori and Yumi Asahi
7. LNAI 14017, Engineering Psychology and Cognitive Ergonomics: Part I, edited by Don Harris and Wen-Chin Li
8. LNAI 14018, Engineering Psychology and Cognitive Ergonomics: Part II, edited by Don Harris and Wen-Chin Li
9. LNAI 14019, Augmented Cognition, edited by Dylan D. Schmorrow and Cali M. Fidopiastis
10. LNCS 14020, Universal Access in Human-Computer Interaction: Part I, edited by Margherita Antona and Constantine Stephanidis
11. LNCS 14021, Universal Access in Human-Computer Interaction: Part II, edited by Margherita Antona and Constantine Stephanidis
12. LNCS 14022, Cross-Cultural Design: Part I, edited by Pei-Luen Patrick Rau
13. LNCS 14023, Cross-Cultural Design: Part II, edited by Pei-Luen Patrick Rau
14. LNCS 14024, Cross-Cultural Design: Part III, edited by Pei-Luen Patrick Rau
15. LNCS 14025, Social Computing and Social Media: Part I, edited by Adela Coman and Simona Vasilache
16. LNCS 14026, Social Computing and Social Media: Part II, edited by Adela Coman and Simona Vasilache
17. LNCS 14027, Virtual, Augmented and Mixed Reality, edited by Jessie Y. C. Chen and Gino Fragomeni
18. LNCS 14028, Digital Human Modeling and Applications in Health, Safety, Ergonomics and Risk Management: Part I, edited by Vincent G. Duffy
19. LNCS 14029, Digital Human Modeling and Applications in Health, Safety, Ergonomics and Risk Management: Part II, edited by Vincent G. Duffy
20. LNCS 14030, Design, User Experience, and Usability: Part I, edited by Aaron Marcus, Elizabeth Rosenzweig and Marcelo Soares
21. LNCS 14031, Design, User Experience, and Usability: Part II, edited by Aaron Marcus, Elizabeth Rosenzweig and Marcelo Soares

47. CCIS 1836, HCI International 2023 Posters - Part V, edited by Constantine Stephanidis, Margherita Antona, Stavroula Ntoa and Gavriel Salvendy

https://2023.hci.international/proceedings

Preface

The 11th International Conference on Distributed, Ambient and Pervasive Interactions (DAPI 2023), an affiliated conference of the HCI International Conference, provided a forum for interaction and exchanges among researchers, academics, and practitioners in the field of HCI for DAPI environments. The DAPI conference addressed approaches and objectives of information, interaction, and user experience design for DAPI Environments as well as their enabling technologies, methods, and platforms, and relevant application areas.

The DAPI 2023 conference covered topics addressing basic research questions and technology issues in the areas of new modalities, immersive environments, smart devices, etc. On the other hand, there was an increase in more applied papers that cover comprehensive platforms and smart ecosystems addressing the challenges of cyber-physical systems, human-machine networks, public spaces, smart cities, and nature preservation. The application areas also include education, learning, culture, art, music, and interactive installations.

Two volumes of the HCII2023 proceedings are dedicated to this year's edition of the DAPI Conference. The first volume focuses on topics related to designing and evaluating intelligent environments, user experience in intelligent environments, and pervasive data. The second volume focuses on more applied topics related to smart cities and environment preservation, media, art and culture in intelligent environments, and supporting health, learning, work, and everyday life.

Papers of these volumes are included for publication after a minimum of two single–blind reviews from the members of the DAPI Program Board or, in some cases, from members of the Program Boards of other affiliated conferences. We would like to thank all of them for their invaluable contribution, support, and efforts.

July 2023

Norbert A. Streitz
Shin'ichi Konomi

11th International Conference on Distributed, Ambient and Pervasive Interactions (DAPI 2023)

Program Board Chairs: **Norbert A. Streitz,** *Smart Future Initiative, Germany*, and **Shin'ichi Konomi,** *Kyushu University, Japan*

Program Board:

- Pedro Antunes, *University of Lisbon, Portugal*
- Kelvin Joseph Bwalya, *University of Johannesburg, South Africa*
- Morten Fjeld, *Chalmers University of Technology, Sweden*
- Nuno Guimarães, *Instituto Universitário de Lisboa - ISCTE, Portugal*
- Kyungsik Han, *Hanyang University, South Korea*
- Jun Hu, *Eindhoven University of Technology, The Netherlands*
- Eiman Kanjo, *Nottingham Trent University, UK*
- Nicos Komninos, *Aristotle University of Thessaloniki, Greece*
- Maristella Matera, *Politecnico di Milano, Italy*
- H. Patricia McKenna, *AmbientEase/UrbanitiesLab Initiative, Canada*
- Tatsuo Nakajima, *Waseda University, Japan*
- Guochao (Alex) Peng, *Sun Yat-sen University, P.R. China*
- Elaine M. Raybourn, *Sandia National Laboratories, USA*
- Carsten Röcker, *TH OWL, Germany*
- Tomoyo Sasao, *University of Tokyo, Japan*
- Reiner Wichert, *Darmstadt University of Applied Sciences, Germany*
- Chui Yin Wong, *Intel Corporation, Malaysia*
- Woontack Woo, *KAIST, South Korea*
- Takuro Yonezawa, *Nagoya University, Japan*
- Chuang-Wen You, *National Tsing Hua University, Taiwan*

The full list with the Program Board Chairs and the members of the Program Boards of all thematic areas and affiliated conferences of HCII2023 is available online at:

http://www.hci.international/board-members-2023.php

HCI International 2024 Conference

The 26th International Conference on Human-Computer Interaction, HCI International 2024, will be held jointly with the affiliated conferences at the Washington Hilton Hotel, Washington, DC, USA, June 29 – July 4, 2024. It will cover a broad spectrum of themes related to Human-Computer Interaction, including theoretical issues, methods, tools, processes, and case studies in HCI design, as well as novel interaction techniques, interfaces, and applications. The proceedings will be published by Springer. More information will be made available on the conference website: http://2024.hci.international/.

General Chair
Prof. Constantine Stephanidis
University of Crete and ICS-FORTH
Heraklion, Crete, Greece
Email: general_chair@hcii2024.org

https://2024.hci.international/

Contents – Part I

User Experience in Intelligent Environments

Pervasive Data

Contents – Part II

Media, Art and Culture in Intelligent Environments

Supporting Health, Learning, Work and Everyday Life

Designing and Evaluating Intelligent Environments

DeforVerFace: Modular Linear-Deformable Vertical Surface

Takuma Anakubo and Kaori Fujinami(✉)

Daily Life Computing Laboratory, Tokyo University of Agriculture and Technology,
Koganei, Tokyo, Japan
fujinami@cc.tuat.ac.jp
http://tuat-dlcl.org/welcome_en/

Abstract. In recent years, shape change interfaces have been the focus of attention, where novel interaction techniques and application possibilities have been explored through the incorporation of shape change into static objects. In this paper, we focus on the interaction with shape-changing vertical surfaces. Existing work on vertical plane interaction is mainly concerned with visual representation using projection mapping or shape change to present interaction results. We believe that the reason for the limitation of the interaction method is that the vertical surface, such as the wall and the door, is inherently fixed. In this paper, we propose a shape-changing vertical surface that goes beyond mere 2D interaction space, which we call DeforVerFace. DeforVerFace consists of a set of linear deformable elements and modules for sensing the nearby environment. In this paper, we design and implement DeforVerFace and present a user study aimed at understanding the possibilities of a shape-changing vertical surface in our everyday building environment.

Keywords: Shape-changing interface · Interactive surface · Ambient displays

1 Introduction

Human-computer interaction is a vibrant area of study. Shape-changing interfaces, which pursue new interactions by incorporating shape changes in inherently static objects, have attracted much attention. Shape-changing interfaces [1] use shape changes for input and output, allowing more intuitive operation than conventional non-deformable interfaces, as well as more expressiveness through the use of affordances. Research on shape-changing interfaces includes studies using table-type [1], handheld devices [4,6,9], string-like devices [5], and metaphoric objects, e.g., flower to represent the posture of a person [2]. In this paper, we focus on the interaction with shape-changing vertical surfaces. There are studies of interaction using walls as vertical surfaces; however, most of these are visual interactions using projection techniques with walls as screens [8], or using shape changes as a means of expressing information [7,10]. We consider that this is

© The Author(s), under exclusive license to Springer Nature Switzerland AG 2023
N. A. Streitz and S. Konomi (Eds.): HCII 2023, LNCS 14036, pp. 3–12, 2023.
https://doi.org/10.1007/978-3-031-34668-2_1

because vertical surfaces such as walls and doors are inherently fixed, which limits interaction methods. Therefore, we propose deformable vertical surfaces called DeforVerFace to overcome the limitation and enable new interactions with architectural elements. DeforVerFace not only present information by its appearance change, but also react to the change of nearby objects and act on surrounding objects, so that vertical surfaces could go beyond mere two-dimensional surfaces.

The remainder of this paper is organized as follows: Sect. 2 presents the design and implementation of DeforVerFace. A user study was performed to investigate the characteristics of deformable vertical surface in Sect. 3. Finally, Sect. 4 concludes the paper.

2   Design and Prototype Implementation of DeforVerFace

2.1   Taxonomy of Interaction

We define three aspects in the interaction with DeforVerFace:

– Autonomy in deformation
– Presentation through deformation
– Effect of deformation

The *autonomy* aspect represents the trigger of shape change, which corresponds to attributes of *manual* (from user) and *automatic* (from the system). The *presentation* aspect has attributes of *direct* and *indirect*. Direct presentation means that the shape of the surface itself represents some information, whereas indirect presentation acts surrounding environment to communicate with the user. Finally, *inductive* and *restrictive* are the attributes of *effect* aspect. The inductive effect is so-called affordance, and the restrictive effect prevents the user from performing an activity by shape change. By combining the attributes in autonomy aspect with those of presentation and effect aspects, we can obtain eight patterns of interaction as shown in Table 1. Note that we consider that "ManuInduc" hardly exists because manual control of the shape and inductive nature of the shape change are conflicting concepts each other.

Table 1. Aspects and attributes in shape change

		Presentation		Effect	
		Direct	Indirect	Inductive	Restrictive
Autonomy	Automatic	AutoDir	AutoIndir	AutoInduc	AutoRestr
	Manual	ManuDir	ManuIndir	ManuInduc	ManuRestr

2.2   Assumed Interaction with DeforVerFace

We introduce application assumed for interaction with DeforVerFace with mapping to the aspects defined above.

Dynamic Switch that Changes the Position and Size: Conventionally, switches for controlling electronic devices such as room lighting and air conditioning are embedded in the wall, and their position or size is not easy to change. However, the issue can be addressed by deformable vertical surface. For example, when a short child tries to press a switch, the convenience is improved by lowering the switch to a position where the child can reach it (Fig. 1 (a)). By representing a switch with a deformable vertical surface, the affordance of the vertical surface is changed, and the user is induced to perform an action by pressing the switch. Therefore, this example is classified as "ManuInduc". On the other hand, if a switch is deliberately hidden so that it cannot be pressed, this is considered to be "AutoRestr" because the user is being restricted.

Doorknob that Changes the States Depending on Situations: In this example, a door handle created with a deformable vertical surface appears when the user enters a space, and disappears when they are denied access (Fig. 1 (b)). The user may not feel restricted, as this does not explicitly restrict the user's behaviour. By applying this system, a room that only children are not allowed to enter can be realised naturally by moving the position of a doorknob to a place that is out of reach of children. This is another example of "AutoRestr".

Rain Notification by Moving Umbrellas: This is an interaction that notifies the user of weather information, such as a rain forecast, through the shaking or dropping of an umbrella on a deformable vertical surface as the user approaches the front door on a rainy day (Fig. 1 (c)). The user is highly engaged with the content of the message by actually moving a real object associated with rain, rather than receiving information through text messages from a smartphone or other device. This example falls into category "AutoInduc" because the information is presented indirectly using a real object.

Interactive Information Display by Shape: Information is communicated by the change in shape of a deformable vertical surface (Fig. 1 (d)), rather than by a device held by the user, such as a smartphone. It makes use of the high visibility of vertical surfaces like walls. In addition, by making it possible to respond to a notification by touching the deformed vertical surface, it is possible to improve the accessibility of information, for example, by providing detailed information. In contrast to the above third case, this belongs to "AutoDir" because it presents information directly by the deformed shape of the surface itself.

Substitutes for Any Existing Object: For example, when a bookshelf is required in a room, the vertical surface temporarily acts as a bookshelf by deforming like a shelf when the position and size are specified (Fig. 3 (e)). In this example, it is considered to be "AutoInduc" until the bookshelf appears and induces the user to place a book on it, and "AutoRestr" when the book is actually placed on the bookshelf, since it restricts the free fall behaviour of the book.

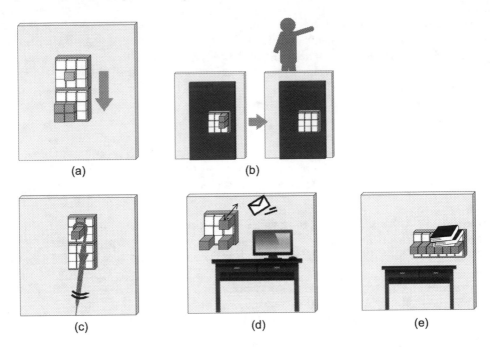

Fig. 1. Assumed interactions with DeforVerFace: (a) dynamic switch, (b) doorknob with dynamic restriction, (c) rain notification by actuated umbrella, (d) information display by shape, and (e) ad-hoc bookshelf.

Note that all of the above are *automatic* cases, where the deformation is triggered by the environment; however, if the deformation is triggered by explicit instructions from the user, the presentation and effect attributes corresponding to "manual" in the *autonomous* aspect are assigned, such as "ManuDir" and "ManuRestr".

2.3 Prototype System

Figure 2 shows the functional and hardware components in the prototype DeforVerFace system; a unit of deformable surface consists of 2×2 independently expanding and contracting elements (linear actuator) to generate concave or convex. To respond to the user's touch, a force sensitive resistor (FSR) was placed on the surface of each block. Infrared (IR) distance sensors were also placed on each edge to detect the user's approach from a distance of approximately 70 cm. They are also used to detect the direction of movement up, down, left or right by combining the inputs from two sensors.

Furthermore, each unit can communicate each other to realize large deformable surface (Fig. 3), in which four units are connected to an aggregation node via Bluetooth (b), and the aggregation nodes also communicates each other over Bluetooth including a user's terminal (c). An aggregation node can be a microcontroller without rich user interface; in the prototype system, we used smart phone terminals as aggregation nodes. We assume that the vertical and horizontal positional relationships between adjacent nodes, as well as a set of four units managed by one aggregator, are pre-registered at the time of installation into wall. Application-specific settings, such as actuation rules and patterns, are also assumed to be specified by a user's terminal and stored on the memory of ArduinoMega.

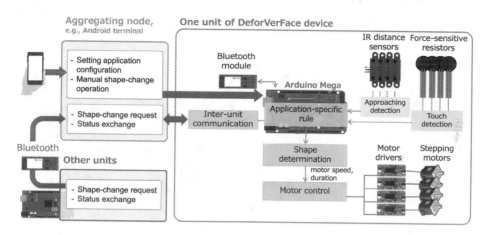

Fig. 2. Major functional and hardware components in the DeforVerFace system.

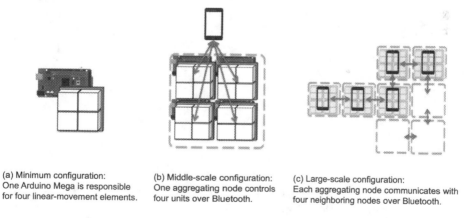

(a) Minimum configuration: One Arduino Mega is responsible for four linear-movement elements.

(b) Middle-scale configuration: One aggregating node controls four units over Bluetooth.

(c) Large-scale configuration: Each aggregating node communicates with four neighboring nodes over Bluetooth.

Fig. 3. Configuration of DeforVerFace.

To realize linear actuation, we applied the mechanism proposed by Iwata et al. [3] as a reference. A stepper motor turns a bolt and moves the nut up and down, causing the block itself, which is coupled to the nut, to move up and down (Fig. 4 (a)). Linear actuation was assumed to be able to follow the user's hand movement speed, expanding and contracting at 1 cm/s. The speed of expansion and contraction is determined by the speed of the motor and the pitch of the screw (distance between threads), but the commercially available screws (M4; 0.7 mm pitch) were not fast enough. Hence, the pitch was set to 8 mm and, after some trial and error, a bolt and nut were 3D printed; the diameter of the bolt was set at 8 mm for robustness. Each motor (Pololu, SY28STH32-0674A) is controlled by ArduinoMega via a stepper motor driver EasyDriver. The maximum deformation distance was 7.2 cm, and the deformation speed at fastest (one block is operated) and slowest (nine blocks were operated simultaneously) were 3.02 cm/s and 1.40 cm/s, respectively (Fig. 4 (b)).

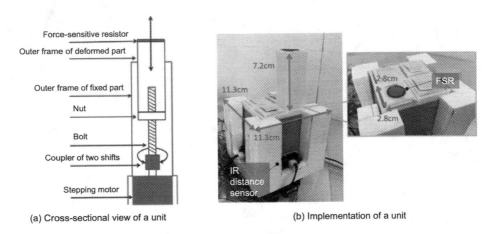

(a) Cross-sectional view of a unit   (b) Implementation of a unit

Fig. 4. Prototype of DeforVerFace system.

3   Experiment

An evaluation was carried out to understand the characteristics of deformable vertical surface realized by DeforVerFace.

3.1   Method

Ten university students (8 males and 2 females) participated, in which the participant compared the information presentation by DeforVerFace and wall-projection to assess the effectiveness of shape-changing in three aspects and attributes from Table 1:

- 1) Direct presentation of remaining time of a task
- 2) Indirect presentation of weather condition
- 3) Inductive effect of a protrusion as a touchable object (switch)

For the case 1), a "timer" that represents the remaining time of 30 s with the height of the protrusion on the wall (DeforVerFace) or the length of the projected bar (Projector) (Fig. 5 (a)). This is categorized in "AutoDir" because the shape itself indicates the information, i.e., the remaining time. The case 2) is indirect presentation of weather condition (Fig. 5 (b)), which is a concrete example introduced in Sect. 2.2 as an example of "AutoInduc". The projection-based presentation was realized by blinking the area around the umbrella. In these cases, the participants viewed the display from a total of nine different positions and orientations: from the front of the unit, 45° to the left of the front, 90° to the left of the front, and at three different distances (50 cm, 100 cm and 200 cm) from the unit. Finally, in case 3), a protrusion appeared randomly while the participant was working on a computer at a desk. He/she was asked to touch the top of the protrusion as soon as he/she noticed it (Fig. 5 (c)). This case was intended to realize "AutoInduc". A red rectangle was projected on the wall in the projection condition.

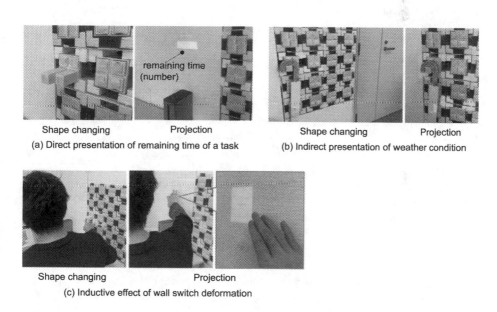

Fig. 5. Three types of shape changing and projection interface in the experiment. (Color figure online)

Participants wore headphones and listened to music to cancel out the noise of the stepper motors in all cases. In the case of DeforVerFace, only two units were actually implemented, while other units were dummy units, with the printed appearance of the front view of DeforVerFace pasted onto styrofoam board, to give the user the impression that a large area of the wall was DeforVerFace-enabled. Additionally, in the case of projection, experiments were carried out in two patterns: with the room lighting on and off, because the brightness of the room has a major impact on the visibility of information. After experiencing the interaction modes, the participants were asked about their impressions. The order in which the participants experienced the three cases was counterbalanced.

3.2   Result and Discussion

Direct Information Presentation Through Shape Visualization: The fact that there were opinions that "the size of the presented information can be understood intuitively from the size of the deformation" when using DeforVer-Face compared to the projection display suggests that the deformation is more intuitive for understanding the presented information (remaining time). On the other hand, there were also opinions that "detailed information cannot be obtained" and "it is possible to express a short time by deformation, but it is difficult to understand changes in a long time" as characteristics of information presentation by deformation. This suggests that, compared to the presentation of numerical values by projection, information presented by deformation is not suitable for presenting detailed information or information that changes slowly.

We asked the participants about the preference for the information presented with DeforVerFace. They replied that it was information that indicated whether the device was in a particular state or not, such as "the end of a process performed by an appliance such as a washing machine or microwave oven", "the humidifier is out of water", or "the light bulb is out". Relative information was also preferred, such as "information about having gained or lost weight". These responses support the above findings from the comparison of the "remaining time presentation" in DeforVerFace and projection.

Furthermore, as described in Sect. 3.1, the information was provided with nine combination of viewing angle and distance. There was no mention of differences due to distance with regard to the deformation method and the projection method. On the other hand, opinions were obtained about the characteristics of the angle, such as: "the information could be seen from a flat angle (almost parallel to the wall surface), but it was difficult to see from the front" (deformation version), "the information could not be seen from a flat angle" (projection version), and "it was easier to see from the front than with deformation" (projection version). Therefore, for example, when information is presented to a person moving parallel to a wall in a train station, we consider it easier for the person to notice if the information is deformed rather than projected or printed directly onto the wall. Furthermore, combine the two methods would achieve a synergistic effect; in the example of a timer displaying remaining time, it is conceivable to first make the user aware and get an overview of the remaining time by using deformation, which is considered easy to perceive, and then provide detailed information by projecting numerical information around.

Indirect Information Presentation Through Actuation on Surrounding Objects: Eight out of nine participants preferred the actuated type (DeforVer-Face) in the case 2) experiment, in which the rain forecast was communicated by actuating or projecting flashing patterns on umbrellas. The reasons given were "the deformable type was easier to notice because the real object moves in three dimensions", "there were shiny objects in everyday life, but the movement of a real object was unusual and striking", and "the whole umbrella changed in the deformable type, whereas only a part of the umbrella changed in the projection type, so it was dynamic and striking". The three-dimensional, large movements and unusual changes caused by the movement of a real object are thought to be the underlying factors. This suggests that advertising can be more eye-catching using DeforVerFace instead of a projector or monitor.

Interesting comments were made by the participants who preferred DeforVer-Face: "I felt that the wall wanted me to hold the umbrella", "The wall told me with its movement that I had to hold it" and "I thought it was cute that it was swinging". This is an indication that the participants had the same feeling towards the wall and the umbrella as they had towards living creatures; this is because the walls themselves move, i.e., change shape, and makes them feel as if the walls are anthropomorphic, and thus they may have some biological feeling towards the walls.

In terms of the viewing angle, similar to the experiment in case 1), the deformable type seemed to be better at flat viewing angles and the projector at frontal viewing angles.

Interaction with Inductive Elements in the Environments: In the case 3) experiment, the ease of inducing behaviour from the presentation of "switch-like" stimuli was investigated, which was performed by changing the shape or projection. Feedback from participants indicated that, as in the previous two cases, the deformable version was easier to find when viewed from flat viewing angles, whereas the projected version was easier to find when viewed from the frontal angles. Participants also insisted that the deformable version provided a clearer sense of touch than the projected version.

4   Conclusion

In this study, we proposed a modular system DeforVerFace that realizes deformable vertical surface and validated the concept by comparing non-deformable surface employing projection-based interface. The result revealed the characteristics of the interaction with shape-changing vertical surface and possibility of applications: 1) the presentation of information by deformation was suitable for intuitively communicating a rough amount of change, not for presenting detailed information such as numerical values; 2) the information presented by making the surrounding objects move through deformation could draw more attention than the information presentation by projection; 3) tangible switches using deformations could provide more concrete feedback to the user than switches using projection with touch detection. The actual installation does not need to be full scale from the beginning, although there are issues such as supplying high power for motor control and reducing weight; the modular architecture of DeforVerFace allows scaling of vertical surfaces within a building by specifying the installation location and area as required.

References

1. Follmer, S., Leithinger, D., Olwal, A., Hogge, A., Ishii, H.: inFORM: dynamic physical affordances and constraints through shape and object actuation. In: Proceedings of the 26th Annual ACM Symposium on User Interface Software and Technology, pp. 417–426. ACM, New York, October 2013. https://doi.org/10.1145/2501988.2502032
2. Hong, J.K., Song, S., Cho, J., Bianchi, A.: Better posture awareness through flower-shaped ambient avatar. In: Proceedings of the Ninth International Conference on Tangible, Embedded, and Embodied Interaction, pp. 337–340. ACM, New York, January 2015. https://doi.org/10.1145/2677199.2680575
3. Iwata, H., Yano, H., Nakaizumi, F., Kawamura, R.: Project FEELEX: adding haptic surface to graphics. In: Proceedings of the 28th Annual Conference on Computer Graphics and Interactive Techniques, pp. 469–476. ACM, New York, August 2001. https://doi.org/10.1145/383259.383314
4. Jang, S., Kim, L.H., Tanner, K., Ishii, H., Follmer, S.: Haptic edge display for mobile tactile interaction. In: Proceedings of the 2016 CHI Conference on Human Factors in Computing Systems, pp. 3706–3716. ACM, New York, May 2016. https://doi.org/10.1145/2858036.2858264
5. Nakagaki, K., Follmer, S., Ishii, H.: LineFORM: actuated Curve Interfaces for Display, Interaction, and Constraint. In: Proceedings of the 28th Annual ACM Symposium on User Interface Software and Technology - UIST '15 (2015). https://doi.org/10.1145/2807442.2807452
6. Park, J., Park, Y.W., Nam, T.J.: Wrigglo: shape-changing peripheral for interpersonal mobile communication. In: Proceedings of the 32nd Annual ACM Conference on Human Factors in Computing Systems (2014). https://doi.org/10.1145/2556288.2557166
7. Rydarowski, A., Samanci, O., Mazalek, A.: Murmur: kinetic relief sculpture, multi-sensory display, listening machine. In: Proceedings of the 2nd International Conference on Tangible and Embedded Interaction, pp. 231–238. ACM, New York, February 2008. https://doi.org/10.1145/1347390.1347442, https://dl.acm.org/doi/10.1145/1347390.1347442
8. Shoemaker, G., Tang, A., Booth, K.S.: Shadow reaching: a new perspective on interaction for large displays. In: Proceedings of the 20th Annual ACM Symposium on User Interface Software and Technology, pp. 53–56. ACM, New York, October 2007. https://doi.org/10.1145/1294211.1294221
9. Strohmeier, P., Carrascal, J.P., Cheng, B., Meban, M., Vertegaal, R.: An evaluation of shape changes for conveying emotions. In: Proceedings of the 2016 CHI Conference on Human Factors in Computing Systems - CHI '16, pp. 3781–3792. ACM Press, New York (2016). https://doi.org/10.1145/2858036.2858537, http://dl.acm.org/citation.cfm?doid=2858036.2858537
10. Yu, B., Bongers, N., van Asseldonk, A., Hu, J., Funk, M., Feijs, L.: LivingSurface: biofeedback through shape-changing display. In: Proceedings of the TEI '16: Tenth International Conference on Tangible, Embedded, and Embodied Interaction, pp. 168–175. ACM, New York, February 2016. https://doi.org/10.1145/2839462.2839469

User-Developer Interaction in a Living Lab: A Case Study of an Exercise Support System for the Elderly

Fujian Ding$^{(\boxtimes)}$ and Momoko Nakatani

School of Engineering, Tokyo Institute of Technology, 4259-G2-5, Nagatsuta-cho, Midori-ku, Yokohama-shi 226-8503, Japan
`ding.f.ab@m.titech.ac.jp`

Abstract. It is difficult to effectively co-create a system used by the elderly over a long period because the elderly and the developers change along with the system improvements made during long-term co-creation. We analyzed the changes that occurred during long-term co-creation using the development of an exercise support system for the elderly as a case study. We held three workshops and interviewed users and developers several times over six months. After qualitatively analyzing the transcript of workshops, we found evidence that even the elderly who are digitally challenged can provide ample interesting feedback to an ICT system. We also found that long-term participants are more likely to help develop the system. So, as a result, we recommend developers to co-design the product with target users even in the prototyping phase.

Keywords: Participatory design · Seniors · Living labs

1 Introduction

It is not easy to design digital devices for the elderly because they have various physical, psychological, and cognitive differences. Furthermost, most human-computer system interfaces for general use have been designed, either deliberately or by default, for a "typical" younger user [1–4], and young designers often have difficulty in creating appropriate technology for the elderly [1].

The first half of the 20th century was an age of manufacturing in which "product quality" was of great importance. After that, we passed through the Age of Distribution, in which distribution networks were developed, and the Age of Information, which emphasized increased consumer recognition. We then entered the Age of the Customer, in which the development of distribution networks and the spread of the internet from about 2010 began to emphasize customer experience [5]. As more importance is placed on better user experience in business, rather than just product specifications, S-D logic (service-dominant logic) has become the focus of attention. Service design, born out of this historical background, is becoming more generalized as an approach linked to human-centered design and design thinking.

N. A. Streitz and S. Konomi (Eds.): HCII 2023, LNCS 14036, pp. 13–28, 2023.
https://doi.org/10.1007/978-3-031-34668-2_2

In design thinking, being user-centered is important; developers, end-users, and related stakeholders must co-create to develop better user experiences with products or services [6]. Many good ideas for new product development and improvement come from end users [7]. By co-creating with users, systems, products, and services that are more satisfactory and easier to learn and use can be developed [8].

In particular, living labs (LL), an approach in which users participate in the design process on a long-term basis, have attracted much attention in recent years [9–11]. The process of living labs encompasses profound learning opportunities for developers and users, bringing high value to both parties and leading to good product development [12]. However, co-creating over an extended period requires considerable cost and cooperation with many parties. As a result, many workshops (WSs) that include a user co-creation process end after only one session (e.g., [13, 14]).

User reaction will influence the system's evolution; as users participate in the WS over time and improve the design, much will be learned, and not only the system but also the perceptions of the users and developers will change. Helping the elderly understand the functionality of an unfinished prototype, especially in the early stages of development, will be difficult, making obtaining valuable feedback difficult. The developer must appropriately understand users' reactions and improve the prototype. However, in the early stages of co-creation, the developer's understanding of the elderly may be insufficient, and their perceptions may gradually change. Therefore, this study reports on those changes, using the design of a specific IT device as a case study. Specifically, this study answers the following research questions by investigating the development process of an exercise support system (ESS) for the elderly.

- RQ1. How do elderly people who participate in a system's design process respond to its prototype in its early stages? Is it possible to elicit opinions and suggestions that help the system evolve?
- RQ2. How do the perceptions of developers and older adults change throughout long-term co-creation, and how do these changes help the system evolve?

This study takes an exercise support system (ESS) for the elderly as its subject and reports on this system's actual development process to answer RQ1 and RQ2.

2   Related Work

2.1   Co-creation with Users in Living Labs

In living labs (LLs), end-users actively participate in the service design process over an extended period. LLs differ depending on objectives and design approaches [10, 16, 17]. For example, some LLs aim to solve social problems in a particular city or region [18]. In other cases, LLs have been held to develop new technologies [19]. Because LL research is based on long-term co-creation with users, it requires more direct or indirect communication and collaboration with users than ordinary service design [15]. Therefore, researchers should understand not only service design but also how users change during long-term co-creation. LLs provide positive learning experiences for both users and developers [9], but the content of these experiences and how they change during the development process is unclear. As a case study, we detail the process of conducting repeated workshops. This paper reports the contents of workshops, users' reactions to them, how the system was improved in response to feedback, and how the developers' perceptions changed.

2.2 ICT Design for the Elderly

Regarding physical aspects, chronic illnesses, such as arthritis, impact senior citizens' physical abilities and mobility [25]. On the cognitive side, the elderly often suffer from a reduced attention span when working on complex tasks [24, 25]. Decrements in episodic memory and variances in working memory performance affect problem-solving skills and information processing [24, 26]. Therefore, these situations should be fully understood when designing services and products for the elderly. Particular consideration should be given when designing ICT devices because they have many functions that are not physically visible, making it especially difficult for the elderly to learn how to operate them.

In the case of the development of a mobile healthcare application for the elderly, the service concept was co-created with elderly people unfamiliar with smartphones [11]. The design process is even more challenging when there is an actual prototype device, as both the service concept and the device should be improved. It remains unclear how input from the ideas and opinions of the elderly who understand current prototypes can help in their development. Many researchers have tried to involve the elderly in the design of smartphones and internet technologies [20–22]. Generally, users are regarded as "experts by experience" or experts of their "lifeworld" [27]. Therefore, it is essential to involve the elderly in the design process to generate appropriate ICT designs.

Our study involved elderly people in developing an exercise support system (ESS) as a case study. They were asked to help develop a system that is easy to use and valuable. ESS uses devices highly controlled using AI, which makes it challenging to understand.

3   Method

3.1   Overview of the Design Process

System Improvement Process
The ESS prototypes under development were presented to the users many times in the workshops, leading to repeated improvements. Figure 1 illustrates the process. After the participants experienced the prototype, they provided feedback on their usage, impressions, opinions, and desired features (WS0-3). The developers then improved the prototype based on their feedback (Improvement 1, 2). This cycle was repeated several times.

In a broad sense, the prototype and users (participants) can be viewed as one system in the design process. In other words, the prototype's performance was improved, and the entire experience, including user interaction, was designed through this process. Obtaining feedback from users in the early stages of development is crucial to prevent development rework. However, in the early stages of development, the prototype is quite immature, and it could be difficult for the elderly to understand. The system developers also would not know which of the multiple functions implemented in the prototype should be introduced to the user as essential functions; thus, the explanation to the user may also be lacking, making it difficult to obtain appropriate user feedback. In contrast, if development proceeds with repeated user feedback, the prototype will be refined, users will better understand the system, and user opinions obtained from the workshop will change.

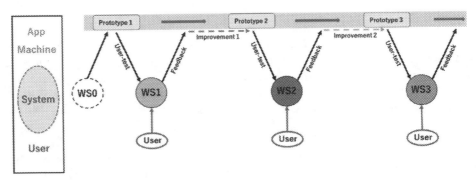

Fig. 1. Overview of system and procedure

This study details how the elderly who had difficulty using digital devices understood the prototypes (Prototype 1–3) in the early stages of development and how the developer improved the system based on their feedback (RQ1). We introduce the design of the workshops (WSs1-3) and report on how participants' and developers' perceptions changed. To answer RQ2, we conducted in-depth interviews with developers and users who participated in the design process multiple times.

Exercise Support System (ESS). The exercise support system (ESS) was developed and improved through the workshops. The system was being developed by WisH Lab, Inc. [28] to promote exercise among the elderly. To support user immersion in exercise, the core concept is a mechanism that changes the playback speed of the video in accordance with users' movement speeds. ESS can be described as a PC-driven application. AI-based techniques capture the left-right movement of an exercising person's head and easily capture the person's walking speed without physical sensors. The video content contains landscapes from around the world, mainly in Japan. For example, there is a video of cycling along a road (Cycling), a video shot from above by a drone (Sky Walk), and a tourism-promotion video. ESS has two main functions: (1) exercise support, a function that immerses people by changing video playback speed while they exercise; and (2) gait measurement, a function that measures a person's walking posture with a camera and displays information such as stride length, walking speed, and posture propriety. Regarding the exercise support function, a quiz function is included to help prevent dementia in the elderly (Fig. 2).

Procedures. To answer the RQs, we qualitatively investigated the process of the workshops. Three workshops were held between August 2022 and January 2023. A detailed schedule is shown in Fig. 3. The workshops were conducted in a community space

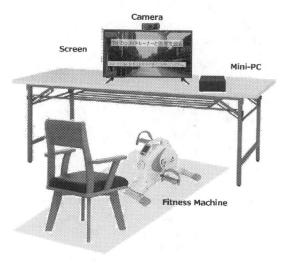

Fig. 2. ESS with the Fitness Machine. The Fitness Machine can be replaced with systems that replicate walking or cycling movements (e.g., cycle trainer).

owned by a nursing station (Fig. 4a) in the Susukino district of Aoba Ward, Yokohama, where the population is aging noticeably. Participants were primarily residents of the surrounding area and were elderly people with no difficulty in walking or exercising. To gather workshop participants, we notified residents by distributing flyers and encouraging them to invite acquaintances. The second and third workshops were designed to be held in conjunction with the smartphone workshops organized by the authors to attract more participants unfamiliar with IT devices. After the workshop, three interviews with developers were conducted. We also interviewed one user for an hour after WS2 to understand the changes in feelings toward the system among those who participated multiple times.

Fig. 3. Schedule of the whole investigation

Workshop. Each workshop was designed to be specific to the development context. All WS remarks were recorded with voice recorders and video cameras. The authors acted as facilitators to facilitate workshop discussions.

The first workshop (WS1) was held for 1.5 h with six elderly participants, primarily to collect first impressions and opinions of using ESS. WS1 consisted of two parts:

experience of the ESS and discussion to improve the ESS. During the experience phase, developers explained and demonstrated the system to participants. Then, participants experienced the gait measurement and exercise support functions. In WS1, a cycle trainer the same size as a bicycle was used as the Fitness Machine. Facilitators wrote down participants' complaints or opinions about the ESS on sticky notes and large sheets of paper. Results are shown in Fig. 4 (second from the left).

WS2 was held in two parts—in the morning and afternoon—with 11 elderly participants and included a smartphone class. Each event lasted 1.5 h, and the smartphone class and the workshop were each 45 min long. The structure of WS2 differed from WS1 because the system had undergone various improvements between the workshops, and the purpose was not only to collect opinions but also to share the improvements with the participants and obtain their reactions. The first 8 min were spent explaining the importance of exercise for the elderly and an overview of dual tasks and the ESS. After approximately 25 min of experience time, the last 15 min were set aside for suggestions about the ESS. An image of this period is shown in Fig. 4 (third from the left).

Fig. 4. Image of nurse station and workshops

WS3 was basically the same as the second, with 12 elderly participants in the morning and afternoon. Unlike WS2, there was no obvious improvement in the ESS in WS3. Since a lot of feedback had already been obtained, we spent some time explaining common previous opinions that we carded and asked participants to evaluate them. The goal was to increase participants' understanding of the system while validating the usefulness of past opinions. An image from WS3 is shown in Fig. 4 (fourth from the left). Cards with illustrations and text describing the functions of the system (Fig. 5) were prepared, and opinions were gathered.

User Interview. To answer RQ2, we interviewed an elderly person who had participated in the WS twice; since there were only two elderly people who had participated twice, we interviewed one of them. The interviews aimed to clarify the following two questions.

(1) After WS2, how had your feelings about participating changed from WS1?
(2) Has your perception of this ESS changed after participating multiple times?

At the beginning of the interview, we asked the participant frankly, "What do you think about ESS?" Then, we presented what she said at the WS and asked her to recall WS. Next, we discussed again the opinions we had obtained and exchanged ideas on how the system could be improved.

Developer Interview. To answer RQ1, we interviewed the developers after each WS. The interview was with three developers and lasted approximately an hour. At first, they talked about their motivation to develop such a product and their painful experiences in product development. The developers had already had experience listening to users' voices in Soka City before WS1. We asked them about the differences between the workshop in Soka City (WS0, in Fig. 1) and the WS in Susukino district (WS1). Finally, we asked the developers what they thought about the feedback they received from the participants. The second interview was with three developers and lasted an hour. It focused on changes in developers' attitudes toward WS. The third interview was with two developers and lasted 25 min. We shared opinions on the relative importance of users' and developers' perspectives.

4 Results

4.1 Data Extracted from Workshops

We classified responses from the WSs into four categories based on the previous study [23]: (1) evaluation of existing functions and tools; (2) proposal of new functions and experiences; (3) post-implementation forecast; and (4) reasons for proposal and evaluation. A summary of the results of WS1 and WS2 is shown in Table 1. As shown in Table 1, a similar number of opinions were obtained on (1) the evaluation of existing functions and (2) the proposal of new functions. However, more feedback on (3) imagining how functions could be used in one's life and (4) reasons for suggestions and evaluation was received in WS2 than in WS1.

WS1. Despite the hands-on experience with a series of functions in WS1, there were many occasions when participants were unable to understand the system. The following transcript is an example of a conversation just after all participants had experienced the ESS and the facilitator (F) posed a question to the participants (P).

F: Where would you like to use this ESS? At home or in a community like here?

P1: I wouldn't do it at home.

F: Why not?

P2: I have time, though.

P3: I think the screen is very beautiful (1), but it's too big.

This is a typical example of the system not being properly understood by participants. This system could be used as long as a camera and a computer are available, and the equipment used as a Fitness Machine does not necessarily have to be a big bicycle. The bicycle was just an example of an exercise method offered to participants; the essence of the ESS was not conveyed to them. Thus, they responded that they did not want to do it at home because of a lack of space (such as for a bicycle) in their homes.

Other elderly participants were dubious about the purpose of the system; they did not understand it. For example, the following statement shows P3 not understanding the system and the participants around him following him.

P3: But I can't get it... If the goal is to exercise, you can increase that load yourself, or the speed of it, so [...]

P2: You can do that, that's…

P3: You can do that, right?

F: You can do that. Yes, I can.

P3: Like keeping it, and then speeding it up, and so on.

F: If you can't do that, then what's the point?

P3: I don't understand, that's what exercise is for in the first place, right?

In contrast, participants who correctly understood the system provided useful feedback for development. However, as shown in the following examples, there were often situations where opinions were divided among participants.

P1: This is quite a personal opinion, but I was so shocked when the staff at the nursing home called me by my reception number. So, I don't like it when the system calls my number when measuring my gait…It's my opinion but…. *[categorized as (1) in Table 1]*

F: Ah, I see!

P2: Calling number, it's just because of anonymity, right?

P1: If that's all, yes, yes… If it's just for anonymity reasons, it's OK. In short, we all have our own names, so it's a great shock to treat us by number, but, well…, okay…

P2: But for me, I don't want the system to call me by name. Sorry.

In this way, the feedback was not only about functionality but also about hospitality, and how the ESS interacts with the users.

Other feedback included requests for improved video content and interaction with the device when using gait measurements. Although the ideas about the video content were quite creative, the suggestions collected in WS1 were mostly just impressions of the participants' experiences with the product and general ideas they formed based on their personal preferences.

WS2. WS2 was notable in that participants raised points for improvement in the functionality of ESS and new suggestions that the developers had not envisioned, unlike in WS1. Those who found the exercises boring when doing them at home made this suggestion.

P4: I think it is still boring, so I'd rather watch a TV show and no quiz. *[categorized as (2) in Table 1]*

P5: Quizzes are, well, okay to have, but

P4: Yes, we could do it just to row.

P5: But is it good to exercise while watching a TV show?

The most interesting aspect is that one participant suggested content completely different from that in the video offered by developers.

P4: I hope I can read a novel, though.

F: A novel?

P4: No, no, the system read it out loud. If it could display some pictures or a screen or something according to the novel, that would be interesting. *[categorized as (2) in Table 1]*

P2: Like art or something that isn't usually familiar!

P4: Yes, I would like to be cultured. I'd like to be able to read (listen to) a haiku or something and see the related images.

Table 1. Qualitative data of WS1 and WS2

Category	Num(1)	WS1	Num(2)	WS2
(1) Evaluation of existing functions or tools	10	"Screen transitions that match the speed of motion should be realistic." "I need time to correct my posture before starting the gait measurement."	11	"I'm a little unconvinced by the gait measurement results." "I didn't notice the quiz. But it might be nice to have something like that."
(2) Proposal of new functions and experiences	11	"I would like to be able to send the number of steps to my phone. Because I want to save my steps." "Maybe we can put our own video into the system. We can taste it again"	10	"(Walking posture) Make it easy to see the difference between this time and the previous time." "I like to chat with friends online while exercising (without having to show up)."
(3) Post-implementatio n forecast	1	"It's good to have when you go to the gym or some other facility to do it, even if you have it at home, it's not easy to use it."	8	"Walking outside is fine, but at home, you can do it without being affected by temperature and pollen."
(4) Reasons for proposal/evalu ation	1	"I may get tired of the video patterns over time."	5	"If I put it in my house, it might get dusty. It would be nice to be able to talk with other people. Even if it's only by voice."

(1) Number of responses obtained in WS1   (2) Number of responses obtained in WS2

Listening to readings while exercising is creative. Moreover, some participants imagined how they would do it at home.

P5: I think it shouldn't be put in my house. It will be dusty because I think I won't do it alone.

P2: If I can do it while chatting or something, I might be more willing to do it at home. *[categorized as (2) in Table 1]*

P5: Yes, that's right. That's a good idea. Women prefer to chat with other women.

F: Do you mind showing your face?

P2: I don't care about the face. Umm, if I am at home, I'd be doing it in my pajamas *[categorized as (4) in Table 1]*.

Some participants developed clear purposes for using the ESS. One participant, a man who could do Kyudo, tried to validate his own walking style. Kyudo practitioners are required to walk such that the body's center of gravity does not shift up and down when moving forward. The participant wanted to see his gait measurement results from intentionally walking with Kyudo posture.

In WS2, participants made useful remarks based on a correct understanding of the system. Overall, it can be said that the data acquired was clearly richer than in WS1. Moreover, as Table 1 shows, there was a marked increase in the number of statements about using the functions in daily life and statements about the reasons for proposing the function.

WS3. WS3 helped the developers prioritize opinions and suggestions obtained in previous workshops. Further, new opinions collected were useful for developers (e.g., "If an AI character appears on the screen and interacts with the user, it will motivate the user to exercise"). Another example of meaningful feedback is shown below:

P6: I think it will be interesting to be able to change the posture and load while pedaling the bicycle (uphill or downhill), to see how the load changes by itself. I don't think it is interesting to adjust it beforehand.

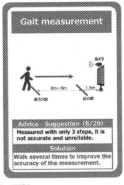

* Japanese cards were used in WS3

Fig. 5. Sample cards used in WS3

The participants did not merely express their likes and dislikes about ESS but also consciously sought to provide feedback to make it interesting, fully understanding the concept of ESS to immerse people in the exercise. The following is an example of such feedback.

P6: Yes. I don't have a clear goal yet for how I'm going to do it. I think it is better to have a goal. Like how many steps I'm going to walk with this, if I set a goal of 10,000 steps, yes, I'm going to do my best to achieve it. You better make a monthly or weekly goal!

Setting goals may make users feel a sense of accomplishment or obligation, which may encourage them to exercise. These statements show that the participants fully understood that the application was designed to facilitate long-term exercise.

4.2   Changes in Application Design in Response to User Feedback

The ESS gradually improved in response to user feedback. In the first improvement after WS1 (Improvement 1 in Fig. 1), modifications were made considering that the purpose and essence of the application were not communicated to the elderly. For example, the processing speed of the program was improved to help users understand that their movement controls the video speed. In addition to functionality, other aspects were also improved. For example, exercise equipment was downsized for WS2. It became clear in WS1 that the equipment's size was an important component of the user experience. We also modified the graphs of gait measurement results, which were difficult for users to understand.

Improvement 2 mainly involved operational modifications. WS2 users offered various novel ideas, many of which were expensive to develop and difficult to implement immediately, so modifications are ongoing.

User feedback was not limited to ESS functions. As a new idea, video content played during exercise was not necessarily prepared only by the developer but also by the users because they want to collect the videos by themselves. In other words, not only the direction of increasing the sophistication of application functions and content but also the direction of incorporating users as part of the system was born through co-creation with the users.

4.3   Voice of User Who Participated Several Times

Differences between WS2 and WS1 were described in an interview with a participant who attended both workshops:

P: The participants were different between the workshops. I just thought the bikes were smaller, so maybe a little improved, but the distance of the walking measurement was the same, wasn't it?

While improvements in response to user feedback (e.g., downsizing exercise equipment) were well received, the participant also noted that issues she had raised had not improved. She also pointed out that she didn't understand ESS well in WS1:

P: There were a lot of things I didn't understand at the beginning, you know.

Although it was difficult for her to understand the new IT device, repeated participation improved her understanding. She also provided constructive suggestions that the target users of ESS should be refined.

P: You should narrow down the target audience a little more. (snip) Probably as I get into my 80s and 90s, I will be gradually losing my footing. It would be more effective to target such people. Healthy people can go out without the system.

She also provided other constructive feedback about improving systems. For example, "It would be easier to see the difference if the standard pattern of walking posture and the pattern of measurement results were displayed in different colors;" "It would be nice if the interface were simplified and as convenient as possible so that you can do what you want by pressing once;" and "Since I am an elderly person, it is great to exercise while watching shows or favorite actors I have watched in the past." These comments and feedback suggested that those who participated more than once were more interested in the system.

When we asked her if she was happy to see her opinion reflected in the system's evolution, we received an unexpected answer.

P: It wasn't just one participant, you know. We all had the same kind of opinion. So, it means that we are all thinking the same thing, not just my opinion, so I am not delighted about the fact that my opinion was reflected.

Indeed, there were often suggestions that all participants supported. We also asked her how her perception of ESS had changed.

P: I have a feeling that I hope the system will get better to a level where it doesn't matter where you put them out. I hope it will be something that you will not be ashamed of because I know that all the members (developers) are working very hard.

Participating multiple times and being partially involved in the system's development increased user support for its development.

4.4   Benefits of Repeated User Feedback from the Developers' Perspective

The developers are experts in image processing. They aim to create a system related to exercise support using their unique technology. However, they were unsure how to convert the technology into a product that users would accept and hoped to improve it by listening to user feedback. For example, developer (D) stated the following:

D: When I first experimented alone in my room, I saw only one face on the screen for face detection, and (snip) I thought, "Oh, it worked!" and then I took it to Soka (user community), but there were many people behind me, and when different people raised hands, it happened to react! Because there were a number of faces, [the face detection] reacted with different faces.

Improved flaw detection is an obvious advantage of user co-creation, but the developers also mentioned the benefits of co-creating with the elderly multiple times and in different settings. In the workshop conducted by the developer in Soka City (WS0) prior to WS1, there were significant differences in the characteristics of elderly participants. Compared to WS0 participants, WS1-3 participants were healthier but had fewer social relationships. As a result, the developers felt that they received more critical remarks from the participants than in WS0.

D: I was surprised when I went there in August (WS1). What surprised me was that everyone in Susukino was already in good spirits, and the users were so different. They said some pretty tough things to me. They were the kind of people who originally go to training machines and gyms, so I thought, well, they are a different target group.

The new points raised by different communities in WS1 helped developers reconsider the concept of the product and its target users. To improve the results of the gait measurement, which participants in WS1 characterized as difficult to understand, the developers reviewed relevant literature.

D: I began to question whether I was communicating correctly, so I started referring to walking books published by sports manufacturers. I looked into it […] When I gave such a diagram, it was certainly easier to understand than in WS1.

The advantage of conducting both WS0 and WS1 was that developers could obtain input from different user groups. However, developers also felt they benefited from repeated user co-creation in the same location.

D: We worked in the same place [for WS1, WS2, and WS3], so […] we could compare [responses] like "It was bad last time, and much better this time." If we didn't do it in the same place, it would be blurred and other parameters would come into play, but we repeatedly did it in the same place […] I am grateful for that.

The developers also saw the benefit of getting up-to-date feedback each time they improved a feature, but they ignored the repeated participation of the same users.

D: (To those who participated last time) If there was a definite change, I would like to ask [participants] about how it changed […] But in the workshops, I noticed later that the same person came last time! I was too busy doing demonstrations.

5 Discussion

5.1 Helping Participants Understand the System and Elicit Useful Opinions (RQ1)

It was challenging for the elderly to understand the essence of the functionality of the application being developed; in WS1, the objectives of the system were not communicated to participants. The feedback received was not related to the system's functionality.

However, the developers felt that this user feedback was useful. In response to WS1, developers made many improvements.

Insight into how to effectively help the elderly understand the system can be found in the significant differences in the feedback obtained from WS1 and WS2-3. Unlike WS1, WS2 and WS3 involved additional explanations about the essence of the past user feedback and improvements which might have helped participants better understand the discussions. The explanations were about the importance of lower limb exercise and the improvements made in response to previous workshops. By explaining system improvements, the points that the developers focused on were communicated to the participants, which might encourage them to realistically imagine using the system in their daily lives. Moreover, explaining system improvements allowed developers to obtain more of the feedback they sought. In WS3, each of the functions that had been proposed was explained using cards shown in Fig. 5, which may have attracted the participants' attention because the important points were prominently explained. To communicate the essence of the system to the elderly, it may be effective not only to have them experience the prototype that has already been implemented but also to use such tools and to widely present multiple proposed functions to solicit their feedback.

5.2 Benefits of Long-Term Design with the Elderly (RQ2)

The type of feedback received during WS2 varied more than those received during WS1. In WS2, there were significantly more reasons for forecasts and suggestions after implementing new features. User understanding of ESS also increased in WS2. In the Workshop, as mentioned earlier, explanations to participants were refined, but through repeated user co-creation, the ESS evolved into an elderly-friendly system.

Users who could participate in more than one workshop showed (1) better understanding of the system, (2) greater ability to offer rational feedback, and (3) greater willingness to help the system evolve.

These findings suggest that conducting a living lab consisting of multiple workshops over an extended period allows for the collection of diverse data but requires careful consideration of collection methods; Asking users' opinions on the subject of different living labs helped to clarify the target users and refine the concept of the system. However, focusing on a specific living lab and repeatedly holding workshops allows for focusing on a specific target user group. Thus, changes can be observed without being distracted by different factors, leading to consistent system improvements. For example, one can filter out personal preferences, making it easier to find opinions that are more important to the target users. This could lead to more user-friendly and attractive product designs for older adults.

5.3 Limitations

After conducting this study for six months, several limitations prevented the experiment from proceeding as expected. Firstly, because of the small number of participants who could participate multiple times, it was not possible to interview enough repeat participants to thoroughly investigate long-term changes in participants during the living lab. Another limitation is that because we could hold only one workshop once in a while, few people could experience the system. Preparing a system that would allow more people to experience it would allow for collecting more diverse data.

We plan to leave the ESS in the community for an extended period and prepare an environment where the surrounding residents can easily experience it at any time. In addition, a mechanism should be in place to collect users' opinions even when the ESS is left unattended for an extended period.

6 Conclusion

Involving the elderly in the development of ICT services on a long-term basis has significant benefits. This study focused on a particular system, ESS, and detailed the process of refining it in a living lab. Even if participants did not initially understand the essence of the system, the developers gained insight into how the system should be communicated to users, which they used to refine the concept. Although communicating the essence of the system to the elderly was challenging, we showed that workshop design, tools, and repeated WS sessions helped improve user understanding. Long-term participants could more significantly contribute to the development of the system. We plan to collect feedback from more long-term participants to establish guidelines for obtaining useful feedback.

References

1. Gregor, P., Newell, A.F., Zajicek, M.: Designing for dynamic diversity: interfaces for older people. In: Proceedings of the Fifth International ACM Conference on Assistive Technologies (Assets 2002), pp. 151–156. Association for Computing Machinery, New York, NY, USA (2002). https://doi.org/10.1145/638249.638277
2. Newell, A.F.: Extra-ordinary human computer operation. In: Edwards, A.D.N. (ed.) Extra-Ordinary Human-Computer Interactions. Cambridge University Press (1995)
3. Newell, A.F., Gregor, P.: Human computer interfaces for people with disabilities. In: Helander, M., Landauer, T.K., Prabhu, P. (eds.) Handbook of Human-Computer Interaction, pp. 813–824. Elsevier Science BV (1997). ISBN 0 444 81862 6
4. Newell, A.F., Cairns, A.Y.: Designing for extraordinary users. Ergon. Des. **1**, 10–16 (1993)
5. 長谷川 敦士, サービスデザインの時代: 顧客価値に基づくこれからの事業開発アプローチ, 情報管理, **59**巻(7)号, 441–448 (2016)
6. Stickdorn, M., Schneider, J.: This is Service Design Thinking: Basics, Tools, Cases, p. 26
7. Von Hippel, E.: Lead users: a source of novel product concepts. Manag. Sci. **32**(7), 791–805 (1986)
8. Joyce, K., Williamson, J., Mamo, L.: Technology, science and ageism: an examination of three patterns of discrimination. Indian J. Gerontol. **21**, 110–127 (2007)
9. Bergvall-Kåreborn, B., Stahlbrost, A.: Living Lab: an open and citizen-centric approach for innovation. Int. J. Innov. Reg. Dev. **1**(4), 356–370 (2009)
10. Hossain, M., Leminen, S., Westerlundd, M.: A systematic review of living lab literature. J. Clean. Prod. **213**, 976–988 (2018)
11. Schuurman, D., De Marez, L., Ballon, O.: Living Labs: a systematic literature review. In: Proceedings of the Open Living Lab Days (2015)
12. Nakatani, M., Nakane, A., Akasaka, F., Ishii, Y., Watanabe, M.: Potential of the dialogue in the living lab: case study on "Service Lab for Nurturing." Trans. Hum. Interf. Soc. **21**(4), 391–404 (2019)

13. Davidson, J.L., Jensen, C.: Participatory design with older adults: an analysis of creativity in the design of mobile healthcare applications. In: Proceedings of the 9th ACM Conference on Creativity & Cognition (C&C 2013), pp. 114–123. Association for Computing Machinery, New York, NY, USA (2013)

14. Kanstrup, A.M., Bertelsen, P.: Bringing new voices to design of exercise technology: participatory design with vulnerable young adults. In: Proceedings of the 14th Participatory Design Conference: Full Papers - Volume 1 (PDC 2016), pp. 121–130. Association for Computing Machinery, New York, NY, USA (2016)

15. Akasaka, F., Yasuoka, M., Nakatani, M., Kimura, A., Ihara, M.: Patterns for Living Lab practice: describing key know-how to promote service co-creation with users. Int. J. Autom. Technol. **14**巻(5号), 769–778 (2020)

16. Leminen, S., Westerlund, M., Nyström, A.G.: Living Labs as open-innovation networks. Tech. Innov. Mgmt. Rev. **2**(9), 6–11 (2012)

17. Schuurman, D., Mahr, D., De Marez, L., Ballon, P.: A fourfold typology of living labs: an empirical investigation amongst the ENoLL community. In: International Conference on Engineering, Technology and Innovation (ICE) & IEEE International Technology Management Conference, pp. 1–11 (2013)

18. Emilson, A., Hillgren, P.A., Seravalli, A.: Designing in the neighborhood: beyond (and in the shadow of) creative communities, Chap. 3. In: Making Futures: Marginal Notes on Innovation, Design, and Democracy, pp. 35–61. The MIT Press (2014)

19. Castelli, N., Ogonowski, C., Jakobi, T., Stein, M., Stevens, G., Wulf, V.: What happened in my home?: An end-user development approach for smart home data visualization. In: Proceedings of the CHI 2017, pp. 853–866 (2017)

20. Kankainen, A., Lehtinen, V.: Creative personal projects of the elderly as active engagements with interactive media technology. In: Proceedings of the 8th ACM Conference on Creativity and Cognition, pp. 175–184. ACM (2011)

21. Lorenz, A., Mielke, D., Opperman, R., Zahl, L.: Personalized mobile health monitoring for elderly. In: Proceedings of the 9th International Conference on Human Computer Interaction with Mobile Devices and Services, pp. 297–304. ACM (2007)

22. Massimi, M., Baecker, R.M., Wu, M.: Using participatory activities with seniors to critique, build, and evaluate mobile phones. In: Proceedings of the 9th International ACM SIGACCESS Conference on Computers and Accessibility, pp. 155–162. ACM (2007)

23. Aner, K.: Discussion paper on participation and participatory methods in gerontology. Zeitschrift fur Gerontologie und Geriatrie **49**(Suppl. 2), 153–157 (2016)

24. Birren, J.E., Schaie, K.W.: Handbook of the Psychology of Aging. Academic Press, San Diego, CA, USA (2001)

25. Czaja, S.J., Lee, C.C.: Information technology and older adults. In: Sears, A., Jacko, J.A. (eds.) The Human Computer Interaction Handbook. Lawrence Erlbaum Associates, New York, USA (2008)

26. Gamberini, L., Alcaniz, M., Barresi, G., Fabregat, M., Ibanez, F., Prontu, L.: Cognition, technology and games for the elderly: an introduction to ELDERGAMES Project. PsychNology J. **4**(3), 285–308 (2006)

27. Beimborn, M., Kadi, S., Köberer, N., Mühleck, M., Spindler, M.: Focusing on the human: interdisciplinary reflections on ageing and technology. In: Domínguez-Rué, E., Nierling, L. (eds.) Science Studies. Ageing and Technology: Perspectives from the Social Sciences, vol. 9, pp. 311–333. Transcript, Bielefeld (2016)

28. http://wishlab.co.jp/

Human-Computer-Building Interaction: An Integrated Experience of the Digital and Physical Environments

Panharith Ean[✉]

Slalom, New York, NY 10007, USA
eanpanharith@gmail.com

Abstract. The paper discusses the role of human-computer interaction in the context of the built environment. It looks into how technology could be integrated into the three stages of the building life cycle: pre-inhabitant, inhabiting, and post-inhabitant. In each stage, the paper investigates the current relationship between people, technology, and building and how it could be strengthened to have a positive impact on the environment and people. Before inhabitation, the research examines processes around design and construction and how they can be innovated with a collaborative digital platform that leads to automated processes and trackable systems. During inhabitation, the notion of adaptive architecture is discussed with a focus on adaptation to the environment, people, and data. To achieve the circular promise of the building life cycle, in post-inhabitant, the paper explores technology retrofit to revitalize an aging building for better performance. It also discusses material reusability and technology-enabled waste management. Using the framework of building life cycle, the research analyzes through case studies of existing models and their synthesis. The guiding question behind the research is, how might we integrate technology to create a holistic system that improves the built environment throughout its life cycle?

Keywords: Human-machine-building interaction · Human-building interaction · building life-cycle

1 Introduction

The rapid growth in technology, especially in personal devices and smart home systems, changes how we communicate, live, work, and play. It challenges how we build and interact with physical spaces. The recent increase in work/live hybrid causes behavioral and cultural changes that challenge the adaptability of spaces and how they function and accommodate different needs. Climate change demands drastic measures in constructing and operating buildings on a larger scale. Human-computer-building interaction needs to be a holistic system that integrates technology into the built environment and responds and adapts to these different needs.

Today's "smart buildings" are rarely holistically integrated. Digital interaction and physical space are developed as two disparate systems. Touch screens and smart-home devices are foreign objects introduced to activate the physical space. The two systems are not fundamentally designed as one; thus, there is always a discrepancy in the experience and functionality. To fully reach a holistic integration system, the practice of digital interaction and the built environment need to overlap from start to finish and at different levels.

This research investigates the relationship between people, technology, and building. It looks into how technology can be integrated into the built environment throughout its life cycle and how human-computer interaction can be tangible with spatial and cognitive experience, enabling different ways one lives, works, and plays. Through case studies and their synthesis, the paper outlines opportunities in a holistic human-computer-building interaction throughout the three stages of the building life cycle.

2   Building Life Cycle Framework

The American Institute of Architects defines the building life cycle in four phases: material manufacturing, construction, use and maintenance, and end of life [1]. This framework dates to the 1960s, mapping out the relationship between the built environment and the raw materials and energy resources needed for its operation [2]. This paper reconsiders the building life cycle from a user's and inhabitant's point of view into three phases: pre-inhabitant, inhabiting, and post-inhabiting. This allows a close study of the relationship between people, technology, and building.

Pre-inhabitant: innovates design and manufacturing processes that minimize material, time, and effort with a cohesive system that communicates between industry professionals, stakeholders, and end-users. The research examines tools and methods that aid the design and manufacturing processes including integrated Building Information Modeling (BIM), automated construction, and embedded Radio-Frequency Identification (RFID) in fabrication and transportation systems.

Inhabiting: focuses on how technology augments physical spaces to adapt to environmental, societal, and behavioral changes. These changes require the space to be dynamic in its physicality, functional program, and material and energy performance. It also prompts the rethinking of better integrating digital and physical spaces for a seamless experience between the two. This research portion explores how physical spaces can adapt to the surrounding environment, the inhabitant, and data-driven reconfiguration.

Post-inhabitant: enables technology intervention to redefine the building's end of life. The linear tendency of a building's life cycle causes huge concerns with the limited availability of materials and energy. Therefore, bridging the loop between the building's end-of-life and its reusability potential is crucial. What, then, is the role of technology and computer interaction in maintaining and extending the longevity of physical spaces? This research portion focuses on the lens of retrofit, adaptive reuse, and recycling and waste management that bridges the gap between post- and pre-inhabitant and revitalizes its inhabiting capacity.

3 Pre-inhabitant

This stage begins with material manufacturing, design, and construction in the built environment. It goes further back to extracting raw materials from the earth, processing and transporting them to warehouses and construction sites [3]. Design development happens adjacent as a separate workflow that instigates the construction process. The construction process includes the use of power tools and machinery for fabrication and installation [1]. All of these touchpoints, from material extraction to manufacturing, transportation, design, and construction, could be made more efficient to minimize energy, time, and money. Three main technological systems that will be discussed here are the Building Information Modeling (BIM) and its integration with Augmented and Virtual Reality (AR/VR), automated construction, and the implementation of Radio-Frequency Identification (RFID) into fabrication and transportation.

3.1 Building Information Modeling (BIM) and AR/VR

BIM is a "collaborative way for multidisciplinary information storing, sharing, exchanging, and managing throughout the entire building project life cycle" [4]. It is a process of producing three-dimensional work in the digital space and coordinating it with the physical environment. More importantly, it is a management tool that is shared between the many professionals involved in the project. With one collaborative digital model, BIM enables the editing and coordination of different types of information, including visualization for both design and construction purposes, detailed construction, material, equipment quantities, cost estimation, scheduling, fabrication data, and toolpaths [5]. The concept of BIM dates back to the 1970s, with its first software tools coming out in the late 1970s and early 1980s [6]. However, it was not until the early 2000s that 3D computer-aided design (CAD) and BIM were more widely used [5]. One of the early users of BIM is the architecture firm Gehry Partners, known for designing and building complex geometric architecture. 8 Spruce Street project, a 76-story residential tower in New York, exemplifies the power of BIM as a technology enabler for the project's success. The tower facade consists of highly curved 10,500 unique panels [7]. The BIM system and the firm in-house software, CATIA enable precise fabrication and optimization that drive the cost of design and construction to the same price point as a typical flat glass curtain wall.

Layering on BIM with augmented reality (AR) and virtual reality (VR) technologies would further expand the potential of the design and construction. AR allows users to interact with the virtual objects in the physical space: scaling, editing, or repositioning. It also allows users to obtain information about the physical space: measuring the distance, geo-locating, or triggering audio responses. In constructing complex buildings, assembly accuracy can be sharpened with AR technology. For example, in building an intricate pattern brick wall, the University of Tasmania uses Fologram technology to equip construction workers with AR glasses to precisely lay the brick in the designed pattern [8, 9]. Fologram positions the 3D digital model into the physical space and produces real-time layout guidelines for workers to follow. The technology connects the digital design with the actual construction to ensure accurate execution in minimal time.

Integration between BIM and AR/VR technologies enables precise visualization that leads to clear communication, allowing people to see design and construction details instead of interpreting conventional 2D documentation. Seeing and interpreting documentation is a distinction that AR/VR technology can advance. Expanding on the BIM collaboration process, AR/VR's open collaboration capacity, yielding from its precise visualization, enables different teams to view and edit in real-time, a process that would otherwise require back-and-forth communication with a high margin of miscommunication. AR/VR enables the simulations of processes by letting users make different design decisions and observe the outcomes in real-time. A study showed that more decisions were made by seeing the result in VR in an hour than if the process were to be on the field [10]. This cuts down the cost and time that are typically required for physical mockups. With these design changes, the costs relating to change can be updated automatically, aiding decision-making and accurate cost estimation [11]. AR can help visualize the process of assembling different construction elements that correspond with the model in the BIM system [12]. From an on-site worker perspective, it can further aid by providing the precise step-by-step assembly process to minimize safety risks and ensure as-designed accuracy.

3.2 Automated Construction

Robotic and automated manufacturing have already been employed in automobiles, aircraft, electronic, food, and packaging factories. The common thread in these operations is using a robotic system in a controlled environment, doing preassigned repetitive tasks. It is not widely used in the construction process due to the uncertain nature that varies in all construction sites. The robotic system requires a robust "understanding of the geometric, computational, and physical phenomena that underlies the problem" [13]. However, steady development has been made to answer the demand for more efficient and safer construction and assembly processes. Two main processes that could be benefited from an automated system are the construction of different components and the in-situ assembly of parts, which is more challenging. 3D-printed construction, one of the more common methods, utilizes additive manufacturing, printing out different materials from concrete to glass, and steel. Innovations around the nozzle and gantry system allow printing in new materials, more complex forms, and larger scales.

From printing to assembling, Spatial Timber Assemblies, a collaboration between Gramazio Kohler Research, ETH Zurich, and ERNE AG Holzbau, develop a fabrication process that employs multiple robotic arms that not only assemble the timber structure but also saw and drill the timbers to exact specifications. The team is developing "new robotic timber joining techniques to expand the design space of additive digital timber construction" [14, 15]. The design-build is a circular system from a digital model to fabrication and assembly by the robotic arms.

Another research project by MIT's Mediated Matter Group, FIBERBOTS, aims to shift the automated fabrication from the current two manufacturing attributes, fabrication units, and how tailorable the material is [16]. These constraints set limits on the resulting structure in terms of geometric form and the need to predefine the behavior of the fabrication robot that does not allow for on-the-go adjustment in response to the changing nature of the physical world. The FIREBOTS are a swarm of 16 robots designed to autonomously weave fiberglass filaments around themselves and form tubular structures with high strength [17]. Each robot has an inflated silicone membrane covering its main body. The robot attaches itself to a pre-existing structure by inflating its membrane. The storage system on the ground would then supply a "mixture of fiberglass thread and resin" that is "fed through to an extended, winding arm on the robot" [17]. The nozzle of the robot mixes the materials and weaves the "wetted fibre around itself" [17]. When the structure solidifies, the robot deflates itself and moves upwards along its structure, and repeats the process. The use of these smaller multi-robot systems gains the fabrication flexibility that uniaxial fabrication methods like a robotic gantry cannot afford. This method can also scale up and down, from fabricating at a product scale to a large-scale architecture.

Automated construction creates a closed-loop design and construction system. When the design is changed, the fabrication process will adjust accordingly, constantly syncing communication between the designer, the digital model, the robotic system, and the assembled construction. This integration bridges the gap between design and execution, allowing real-time changes and simultaneous feedback communication.

3.3   Radio-Frequency Identification (RFID) Tracking System in Construction

The appeal of Radio-Frequency Identification (RFID) lies in its non-contact wireless system, transferring data via electromagnetic signals, consisting of the RFID tag and reader [18, 19]. Many applications of RFID are used in everyday life, from subway cards to door fobs. In the construction industry, this technology enables tracking of material, machinery, and labor, which will then accumulate cross-referenced data to optimize time, efficiency, and cost, and to also improve labor safety. From a management standpoint, a study outlines how RFID advances construction projects: logistic and supply chain management, inventory, quality assurance, waste management, access control for labor, worker safety, and tracking of machines and tools in operation and maintenance [20].

In the design and construction of the Barclays Center in Brooklyn, SHoP Architects built an integrated data system in BIM during the design development. They developed an iPhone app that tracks the production, transportation, and installation of the 12,000 unique facade steel panels [21]. A barcode is attached to each panel as a tag that transmits data to the app. This allows the architects, engineers, construction managers, and other building consultants to view the update in real-time at every stage. The achievement of this project is the control and management of the building's complex geometry and different aggregate parts.

More recently, a Dutch modular construction company De Meeuw has been implementing RFID-based solutions using Nova RFID Asset Management provided by Aucxis RFID Solutions [22]. De Meeuw is able to track its modules both during on-site installation and off-site assembly. Traditionally, this process has been done manually with serial numbers that were printed and applied to each module. The workers have to find the number and coordinate with the transportation and construction. The RFID system allows this process to be automated, speeding up the installation by 50 percent faster than the typical construction process [22]. Nova RFID Asset Management is an integrated hardware, middleware, and software system that optimizes "tracking & tracing, stock management, inventory, specialized access control, warehouse management, controlling processes etc." [23]. De Meeuw's building modules have two or three passive Ultra High Frequency (UHF) RFID on-metal tags attached. Each tag's distinct ID number is encoded and stored in the software, along with a link to the module's serial number [22]. To build location and status information for the modules, handheld and fixed gateway readers are used to interrogate the tags. Aucxis's middleware would interpret and filter the data and send those to Aucxis's cloud-based software [22]. This system could also be applied to the construction machinery and tools to track their usage, when they are available, and their locations. It would be built into the project time management and scheduling to ensure that each piece of machinery is being used at the right time for the proper function and minimize the amount of space needed on site to store them. It also provides users visibility across different teams.

Another use case of a tracking RFID-like system is to improve the safety of workers, construction workers, truck drivers, and other personnel who might be exposed to a high-risk working environment. Swanholm Tech has developed a wearable safety vest equipped with a machine-learning system from Imagimob [24]. The vest detects the movements of the person in it and alerts the system should they be in critical conditions like falling. The built-in processor analyzes the data of the movement, alerts the individual, and forwards a text message to an authorized manager after a grace period, identifying that the individual is in actual danger. There are three types of alerts that the vest triggers: "one to alert management of a fall, based on sensor analysis via AI; a second to enable manual alerts triggered by workers; and a timer alarm to notify workers if they remain in a hazardous environment beyond a limited time" [25]. The system can be customized to the company's needs and conditions. This unlocks the potential for increasing safety in construction worksites, often requiring extreme caution.

A construction site has many moving parts, from material transportation, machinery, and power tools in use, labor tasks, and the actual assembling and constructing, not to mention non-physical moving parts of communication and management. This presents a significant challenge in controlling and maintaining a safe and cooperative environment. RFID-based solutions aim to regain control with the ability to track, locate, and obtain different information.

4 Inhabiting

This is the broadest stage of the building life cycle, encompassing our daily lives from live, work, and play. It is the stage we are most familiar. Our interactions with the physical environment: our home, offices, schools, gyms, restaurants, and public parks are progressively heightened by the technology inherited in those spaces: smartphones, WiFi, HVAC systems, etc. From the technical standpoint, this phase also considers our day-to-day energy consumption, water use, and general environmental waste [1]. It is imperative, then, that the relationship between technology and physical spaces are complementary to advance the well-being of the surroundings, the planet, and people. How might the built environment adapt to these different changes? Adaptive, responsive, and interactive architecture are topics in the literature that discusses such questions.

Adaptive architecture, as defined in research by Holger Schnädelbach, is "concerned with buildings that are designed to adapt to their environments, their inhabitants and objects as well as those buildings that are entirely driven by internal data" [26]. An important notion here is that physical space cannot remain static in the constant flux of its surroundings. How might this idea of adaptive spaces be more systematic in answering today's pressing questions? It is now more urgent with the climate crisis that demands the recalibration of our energy consumption, the housing crisis that demands better policy and rethinking of ways to construct and retrofit space, and our recent behavioral change with remote work. The paper will discuss adaptive architecture concerning the environment, the inhabitants, and data.

4.1 Responsive Facade

The built environment exists in the larger and ever more complex natural environment. The friction between buildings and natural phenomena elicits immediate responses, especially because the building industry is one of the most polluting industries, consuming effusive energy and producing enormous greenhouse gasses. The building envelope is the layer that draws the boundary between the inside of the building and the outside of the natural environment. It encloses the building's interior and its inhabitants; it is the foremost layer, regulating external forces like weather and noise for internal comfort and safety. With emerging technology and environmental policies, it is also where a lot of environmental responses are taking place: optimized sun-shading to reduce energy consumption, photovoltaic (PV) panels to generate energy and dynamic operable louvers for natural ventilation.

In the extreme heat of Abu Dhabi, the Al Bahar Towers, designed by Aedas Architects, are enclosed with a dynamic facade that responds to the sun movement and in relation to working hours when the building is occupied [27]. The facade is composed of triangular solar screen units that automatically fold and unfold to regulate heat, light, and view [28]. The system reduces solar gain, which minimizes air-conditioning cooling loads; it controls solar glare, visibility and privacy, which reduces artificial lighting needs and corresponds to the user's preference between visibility and privacy.

Combining the idea of a dynamic movable facade panel with solar energy capturing, Svetozarevic et al. developed a dynamic photovoltaic building envelope system. The system optimizes capturing sunlight as the sun moves throughout different seasons while providing shading that regulates heat and view for the building occupants [29]. The facade system comprises smaller PV or mirror panels on the two-axis soft actuator attached to a diamond-grid rod-net structure. The system allows the individual panel to move automatically for energy consumption or in response to user interaction. A user interface enables one to control each panel or different parts of the facade. This solution can accommodate different building functions and user preferences in terms of customizable lighting and view while actively capturing solar energy.

A building envelope is a primary interface mediating between inside and outside. It is often thought of as a literal barrier between the two, thus disengaging external climate and other contexts to enclose the interior space with artificial lighting, heating, and cooling. The consequence of this spikes energy consumption and produces architecture indifferent to its context and people. Shifting from thinking of a building envelope as a barrier to it as a mediator opens a broader conceptual framework that allows technology to intervene in creating an adaptive and responsible architecture within the environment.

4.2   Personalized Spaces

Many advancements have been made to tailor physical spaces to our specific needs. Smaller and localized operations have been commercialized and put into use, like movable partition wall modules, automatic blinds, lighting, and temperature adjustments. These systems are manually or mechanically operated or built into automatic smart home devices. They respond to a user's preferences, whether set to a specific configuration or automatically adjusted to a different time of the day or the different types of room functions. More holistic configurations can be adjusted to the user's physiological data: heart rate, body temperature, respiration, brain activity, etc. [30].

As discussed in the previous section about regulating external weather and environmental forces, here, the research looks inward into interior spaces and the dynamic between users and the heating, ventilation, and air conditioning (HVAC). The HVAC system has a standard configuration in most office buildings and may allow for local customization in a residential building. However, its broad standardization accounts for energy inefficiency and discomfort in indoor climates. A personalized HVAC control system, developed by the Responsive Environments Group at MIT Media Laboratory, responds to various occupants' levels of comfort [31]. The system is composed of four main components. First are portable nodes, equipped as wearable on a user and fixed to an existing room's thermostat and on the exterior of the building. They sense the "local temperature, humidity, light level, and inertial activity level of the user" [31]. Users can also input their comfort scale. The second is a room node, placed inside the room to receive data from the personal nodes. The third is a control node placed on a motorized operable window and the variable-air-volume dampers. The control nodes regulate the opening and closing of their associated mechanical elements. The fourth is the central network hub, a "computer that receives all of the data over ethernet and processes it according to the comfort and control algorithms" [31]. These four types of nodes communicate with each other wirelessly to track user comfort level and location and adjust the appropriate airflow sources.

Reconfiguration of the interior spaces itself can be done manually and mechanically with movable wall systems as seen in most conference rooms. It can also alter the ambient environment of light, audio, and smell. Inhabitants' physiological data could inform and reconfigure the space they are in for a truly personalized experience. It is especially beneficial when this technology is applied in medical spaces and care centers, where the physical environment can alleviate the patient's condition. Overall, it provides a closer relationship between people and the space they are in, creating a synchronized feedback loop that allows the building to perform better for the environment and the inhabitant.

4.3   Data-Driven Digitally Embedded Material

The data-driven design process, as discussed previously in BIM systems and automated construction, provides a foundation for a truly adaptive architecture that can adjust based on a data feedback loop from its surrounding environment, the inhabitants, and objects inside. Today's most common data feedback is to display information, entertainment, or notification. Visual communication is made visible with digital displays in a physical environment. The boundary between what is digital and what is physical is getting thinner as the development of mixed reality (MR), AR, and digitally embedded architectural elements advances. Similarly, physical space configuration with digital inputs has become more common in today's buildings in addition to manual and mechanical alterations.

Digital displays, including building-scale LED screens, are not a novel idea. Despite their increase in size and display quality, they are essentially large screens attached to buildings, be it as a digital banner or as interior interactive way findings. Recent development of LED embedded glass "GLAAM Media Glass" inches closer to seamless digital integration [32]. It is a micro-LED technology embedded into the transparent construction-grade glass, with the capacity for digital display without obstructing views. AR has also become more widely used in everyday life, from social media filters to measuring rooms with smartphones or trying on digital fashion and accessories. But how might fully embedded digital-physical material be? How might data-driven physical reconfiguration happen at a material level?

Manuel Kretzer writes about "information materials" as a distinct type of dynamic material that has the "capability to contain and harvest (digital) information and transform it into physical representation" [33]. Information materials are also based on information technology. "They are artificially created on a symbolic level by combining formerly distinct elements into functional assemblies using digital technologies" [33, 34]. The reconfiguration happens at the material atomic level. Seth Goldstein and Todd Mowry started the Claytronics project, "researching the production of nanoscale computers and robots, referred to as claytronic atoms, or catoms that can form tangible three-dimensional objects that users can interact with" [33, 35]. Goldstein and Mowry believe that this development of programmable matter "will allow us to take a (big) step beyond virtual reality, to synthetic reality, an environment in which all the objects in a user's environment (including the ones inserted by the computer) are physically realized" [36]. Claytronic aims to build 3-Dimensional forms with the aggregation of catoms, which allows the form to be fully dynamic [37]. This promises that information can be communicated with the physical form on the composite level of the material, which means on the building scale, the adaptation of space could be informed by many sets of data. It also implicates the possibility of self-assembly and repair, which is particularly revolutionary at an architectural scale.

Most work in information materials and programmable matter exists in research labs and on a small prototype scale. But it opens up the future possibilities of how architecture could evolve with its surroundings and inhabitants seamlessly. The idea of synthetic reality would allow for entire user interaction between people and building, with technology as the invisible agent existing at the atomic scale.

5 Post-inhabiting

Post-inhabiting is categorized as the building's end of life. From an energy standpoint, it necessitates the energy needed for "building demolition and disposal of materials to landfills," including transportation of those materials and the environmental waste produced [1]. From a technical standpoint, care and maintenance is part of the inhabiting phase. However, the research will discuss here the extension of those activities as well as recycling and reusing, with technology enablement, to elongate the longevity of a building. This is also where the linear framework of the building life cycle is challenged to shift from this being the end to circle back to the stages of inhabiting and constructing. The research will explore retrofitting old buildings, innovations in material reusability, and technology-enabled waste management.

5.1 Retrofitting

Building's average life span, from an operational standpoint assumed by life cycle assessment (LCA), is approximately 50 years [38]. This number varies drastically depending on the building's functions, material, and geography. In many cities, the average building's age is much older than that. For example, the median residential building age in New York City is around 90 years old [39]. This means many of these buildings outdate the policies and technologies that have been developed and used in recent years. A huge undertaking in the building industry is retrofitting old buildings to meet current environmental and living standards. Green retrofit, as defined by the U.S Green Building (USGBC), is "any kind of upgrade at an existing building that is wholly or partially occupied to improve energy and environmental performance, reduce water use, and improve the comfort and quality of the space in terms of natural light, air quality, and noise—all done in a way that it is financially beneficial to the owner" [40, 41]. Combined with technology integration, retrofitting is a prominent solution for extending the building life.

Harvard Center For Green Buildings and Cities worked with an architectural firm Snøhetta in retrofitting a pre-1940 residential house in Cambridge, MA, to be the Center's headquarters [42, 43]. Nine main renovations were made: zero heating and cooling system through underground geothermal wells, thermal energy storage, power production, improved envelope, 100% natural ventilation, 100% daylight autonomy, solar chimney, green roof, rain garden, and landscape. Named HouseZero, the Center's goal is to achieve the following:

1. Almost zero energy required for heating and cooling (No HVAC system)
2. 100% natural ventilation
3. 100% daylight autonomy (No daytime electric light)
4. Zero carbon emissions, including embodied energy in materials [43].

The building functions as a living laboratory with data sensors embedded in each building's component, transmitting those data to the building software's algorithms, which will "prompt the building to adjust, reconfigure, and harmonize its daily operation based on future weather forecasts" [43]. The building computation also studies user behavior, providing a feedback loop for the building to adjust. This retrofit revitalizes a building at the end of life into a newly data-driven space that promotes "energy-efficiency, health, and sustainability" [43].

Incorporating cutting-edge technology with a focus on environmental performance and adaptation to both external context and user behavior, the approach to HouseZero can be replicated. The various renovated systems and components in this project provide a menu of options for other projects to pick and choose what is appropriate, all of which would arrive at the same goal. The goal is to retrofit, care for, and maintain existing buildings instead of demolishing them. HouseZero exemplifies that it does not have to be a new construction to be technologically advanced; it utilizes old structures and equips them with new systems responsive to the environment and people.

5.2 Material Reusability

The potential of information materials and programmable matter, discussed in the inhabiting section, presents vast opportunities in ways that material and architectural elements can be reused. The kits-of-part inherent in the material and more minor building components allows for localized repair, maintenance, and adaptation instead of the entire retrofitting approach. Data information from programmable material can alert the building inhabitant of its performance, age, and necessary repairs. With non-programmable material, AR technology, particularly AR-Simultaneous Localization and Mapping (AR-SLAM), can help achieve a similar data-driven repair and maintenance process [44].

Integrating AR-SLAM with the BIM process during the construction phase would allow complete data control of different building parts throughout the building life cycle and enable appropriate repair or replacement in a more accurate assessment. BIM on its own cannot provide the real-time location of each building part for facility management. This is where AR-SLAM comes in. Markerless AR uses "localization methods to link the virtual world with the real world" [45]. This allows AR to track the locations of hidden mechanical parts and obtains their information. The process enables real-time information updates and location to assess the status of all buildings' hidden components.

Material reusability has been done more manually through the design process by intentionally designing for components to assemble and disassemble. Alternatively, new construction is built by sourcing local salvageable materials, as seen in the work of architects Santiago Cirugeda [46], or Yatin Pandya [47], or the Resource Row housing complex by Lendager Group [48]. Sourcing through old materials to construct new buildings is a circular design approach that could be made more efficient when the different building components can be tracked and identified more robustly. With a material database created with BIM during the design and construction, this information could only benefit the recycling and waste management at the material's end of life. Arup engineering partners with Frener & Reifer, BAM, and the Built Environment Trust demonstrated this design process in the Circular Building for the London Design Festival in 2016. In thinking through a circular economy of supply chain, the manufacturers and Arup's designer input material information using a cloud-based platform that communicates the BIM model with the Circular Building's website [49]. Integrated materials database with BIM system allows complete and transparent information about every part of the building throughout different phases and eventually be able to provide accurate ways to recycle and manage waste properly.

Locating and identifying different construction materials and components is one of the main challenges. Again, the ideal solution would take place at the beginning of the design process by proactively inputting different material data into BIM and distributing those data in an accessible and usable way. However, with existing buildings, AR-based solutions and image recognition, which will be further discussed in the following section, can be deployed to maximize the lifespan of materials and, subsequently, the building.

5.3 Technology-Enabled Waste Management

The construction industry produces around 35% of the total generated waste [50]. The different material composites, including hazardous materials in construction waste, make it difficult to sort for recycling. The disposal of these materials causes further complications of soil, water, and air pollution [51]. As discussed in the previous section, sufficient data accuracy of materials and construction components is foundational to effective waste management. Alternatively, artificial intelligence with image recognition can be one of the key solutions with existing buildings that do not have embedded material data.

The utilization of AI in waste management takes on various functions, from automated waste recognition and sorting to detecting toxic material, optimizing transportation routes, and localizing waste facilities [52]. This would accelerate the collecting, sorting, disposing, and recycling processes drastically. The same principle can be applied to construction waste. An AI model, developed by Na et al., is trained to recognize construction waste by "applying image data augmentation and transfer learning" [53]. The team trained the model with images directly taken at the waste facility and images via web crawling. As a result, the AI model was able to "differentiate between five types of construction waste" which was achieved "through transfer learning of the AI model using segmentation" with improvements that could be made "by developing data quality assessment methods and refinement techniques" [53]. This study shows how AI could be an integrated tool in categorizing complex construction wastes. Outside of the research and into practice, Kuljetusrinki Ltd., an environmental service provider based in Finland, used an AI-automated sorting robot to process construction waste. The robot "scans the waste on the sorting belt by using several sensors"; it recognizes and sorts "almost any material at a speed of 6000 picks per hour" [54]. More importantly, the collected data is used to feed and improve the system through the scanning process.

Creating a building material database as a standard practice shared among different industries and users gives accurate and necessary information for care, dismantling, recycling, and disposal. Additionally, the emergence of artificial intelligence and robust training models assist in sorting and managing waste. From retrofitting to material reuse, lastly, at the definite end of building life, recycling and disposal of construction waste can be streamlined and effectively sorted to ensure maximum recyclability and minimum environmental impact.

6 Discussion

The paper outlines nine technology interventions that could be integrated in each phase of the building life cycle and analyzes the methodologies through case studies ranging from prototypes in research labs to constructed architecture projects. Starting with BIM technology as an all-in-one collaborative platform for all disciplines within the AEC industry and beyond builds a strong foundation for digital data to be assessed and analyzed. A feedback loop is a constant theme throughout the research, and BIM enables this sharing of information across different phases of the building. Automated construction with robotic systems bridges the gap between design and execution and allows for real-time adjustment between the two. The many moving parts of a construction site raise safety, material, and machinery efficiency concerns. Through tracking these different parts with RFID, the site can be a more controlled environment that ensures safety for workers and optimizes the use of different materials and machinery.

As the building enters an inhabiting stage, the research investigates how the spaces can adapt to different parameters, external environments, people's behavior, and data. Innovations in building's facade focus on mediating between the outside and inside to minimize energy consumption through working in the environmental context. A responsive facade with movable panels aims to decrease artificial lighting, cooling, and heating, while maintaining desirable view and natural light. The addition of PV panels further generates energy to compensate for the building's energy consumption. A case on personalized HVAC creates a tailored, comfortable interior environment for the inhabitant while reducing the energy consumed by the standard HVAC. This study also pushes the understanding of reconfiguring space beyond its physicality and considering people's physiological data to change the ambient quality of a space. The research investigates an atomic scale of information material and programmable matter. Even though these materials primarily exist in laboratories still, they promise a synthetic reality - one where the integration of digital information happens at a material atomic level.

In shifting from thinking of the building life cycle as a linear journey that ends in a landfill to thinking of it as an actual circular model, emphasis is put on connecting the post-inhabitant stage back to the inhabitant and pre-inhabitant stages. Retrofitting existing and aging buildings is one of the rising practices in sustainable architecture. Harvard HouseZero, acting as a living laboratory, points to various possible retrofitting components that can be replicated in parts or as a whole. Maintaining, repairing, and reusing certain building parts require understanding the parts' material properties and physical location. AR technology, in particular, AR-SLAM, can be integrated with BIM to locate and identify these parts, especially when they are hidden like the mechanical system. Lastly, when buildings get demolished, better systems need to be in place to sort different materials accurately and effectively for recycling and disposal. With more and more sufficient training models, AI and image recognition can assist and manage this process.

7 Conclusion

The difference in speed between technology and the built environment creates much friction in design and development. This requires an integration system that engages with all phases of the building life cycle. The system needs to be adaptable to different needs and leaves room for technical and social ambiguity. Human-computer-building interaction aims to ensure the well-being of our surroundings, the planet, and ourselves. Mapping the interaction between people, technology, and building into the building's life cycle is a holistic approach seamlessly integrating digital and physical environments. At each touchpoint, there is an opportunity to investigate and improve relationships between different users, the spaces they are engaged in, and the function they are performing. The research affirms that technology integration into the physical space needs to happen even before the space is constructed. Instead of just accessorizing the constructed building with smart devices, technology integration should be implemented through all stages of the building life cycle. Doing so ensures smoother and safer design and construction processes, enhances the living experience, increases material reusability, and minimizes waste. More importantly, this integration shifts the linear operation of buildings ending in landfill, causing environmental harm, to an actual circular relationship where building life can be extended and revitalized.

References

1. Bayer, C., Gamble, M., Gentry, R., Joshi, S.: AIA Guide to Building Life Cycle Assessment in Practice, pp. 48–49 (2010)
2. SAIC: Life Cycle Assessment: Principles & Practice, p. 88. EPA (2006)
3. Guinée, J.B., Huppes, G., Heijungs, R.: Life Cycle Assessment - An Operational Guide to the ISO Standards (2001)
4. Tang, L., Chen, C., Tang, S., Wu, Z., Trofimova, P.: Building Information Modeling and building performance optimization. In: Encyclopedia of Sustainable Technologies, pp. 311–320 (2017). https://doi.org/10.1016/b978-0-12-409548-9.10200-3
5. Shelden, D.: Entrepreneurial practice: new possibilities for a reconfiguring profession. Disruptors: Technol.-Driven Archit.-Entrepreneurs **90**(2), 6–13 (2020). https://doi.org/10.1002/ad.2541
6. Eastman, C., Fisher, D., Lafue, G., Lividini, J., Stoker, D., Yessios, C.: An Outline of the Building Description System. Institute of Physical Planning, Carnegie-Mellon University (1974)
7. Gehry, F., Lloyd, M., Shelden, D.: Empowering design: Gehry Partners, Gehry Technologies and architect-led industry change. Disruptors: Technol.-Driven Archit.-Entrepreneurs **90**(2), 14–23 (2020). https://doi.org/10.1002/ad.2542
8. Franco, J.T.: Assim É construída uma parede de tijolos utilizando realidade aumentada. ArchDaily Brasil (2019). https://www.archdaily.com.br/br/908796/assim-e-construida-uma-parede-de-tijolos-utilizando-realidade-aumentada?ad_medium=gallery. Accessed 03 Feb 2023
9. Fologram (n.d.). https://fologram.com/. Accessed 03 Feb 2023
10. Sacks, R., Gurevich, U., Belaciano, B.: Hybrid discrete event simulation and virtual reality experimental setup for construction management research. J. Comput. Civ. Eng. **29**(1), 04014029 (2015). https://doi.org/10.1061/(asce)cp.1943-5487.0000366
11. Davidson, J., et al.: Integration of VR with BIM to facilitate real-time creation of bill of quantities during the design phase: a proof of concept study. Front. Eng. Manag. **7**(3), 396–403 (2019). https://doi.org/10.1007/s42524-019-0039-y
12. Cuperschmid, A.R., Grachet, M.G., Fabrício, M.M.: Development of an augmented reality environment for the assembly of a precast wood-frame wall using the BIM model. Ambiente Construído **16**(4), 63–78 (2016). https://doi.org/10.1590/s1678-86212016000400105
13. Diankov, R.: Automated Construction of Robotic Manipulation Programs, p. 2. The Robotics Institute Carnegie Mellon University, Pittsburgh (2010)
14. Spatial timber Assemblies: DFAB HOUSE (n.d.). https://dfabhouse.ch/spatial_timber_assemblies/#:~:text=Spatial%20Timber%20Assemblies%20is%20an,the%20level%20of%20structural%20complexity. Accessed 29 Jan 2023
15. Spatial Timber Assemblies: dfab (n.d.). https://dfab.ch/streams/spatial-timber-assemblies. Accessed 29 Jan 2023
16. Kayser, M., et al.: FIBERBOTS: design and digital fabrication of tubular structures using robot swarms. In: Willmann, J., Block, P., Hutter, M., Byrne, K., Schork, T. (eds.) ROBARCH 2018, pp. 285–296. Springer, Cham (2018). https://doi.org/10.1007/978-3-319-92294-2_22

17. Hitti, N.: Neri Oxman's Swarm of Fiberbots Autonomously Build Architectural Structures. Dezeen (2018). https://www.dezeen.com/2018/10/05/neri-oxman-fiberbots-mediated-matter-lab-mit-architectural-structures/#. Accessed 29 Jan 2023
18. Shen, X., Chen, W., Lu, M.: Wireless sensor networks for resources tracking at building construction sites. Tsinghua Sci. Technol. 13(Suppl. 1(0)), 78–83 (2008). https://doi.org/10.1016/S1007-0214(08)70130-5
19. Domdouzis, K., Kumar, B., Anumba, C.: Radio-Frequency Identification (RFID) applications: a brief introduction. Adv. Eng. Inform. 21(4), 350–355 (2007). https://doi.org/10.1016/j.aei.2006.09.001
20. Lu, W., Huang, G.Q., Li, H.: Scenarios for applying RFID technology in construction project management. Autom. Constr. 20(2), 101–106 (2011). https://doi.org/10.1016/j.autcon.2010.09.007
21. Barclays Center: SHoP (n.d.). https://www.shoparc.com/projects/barclays-center/. Accessed 22 Jan 2023
22. Swedberg, C.: Builder tracks housing modules via IoT technology. RFID J. (2022). https://www.rfidjournal.com/builder-tracks-housing-modules-via-iot-technology. Accessed 23 Jan 2023
23. Aucxis: (n.d.). https://www.aucxis.com/en/rfid/rfid-solutions#Nova. Accessed 24 Jan 2023
24. Halfacree, G.: Swanholm Tech's Connected Safety Vest Is a Wearable TinyML Lifesaver. Hackster.io (n.d). https://www.hackster.io/news/swanholm-tech-s-connected-safety-vest-is-a-wearable-tinyml-lifesaver-c472f6ac8d17. Accessed 25 Jan 2023
25. Swedberg, C.: Connected vest protects workers via AI, BLE. RFID J. (2022). https://www.rfidjournal.com/connected-vest-protects-workers-via-ai-ble. Accessed 23 Jan 2023
26. Schnädelbach, H.: Adaptive architecture - a conceptual framework. MediaCity 197, 524 (2010)
27. Cilento, K.: Al Bahar Towers Responsive Facade/Aedas. ArchDaily (2012). https://www.archdaily.com/270592/al-bahar-towers-responsive-facade-aedas. Accessed 04 Feb 2023
28. Karanouh, A., Kerber, E.: Innovations in dynamic architecture. J. Facade Des. Eng. 3(2), 185–221 (2015). https://doi.org/10.3233/fde-150040
29. Svetozarevic, B., Begle, M., Jayathissa, P., et al.: Dynamic photovoltaic building envelopes for adaptive energy and comfort management. Nat. Energy 4, 671–682 (2019). https://doi.org/10.1038/s41560-019-0424-0
30. Schnädelbach, H.: Physiological data in adaptive architecture. In: International Adaptive Architecture (2011)
31. Feldmeier, M., Paradiso, J.A.: Personalized HVAC control system. In: 2010 Internet of Things (IOT) (2010). https://doi.org/10.1109/iot.2010.5678444
32. Wooten, J.: World's First Digital Media and Interactive Glass Building Material Enters U.S. Market. SignShop (2020). https://www.signshop.com/lighting-electric/digital-signage/worlds-first-interactive-glass-building-material/. Accessed 24 Jan 2023
33. Kretzer, M.: Information Materials, pp. 52–53. Springer, Cham (2017). https://doi.org/10.1007/978-3-319-35150-6
34. Bühlmann, V., Hovestadt, L.: Introduction: printed physics. In: Printed Physics, pp. 71–112 (2013)
35. Goldstein, S.C., Campbell, J.D., Mowry, T.C.: Programmable matter. Computer 38(6), 99–101 (2005)
36. Copen, G.S., Mowry, T.C.: Claytronics: an instance of programmable matter. In: Wild and Crazy Ideas Session of ASPLOS (2004)
37. Claytronics: Claytronics - Carnegie Mellon University (n.d.). https://www.cs.cmu.edu/~claytronics/. Accessed 07 Feb 2023
38. Grant, A., Ries, R.: Impact of building service life models on life cycle assessment. Build. Res. Inf. 41(2), 168–186 (2012). https://doi.org/10.1080/09613218.2012.730735

39. Building Ages and Rents in New York. RentHop. https://www.renthop.com/studies/nyc/building-age-and-rents-in-new-york. Accessed 05 Feb 2023
40. Al-Kodmany, K.: Green retrofitting skyscrapers: a review. Buildings **4**(4), 683–710 (2014). https://doi.org/10.3390/buildings4040683
41. Department of Energy (DOE). http://www.energy.gov/. Accessed 05 Feb 2023
42. Future Home: House Zero, a Zero Energy Retrofit. Harvard Center for Green Buildings and Cities (2022). https://harvardcgbc.org/research/housezero/. Accessed 04 Feb 2023
43. Harvard HouseZero: Snøhetta (n.d.). https://snohetta.com/project/413-harvard-housezero. Accessed 04 Feb 2023
44. Schiavi, B., Havard, V., Beddiar, K., Baudry, D.: BIM data flow architecture with AR/VR technologies: use cases in architecture, engineering and construction. Autom. Constr. **134**, 8, Article id 104054 (2022). https://doi.org/10.1016/j.autcon.2021.104054
45. Chen, K., Chen, W., Li, C.T., Cheng, J.C.: A BIM-based location aware AR collaborative framework for facility maintenance management. J. Inf. Technol. Constr. **24**, 360–380 (2019)
46. Recipes for Urban Subversion: Design Indaba (n.d.). https://www.designindaba.com/articles/creative-work/recipes-urban-subversion. Accessed 04 Feb 2023
47. Sundar, N.: Style and Substance, from Waste. The Hindu (2016). https://www.thehindu.com/features/homes-and-gardens/green-living/style-and-substance-from-waste/article8509146.ece. Accessed 04 Feb 2023
48. Resource Rows: Lendager (2022). https://lendager.com/project/resource-rows/#:~:text=What%20if%20we%20simply%20cut,an%20atmosphere%20of%20allotment%20gardens. Accessed 04 Feb 2023
49. Gorgolewski, M.: Resource Salvation: The Architecture of Reuse, p. 57. Wiley, Hoboken (2018)
50. Huang, X., Xu, X.: Legal regulation perspective of eco-efficiency construction waste reduction and utilization. Urban Dev. Stud. **9**, 90–94 (2011)
51. Polat, G., Damci, A., Turkoglu, H., Gurgun, A.P.: Identification of root causes of construction and demolition (C&D) waste: the case of Turkey. Proc. Eng. **196**, 948–955 (2017). https://doi.org/10.1016/j.proeng.2017.08.035
52. Mahendra, S.: Artificial Intelligence in Waste Management. Artificial Intelligence+ (2023). https://www.aiplusinfo.com/blog/artificial-intelligence-in-waste-management/. Accessed 06 Feb 2023
53. Na, S., Heo, S., Han, S., Shin, Y., Lee, M.: Development of an artificial intelligence model to recognise construction waste by applying image data augmentation and transfer learning. Buildings **12**(2), 175 (2022). https://doi.org/10.3390/buildings12020175
54. AI and Autonomous Robot for Waste Management: Construction Technology (2022). https://www.constructiontechnology.media/news/ai-and-autonomous-robot-for-waste-management/8023806.article. Accessed 06 Feb 2023

Living Labs Are the Silver Lining for Creating Sustainable Health and Care for the Future

Peter Julius[1]([✉]), Martin Hannibal[2], and Alexander Weile Klostergaard[1]

[1] Public Intelligence, Billedskærervej 17, 5230 Odense, Denmark
{peter,alexander}@publicintelligence.dk
[2] Department of Business and Management, SDU, Campusvej 55, 5230 Odense, Denmark
mhk@sam.sdu.dk

Abstract. Aging populations and the consequent exponential rise in health care costs are a challenge to many developed societies. This paper provides insights to how the Living Labs methodology can address this challenge by involving citizen insights to drive co-creation innovation processes to secure a sustainable future in the healthcare services. The point of departure for this paper is Public Intelligence' Living Lab methodology, which facilitates sharing knowledge between sectors, domains, and cultural differences. The paper provides evidence from two distinct implementations of the innovation design and compares the processes. The research shows that the Living Lab design is valuable in diverse contexts. Subsequently the paper is concluded by discussing the cross-cultural dissemination of the methodology in relation to prospected internationalization to Japan.

Keywords: Living lab · Design Thinking · Service design · co-creation · smart cities · participatory design · insight-driven healthcare

1 Introduction

Aging populations and rising cost of healthcare and services describe one of many mega trends that have already impacted many developed societies [1–3]. Commentators, professionals, and researchers [4, 5] have identified innovation, increased digitalization and technological developments as means to stifle the increasing workloads and attain efficient use of the limited resources in the healthcare sector [6]. However, this and the technologies and data involved will often drive a radical turn in the business approach for firms in the sector.

This paper introduces a structured framework for innovation which embraces and thrives on shift. The Living Lab methodology has been developed by Public Intelligence (PI) across a decade of intensive work related to the health and care sector and has been used in different settings in Denmark, Japan, United Kingdom, and Germany. The paper will argue that businesses need an innovation methodology based on sustainable value creation with both citizen data and the organization who looks to solve a problem. Living Labs oppose innovation that tends to favor the creative mind. Misconceptions like "I got the idea under the shower" or "Innovation is about getting the right idea and deploying it", illustrate a focus on the creative part and indicate that the idea is the dominant initiator of innovation. Instead, we emphasize an approach that is structured over six phases and many activities to ensure that innovation is not luck but a set of activities that is tailored to meet the challenges at hand.

The paper is structured in chapters including a short overview of the research method, followed by an introduction to the Public Intelligence Living Lab methodology. Subsequently, two different case studies will be presented, and key results will be accounted for and discussed using eight points of view. On this basis concluding remarks are given as well as ideas for future research are proposed.

2   Theory

2.1   Innovation of Health Services

Innovation has proven to be a strong driving force to form new markets and base value networks. Disruptive innovation provides leeway for displacement of established market leading firms through formation of new alliances and by introducing new products and/or service and alliances [7]. Following these seminal thoughts, theories and perspectives on innovation aim to explain how organizations can harness their innovative potential to drive change and achieve breakthroughs in product or service delivery.

Leading research on innovation has emphasized intrinsic motivation and a supportive environment for promoting innovation in industries [8]. Accordingly, innovation in healthcare is the result of a complex interplay between individual factors, such as skills, knowledge, motivation of the service providers, and organizational factors, such as organizational culture, resources, and structure of healthcare organizations. In particular, it is argued that creativity is enhanced when service providers are motivated by a sense of purpose and challenge. This is further amplified when organizational environments support creativity through practices such as fostering autonomy, providing resources and feedback, and encouragement of risk-taking behavior [8].

The role of networks has traditionally been perceived to have strong explanatory power in researching innovation processes [9]. It is argued that knowledge and innovation in industries results from interactions between service providers and communities. This suggests that organizations can promote innovation through creating (new) networks that facilitate knowledge sharing and collaboration [9].

Innovation research highlights the importance of innovation in driving sustainable change in value delivery. The literature suggests that innovation is not exclusively ideation. Innovation also involves translation of these ideas into practical solutions which address complex and pressing challenges in service or product delivery [10]. In following these thoughts this line of literature suggests that organizations can drive sustainable change by promoting innovation through wikicapital eg. the capital arising from networks. This leverages the value created by networks of healthcare providers, organizations, and institutions that are collaborating and sharing knowledge, information, and resources [10].

2.2 Living Labs

Since Living Labs first emerged as a term to describe cooperating partnerships and live field trials [11], they function in different business domains and have developed in many ways. Recent years have brought several endeavors to elaborate on what is a Living Lab and which methods are used to drive new insights and innovation. A literature review has detected a convergence towards areas such as "Aging problem of societies", "Smart cities", "Urban Living Labs", "Overall sustainability", and 80% of the literature on Living Labs have been published since 2015 [12]. Living Labs have also emerged as a specific approach to open innovation processes in the context of publics across the EU, and research has categorized the purpose of Living Labs in three scenarios: *Living Labs for "grand" challenges*, *Living Labs for domain specific challenges* and *Living Labs as citizen-led initiatives targeting public value*. This implies that practitioners need to reflect on what meaning user involvement should have for the final decision-making processes [13].

Finally, by integrating living labs into theories on creativity and innovation, healthcare organizations can create supportive environments that encourage change in health services, foster knowledge sharing and collaboration among relevant stakeholders. Change in public innovation has been identified in three frames in a Living Lab context: *Processual learning, restrained space*, and *democratic engagement* [14]. These frames vary on several parameters such as type of process (incremental, systemic transformative or conceptual innovation), degree of intensity of stakeholder involvement (from low to high) and problem area (mainly local, global, or local-global). To different extent Living Lab drives sustainable change in health and care services according to the purpose of the organization.

3 Methodology

This section presents and discusses the research design of the research study. The study employs a qualitative approach to achieve insights on participants' meanings to facilitate a richer holistic perspective on the Living Lab approach [15, 16]. In addition to the formal interviewing data has been obtained through participant observation inspired by seminal ethnographic research [17, 18]. Hence, two of the authors are integral part of the management team in PI whilst one the CEO have had a leading role in the exemplar case from Harbor Town & Southgate.

Data has been gathered through a period of 21 years. Because of the research designs embedded approach, data has been collected from the inception of each case up until present day. The data composition for each case is unique building on personal records, archival data, internet sources, coffee chats, workshop materials, project meetings, management seminars, etc. This diverse body of materials has supported a richness of data to provide deep insights on the Living Lab methodology [19]. The data has been discussed among the authors to increase reliability and decrease biases throughout the process of analysis. Thus, as an example of this, written sources and interview transcripts have been through a process resembling intercoder reliability checks.

The below Table 1 provides an overview of interviewees and observing participants.

Table 1. Overview of interviewees and observations

Name/Pseudo	Type	Case	Role	Interview Date	Interview Length	Key takeaways
Peter	Internal - PI	E-Health City Harbor Town + The Virtual Nursing Home Southgate	CEO	N/A	N/A	Conducting living labs across private and public sector
Alex	Internal - PI	(E-Health City Harbor Town + The Virtual Nursing Home Southgate)	Consultant	N/A	N/A	Document harvest and elaboration
Berit	Internal – PI	E-Health City Harbor Town + The Virtual Nursing Home Southgate	COO	N/A	N/A	Conducting living labs across private and public sector
Jens	Internal - PI	The Virtual Nursing Home Southgate	Consultant	N/A	N/A	Constructing theoretical background and descriptions
Lene	Internal - PI	E-Health City Harbor Town	Senior Project Manager	N/A	N/A	Managing, planning and recruiting for living lab
Peder	External, University Hospital	E-Health City Harbor Town	Strategic Core Group	31/1/2023	1h 55m	Focus on health created in and through communities, innovation through citizen collaboration
Rolf	External, Municipality	The Virtual Nursing Home Southgate	Director	19/1/2023	4h 00m	Innovation management, strategic fit in the service portfolio
Louise	External, Municipality	The Virtual Nursing Home Southgate	Head of Senior Rehabilitation and Development	25/11/2022	2h 25m	management of concept and organization
Becca	External, Municipality	The Virtual Nursing Home Southgate	Project Coordinator	19/1/2023 25/4/2022	0h 30m 3h 25m	User and employee experience in conceptualization
Claus	External, Municipality	The Virtual Nursing Home Southgate	Analysis Consultant	20/4/2022	1h 20m	Economic assessment of project potential

4 Findings

This section will provide an overview on the two exemplar cases where the living lab methodology has been employed. Before presenting these cases, we will describe the Living Lab methodology and provide a short background about PI.

4.1 Public Intelligence - Living Lab Methodology

Public Intelligence (PI) was founded in 2007 aiming at creating sustainable health and care services through innovation e.g., by bringing healthcare service to the user at their home. Today PI operates primarily as a consultancy firm with 10 full time employees. PI has been specializing in welfare and health service innovation and development with the main office in Odense, Denmark. PI functions in the intersection between the public and private sectors including municipalities/public organizations and private companies.

Sustainability is for PI incorporated in working with the benefit of the triple bottom line (the planet, people, and profit). Sustainability is a central framework for not only environmentally responsible green technology, but also protecting citizens and the workforce and ensuring a world where the business can continue to operate and provide value to clients and stakeholders. A major focus in sustainability is also to ensure that there are good health and welfare services in the years to come.

PI tries to set a sustainable discourse for how we perceive change management in complex systems. The current discourse on innovation (IDEO etc.) presents linear goals of continual improvement of past services and technologies. Linear innovation does not address the issues we have in future societies, where a different view on demographic change and planetary resources defines the requirements for organizations and business.

One of the core services offered by PI is the Living Lab methodology (see Fig. 1 below). In many innovation frameworks users are perceived as important initiators for any innovation process. However, for PI the key initiator is the organization that 'owns' the challenge at hand. For instance, this could be a municipality responsible for services tailored to elderly people or a Japanese insurance company with an interest in delivering a cost-effective quality service or other organizations with something at stake within the health and care sector.

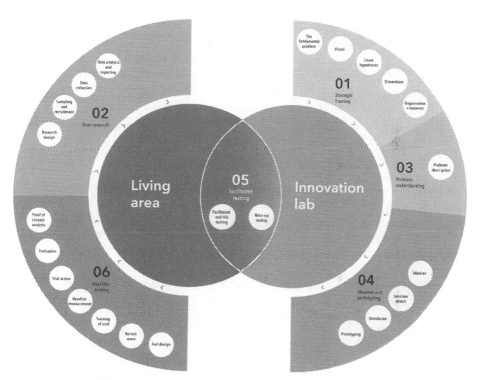

Fig. 1. The Public Intelligence Living Lab Methodology

4.2   Case: Harbor Town - eHealth City

eHealth City Harbor Town, is a public-private-innovation partnership between the municipality, the regional University Hospital (OUH), the regional University of Southern Denmark (SDU) and Public Intelligence (PI). In October 2017 Harbor Town became the world's first user-oriented test city for health services, when eHealth City Harbor Town was launched. The citizens play a key role in developing health and social care services. This Living Lab turns the normal innovation process upside down. Accordingly, citizens' needs provide the starting point of the innovation process instead of taking point of departure in specific technologies or the health sector. In other words, solution health and social care providers citizens co-create tomorrow's solutions starting in the lived experience. eHealth City Harbor Town consists of both a living arena and an innovation-lab.

The living arena comprises 258 households that are representative for the entire town. The innovation-lab is situated in a great hall furnished to incorporate workshops with decision-makers, users and health and care professionals. All four partners pay an annual fee to support the governance of and access to the Living Lab with its living-arena and innovation-lab. For every project conducted in the Living Lab, 5% of the total project funding is paid to support the Living Lab.

The overall project was divided into three stages: Agreement, Establishment and Operations. Because of the cross sectoral focus of the Living Lab, preliminary agreements were needed between the partners. The governance structure was decided along with the business model of the living lab during four meetings with strategic decision makers. The living arena was established through framing and organizing the geographic living-arena to be representative of the city. To this end, socio-economic and health data were compiled with emphasis on criteria based on national health surveys and specific strategic needs of the four partners. Subsequently, letters were sent to all 258 households aiming to engage the citizens in the living lab. The letter described the purpose of the living lab and upcoming activities. To ensure the participation of marginalized citizens, local health and care workers followed up with physical visits accompanied by an innovation consultant.

These two steps were followed up by information meetings. These had the dual purpose to inform the citizens about the living lab and to enlist those with interest in participating more directly in innovation activities. Finally, a survey was distributed focusing on the experienced state of health of each user, their diagnosed illnesses, the number, and characteristic of visits to a health and/or care institution, and their network and relations.

Operations of the living lab could proceed. The first innovation activity of the living lab was the completion of in-depth interviews with a representative sample of users focusing on personal experiences with the health care system and their dreams and ideas. Drawing on this, four strategic visions were created to guide the subsequent innovation process. The four visions were:

- Harbor Town as world leader within prevention
- Health created in and through communities
- No patients with chronic diseases should be hospitalized
- A health and care system which is always accessible

The strategic core group decided to proceed with innovating on the second vision to improve community supported health. Workshops with citizens assisted in co-creating on how citizens could help improve each other's physical, mental and social health. This resulted in 10 trial actions where citizens themselves tried new ways of socializing with a focus on health and care.

Presently and building on the initial steps of the Living Lab University of Southern Denmark and the regional University Hospital has attained national funding to a project on prevention. This project aims to prevent people with chronic illnesses from being hospitalized unnecessarily through testing new innovative health care technologies on socially marginalized first-time parents.

4.3   Case: Southgate - Virtual Nursing Home

The Virtual Nursing Home was administered as a Living Lab from 2019–2021 in collaboration with a rural municipality in Denmark, and by the end of 2021 eight citizens lived in their own homes as an alternative to a traditional nursing home. Over the course of fourteen month Living Lab, various activities were conducted toward five deliverances. The Living Lab worked as means to create a successful solution on the co-creation of nursing homes without beds with multi-stakeholder inputs. These inputs derived from both citizens, employees, and relevant decision makers in the municipality's Adult and Health Service.

The key moments in the development were Contracting, Start-up meeting, Start-up seminar, Phase 1: Core Lab, Phase 2: The opportunities no one knows about, Phase 3: The details that make the difference, Phase 4: Real world testing, Phase 5: The overall solution. The development was followed up by scaling, since The Virtual Nursing Home continued operations, and in 2022 it included sixteen citizens.

The key outcomes were the description of the problem (How can citizens - who today have to go to nursing homes - be given the opportunity to stay longer in their own homes if they wish to do that?), thorough data collection and user research, creation of future scenarios based on ideation, delivering test material, business cases on tests, and creation of a final, comprehensive solution in a cohesive concept including visual elements and a preliminary implementation plan, including expected resource consumption.

The story behind the innovation project is that Southgate, a municipality, assumed the need for increased flexibility for citizens and relatives, the use of new opportunities for employees to create value for the citizens and the benefits of more efficient use of resources for the organization. They sought to make a service for all citizens who wanted to stay in their home as long as possible.

The Virtual Nursing Home was targeting the 15% least care-intensive citizens in nursing homes today and the 5% most care-intensive citizens in home care. Six terms for the target group for the service were discovered: The citizen 1) Has physical and / or cognitive impairment which requires help in nursing homes that home care cannot offer, 2) Wants to stay in their own home rather than going to a nursing home, 3) Wants to manage themselves in their own home, 4) Wants and manages to use technology as their personal helper, as a supplement to the municipality's physical help, 5) Lives in a home where the physical environment allows or can be changed, to enable the citizen to receive the necessary help, while at the same time meeting the legislation for the employees' working environment, 6 Accepts the use of sensor - and GPS – technology.

The foundation of The Virtual Nursing Home is structured around three main pillars: Physical Adoption, Ethical Foundation, and Employee Professional Foundation. These pillars encompass a broader range of considerations, including infrastructure, ethical and regulatory compliance, involvement of residents and their families, and the professional development and attitudes of staff members.

The development of key elements for The Virtual Nursing Home was made in prototyping with citizens and staff. This process resulted in several ideas categorized through three experience perspectives: 1) Experience of presence (Good morning service, virtual eat together service etc.), 2) Experience of short response time (Virtual response within 30 s service, local network as first responders service etc.), and 3) Experience of coordination (Common digital overview service, Daily team coordination morning check-in). Thus, the concept can provide high-quality, personalized care that is enabled by technology, while maintaining a strong focus on the wellbeing and autonomy of residents.

5 Discussion

Below the processual step for implementing the Living Lab in the two cases is compared in relation to eight processual steps. Table 2 describes the two cases and subsequently the distinct steps are discussed in view of similarities and discrepancies.

Table 2. Living Lab – Processual and comparative overview

Processual step	Harbor Town (HT)	Southgate (SG)
Strategic framing to create the fundament and governance needed to move forward	Steering group did a workshop across all participants	Public Intelligence workshop with management
User research as input and triangulation	Insights were formed into 13 general main insights as offspring for innovation	Insights were gathered to gain specific knowledge regarding the problem at hand
Problem understanding and description as the scope for ideation	There was no original problem. HT was built as an innovation engine tailored to a vision	The problem was concrete and centered around capacity building in the organization.
Ideation and prototyping	Process was tailored to fit different problems in the process. Mainly citizen oriented.	The process was tailored to fit the concrete problem. High employer voice in the process.
Facilitated tested in a controlled environment	Peoples were invited to workshops at different locations	The organization created a system for simulation
Test in real life	The prototypes were tested in reality	The prototypes were tested in reality
The importance of organization	The involved organizations (4 in all) participated on equal terms. Cross-organizational collaboration was key for success.	The organization was important as an owner for the process and to implement the new concept.
Creation of value in the quest for a sustainable future	The result was mainly interorganizational learning. The process also gave inputs for further model alterations and adjustments.	The result was the design of a completely new health and care service with high impact

In the first case eHealth City Harbor Town, *wikicapital* arises from networks through the Living Lab by creating a foundation using workshops with all participants, and it created interdisciplinary and interorganizational learning, which provides value in making inputs for future development processes. The citizens play a key role in developing health and social care services, and the project aims to improve community-supported health, prevent people with chronic illnesses from being hospitalized unnecessarily, and create a health and care system that is always accessible. Thus, the project is an example of how smart cities can create sustainable and livable urban environments that enhance the quality of life for their residents by leveraging technology and innovation to provide accessible and inclusive health and care services.

In the second case The Virtual Nursing Home Southgate, *wikicapital* arises through the involvement of citizens, employees, and relevant decision-makers in the municipality's Adult and Health Service in the innovation of homes with multi-stakeholder inputs. The Living Lab was used to create a cohesive concept including visual elements, a preliminary implementation plan, and expected capacity expansion to deliver a comprehensive solution. Furthermore, Virtual Nursing Homes can contribute to the overall sustainability and resilience of Smart Cities by reducing the need for physical infrastructure such as hospitals and nursing homes. This can free up resources for other critical services such as transportation, education, and public safety.

The Living Labs established citizen insights in different contexts. The Virtual Nursing Home Southgate can be described as a *retained space* which resulted in transforming service in health and care with ideation based on a defined problem area. More stakeholders were involved in eHealth City Harbor Town and the type of innovation was radical based on local-global problem areas. This context reassembled *democratic engagement* and greater interorganizational learning.

Overall, the two cases discuss the relevancy of a thoughtful and integrated approach like the Living Lab methodology introduced, which addresses the technological, ethical, and professional dimensions of care provision. They share some common themes, such as the importance of utilizing technology to provide remote care, personalized care plans, and comprehensive services to meet the needs of the citizens.

6 Conclusion

The two cases show that the Living Lab design can be used in diverse contexts. The distinct design features promote innovation processes led through new or intensified networking of collaborating stakeholders - healthcare providers, institutions etc. sharing knowledge, information, and goals [9]. The literature provides evidence of the value of this in innovation processes [10]. Thus, Living Labs can be a strong tool for building better health services going into the future through creating value across the organization, the municipality, end-users, and the employees at the same time. This research paper emphasizes wellbeing, health, and care. The research suggests that Living Labs designs can work across industries and has the potential to create insight-driven frameworks for companies or even cities. The consequent innovation process is guided by the values and goals of the managing organization whilst being anchored in citizen-centered design data to secure a path to tomorrow's solutions.

7 Further Research

Living Lab has a strong internationalization potential as nearly all developed societies are challenged with an aging population and an ensuing need for more efficient healthcare systems. Among other countries, Japan could be a potential market to enter with a population twenty times the size of the Danish home market and high similarity in terms of the demography. Market entry could potentially be challenged by cultural differences in relation to the Living Lab Design. In general, the export of the specific design would result in some elements being lost in translation. The current Living Lab design has been nurtured to fit a Danish setting and successful market entry will demand prudent cultural translation of the design. Following seminal literature [20], this could be administered through building strong ties to local networking partners. However, this process would need strong commitment from both sides [21].

IDEO's design thinking framework emphasizes an iterative process to create products or solutions that are both functional and natural for users. These processes allow for constant iteration, improvement and refinement of ideas based on citizen-insights, prototyping and testing. Nevertheless, IDEO frameworks are not cyclical. In contrast, Living Labs establishes a foundation that makes continuous ideation and real-life testing services possible. We suggest that future studies examine the governance structure of different Living Labs and the IDEO framework to evaluate and compare the recyclability of methods. This research could provide value into how design thinking can be leveraged to drive sustainable innovation, such as how it changes the way organizations approach innovation, and how it impacts the work culture.

References

1. Kimble, C.: Business models for e-health: evidence from ten case studies. Glob. Bus. Org. Excell. **34**(4), 18–30 (2015)
2. Kinsella, K.G., Phillips, D.R.: Global aging: the challenge of success, vol. 60. Population Reference Bureau Washington, DC (2005)
3. Steverson, M.: Ageing and health (2018). https://www.who.int/news-room/factsheets/detail/ageing-and-health
4. Accenture: Digital Health Tech Vision (2019)
5. Lamarre, E., Eloot, K., Atluri, V., Fernandes, P.,Wüllernweber, J.: The Internet of Things: how to capture the value of IoT. Retrieved from McKinsey & Company (2018)
6. Sundhedsdatastyrelsen: Digital Health Strategy 2018–2022: A Coherent and Trustworthy Health Network for All (2018)
7. Christensen, C.M.: The Innovator's Dilemma: When New Technologies Cause Great Firms to Fail. Harvard Business School Press, Boston, MA (1997)
8. Amabile, T.M.: A model of creativity and innovation in organizations. Res. Org. Behav. **10**(1), 123–167 (1988)
9. Gurteen, D.: Knowledge, creativity and innovation. J. Knowl. Manag. (1998)
10. Yusuf, S.: From creativity to innovation. Technol. Soc. **31**(1), 1–8 (2009)
11. Lasher, D.R., Ives, B., Jarvenpaa, S.L.: USAA-IBM partnerships in information technology: managing the image project. MIS Q. **15**(4), 551–565 (1991)
12. Huang, J.H., Thomas, E.: A review of living lab research and methods for user involvement. Technol. Innov. Manag. Rev. **11**(9/10), 88–107 (2021)
13. Vorre Hansen, A., et al.: Living Labs for Public Sector Innovation: insights from a European case study. Technol. Innov. Manag. Rev. **11**(9/10), 47–58 (2021)
14. Fuglsang, L., Hansen, A.V.: Framing improvements of public innovation in a living lab context: processual learning, restrained space and democratic engagement. Res. Policy **51**(1), 104390 (2022)
15. Eisenhardt, K.M., Martin, J.A.: Dynamic capabilities: what are they? Strat. Manag. J. **21**(10/11), 1105–1126 (2000)
16. Yin, R.K.: Applications of Case Study Research, 3rd edn. SAGE, Newcastle upon Tyne (2012)

17. Aktinson, P., Hammersley, M.: Ethnography and participant observation. In: Strategies of Qualitative Inquiry, pp. 248–261. Sage, Thousand Oaks (1998)
18. Parry, S., Jones, R., Rowley, J., Kupiec-Teahan, B.: Marketing for survival: a comparative case study of SME software firms. J. Small Bus. Enterp. Dev. 4(19), 712–728 (2012)
19. Eisenhardt, K.M.: Building theories from case study research. Acad. Manag. Rev. 14(4), 532–550 (1989)
20. Granovetter, M.: Getting a job: a study of contacts and careers. University of Chicago Press, Chicago (1974)
21. Zucchella, A., Siano, A.: Internationalization and innovation as resources for SME growth in foreign markets: a focus on textile and clothing firms in the Campania Region. Int. Stud. Manag. Org. 44(1), 21–41 (2014)

PURPOSE MODEL - Visual Method for Mutual Understanding in Co-creation Projects

Yurie Kibi[1]([⊠]) [iD] and Tetsuro Kondo[2]

[1] NIKKEN SEKKEI LTD., 2-18-3 Iidabashi, Chiyoda-ku 102-8117, Tokyo, Japan
kibi.yurie@nikken.jp
[2] Zukai Institute, Inc., 1-5-10 Sekiguchi, Bunkyo-ku 112-0014, Tokyo, Japan
cha@zukai.co

Abstract. This paper develops a new visual communication method for mutual understanding in Co-creation projects, the **Purpose Model**, and discusses its effectiveness. To create the tool, 30 cases of Co-creation projects were investigated and four elements of sustainable and better Co-creation projects were extracted. We also summarized seven items used in several tools for visualizing stakeholders used in the areas of project management and service design.

Following these elements as well, a new model is proposed to visualize Co-creation and promote mutual understanding among concerned persons. The features of this style are that it focuses on the 'common purpose', which is important for Co-creation projects, and that it can be used for fixed-point observation by writing in the same format, including changes from the initial, ambiguous stage.

In the process of devising the Purpose Model, the needs for communication tools in projects involving multiple stakeholders were identified, while disseminating the information on SNS and providing toolkits and web tools as open source.

As examples of use in actual projects, I introduce the use of the tool in the kick-off of a Living Laboratory for public-private-academic collaboration in a smart city, and its use in communication within and between teams in a commercial facility involving citizens in a redevelopment project.

Keywords: Co-creation · Participatory Design · Living Lab · Visual Method · Mutual Understanding · Communication tool · Smart Cities

1 Introduction

In this paper, a new visual communication method for mutual understanding in Co-creation projects is devised and its effectiveness is clarified.

In Co-creation projects, it is essential for stakeholders to communicate with people and organizations from different positions and perspectives. However, the more stakeholders there are, the more complex the project becomes, so there are many communication challenges.

In response to such challenges, communication tools have been widely developed in the fields of service design and project management to organize such multiple stakeholders and enable dialogue between concerned persons.

N. A. Streitz and S. Konomi (Eds.): HCII 2023, LNCS 14036, pp. 56–75, 2023.
https://doi.org/10.1007/978-3-031-34668-2_5

For example, the 'Stakeholder Map [1, 2]', which visualizes the main stakeholders and depicts their positioning, the 'Net Map [3]', which visualizes the relationship between stakeholders as well as their influence, and the 'Stakeholder Matrix [4–6]', which lists the expectations and influences of each stakeholder in a tabular form.

Many of these tools focus on stakeholders, with the objectives and issues being self-evident, and have mainly built an understanding of the current situation and triggered dialogue by capturing their interests and influences.

The following seven elements were identified in the items of these tools.

- Stakeholders
- Roles/Characteristics/capacities
- Influence/Power
- Relation
- Interests/expectations
- Implications for planning
- Attitude (positive, neutral, negative)

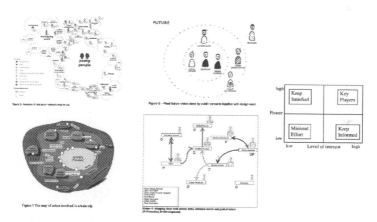

Fig. 1. Visualization tools for different types of stakeholders [3, 4, 7–9]

Of these tool elements, only the "stakeholder" item is common to each tool. Other items are used differently depending on the purpose or scene in which the tool is used.

For example, the stakeholder map was expressed by combining the elements of "stakeholders" and "size of influence/power" [7–9], and the stakeholder matrix included four elements: stakeholders and characteristics/capacities, objectives (expectations/interests), and measures/implications [4].

In addition, many of the tools differed in the elements written and the way they were expressed despite having the same name, and there was a large degree of freedom in the way they were written (see Fig. 1).

In proposing "a new visual communication method for mutual understanding in Co-creation projects," the element that differs from the above items is the common purpose (Co-Purpose): "What does this project exist for and what does it do?" This is one of the unique aspects of this study.

Seen from the research case study described below, a common purpose that can be shared among stakeholders in different positions is important to the success of a Co-creation project.

As in the past, it has become difficult to align the sense of purpose of all the various stakeholders, if the purpose is only economic in nature to gain innovation and growth or to solve social issues. Therefore, it is important to It is necessary to delve into the interests of each concerned person and foster objectives that incorporate both economic and social aspects [10, 11].

As Sanders & Stappers' Co-Design process states that the first stage of co-creation is the fuzzy front end, common objectives are often vague in the initial stages and are gradually developed (see Fig. 2) [12].

This is why it is necessary to continuously share the direction and goals of the project with stakeholders, and to do so, a "model that can capture change" is required. Therefore, a rule was established to "write a Co-creation project in a common format" in order to capture change. This is another feature of this study.

In this study, we put the common purpose of the project in the middle and created a model that expresses who is involved as stakeholders, in what roles, and for what purpose, in a single sheet. This is called the Purpose Model. To summarize the differences from previous tools, the common purpose is positioned as an important element, and the rules are written in a common format to make it easier to grasp changes.

From this point, we will explain the origins of this tool and clarify its effectiveness in facilitating mutual understanding and communication in Co-creation projects.

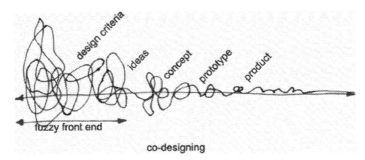

Fig. 2. Sanders, E. and Stappers, P.J. (2008) Co-Design process states that the first stage of co-creation is the fuzzy front end

2   Creating the Model

The research methodology was as follows.

(1) Element extraction based on research and interviews
(2) Modeling and revising
(3) Effectiveness verification

2.1 Element Extraction Based on Research and Interviews

Cases that are not business alliances or collaborations, but rather new challenges that take a step out of existing fields.

First, we selected 30 cases of both national and international co-creation projects, and surveyed the issues to be addressed, the activities, and the concerned persons. Additional interviews were then conducted with the persons in charge of the characteristic cases.

The selection criteria for the cases were as follows.

- Cases that are not business alliances or collaborations, but rather new challenges that take a step out of existing fields.
- The case studies were not one-off projects, but ongoing projects.
- Two or more subjects with different attributes cooperate with each other (e.g., companies and users, universities and citizens, and local governments). Additional interviews were then conducted with the persons in charge of the characteristic cases (Table 1).

Table 1. List of Co-Creation Projects studied

No.	Project	Place
1	BONUS TRACK	Tokyo
2	Waag	Amsterdam
3	Dutch skies	Amsterdam
4	Munakata International Ecologycal Summit	Fukuoka
5	DeCeuvel	Amsterdam
6	LEO Innovation Lab	Copenhagen
7	Regenerative Organic Certified	USA
8	g0v	Taiwan
9	PoliPoli	Tokyo
10	COVID-19 Information Website in Tokyo	Tokyo
11	BRING	Tokyo
12	Dove Self-Esteem Project	USA
13	DESCHOOL	Amsterdam
14	B-Corp	USA
15	HIGHLINE	USA
16	Forest Green Rovers	UK
17	ART SETOUCHI	Kagawa
18	Fashion for Good	Amsterdam
19	Ars Electronica	Linz
20	BLOXHUB	Copenhagen
21	SUKURIRE	Tokyo
22	Co-nect	Tokyo
23	NO YOUTH NO JAPAN	Tokyo
24	MEETS · THE · FUKUSHI	Hyogo
25	YOSHINO-Cedar HOUSE	Nara
26	Pnika	Tokyo
27	NOW Project	Seoul
28	HOLZMARKT	Berlin
29	Art Project at Osaka City University Hospital	Osaka
30	Erlangen	Erlangen

The following four elements emerged as common elements in these cases.

- The project has a common purpose that people across positions can sympathize with.
- Diversity of stakeholders
- The roles and objectives of each stakeholder are clear.
- Many stakeholders are proactively involved in the project.

Modeling the project so that these elements can be expressed (see Fig. 4). In doing so, we also referred to the seven elements of the existing tools for stakeholder analysis described in Sect. 1.

2.2 Modeling and Revising

The model is a circle with the common purpose of the project in the center, the concerned persons of the project written around it, and who is involved in what role and for what purpose described in concentric circles (see Fig. 3).

In order to show the diversity of stakeholders at a glance, the model is color-coded in four categories: companies, government, citizens, and universities/research institutions/experts. The upper and lower parts of the model are assigned meaning.

Stakeholders who agree with the common objectives and are actively involved in the project are placed on the lower side, and other stakeholders necessary for the project are placed on the upper side.

We call this line that separates the upper and lower sides the "line of subjectivity". Rather than dividing the stakeholders by the relationship between the value provider and the value receiver, as has been the case in the past, we have represented the various stakeholders who agree with the common goal and have the initiative as those who create value together. In other words, some users may be placed at the bottom of the diagram as proactive co-creation partners, while companies that are not proactive may be placed at the top.

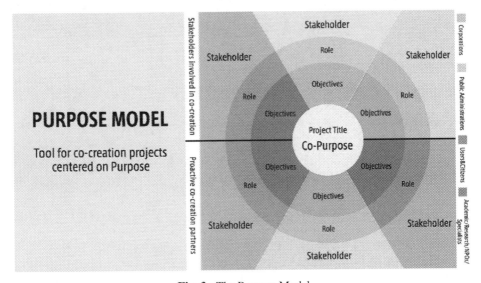

Fig. 3. The Purpose Model

This model was adjusted while applying it to the cases studied, and a beta version was sent out through SNS, and while users were utilizing it, the wording was adjusted, the range of colors to be applied, colors that are easy to distinguish for colorblind people, and design revisions were made to enable information to be easily seen (See Fig. 5).

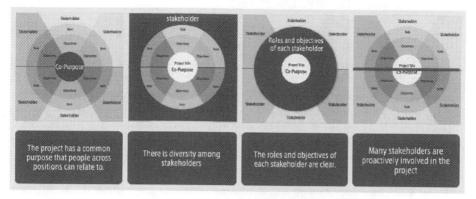

Fig. 4. Correspondence between the Purpose Model and the extracted elements

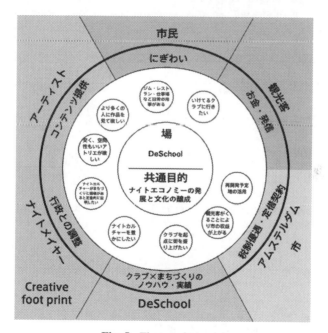

Fig. 5. First study model

3 Effectiveness Verification

To verify the effectiveness of the model, the model was released as an open source tool and a quantitative evaluation was conducted to measure the response to the model, and a qualitative evaluation was conducted based on interviews and observations of actual project personnel utilizing the model and the ease of communication with and without the model.

3.1   Publication of the Toolkit

Articles about the Purpose Model, including case studies and how to use it, were published on SNS (12 articles totaling 182,612 views), and the tool was released as an open-source tool, which has been downloaded more than 900 times (as of January 2023).

The position of those who downloaded the tool was the highest among employees (52.9%), followed by representatives and executive officers (21%), sole proprietors and freelancers (10.6%), students (8.8%), teachers (2%), indicating that the tool is highly used not only in the field but also at the decision-making level, where the overall picture is understood by students and teachers The survey also showed that the system is highly used by students and teachers.

The departments they belong to were innovation and co-creation at 30.3%, new business at 18.9%, corporate planning at 11.9%, consulting at 10.7%, human resource development at 4.7%, and R&D at 2.7%.

Sixty percent of the respondents were in innovation, new business, management planning, and departments that think about the future, with consulting in a supporting role and human resource development and retention objectives such as acquiring co-creative thinking and increasing employee engagement in teams (see Fig. 6).

Fig. 6. Results of questionnaire used to download the toolkit. The answers to the question "Please tell us about your position" (left) and "What is your function or area of responsibility" (right).

Results of responses to the questionnaire when downloading the toolkit. Responses to the question "What is your position?" (left) and what job functions or responsibilities do you have (right).

The most common purpose of use (multiple choices possible) was "To examine the contents of a new project I am involved in and to explain ideas," with 68% of respondents stating that they wanted to use it to think about new projects and to share their ideas with others.

This was followed by 53.2% for "to organize the current status and history of existing projects, and to develop future strategies," and 48.9% for "to build consensus and involve stakeholders," indicating that many respondents wanted to use it to organize projects they are already working on and to involve others (see Fig. 7).

Next, the question was asked about with whom the models are used for communication, 51.9% of the respondents answered "communication within the team," followed by "to partners and clients" at 37.3%, indicating that the models are also used to communicate with external parties (see Fig. 8).

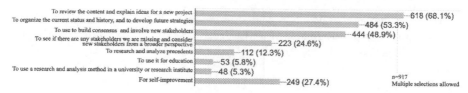

Fig. 7. Results of questionnaire about purpose of use

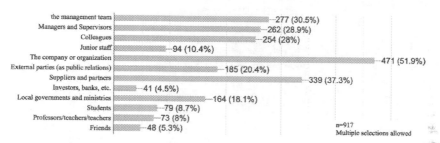

Fig. 8. Results of questionnaire about persons with whom the model will be used to communicate

In addition, after releasing "PURPOSE MODEL STUDIO," a web tool that allows users to freely edit a purposed model intuitively by drag-and-drop, the number of individual users who accessed the site reached more than 2,300 within five months after its release.

These results suggest that in today's age of increased opportunities to work on projects with multiple concerned persons, the Purpose Model fits the need to organize complex projects and facilitate communication among concerned persons.

3.2 Case Study in an Actual Project

Next, the model was used in two actual projects (a Living Lab project in a smart city and a redevelopment project created through Co-creation with citizens), and its effectiveness was verified through interviews with the people in charge of the projects.

Case1. Kashiwa-no-ha Minna no Machizukuri Studio. In Kashiwa-no-ha Smart City (Chiba, Japan), a Living Lab project called "Kashiwa-no-ha Minna no Machizukuri Studio" is taking place, in which companies bring in issues and work with citizens to find solutions.

UDCK, a public-private-academic partnership organization, acts as the link between each stakeholder, bringing together concerned persons from various sectors such as universities, real estate companies, companies with issues, city departments, and citizens to facilitate the project.

The challenge with this initiative was that, while agreeing on the major objective of solving social issues, the project often proceeded without the concerned persons knowing each other in depth, resulting in a lack of communication among the stakeholders along the way, which prevented the project from producing the desired results.

Therefore, the Purpose Model was used in the kick-off meeting of the new Living Lab in order to share the awareness of the respective issues from the initial stage and to make the participants aware that they should work with a common understanding of the issues.

Fig. 9. Scene of the workshop   **Fig. 10.** Purpose Model worksheet

Workshop participants included the director of UDCK (Urban Design Center Kashiwa-no-ha), the public-private-academic partnership organization that owns the Living Lab, people from companies that bring in issues, people from city planning companies, people from the city government, and researchers from the Hitachi and University of Tokyo Laboratory (H-UTokyo Lab) (see Fig. 9). The flow of the workshop was as follows (see Fig. 11).

1. First, self-introductions were made and participants shared their awareness of the issues and thoughts on what they usually do and on this initiative, followed by fieldwork in Kashiwa-no-ha Smart City, where they will work together as a living laboratory.
2. Next, the companies bringing in their issues told us why they wanted to work on this issue.
3. Then, the participants gave an explanation of the Purpose Model and provided input on co-creation with citizens, using examples.
4. Then we conducted a workshop using a dedicated worksheet (see Fig. 10).

Figure 10 shows the Purpose Model worksheet used that day. This worksheet was made so that participants could work with four colors of sticky notes that corresponded to the Purpose Model.

Since this was the first time, the common objectives were tentatively set by the companies that brought in the issues to be addressed. First, each person describes the Purpose Model for this project. At that time, it is acceptable if there are blanks in the objectives and roles.

5. Then, share it with everyone. First, one by one, talk about the stakeholders to whom you belong and the people you want to involve and deliver value to (stakeholders you want to be on the top side of the model) in the following items
   • What are your thoughts on the project?
   • What objectives you hope to achieve to sustain your activities (objectives, expectations, and interests)

- What role you can play in the project (role/capacity)
- Who you want to involve and to whom you want to deliver value

After the participants from that stakeholder have finished speaking, the other participants can express their requests and expectations, such as "I expect you to play this role as well" in addition to what the stakeholder is aware of, or conversely, they can propose what they can do, such as "I can answer these expectations".

6. At the end, the model with everyone's thoughts was integrated and set up as an ideal form.

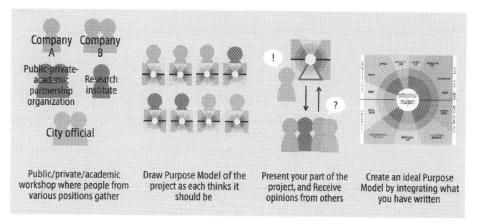

Fig. 11. Overview of this work: Kick-off of Co-creation project involving people from various walks of life

After going through this work, we asked, "How has the Purpose Model helped you in your work?" and received the following answers.

Mr. H (UDCK): It was useful for sharing awareness during the kickoff. By using the model, thoughts were less likely to be scattered all over the place, which was very effective as a first step. Also, many people filled in the "stakeholders who were not there" form, which we did not expect so much this time, and we could sense the participants' expectations by being able to imagine the expansion of the project in the future.

Ms. S (H-UTokyo Lab): It is natural that each organization has its own aims and objectives for the project, and it would be ideal if the program could take advantage of these, but it is really difficult to understand each other deeply at the beginning stage.

This time, by trying to draw each person's Purpose Model based on self-introductions and comparing them with each other, we were able to learn what the people around us expected of our organizations and openly communicate in a good atmosphere what roles we expected of the other person. I feel that it became easier for each organization to draw their future steps.

Thus, by talking about their own awareness of the issues, what they wanted to do, and their expectations of each other from the beginning, they were able to empathize with the issues and realize the roles they were expected to play. In addition, I realized that what I wanted to do was unexpectedly easy to achieve with other stakeholders, and this helped to increase my motivation for co-creation.

Through this initiative, there were four effects.

1. Everyone involved in the project had an opportunity to overview the project as a whole.
2. It provided an opportunity to talk about the thoughts and feelings involved and brought the concerned persons closer together psychologically.
3. It enables the adjustment of expectations and recognition of each other. By being aware of one's own role and knowing the role expected of one's partner, it is possible to adjust expectations. In addition, by disclosing their objectives to each other, they were able to cooperate with each other, and their motivation for Co-creation increased.
4. The participants can gain a broad view of the concerned persons seen from their respective standpoints and can share the direction of the project once they have expressed their own opinions, allowing them to prioritize and decide on the first step to take.

It was also possible to indicate who they wanted to involve and who they wanted to approach, and to name various types of target audiences.

This project is ongoing, and they are trying to draw new models at milestones and look back at the models they have drawn in the past to help the project move forward.

Case2. BONUSTRACK. BONUSTRACK is a commercial facility created as part of a redevelopment project of a vacant above-ground lot in Shimokitazawa, Tokyo, following the construction of an underground railroad line (see Fig. 12).

Fig. 12. Scene of BONUSTRACK (left) and, Bird's eye view (right)

Unlike conventional top-down redevelopment projects, the project was initiated by local residents rather than visitors to the commercial facility, with the aim of "enriching the lives of people living within walking distance by supporting the individual stores that are the character of the town together with everyone". The project was created through a user-centered, Co-creation process that began in the initial stages of development with the cooperation of multiple experts, tenants, and residents.

The project attracted a lot of attention from the very beginning and it became a bustling place every day. However, why did it work? There was no way to provide an overview of the project and the co-creation process behind the project.

In addition, as the number of concerned persons increased, the intention was to reaffirm within the team what was important to work on, and to align perceptions by understanding the current situation and envisioning the future.

Therefore, together with the people in charge of the project, we described four Purpose Models in chronological order from the initial stages of the project to visualize the process and share the future vision (see Fig. 13).

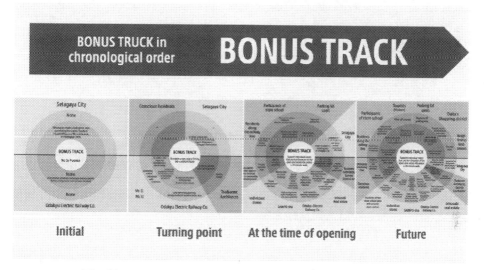

Fig. 13. Chronological change model of Case2 BONUS TRACK

In the initial planning stage, only Odakyu Electric Railway and Setagaya City were involved in the project.

The initial model represents a stage in which the project has no objectives and no image of the place yet (see Fig. 14).

Next is the turning point phase. What is important in the BONUS TRACK is the "exploration" period, which is also a turning point. The model of the turning point depicts the situation during this period.

Odakyu Electric Railway could have turned the site into a parking lot for short-term profit.

However, the company's awareness of the problem, In order to improve this area in the long term, we need a new way of redevelopment that restores Shimokitazawa's individuality. This was a time of trial and error, when they were considering what this area should be like from a broad perspective and with a long-term view.

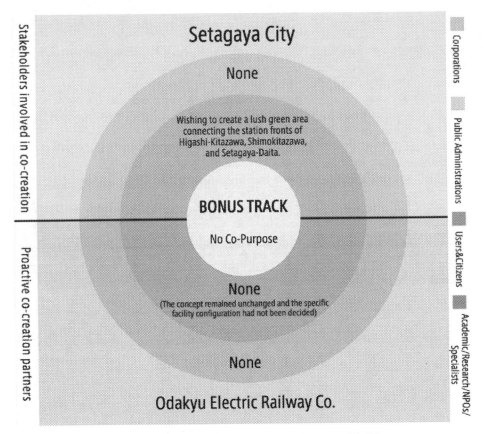

Fig. 14. Case2 BONUS TRACK Initial Purpose Model

After meeting with partners with different specialties who shared this awareness of the issue, the persons in charge of the project held numerous discussions and walked around the surrounding area as if they were painting a map, searching for the kind of place that should be created.

At the same time, they engaged in dialogue with residents who opposed the redevelopment. They took a positive view that the residents opposed the project, because they had strong feelings for this community, took on their pain once and talked about what they could do and the value of what this place could offer from the perspective of the residents who opposed the project, and built a relationship of trust (see Fig. 15).

And at the time of the opening. The current model depicts the situation in the present = "experimental" phase, about one year after the opening of the bonus track.

Mr. O and Mr. U, who had participated as "individuals" in the previous "turning point" stage, established a company called "SAMPO-sha" to operate this place.

In April 2020, the store opened at the Corona Disaster, and according to Mr. T of Odakyu, the number of tenants that could open the store was 60–70% of the total. However, the good side of the situation was that residents came forward to work together to create the space, and the relationship with them was deepened at an early stage.

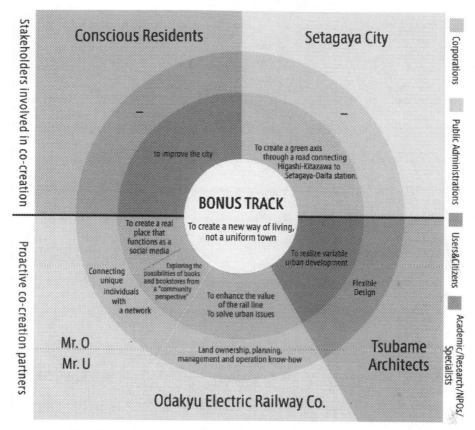

Fig. 15. Case2 BONUS TRACK The turning point of Purpose Model

Some of the "residents along the railway line" shown as "stakeholders involved in Co-creation" in the upper part of the Purpose Model are now showing up as "residents who want to be involved in community development" in the lower part of the model as "proactive Co-creation partners" (see Fig. 16).

Furthermore, at the time, the business model was set up to ensure short-term earnings as an enterprise while using part of the site as a parking lot, but in order not to be dependent on earnings from the rent of the location alone, an online course called *"THE STORE SCHOOL"* was planned for businesses that want to run unique stores, and earnings were generated there as well. In addition, the company is also working to nurture future store openers while generating revenue.

In this way, the experimental period is also a time to update the hypotheses that have taken shape, such as by creating multiple profit models depending on the situation.

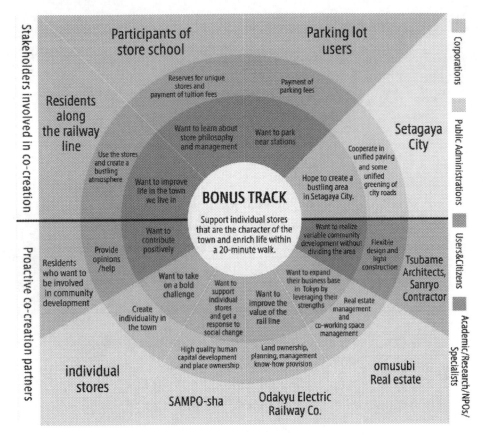

Fig. 16. Purpose Model at the time of the BONUS TRACK OPEN

Finally, there is a look into the future. The model of the future represents the signs that change is actually beginning to occur and that some of the changes are starting to be realized (see Fig. 17).

There are three key points for change here.

In general, residents who are "users of the place" often belong to the "stakeholders involved in co-creation" in the upper part of the model, but in the BONUS TRACK, the "*Shimokita Gardening Club*," a volunteer partner that manages the plantings, and "conscious residents" who pick up trash and deliver their opinions belong to the "proactive co-creation partners" in the lower part of the model, thus transcending the relationship between the operator and the users. The "conscious residents" who pick up trash and provide opinions belong to the "proactive co-creation partners" in the lower part of the model, and go beyond the relationship between the operator and the users. The model is very good at leaving a margin for involvement and nurturing, and creating a mechanism for residents to play a role in the process.

Secondly, looking at the activities of BONUS TRACK, we can see that the number and types of stakeholders have increased as some of the original stakeholders have taken on new purposes and roles, such as a landowner who belonged to the "Residents along

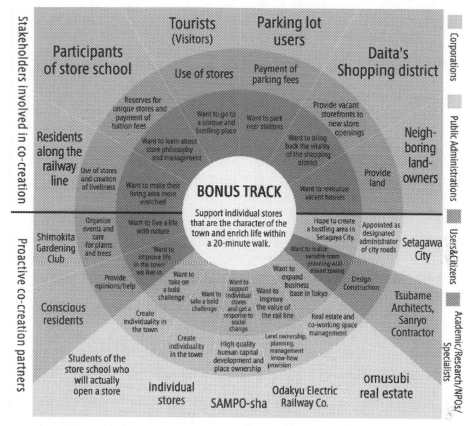

Fig. 17. Case2 BONUS TRACK Purpose Model of the Future

the railway line" during the experimental period asking for advice on utilizing a vacant house or a request to utilize a vacant store in the shopping district at the next station. It is clear that the number and types of stakeholders have increased.

The third key point is that although Setagaya City had cooperated so far in unifying the pavement of the city's roads and the BONUS TRACK site, it has not actively participated in the project, and is now becoming proactively involved, starting to change from a "stakeholder involved in Co-creation" to a "proactive co-creation partner".

Thus, by looking at the changes in each of the four phases in terms of the Purpose Model, we can see how the number of concerned persons increased and took on new roles as the project progressed, and how the common purpose in the middle was brushed up (see Fig. 13). The figure visualizes that this project was not developed in a conventional top-down manner, but was undertaken through Co-creation with various stakeholders who shared the same vision.

Consequently, the process that used to be described in stories can now be explained in a model, facilitating communication both internally and externally. Symbolic of this was the book *"Communityship: The Shimokita Railroad Street Project,"* which summarizes the series of projects. Challenging Regions, Supporting Railroad Companies also included the Purpose Model in the explanation of the project [13].

Mr. T., who is in charge of the project, made the following comments about the Purpose Model.

There are two things that are important in moving forward with a project. One is that all subjects involved in the project should share the same objectives. In the process of progressing a project, there are often disagreements among the various subjects. I feel that the reason for this is often because the means become the objectives. Another is the need to shorten the distance between the "provider" of value and the "receiver". Only when both parties share the risk can they come closer to their respective goals. When we understand each other's risk, the positions of "provider" and "receiver" of value can sometimes be interchanged. I came across the Purpose Model when I was thinking about how to visualize the above. It was great to be able to visualize what we have done so far and what we are thinking of doing in the future. I was able to explain the project more smoothly and use it to share ideas within the team. I also think it could be used to share with new team members when they join.

The model has also been used for other fixed-point observation purposes, such as writing the model again two years after the future was predicted and seeing the differences from what was predicted at the time (see Fig. 18).

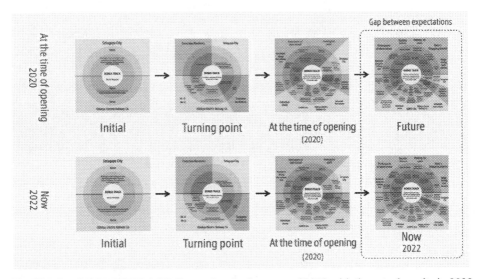

Fig. 18. Case2 BONUS TRACK Comparing the future as of 2020 with the actual results in 2022

In Case1 and Case2 discussed here, the timing and method of writing Purpose Models differed depending on the purpose.

Case 1	Purpose	To gather materials for mutual understanding among stakeholders and to consider the future direction of the project
	Timing	Initial stage of the project
	How to create	Workshop, written by all concerned persons, and summarized by the project manager
Case 2	Purpose	Visualization of important points and processes of the project, and sharing of future vision
	Timing	After the first phase of the project
	How to create	Project leader writes the report by himself/herself and shares it with the team

Although the purpose, timing, and method of creation differed between Case 1 and Case 2, as the participants commented, both promoted mutual understanding and shared recognition of the current status and direction of the project.

4 Conclusions

In this paper, a new tool for visualizing Co-creation projects and facilitating communication, the Purpose Model, was devised, and its needs and effectiveness were verified.

From the preliminary case study and case research, it was confirmed once again that it is important to share a common purpose that can be personalized by people in various positions, rather than the purpose of one organization, because Co-creation involves a variety of stakeholders.

However, the common purpose is not always clear from the beginning. The initial stage of Co-creation is exploratory and the common purpose is vague, so the common purpose itself needs to be brushed up in the course of the project. Therefore, the Purpose Model is not written once and never ends. Because it is difficult to see where one is going, the model must be like a compass that can be looked at many times during a journey, and to which one can return again and again [14].

Moreover, considering the central common purpose from the perspective of citizens and end-users, as well as from a broader perspective of what issues and to whom should be addressed, could lead to involve a wider range of parties.

Meanwhile, having only a common purpose does not mean that activities can continue sustainably. The model has a hierarchy of objectives, writing common purpose and individual objectives and expectations [15]. In order for stakeholders to keep running together, the project is driven by tightly tied objectives that reflect the interests and concerns of each. However, in past projects, there have been few opportunities to share the thoughts and roles of each stakeholder. One of the keys is to openly share thoughts and roles that are difficult to see on the surface, and to build a relationship of mutual ownership.

Through the actual use of the system in the project, new discoveries were made. First, by visualizing the process, it was possible to convey the great value of Co-creation from a medium- to long-term perspective, which could not be conveyed only by the results.

In addition to that, sharing expectations among concerned persons in the project provided an opportunity to build relationships, such as by listening to the other party or by disclosing weaknesses and relying on the other party. As a result, it was also apparent that the expectations led to becoming more aware of one's own role and motivated each concerned person to do the same.

It was also apparent that the people most likely to utilize this model are "those who have an overview of the project". As was indicated in the question "Who do you use this model for and in your position?" in the survey, many people said that they use it to explain and raise awareness within the company and among Co-creation partners, indicating that it is often used by those who have a full picture of the project.

Specifically, the project manager (Case 1), the project leader (Case 2), or the consultant or designer who provides advice to the project leader from the external party, would be suitable for the role of coordinator.

In the future, we would like to explore its potential as a project design tool by examining a series of frameworks that combine it with other tools to delve into issues to consider common objectives, relationships among stakeholders, and the flow of money.

Furthermore, we are also interested in viewing Purpose Models as data. By gathering multiple case studies across disciplines with the same format, it should be possible to systematize points of failure, cross-disciplinary comparisons, and Co-creation projects.

By sharing and systematizing a wealth of examples in the same format and disseminating them, people who are wondering what they can do and what they should do in Co-creation will be able to actually engage in the activities. This will also provide an opportunity for those who are wondering what they can do and how they can do it to actually start their own activities.

In the future, the center of social activities will shift from "power" to "purpose".

That is why the common purpose that is the center of a project will become increasingly important, and to achieve that common purpose, it is necessary to be able to explain the long-term value in a project and to create a situation in which diverse stakeholders can exchange multilayered values. The required role of the Purpose Model is to support that communication.

References

1. IBM: [Stakeholder Map] (n.d.). https://www.ibm.com/design/thinking/page/toolkit/activity/stakeholder-map. Accessed 13 May 2021
2. Stickdorn, Schneider: This is Service Design Thinking. Expectation maps, where stakeholders map their expectations for a service that is meant to solve a social challenge or a part of it. In: This is Service Design Thinking, pp. 176–177 (2011)
3. Schiffer, E.: Net-map toolbox influences mapping of social network. In: International Food Policy Research Institute Presented at the Sunbelt Conference of the International Network of Social Network Analysis, 01–06 May 2007, Corfu, Greece (2007)
4. Persson, U., Olander, S.: Methods to Estimate Stakeholder Views of Sustainability for Construction Projects, pp. 19–22 (2004)
5. Murray-Webster, R., Simon, P.: Making sense of stakeholder mapping. In: PM World Today Tips and Techniques – November 2006, Published in PM World Today - November 2006, vol. VIII, no. 11. "Connecting the World of Project Management" (2006)

6. Thomet, N., Vozza, A.: Project Design Manual, A Step-by-Step Tool to Support the Development of Cooperatives and Other Forms of Self-Help Organization (2010)
7. Giordano, F.B., Morelli, N., De Götzen, A., Hunziker, J.: The stakeholder map: a conversation tool for designing people-led public services. In: Meroni, A., Medina, A.M.O., Villari, B. (eds.) ServDes. 2018. Conference: Service Design Proof of Concept Linköping University Electronic Press. Linköping Electronic Conference Proceedings, no. 150 (2018). http://www.servdes.org/wp/wp-content/uploads/2018/07/48.pdf
8. Stuyfzand, L.J., Jönsson, J.B., de Götzen, A.: How actor-network mapping informs the early stages of system innovation: a case study. In: Lockton, D., Lenzi, S., Hekkert, P., Oak, A., Sádaba, J., Lloyd, P. (eds.) DRS2022: Bilbao, 25 June–3 July, Bilbao, Spain (2022). https://doi.org/10.21606/drs.2022.295
9. Morelli, N., Tollestrup, C.: New representation techniques for designing in a systemic perspective. In: Engineering and Product Design Education Conference (2006)
10. Lee, J.-J., Jaatinen, M., Salmi, A., Mattelmäki, T., Smeds, R., Holopainen, M.: Design choices framework for co-creation projects. Int. J. Des. **12**, 2 (2018)
11. Bushe, G.R., Marshak, R.J.: Revisioning organization development. Diagnostic and dialogic premises and patterns of practice. J. Appl. Behav. Sci. **45**(3), 348–368 (2009)
12. Sanders, E.B.N., Stappers, P.J.: Co-creation and the new landscapes of design. CoDesign **4**(1), 5–18 (2008). https://doi.org/10.1080/15710880701875068
13. Hashimoto, T., Mukai, T., Suita, R.: Community Ship Shimokita Line Street Project. Challenging Community, Supporting Railway Company, Gakugei Publishing (2022)
14. Kibi, Y., Kondo, T.: PURPOSE MODEL - How to Create Co-creation that Involves People. GAKUGEI Publishing, Chiyoda (2022)
15. Konno, N.: FCAJ, Purpose Engineering Institute, WISEPLACE INNOVATION - a method of innovation practice based on purpose engineering, Shoei (2018). https://ci.nii.ac.jp/ncid/BB2741677X

Study on the Identification of Disruptive Technology, Evidence from Nano Science

Yongxin Kong, Bingzong Huang, Yajun Wang, and Guochao Peng[✉]

Sun Yat-sen University, Panyu District, Guangzhou 510000, China
penggch@mail.sysu.edu.cn

Abstract. Disruptive technology is an innovation that initially performs poorly in mainstream markets, but eventually disrupts and replaces existing product. The concept of disruptive technology has been studied at both micro and macro levels. The identification of disruptive technology includes the approaches based on subjective data and objective data. Understanding the nature and dynamics of disruptive technology is important for businesses and policymakers as it can have significant impacts on industries and society as a whole. In this paper, 259,706 nanotechnology papers from 1999 to 2015, are collected to identify disruptive technology in nano field. 53 highly cited paper with more than 1000 citations are analysed, using Disruption index. Study results show that Phosphorene and Polymer solar cells are the top high disruptive technology. In terms of team sizes, disruptive technology in highly cited papers are small teams.

Keywords: Disruptive technology · identification mechanism · nano science

1 Introduction

Disruptive technology, a new technology that breaks the traditional thinking, is used for changing the rule of games, to bring great opportunities for curve overtaking. In this paper, we focus on the identification of disruptive technology and empirical analysis in the field of Nanoscience & Nanotechnology.

Based on literature review, a series of indexes for identifying the disruptive technology is built, which covers subjective indexes and objective indexes. According to the original concept and theoretical basis of disruptive technology, some scholars design the identification index from three perspective: Technological characteristics, Market characteristics, macro-environment.

On the other hand, objective indexes are proposed based on patent data and scientific paper data. In terms of patent data, the identification of disruptive technologies based on patent data is mainly carried out from the following three aspects: patent external features, patent text information, patent citation network. In regard to paper data, Disruption Index (DI) is proposed and constantly improved to become Disruption Index family (DI_5), which is based on literature coupling and literature citation network. Due to the impact of the disruption of scientific knowledge on technological change, some scholars identify disruptive technologies by analyzing the scientific knowledge cited by patents.

N. A. Streitz and S. Konomi (Eds.): HCII 2023, LNCS 14036, pp. 76–90, 2023.
https://doi.org/10.1007/978-3-031-34668-2_6

In this paper, we build the reference network and citation network, use Disruption Index family to study the disruption technology in the field of Nanoscience & Nanotechnology, through the selected paper data from 1999 to 2015 in Web of Science core collection.

2 Literature Review

2.1 Disruptive Innovation

The concept of disruptive technology was first introduced by Professor Christensen of Harvard Business School in his book "The Innovator's Dilemma: When New Technologies Cause Great Firms to Fail" (Christensen 1997). The concept has subsequently been defined from the perspective of both technology push and market pull in the context of discussions on economic development in the early 21st century, which centered on technological determinism and demand determinism theories (Shvidanenko 2020).

According to Christensen (1997), disruptive technology is an innovation that initially performs poorly in mainstream markets, but eventually disrupts and replaces existing products by offering a cheaper, simpler, smaller, and often more convenient alternative. He proposed the disruptive technology model (shown as Fig. 1), which illustrates disruptive technology's performance trajectory compared to mainstream market demand. The performance trajectory of disruptive technology is steeper than that of mainstream market demand, resulting in a technological disruption when the two intersect. In the early stages of its life cycle, a disruptive technology may exhibit poor performance in certain mainstream characteristics. However, it typically offers more flexible, convenient, or lower-priced technology that serves a segment of the market that values its new attributes. As the technology improves over time, the performance of disruptive technology in mainstream attributes improves to a level that meets the needs of mainstream customers, eventually "invading" the mainstream market.

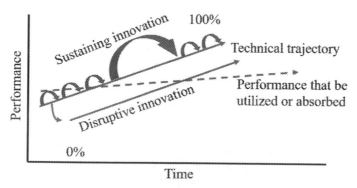

Fig. 1. The disruptive technology model.

Later, Christensen (Christensen, Raynor 2003) proposed an updated version that distinguished between low-end disruption (solving the low-end of existing value networks) and new market disruption (creating new value networks). Low-end disruption does not create a new market, but rather begins at the low end of the mainstream value network. In contrast, new market disruption initially competes with "non-consumption" and, due to its simplicity and affordability, attracts customers from the original low-end value network to the new value network through improved performance (Danneels 2004; Schmidt and Druehl 2008; Sood and Tellis 2011; Henderson 2006).

The concept of disruptive technology proposed by Christensen has received significant attention in academia and industry, leading to the ongoing refinement of the theory (see Table 1). However, due to the complexity of disruptive technology, some scholars have challenged the traditional perspective and further refined the concept (see Table 2).

Table 1. The definition of disruptive technology.

Perspective	Definition	Source
Technology	Disruptive technologies often change the basis of competition by introducing a set of performance indicators that have not been used in competition before	Danneels (2004)
	Disruptive technologies are types of innovation that are highly discontinuous or revolutionary	Thomond & Lettice (2002)
	Disruptive technologies are scientific discoveries that surpass the usual capabilities of products/technologies and provide the basis for new, more competitive paradigms	Tushman & Rosenkopf (1992); Anderson and Tushman (1990); Kassicieh et al. (2002); Kostoff et al. (2004)
	The element of fundamental novelty or suddenness is important in disruptive technologies	Abernathy & Clark (1985)
	Disruptive technologies can be new combinations of existing technologies or entirely new technologies that are applied to problem areas or new commercial challenges. These technologies can lead to significant paradigm shifts in technological products	Kostoff et al. (2004)

(continued)

Table 1. (*continued*)

Perspective	Definition	Source
Market	Disruptive technologies enable discontinuous innovation or products, processes, and/or services to provide exponential value to customers. If a technology's resulting products have different performance attributes that existing customers may not value, then the technology is considered disruptive	Walsh (1996); Lynn et al. (1996); Veryzer (1998)
	Disruptive innovation is a significant change in how consumers or businesses operate, not a new principle or concept, but rather the transfer of existing technology from one domain to another, or the cross of multiple existing technologies	Bower et al. (1995)
	Disruptive technologies create significant new growth in the industries they penetrate by allowing individuals and companies with different skills to provide laddering functional value to existing industries or create new value from the value they offer	Jia et al. (2021)
	Disruptive technologies often emerge from existing businesses and gradually rise in the market, posing a threat to long-term substitutes	Kostoff et al. (2004)
Combining technology and market	Significantly alter the market structure and dominant businesses through a superior "performance trajectory" in key dimensions of customer value, even if they are not necessarily entirely new from a technical perspective	Christensen & Bower (1996)

(*continued*)

Table 1. (*continued*)

Perspective	Definition	Source
	Significantly change the cost-performance frontier and are attractive to existing products due to their superior functional performance rather than cost	Carayannopoulos (2009)
	Disruptive technologies typically emerge from existing businesses and gradually gain market share, thereby threatening the sustainability of long-term substitutes	Cheng et al. (2016)

Table 2. The updating of the theory of disruptive technology.

Perspective	Original theory	Extended content	Source
Creator	Originate from new entrants or start-ups in the market	Originate from incumbent and new entrants	Yu, Hang (2010)
Market attitude	Following a "bottom-up attack" path	The choice of customers actually choose based on complex criteria	Danneels (2004); Dombrowski, Gholz (2009)
Corporate attitude	Being discarded by incumbents	Adopted by incumbent and new entrants	Sood, Tellis (2011)
Market position	Completely replacing existing technologies	Entering first through competition and then cooperation	Naumov (2013)

Research on disruptive technology has also revealed that it operates at both micro and macro levels, as demonstrated by the two-level technology disruption framework proposed by Schuelke-Leech (2018). First-order disruption represents the micro-level disruption based on Christensen's (1997) theory of disruptive technology, while second-order disruption represents the macro-level disruption based on Joseph Schumpeter's (1939a, b) theory. First-order disruption impacts local changes in a market or industry, disrupting the local market, while second-order disruption disrupts organizational structures, social interactions and relationships, public policies, and the physical environment, leading to more significant changes in social, economic, and political norms (Schuelke-Leech 2018).

The characteristics of disruptive technology in emerging economies such as China differ from those in Western economies in terms of technology, institutions, and market trajectories. In terms of technology, the acceleration of knowledge updates, the shortening of technology use cycles, and the emergence of new demands provide an "advantage of being late" platform for emerging economies. Institutions also play a crucial role in the success of newcomers and incumbents in China, with the government providing support (Lee et al. 2017). However, Western companies may have a greater likelihood of obtaining strategic resources than their counterparts in emerging economies. In terms of market trajectories, Chinese companies tend to focus on the low-end and new markets through disruptive technology innovation, while Western companies simultaneously attract customers in the low-end, new, and high-end markets (Grosse 2015; Ruan et al. 2014; Wu et al. 2010).

The concept of disruptive technology has altered the perspective of scholars and managers on technological competition (Adner 2012). Conventional views on technology strategy posit that newcomers can gain an advantage by offering superior performance that can replace the technology of existing companies. Conversely, disruptive technology suggests the possibility that technology that initially performs poorly can eventually disrupt and replace incumbent technology through its offering of a cheaper, simpler, smaller, and often more convenient alternative (Sherif et al. 2009). Disruptive technology refers to a new technology that transforms the fundamental basis of market competition by operating using a distinct set of enterprise performance metrics (Danneels 2004).

2.2 The Approaches to Identify Disruptive Innovation

The Identification of Disruptive Technology Based on Subjective Data. According to Christensen's theory of disruptive technology, disruption occurs when the performance trajectory of technology intersects with the demand trajectory of the market. As disruptive technology evolves, the macro environment also undergoes corresponding changes. Therefore, scholars have constructed a multi-index evaluation framework, based on the concept and mechanism of disruptive technology, to identify disruptive technologies. This framework primarily designs indicators from three aspects: technical characteristics, market characteristics, and macro environment. Data for this evaluation is obtained through methods such as questionnaire surveys and expert interviews, and analyzed using techniques such as the analytic hierarchy process (AHP) and data envelopment analysis (DEA). The technical characteristics indicators are a series of indicators related to the technical performance of the technology, the market characteristics indicators evaluate the impact of the technology on the market from multiple perspectives such as product, enterprise, market, and consumer, and the macro environment indicators are designed to consider factors at the political, economic, and social cultural levels.

Since the early concept and theoretical foundations of disruptive technology, scholars have designed market-oriented indicators to identify enterprises' disruptive technology based on factors such as the maturity of the enterprise's technological products and the market acceptance of the product (Diab 2015; Collins 2011). Moreover, there are many scholars who believe that combining technical and market indicators is crucial for identifying disruptive technology, and on this basis, adding various technical characteristic indicators such as technological breakthrough, technological integration, and technological feasibility (Govindarajan et al. 2006; Wu et al. 2019). As the theory of disruptive technology continues to develop, scholars have increasingly recognized the significant impact of disruptive technology on the macro environment and have expanded the evaluation framework for disruptive technology by designing a range of macro environment indicators, including macro policies, the level of macroeconomic development, supporting systems, social and cultural construction, and atmosphere (Li et al. 2016; Janke 2015) (see Table 3).

Table 3. The indicators to identify disruptive technology.

Technological characteristics	Market characteristics	Macro-environment	Source
	Product cost and quality		Adams et al. (2014)
	The usefulness of the technology, the quality of the technology's output, the utility of the technology, the compatibility of the technology, and the willingness of technology stakeholders to use the technology		Collins (2011)
New attributes of the technology, Uncertainty of the technology	Impact of the technology on the market, Factors that contribute to the technology's ability to disrupt businesses		Sainio (2007)
Breakthroughs in technology performance	New market segments for customers		Govindarajan et al. (2006)
Feasibility, cutting-edge nature, and performance breakthroughs of the technology	Alignment of demand, potential benefits of the technology, and attention to the technology		Adams et al. (2014)

(continued)

Table 3. (*continued*)

Technological characteristics	Market characteristics	Macro-environment	Source
Breakthroughs in technology performance	Net income of the business, marketing budget, marketing channels, customer sentiment		Paap et al. (2004)
Integration, leadership, maturity, diffusion, simplification	Emerging markets, value networks, cost reduction	Policies and macroeconomics	Arianfar (2012)
Technological breakthroughs, feasibility	Market positioning	Government policies	Diab (2015)
Technological performance breakthroughs, impact, universality, feasibility	Differentiation of target markets, maturity of incumbent technologies, acceptance of technology	Coordination of external factors	Guo et al. (2019)
	Investment in technology, diffusion of technology	Macro policies and economic environment, supporting systems and external environmental factors	Paap et al. (2004)

However, these methods have a wide range of indicators and complex evaluation content, largely relying on the subjective judgment of experts to measure the indicators. Many of the evaluation indicators are only suitable for ex post evaluation of disruptive technology, making it difficult to identify disruptive technology in the early stages.

The Identification of Disruptive Technology Based on Objective Data. Identifying disruptive technology through patent literature data. Patents document information on technological innovation activities and patent data is reliable and standardized. Analyzing this data helps to understand the technical characteristics and identify disruptive technologies. Currently, the identification of disruptive technology using patent data mainly focuses on three areas (see Table 4): first, identifying disruptive technology based on external characteristics of patents, such as analyzing indicators such as patent status, patent theme, and the number and changes in citation situations. However, this approach has limitations, such as identifying broad technology themes and difficulty in identifying early-stage disruptive technology. Second, identifying disruptive technology based on the text information of patents, by analyzing co-occurrence and evolution of classification numbers and keywords. However, this approach still has challenges in determining indicators like innovation, impact, and quality for disruptive technology. Third, identifying disruptive technology based on patent citation networks, which allows for measurement of indicators' influence and quality, but requires time to accumulate citation data and therefore cannot be used for identifying early-stage disruptive technology.

Table 4. The indexes to identify disruptive technology based on patent literature data.

Evaluative dimension	Measurement index	Source
Patent external features	Patent application volume, patent grant rate, number of applicants, large number of new applicants, per capita number of patents, per capita increase in application volume, technological reference tree	Buchanan (2010)
	Patent subject's patent application activity, number of times a patent is cited and innovation index symbolizing technological novelty	Luan, Cheng (2016)
	Scientific relevance, technological impact potential, technological breakthrough potential, market attractiveness potential, market competitiveness potential	Luo et al. (2019)
Patent text information	Keyword co-occurrence network proximity and distance in academic publications	Dotsika & Watkins (2017)
	Visual growth rate and diffusion growth rate of keywords	Kim, Park & Lee (2016)
	Ipc classification number restructuring, difference in ipc classification number reference structure, functional characteristics of technology	Huang et al. (2015)
Patent citation network	Patent development path, k-core analysis, theme modeling	Momeni et al. (2017)

Identifying disruptive technology using paper data. The mutation of scientific knowledge can impact technological change, and some scholars identify disruptive technology by analyzing the citation of scientific knowledge in papers. For example, the knowledge difference degree based on the change in keyword frequency (Zhang 2016) and the semantic relevance based on the technical theme (Bai et al. 2017) reveal the mutation of knowledge and can be used to identify disruptive technology. In addition, Bloodworth (2012) designed two indicators, technological advancement and technological performance breakthrough, and used content analysis and one-way ANOVA to determine the importance of key attributes of mainstream technology in order to identify disruptive technology.

Identifying disruptive technology using multi-source data fusion. In order to more accurately and comprehensively identify disruptive technology, scholars mainly combine various types of data, such as patents and papers, for disruptive technology identification research (Kassicieh & Rahal 2007). Shi Hui et al. (2019) integrated paper data and patent manual coding to analyze the change in paper themes and monitor the mutation of patent themes. In addition, Zhao Ge (2017) also added web news data and constructed indicators such as patent three-year citation rate, the average independent claim of the patent, and literature growth rate to identify disruptive technology themes.

3 Data

Developing in the late twentieth century, nanotechnology rapidly penetrated into all fields of science and society at an explosive rate. Many countries regard nanotechnology as one of the disruptive technologies in the future and invest heavily in this field of research. Nanoscience is a very dynamic subject with continuous innovation and multidisciplinary development. Therefore, we focus on the field of nanoscience and nanotechnology, extracted in December 2021 from the Web of Science core collection. We originally select 259,706 nanotechnology papers, which is limited by "Publication Year" to 1999–2015 and by "WoS Category" to nanoscience and nanotechnology (the original paper in 1999).

In this paper, we select papers with a total citation amount of over 1000 in a 5-year citation window as highly cited papers, to identify the disruptive nano innovation with high impact.

4 Method

In this paper, the disruptive indexes (DI and DI_5) proposed by Wu et al. (2019) and Bornmann et al. (2020) respectively, are used to identify the disruptive innovation in nano field. The formula is as follows:

$$DI = \frac{N_i - N_j}{N_i + N_j + N_k} \tag{1}$$

$$DI_5 = \frac{N_i - N_j^l}{N_i + N_j^5 + N_k} \tag{2}$$

where N_i refers to the number of papers that cite focal papers but not cite the references of focal papers, N_j refers to the number of papers that cite both focal papers and the references of focal papers, N_k refers to the number of papers that cite the references of focal papers but not cite focal papers, N_j^5 refers to the number of papers that cite both focal papers and more than 5 references papers.

5   Results

Table 5 summarises the disruption index family of highly cited papers. There are large numbers of FP_cited_ct (the count of papers citing FP), BC_ct (the count of bibliographic coupling between FP and papers citing FP) and Ref_of_FP_cited_ct (the count of papers citing references of FP) in highly cited papers, but there is a small number of, compared with and. The top-ranking publication by DI is "Phosphorene: An Unexplored 2D Semiconductor with a High Hole Mobility" (Liu et al. 2014). Phosphorene is a stable 2D counterpart of layered black phosphorus and, unlike graphene, has an inherent, direct, and appreciable band gap. Phosphorene has broad application prospects in field effect transistors, optoelectronic devices, spintronics, gas sensors and solar cells. The top-ranking publication by DI_5 is titled; "Thermally stable, efficient polymer solar cells with nanoscale control of the interpenetrating network morphology." (Ma et al. 2005). Polymer solar cells, which are thermally stable and efficient compared to silicon-based devices, are lightweight and inexpensive to fabricate, and as such have become a hot area for solar cell research.

The indexes in DI family have different focuses, however, the results indicate that highly cited papers in nanoscience and nanotechnology tend to develop rather than disrupt. In this case, the situation that more than half of is greater than 0 is reasonable, because this algorithm has a disadvantage that can make the number of possible indicators proliferate into disruption "family"(Bornmann et al. 2020).

The reason for this phenomenon is that, although the citation count citing FP is large, the influence of the references cited by FP is significant; moreover, due to the 5-years citation window, the impact of highly cited papers is not significant enough, resulting in showing more consolidation than disruption at this stage.

Table 5. Descriptive statistics of highly cited papers

	Min	Q1	med	Q3	Max	avg	Std
FP_cited_ct	1008	1180	1364	1742	3636	1568.679	619.098
BC_ct	424	931	1106	1295	2850	1192.604	443.195
Ref_of_FP_cited_ct	3100	12667	20390	26473	54101	20651.11	10426.56
Ni	2	139	263	457	1563	376.075	347.667
Nj	424	931	1106	1295	2850	1192.604	443.195
Nk	2255	11537	19466	24325	51997	19458.51	10263.81
DI	−0.14084	−0.07112	−0.04099	−0.02619	0.0367	−0.04818	0.03426
nj5	1	85	263	400	970	273.511	199.605
DI_5	−0.05421	−0.01292	0.00575	0.02477	0.16851	0.01115	0.03752

In addition, Wu, Wang and Evans (2019) proposed that small teams disrupt science and technology. In this paper, we also explore the effect of team size on highly cited papers, respectively. Table 5 shows that highly cited papers are small teams. Highly cited papers with disruption characteristics ($DI_5 > 0$) are published in the team size range between 3 and 11, where the average team size is smaller than that of all highly cited papers (Table 6).

Table 6. Descriptive statistics of count of authors.

	Min	max	median	avg
highly cited papers	1	19	7	7.196
highly cited papers ($DI_5 > 0$)	3	11	7	6.607
full data	1	63	5	5.019

6 Conclusion

In conclusion, this study analyzed 53 high cited paper with more than 1000 citations, selected from 259,706 nanotechnology papers from 1999 to 2015 in order to identify disruptive technology in the nano field. Through the use of the Disruption indexes (DI and DI_5), it was found that Phosphorene and Polymer solar cells were the top high disruptive technologies. Additionally, the research found that disruptive technologies in highly cited papers were often developed by small teams. This information is valuable for businesses and policymakers as it highlights the importance of understanding the nature and dynamics of disruptive technology, to effectively anticipate and adapt to its potential impacts on academic and industries.

Acknowledgement. We acknowledge the financial support from the National Natural Science Foundation of China Grants No. 71974215.

References

Abernathy, W.J., Clark, K.B.: Innovation: mapping the winds of creative destruction. Res. Policy **14**, 3–22 (1985)

Adams, F.P., Bromley, B.P., Moore, M.: Assessment of disruptive innovation in emerging energy technologies. In: IEEE Electrical Power and Energy Conference, pp. 110–115. IEEE Computer Society, London (2014)

Adner, R.: The Wide Lens: A New Strategy for Innovation. Penguin, London (2012)

Anderson, P., Tushman, M.L.: Technological discontinuities and dominant designs: a cyclical model of technological change. Adm. Sci. Q. **35**, 604–633 (1990)

Arianfars, S., Kallenbach, J., Mitts, H., et al.: Back to the future-prediction of incremental and disruptive innovations. In: Finland: Aalto University Multidisciplinary Institute of Digitalisation and Energy (MIDE), pp. 11–16 (2012)

Bai, G.Z., Zheng, Y.R., Wu, X.N., et al.: Research and demonstration on forecasting method of disruptive technology based on literature knowledge correlation. J. Intell. **36**(9), 38–44 (2017)

Bloodworth, I.: A search for discriminative linguistic makers in ICT practitioner discourse, for the ex-ante identification of disruptive innovation. Victoria University of Wellington, New Zealand (2012)

Bornmann, L., Devarakonda, S., Tekles, A., Chacko, G.: Disruptive papers published in Scientometrics: meaningful results by using an improved variant of the disruption index originally proposed by Wu, Wang, and Evans (2019). Scientometrics **123**, 1149–1155 (2020)

Bower, J.L., Christensen, C.M.: Disruptive technologies: catching the wave. Harvard Bus. Rev. **73**(1), 43–53 (1995)

Buchanan, B., Corken, R.: A toolkit for the systematic analysis of patent data to assess a potentially disruptive technology, pp. 1–16. Intellectual Property Office, United Kingdom (2010)

Carayannopoulos, S.: How technology-based new firms leverage newness and smallness to commercialize disruptive technologies. Entrepreneurship Theory Pract. **33**(2), 419–438 (2009)

Cheng, Y., Huang, L.C., Ramlogan, R., Li, X.: Forecasting of potential impacts of disruptive technology in promising technological areas: elaborating the SIRS epidemic model in RFID technology. Technol. Forecast. Soc. Change **117**, 170–183 (2016)

Christensen, C.M., Bower, J.L.: Customer power, strategic investment, and the failure of leading firms. Strateg. Manag. J. **17**(3), 197–218 (1996)

Christensen, C.M., Raynor, M.E.: The innovator's solution: creating and sustaining successful growth. Res.-Technol. Manag. **46**(5), 61 (2003)

Christensen, C.M.: The Innovator's Dilemma: The Revolutionary Book that Will Change the Way You Do Business. Harvard Business School Press, Boston, MA (1997)

Collins, R., Hevne, R.A., Linge, R.R.: Evaluating a disruptive innovation: function extraction technology in software development. In: Proceedings of the 2011 44th Hawaii International Conference on System Sciences, pp. 1–8. IEEE Computer Society, Hawaii (2011)

Danneels, E.: Disruptive technology reconsidered: a critique and research agenda. J. Prod. Innov. Manag. **21**(4), 246–259 (2004)

Diab, S., Kanyaru, J., Zantout, H.: Disruptive innovation: a dedicated forecasting framework. In: Jezic, G., Howlett, R.J., Jain, L.C. (eds.) Agent and Multi-Agent Systems: Technologies and Applications. SIST, vol. 38, pp. 227–237. Springer, Cham (2015). https://doi.org/10.1007/978-3-319-19728-9_19

Dombrowski, P., Gholz, E.: Identifying disruptive innovation: innovation theory and the defense industry. Innovations **4**(2), 101–117 (2009)

Dotsika, F., Watkins, A.: Identifying potentially disruptive trends by means of keyword network analysis. Technol. Forecast. Soc. Change **119**, 114–127 (2017)

Govindarajan, V., Kopalle, P.K.: Disruptiveness of Innovations: measurement and an assessment of reliability and validity. Strat. Manag. J. **27**(2), 189–199 (2006)

Grosse, R.: Emerging Markets: Strategies for Competing in the Global Value Chain. Kogan Page Publishers, London, Philadelphia and New Delhi (2015)

Guo, J.F., Pan, J.F., Guo, J.X., et al.: Measurement framework for assessing disruptive innovations. Technol. Forecast. Soc. Change **139**, 250–265 (2019)

Henderson, R.: The innovator's dilemma as a problem of organizational competence. J. Prod. Innov. Manag. **23**, 5–11 (2006)

Huang, L.C., Cheng, Y., Wu, F.F.: Study on identification framework of disruptive technology. Stud. Sci. Sci. **33**(5), 654–664 (2015)

Janke, A.: Identifying the disruptive potential of the sustainable innovation in the case of e-mobility. In: World Congress on Sustainable Technologies (WCST), pp. 63–64. IEEE, London (2015)

Jia, W.F., Xie, Y.P., Zhao, Y.N., et al.: Research on disruptive technology recognition of China's electronic information and communication industry based on patent influence. J. Glob. Inf. Manag. **29**(2), 148–165 (2021)

Kassicieh, S., Rahal, N.: A model for disruptive technology forecasting in strategic regional economic development. Technol. Forecast. Soc. Change **74**(9), 1718–1732 (2007)

Kassicieh, S., Walsh, S., Cummings, S., McWhorter, J., Romig, P., Williams, D.: Commercialization of disruptive technologies: moving discontinuous innovations into products. IEEE Trans. Eng. Manag. **49**(4), 375–387 (2002)

Kim, J., Park, Y., Lee, Y.: A visual scanning of potential disruptive signals for technology road mapping: investigating keyword cluster, intensity, and relationship in futuristic data. Technol. Anal. Strat. Manag. **28**(10), 1–22 (2016)

Kostoff, R.N., Boylan, R., Simons, G.R.: Science and technology test mining: disruptive technology roadmaps. Technol. Forecast. Soc. Change **71**(1), 141–159 (2004)

Lee, C.-Y., Lee, J.-H., Gaur, A.S.: Are large business groups conducive to industry innovation? The moderating role of technological appropriability. Asia Pac. J. Manag. **34**(2), 313–337 (2017)

Liu, H., et al.: Phosphorene: an unexplored 2D semiconductor with a high hole mobility. ACS Nano **8**(4), 4033–4041 (2014)

Luan, C.J., Cheng, F.: Measuring and forecasting technology market potential based on aggregative indicators of disruptive potential & technology maturity. Stud. Sci. Sci. **34**(12), 1761–1768, 1816 (2016)

Luo, S.P., Kou, C.C., Jin, J., et al.: Disruptive technology prediction based on outlier patents: traditional Chinese medicine patents as an example. Inf. Stud.: Theory Appl. **42**(7), 165–170 (2019)

Lynn, G., Morone, J., Paulson, A.: Marketing and discontinuous innovation: the probe and learn process. Calif. Manag. Rev. **38**(3), 8–37 (1996)

Ma, W., Yang, C., Gong, X., Lee, K., Heeger, A.J.: Thermally stable, efficient polymer solar cells with nanoscale control of the interpenetrating network morphology. Adv. Funct. Mater. **15**(10), 1617–1622 (2005)

Momeni, A., Rost, K.: Identification and monitoring of possible disruptive technologies by patent-development paths and topic modeling. Technol. Forecast. Soc. Change **104**, 16–29 (2016)

Naumov, S.A.: Case study of the competitive behavior of companies in response to disruptive technologies in the dynamic environment of changing user needs. Doctoral dissertation, Massachusetts Institute of Technology (2013)

Paap, J., Katz, R.: Anticipating disruptive innovation. Res.-Technol. Manag. **47**(5), 13–22 (2004)

Ruan, Y., Hang, C.C., Wang, Y.M.: Government's role in disruptive innovation and industry emergence: the case of the electric bike in China. Technovation **34**(12), 785–796 (2014)

Sainio, L.M., Puumalainen, K.: Evaluating technology disruptiveness in a strategic corporate context: a case study. Technol. Forecast. Soc. Change **74**(8), 1315–1333 (2007)

Schmidt, G.M., Druehl, C.T.: When is a disruptive innovation disruptive? J. Prod. Innov. Manag. **25**, 347–369 (2008)

Schuelke-Leech, B.A.: A model for understanding the orders of magnitude of disruptive technologies. Technol. Forecast. Soc. Change **129**, 261–274 (2018)

Schumpeter, J.A.: Business Cycles: A Theoretical, Historical, and Statistical Analysis of the Capitalist Process, vol. 1. McGraw-Hill Book Company Inc, New York, NY (1939)

Schumpeter, J.A.: Business Cycles: A Theoretical, Historical, and Statistical Analysis of the Capitalist Process, vol. 2. McGraw-Hill Book Company Inc, New York, NY (1939)

Sherif, M.H., Seo, D.B.: Government role in information and communications technology innovations. In: Innovations for Digital Inclusions, K-IDI ITU-T Kaleidoscope. IEEE (2009)

Shvidanenko, G., Shvidanenko, O., Sica, E., Busarieva, T.: The role of disruptive technologies in the formation of the world competitive leaders. Manag. Theory Stud. Rural Bus. Infrastruct. Dev. **42**(2), 128–132 (2020)

Sood, A., Tellis, G.J.: Demystifying disruption: a new model for understanding and predicting disruptive technologies. Mark. Sci. **30**, 339–354 (2011)

Thomond, P., Lettice, F.: Disruptive innovation explored. In: 9th IPSE International Conference on Concurrent Engineering. Research and Applications (2002)

Tushman, M.L., Rosenkopf, L.: Organizational determinants of technological change: toward a sociology of technological evolution. Res. Organ. Behav. **14**, 311–347 (1992)

Veryzer, R.: Discontinuous innovation and the new product development process. J. Prod. Innov. Manag. **15**(4), 304–321 (1998)

Walsh, S.: Commercialization of MicroSystems—Too fast or too slow. In: SPIE, International Society for Optical Engineering, pp. 12–26 (1996)

Wu, L., Wang, D., Evans, J.A.: Large teams develop and small teams disrupt science and technology. Nature **566**(7744), 378–382 (2019)

Wu, X., Ma, R., Shi, Y.: How do latecomer firms capture value from disruptive technologies? A secondary business-model innovation perspective. IEEE Trans. Eng. Manag. **57**(1), 51–62 (2010)

Yu, D., Hang, C.C.: A reflective review of disruptive innovation theory. Int. J. Manag. Rev. **12**(4), 435–452 (2010)

Zhang, J.Z., Zhang, X.L.: Overview of radical innovation identification based on scientific references in patents. J. China Soc. Sci. Tech. Inf. **35**(9), 955–962 (2016)

Towards an Interaction Design Framework for IoT Healthcare Systems

Guillermo Monroy-Rodríguez[1], Luis Martín Sánchez-Adame[2]([⊠]) [ID],
Sonia Mendoza[1] [ID], Ivan Giovanni Valdespin-Garcia[1],
and Dominique Decouchant[3]

[1] Computer Science Department, CINVESTAV-IPN, Mexico City 07360, Mexico
{guillermo.monroy,sonia.mendoza,ivan.valdespin}@cinvestav.mx
[2] Computer Engineering Department, UAEM-Valle de México,
State of Mexico 54500, Mexico
lmsancheza@uaemex.mx
[3] Information Technologies Department, UAM-Cuajimalpa,
Mexico City 05348, Mexico
decouchant@cua.uam.mx

Abstract. The rising prevalence of chronic conditions has fuelled the development of numerous devices and IoT systems to improve patients' health outcomes. Despite the abundance of these solutions, their usability remains a significant challenge, hindering their adoption and effectiveness. This paper proposes a conceptual interaction design framework for IoT healthcare systems that prioritises the three critical components of usability: effectiveness, efficiency, and satisfaction. To develop the framework, we conducted a state of the art review and interviewed patients and health experts using the Design Sprint methodology. This resulted in the creation of three personas and their related user stories. Our framework consists of three main components: User Interfaces as Services, Context-Aware Interactions, and User-Centred Data Management. A hypothetical scenario of a digital companion for individuals with diabetes was used to demonstrate the feasibility of the framework. The results of the proposal underscore the importance of considering all stakeholders when designing IoT systems and highlight the potential for individuals to benefit from a more integrated and personalised experience.

Keywords: IoT · Healthcare · IxD

1 Introduction

The Internet of Things (IoT) is revolutionising healthcare, with connected devices and systems transforming how we manage our health and well-being, providing real-time data on patients' health status, enabling early detection of problems and more personalised care [6]. However, there are several challenges to implementing IoT in healthcare, including privacy and security concerns, lack of standarisation, and the need for design and evaluation methods [1]. Overall,

N. A. Streitz and S. Konomi (Eds.): HCII 2023, LNCS 14036, pp. 91–104, 2023.
https://doi.org/10.1007/978-3-031-34668-2_7

these challenges underscore the importance of holistically designing Healthcare Systems rather than focusing on one specific area, such as sensors or communication technologies. By taking into account all aspects of an ecosystem, from hardware to software, IoT solutions can become much more effective [9].

The problem with developing IoT healthcare systems derives from the need to design for a wide range of users, including patients, caregivers, and clinicians [16]. This can be difficult because each group has different needs and expectations. For example, patients may want quick responses from the system, while caregivers may want more information about the patient's condition. Clinicians may need to make complex decisions quickly to provide optimal care for their patients [13]. Moreover, there is a need to consider the complex regulatory environment in which healthcare systems operate. Healthcare providers must comply with various federal and state regulations regarding privacy rights, data security, and clinical trial protocols [20]. In addition, many hospitals are required by law to share electronic health records (EHRs) with other hospitals within their network, so that patients can receive care from multiple sources at once [14].

It is essential to consider the user experience (UX) to realise the potential of IoT healthcare systems. There are several factors to take into account, for instance: the user's needs and preferences; the specific context in which the system will be used; the types of tasks that the user will need to perform; the level of complexity required for each task; and, any potential security or privacy concerns that may need to be addressed [19,23]. To achieve this, Interaction Design (IxD) can help create user-friendly and effective IoT systems. A well-designed system can improve patient outcomes by providing engaging and personalised care. By taking into account the needs of users, interaction designers can create solutions that are both useful and usable. Ultimately, interaction design can play a crucial role in making IoT healthcare systems more successful overall [12,21].

This paper proposes an IxD framework for IoT healthcare systems based on three key concepts: User interfaces as services, Context-aware interactions, and User-centred data management. The information we collected to build our proposal came from two sources: 1) a review of the state of the art to find out what problems have been encountered in usability and UX evaluations of IoT systems, as well as the advances made in the field of IxD; 2) based on a Design Thinking technique [15], the Design Sprint [11], we interviewed various users who have integrated IoT systems to take care of their health, in order to gather functional requirements and build personas based on this.

The paper is structured as follows: In Sect. 2, we review the relevant literature on IoT, healthcare, and interaction design. Next, Sect. 3 depicts the research methodology that we follow. After that, Sect. 4 describes the proposed interaction design framework for IoT healthcare systems. Finally, Sect. 5 concludes the paper and discusses future work.

2 Related Work

To begin with, it is necessary to review what characteristics health-oriented IoT systems have. To this end, the paper presented by Chhiba et al. [3] sets them out as a result of a literature review. This study highlights several key points regarding IoT systems, including their dynamic and constantly changing network structure, limited memory and energy resources, diversity in terms of device types, and the necessity for privacy and security measures when handling sensitive data. In addition, they describe three domains prevalent in this type of systems: those oriented towards healthy living, e.g., helping to monitor exercise routines, dietary regimes, and disease prevention. Another domain includes home care, e.g., self-care monitors, telemedicine, and accident prevention. Finally, there is specialised care, such as that provided by hospitals and health specialists.

Concerning the users of IoT technologies for health, Hossain et al. [8] present an analysis of the possible influences on potential users of these systems. One leverage has to do with interpersonal relationships, i.e., people tend to be encouraged to use specific technology on the recommendation of acquaintances. Another is trustworthiness, as users expect data to be reliable, accurate, and private. A further element is the user's intention to improve their health, whether due to a recent illness, medical recommendation or simply on their initiative; many people seek to start a healthier life and see technology as a means to help them in their purpose. Finally, another factor that can be mentioned is perceived value, as things such as low price, demand for a product, quality and what users get for a given price are elements that help to decide on the adoption of a system.

To understand the relationship between usability and health systems, we consulted the research by Yen and Bakken [22], who created a comprehensive review and categorisation of usability evaluation studies. Among their conclusions, they found that there is no good model or theoretical framework to support this kind of work and that evaluations are often narrowly focused, i.e., they evaluate a feature of a tool with a particular user and then try to extend the results to various scenarios, which leaves out many details and creates an incomplete picture. Additionally, they found that stakeholder feedback was often only integrated at one stage of development and never consulted again.

After reviewing the characteristics of IoT healthcare systems, users and various usability issues, we will discuss a work that presents a model for accepting IoT technologies. Although this research is not specific to healthcare systems, it is a good representation of a proposal incorporating all the elements we have previously described. In their study, Sneesl et al. [17] developed an IoT technology adoption model for a smart campus. By thoroughly reviewing the state of the art, they proposed a model that begins with two main elements: propagation and perceived value. The former element encompasses factors such as replicability, scalability, reliability, security and privacy, and the cost of deployment. The latter element includes utility, enjoyment, technicality, and trust. Through this model, we can note that the challenges in adopting IoT technology in an intelligent campus are similar to those in healthcare systems.

Finally, it is worth mentioning a work that allows us to delve into the needs and challenges faced by IoT environments for healthcare. De Michele and Furini [6] identify security, privacy, and confidentiality as elements to be considered not only by users, but by all those involved in these scenarios, i.e., manufacturers, researchers, technicians, and healthcare professionals. Additionally, they expose unintended behaviour, which refers to situations where users change their behaviour in response to the physiological data provided by the technologies. This can be dangerous, as only a certified physician can indicate a data-driven diagnosis and, based on this, point changes to patients. Otherwise, there is the possibility of unintentional harm.

3 Research Methodology

As a method for investigating, we chose to adapt the approach known as the Design Sprint which encompasses five stages [11,15]:

1. **Understand:** Participants assess the problem they intend to address, the individuals they are designing for, and the format they will utilise.
2. **Diverge:** Participants are urged to let go of preconceptions and engage in various exercises to generate as many ideas as possible, regardless of how feasible or unrealistic they may be.
3. **Decide:** Through different activities, participants decide which ideas to investigate further.
4. **Prototype:** Participants quickly sketch, design, and create a prototype of their ideas, focusing on the User Interface (UI) flow.
5. **Validate:** Participants present their product to users, test it, and are encouraged to provide feedback whenever possible.

Although this approach is not a traditional research methodology, we chose to utilise it because it is an effective way to create valuable products that not only function well and are aesthetically pleasing but also promotes changes in skills and ways of thinking [15]. The goal of this approach, in particular, is to reach a viable solution within five days. However, we modified this aspect as we were more interested in a user-centred design approach and felt that the time constraint would be restrictive.

4 Development

In this section, we detail the various stages of the methodology that were employed in the creation of our proposal. It is important to note that the process outlined here pertains to the initial iteration of the methodology.

4.1 Understand

To gather valuable insights and potential requirements, we researched by reaching out to friends and family members. Based on their characteristics, we divided them into three groups: 1) individuals with a specific health condition or chronic disease; 2) health professionals; 3) people who use electronic devices while exercising.

Through unstructured interviews and casual observation (primarily among those close to us), we understood their daily routines. Subsequently, we developed three personas representing the critical groups within our target population (see Fig. 1).

The next step in this phase was to conduct more specific interviews to uncover the needs and characteristics of each user group, as referenced in Keijzer-Broers and Southall's studies [10,18]. We conducted surveys and interviews with our participants to gather information on the types of devices or systems they would like to incorporate into their daily health routine. We also asked those who were already using such technology to share their feedback on what features were missing and how they could be improved. In the case of the health experts, we inquired about what kind of information they would like their patients to collect. We then used this information to create user stories for each persona, as outlined in Cohn's methodology [5], which can be seen in Tables 1, 2, and 3.

4.2 Diverge and Decide

Based on the personas and their user stories, we were able to come up with an integrative scenario that involves the following elements:

- **Personalised health tracking:** Each user could have a personalised dashboard that tracks their health metrics, such as José's blood glucose and blood pressure levels, Carlos' heart rate, oxygenation, and temperature during exercise, and Melissa's patients' progress with attention deficit hyperactivity disorder (ADHD) management.
- **Integration with wearable devices:** The dashboard could be integrated with wearable devices such as Carlos' smartwatch, which would automatically sync the health data in real-time, reducing the manual effort required to input the data.
- **Reminders and alarms:** The dashboard could also provide reminders and alarms for critical health-related activities, such as José's medication regimen and Carlos' workout schedule.
- **Sharing with healthcare professionals:** The dashboard could allow for secure sharing of health data with healthcare professionals, such as Melissa, enabling her to monitor her patients' progress and provide guidance accordingly.
- **Educational resources:** The dashboard could also provide educational resources, such as healthy recipes and information about the Pomodoro technique and mindfulness practices, to support the users' health journeys.

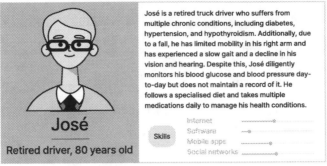

(a) José - Chronic diseases

(b) Melissa - Health professional

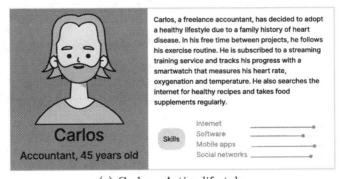

(c) Carlos - Active lifestyle

Fig. 1. The three personas we develop through interviews and observation: a person with chronic diseases (1a), a health professional (1b), and an individual with an active lifestyle (1c).

- **Accessibility:** The dashboard should be accessible and user-friendly, considering José's limited mobility, slow gait, and declining vision and hearing.
- **Data privacy and security:** The platform should ensure data privacy and security, ensuring that the users' health information is protected at all times.

Table 1. User stories for persona José

Requirements	Must-have	Nice to have
Functional	1. Automated tracking and monitoring of blood glucose levels, blood pressure, and medication intake. 2. Ability to easily record and access historical health data. 3. Option to set reminders for medication and dietary restrictions	1. Integration with a wearable device to track physical activity and monitor heart rate and oxygenation. 2. Voice-activated commands for ease of use with limited mobility. 3. Visual aids to improve reading of health data and notifications
User interaction	1. Simple and intuitive interface for tracking and monitoring health data. 2. Ability to share health information with medical professionals. 3. Option to receive personalised health tips and recommendations based on health data	1. Integration with a virtual assistant for easy access to health information and reminders. 2. Option for customising notifications and reminders to suit personal preferences. 3. Ability to set goals and track progress towards maintaining a healthy lifestyle
Social context	1. Ability to connect and communicate with a support network for motivation and encouragement. 2. Option for sharing health data and progress with friends and family. 3. Integration with social media for tracking and sharing healthy recipes and meal plans	1. Option to join virtual communities and participate in challenges with others working towards similar health goals. 2. Integration with health and wellness apps for a holistic approach to health management. 3. Access to a network of health professionals for virtual consultations and advice

This integrative design aligns with the needs and requirements of each persona and provides a comprehensive solution to their health-related concerns. Therefore, we started from these points to find common concepts and discussed them to see which ones were necessary to create a conceptual framework that reflected the acquired insight. Table 4 provides a condensed overview of the ideas we generated, their evaluation outcomes, and the reasoning behind them.

4.3   Prototype

After carefully selecting the dimensions most applicable to our integrative scenario and discussing them in terms of the review of relevant literature, we present our conceptual framework based in the classical usability axes. Drawing inspiration from the work by Gutwin and Greenberg [7], Table 5 summarises our findings.

Table 2. User stories for persona Melissa

Requirements	Must-have	Nice to have
Functional	1. An app that integrates a calendar and reminders to schedule appointments and medication. 2. A journal for patients to track their moods and thoughts. 3. A platform that offers educational resources and videos about ADHD	1. A feature that allows patients to track their sleep patterns. 2. A tool that helps patients to manage their stress levels. 3. A library of guided meditations and mindfulness exercises
User interaction	1. A user-friendly interface with clear instructions and icons. 2. A platform that allows patients to send updates to their therapists. 3. A tool that provides a secure and confidential platform for patients to communicate with their therapists	1. An Artificial Intelligence-powered chatbot that provides personalized support to patients. 2. A platform that offers teletherapy services. 3. A tool that integrates with wearable devices and tracks physical activity
Social context	1. A platform that offers a community of support and encouragement for patients with ADHD. 2. A feature that enables patients to connect with others who share their condition. 3. A tool that provides resources for family members and caregivers	1. An app that integrates with popular social media platforms. 2. A platform that offers peer-to-peer support groups. 3. A tool that provides resources for schools and teachers

In addition to presenting the three dimensions according to the usability axes, we also created their corresponding definitions:

- **User Interfaces as Services:** This framework aspect focuses on designing and implementing user interfaces as independent, modular, and scalable services. The goal is to provide users with a seamless experience across multiple devices and platforms while maintaining the interface more accessible.
- **Context-Aware Interactions:** This framework feature emphasises the importance of understanding and utilising the user's context to create more personalised and meaningful interactions. This can include taking into account the user's location, time, device, physical conditions, and other relevant factors to provide relevant information and recommendations.
- **User-Centred Data Management:** The framework's final dimension prioritises managing user data based on their needs and preferences. This includes ensuring privacy, security, control over their personal information and offering tools for users to understand better and make decisions about their data.

Table 3. User stories for persona Carlos

Requirements	Must-have	Nice to have
Functional	1. A smartwatch that tracks heart rate, oxygenation, and temperature. 2. An app that tracks exercise routines and progress. 3. A platform that provides healthy recipe suggestions	1. A tool that integrates with a wearable device to track physical activity. 2. A feature that provides a nutrition database and suggests meal plans. 3. A platform that integrates with a wearable device to track hydration levels
User interaction	1. A user-friendly interface with clear instructions and icons. 2. A platform that integrates with a smartwatch. 3. An app that provides real-time feedback on progress	1. A tool that provides motivational messages and rewards. 2. An app that provides audio cues and verbal instructions. 3. A platform that integrates with social media and allows users to share their progress with others
Social context	1. A platform that provides a community of support and encouragement for people who want to live a healthy lifestyle. 2. A tool that provides resources for people with a family history of heart disease. 3. An app that integrates with social media to connect with friends and family	1. A platform that offers peer-to-peer support groups. 2. An app that integrates with social media to track friends and family's progress. 3. A feature that allows users to compete with friends and family in healthy challenges

4.4 Validate

The validation of our conceptual framework can be demonstrated by exploring its application in developing a digital companion for individuals with diabetes. To realise this, let us consider a hypothetical scenario in which a person with diabetes uses a digital companion developed using our framework. We chose diabetes because it is one of the most prevalent chronic conditions in Mexico [2]. Table 6 summarises this proposal according to our framework.

First, User Interfaces as Services will enable the digital companion to provide personalised user interfaces that cater to the specific needs of individuals with diabetes. This can be achieved by integrating wearable devices, such as a smartwatch or a fitness tracker, and mobile applications, such as apps that complement continuous glucose sensors specifically designed for people with diabetes. The smartwatch will display essential health metrics, e.g., glucose levels, blood pressure, and heart rate. At the same time, the mobile app will provide a platform for logging food intake, tracking physical activity, and setting reminders for medication.

Table 4. Proposals for possible dimensions of our framework

Proposal	Outcome	Evaluation
Health prediction	Rejected	This may raise concerns about data privacy and security, as well as the accuracy of the predictions, which may have a negative impact on the users' health
Integration with medical devices	Rejected	Medical devices may require regulatory approval, which may be a significant barrier to implementation and are way beyond our scope
Gamification	Rejected	This may not be well-received by all users, as some may prefer a more serious approach to health tracking and monitoring
User interfaces as services	**Accepted**	This feature meets the accessibility requirement, ensuring a user-friendly and accessible experience for those with mobility limitations and sensory impairments
Context-aware interactions	**Accepted**	This dimension supports the provision of relevant reminders, aligning with the platform's goal to assist users on their health journeys. It also satisfies the educational resources requirement, by offering resources to support users' health
User-centred data management	**Accepted**	This proposal advances the platform's goal of allowing users to securely share their health data with healthcare professionals. It also addresses the requirement of data privacy and security, by protecting users' health information

Next, Context-Aware Interactions will allow the digital companion to understand the context in which the individual is using the system and to provide relevant information and recommendations. For example, let us suppose the person is searching for a healthy meal option. In that case, the digital companion can use GPS and Internet data to determine the location and provide a list of healthy options on the restaurant's menu. Additionally, the digital companion can integrate with health and wellness platforms to provide personalised recommendations based on the individual's dietary preferences, health conditions, and goals.

Finally, User-Centred Data Management will ensure that the digital companion's data is stored, managed, and controlled by the user. The digital companion will be designed to use secure and encrypted storage solutions through Health Insurance Portability and Accountability Act (HIPAA)-compliant platforms [4], to store health data and will provide users with the ability to share their data with healthcare providers if they so choose.

Table 5. Interaction design framework for IoT healthcare systems

Components of Usability	User Interfaces as Services	Context-Aware Interactions	User-Centred Data Management
Effectiveness	Provides users with the necessary information and tools to manage their health effectively	Detects users' context and presents them with relevant information	Enables users to manage and understand their health data in a personalized and meaningful way
Efficiency	Streamlines user interactions with the system to minimize the number of steps required to complete tasks	Anticipates user needs based on the context and provides relevant information without the user having to actively seek it	Allows users to access and manipulate their health data easily and quickly
Satisfaction	Offers a positive and user-friendly experience that encourages users to use the system regularly	Creates a sense of awareness and control for users over their health and well-being	Allows users to feel confident in their understanding of their health and how to manage it effectively

In this way, combining our framework into existing IoT devices and platforms may provide users with a seamless and integrated experience and represents an intent to amalgamate the growing body of research in this area.

Table 6. Interaction design concepts of a digital companion for individuals with diabetes

Components of Usability	User Interfaces as Services	Context-Aware Interactions	User-Centred Data Management
Effectiveness	Personalised user interfaces tailored to the specific needs of individuals with diabetes, such as a smartwatch displaying glucose levels, blood pressure, and heart rate, and a mobile app for logging food intake and tracking physical activity	Relevant information and recommendations based on the individual's location, dietary preferences, health conditions, and goals	Ability for users to share their data with healthcare providers if they so choose
Efficiency	Integration of wearable devices, such as smartwatches or fitness trackers, and mobile applications, to provide real-time health metrics and personalised recommendations	Use GPS and Internet data to provide relevant information and recommendations in real time	Secure and encrypted storage solutions to store health data
Satisfaction	Customisable interfaces that cater to individual preferences, making the system easier to use and understand	Context-aware recommendations that provide value to the user, increasing their sense of control over their health	Ownership and control of data, giving users peace of mind and confidence in the system

5   Conclusions and Future Work

The increasing prevalence of chronic conditions and the need for better patient outcomes have motivated the development of various devices and IoT gadgets to support individuals with their health and wellness goals. However, existing solutions often need to be improved in terms of usability, which can limit their adoption and effectiveness. Our paper proposes a conceptual interaction design framework for IoT healthcare systems that considers the three classical key components of usability: effectiveness, efficiency, and satisfaction.

We conducted a comprehensive review of the state of the art to understand the current trends and challenges in the design and development of health-oriented IoT systems. To address this gap, we employed the Design Sprint methodology [11], conducting interviews with patients and health experts to develop three personas that represent common groups of users for health-based IoT systems: those with a disease seeking to improve their condition, health experts who require more tools to support their patients; and people who want a healthier life.

Through these personas and their corresponding user stories, we proposed a conceptual framework that consists of three main components: User Interfaces as Services, Context-Aware Interactions, and User-Centred Data Management. We can design systems that provide personalised, context-aware, and user-centred experiences by applying these concepts. To demonstrate the viability of our framework, we presented a hypothetical scenario of a digital companion for individuals with diabetes, which incorporates the concepts of our framework.

The results of our proposal highlight the importance of considering all stakeholders when designing IoT systems. By integrating our framework into existing IoT devices and platforms, individuals can benefit from a seamless and integrated experience, which can help them achieve their health and wellness goals. However, our work has limitations, such as the need for further research to validate our framework and explore its application in other domains.

In terms of future work, there are several avenues to be explored. For instance, developing customised user interfaces for different types of chronic conditions, such as heart disease or mental health disorders, could be beneficial. Additionally, there is a need to consider the ethical and privacy implications, especially in terms of data management and sharing. Furthermore, developing a toolkit or design guidelines based on our framework could support the design and development of systems and help practitioners implement our framework in practice.

References

1. Calvillo-Arbizu, J., Román-Martínez, I., Reina-Tosina, J.: Internet of things in health: requirements, issues, and gaps. Comput. Methods Programs Biomed. **208**, 106231 (2021). https://doi.org/10.1016/j.cmpb.2021.106231
2. Campos-Nonato, I., Ramírez-Villalobos, M., Flores-Coria, A., Valdez, A., Monterrubio-Flores, E.: Prevalence of previously diagnosed diabetes and glycemic control strategies in Mexican adults: Ensanut-2016. PLOS ONE **15**(4), 1–11 (2020). https://doi.org/10.1371/journal.pone.0230752

3. Chhiba, L., Marzak, A., Sidqui, M.: Quality attributes for evaluating IoT health-care systems. In: Ben Ahmed, M., Boudhir, A.A., Karas, İR., Jain, V., Mellouli, S. (eds.) SCA 2021. LNNS, vol. 393, pp. 495–505. Springer, Cham (2022). https://doi.org/10.1007/978-3-030-94191-8_40
4. Cohen, I.G., Mello, M.M.: HIPAA and protecting health information in the 21st Century. JAMA **320**(3), 231–232 (2018). https://doi.org/10.1001/jama.2018.5630
5. Cohn, M.: User Stories Applied: For Agile Software Development. Addison-Wesley Professional, Boston (2004)
6. De Michele, R., Furini, M.: IoT healthcare: benefits, issues and challenges. In: Proceedings of the 5th EAI International Conference on Smart Objects and Technologies for Social Good. GoodTechs '19, pp. 160–164. Association for Computing Machinery, Valencia (2019). https://doi.org/10.1145/3342428.3342693
7. Gutwin, C., Greenberg, S.: The mechanics of collaboration: developing low cost usability evaluation methods for shared workspaces. In: Proceedings IEEE 9th International Workshops on Enabling Technologies: Infrastructure for Collaborative Enterprises (WET ICE 2000), Gaithersburg, MD, USA, pp. 98–103 (2000). https://doi.org/10.1109/ENABL.2000.883711
8. Hossain, M.I., Yusof, A.F., Hussin, A.R.C., lahad, N.A., Sadiq, A.S.: Factors influencing adoption model of continuous glucose monitoring devices for internet of things healthcare. Internet Things **15**, 100353 (2021). https://doi.org/10.1016/j.iot.2020.100353, https://www.sciencedirect.com/science/article/pii/S2542660520301840
9. Kashyap, V., Kumar, A., Kumar, A., Hu, Y.C.: A systematic survey on fog and IoT driven healthcare: open challenges and research issues. Electronics **11**(17) (2022). https://doi.org/10.3390/electronics11172668
10. Keijzer-Broers, W.J.W., de Reuver, M.: Applying agile design sprint methods in action design research: prototyping a health and wellbeing platform. In: Parsons, J., Tuunanen, T., Venable, J., Donnellan, B., Helfert, M., Kenneally, J. (eds.) DESRIST 2016. LNCS, vol. 9661, pp. 68–80. Springer, Cham (2016). https://doi.org/10.1007/978-3-319-39294-3_5
11. Knapp, J., Zeratsky, J., Kowitz, B.: Sprint: how to solve big problems and test new ideas in just five days. Simon and Schuster (2016)
12. Lemoine, F., Aubonnet, T., Simoni, N.: IoT composition based on self-controlled services. J. Ambient. Intell. Humaniz. Comput. **11**(11), 5167–5186 (2020). https://doi.org/10.1007/s12652-020-01831-4
13. Pradhan, B., Bhattacharyya, S., Pal, K.: IoT-based applications in healthcare devices. J. Healthc. Eng. **2021**, 6632599 (2021). https://doi.org/10.1155/2021/6632599
14. Riad, K., Hamza, R., Yan, H.: Sensitive and energetic IoT access control for managing cloud electronic health records. IEEE Access **7**, 86384–86393 (2019). https://doi.org/10.1109/ACCESS.2019.2926354
15. Sari, E., Tedjasaputra, A.: Designing valuable products with design sprint. In: Bernhaupt, R., Dalvi, G., Joshi, A., K. Balkrishan, D., O'Neill, J., Winckler, M. (eds.) INTERACT 2017. LNCS, vol. 10516, pp. 391–394. Springer, Cham (2017). https://doi.org/10.1007/978-3-319-68059-0_37
16. Selvaraj, S., Sundaravaradhan, S.: Challenges and opportunities in IoT healthcare systems: a systematic review. SN Appl. Sci. **2**(1), 1–8 (2019). https://doi.org/10.1007/s42452-019-1925-y
17. Sneesl, R., Jusoh, Y.Y., Jabar, M.A., Abdullah, S.: Revising technology adoption factors for IoT-based smart campuses: a systematic review. Sustainability **14**(8), 4840 (2022). https://doi.org/10.3390/su14084840

18. Southall, H., Marmion, M., Davies, A.: Adapting Jake Knapp's design sprint approach for AR/VR applications in digital heritage. In: tom Dieck, M.C., Jung, T. (eds.) Augmented Reality and Virtual Reality. PI, pp. 59–70. Springer, Cham (2019). https://doi.org/10.1007/978-3-030-06246-0_5
19. Suryandari, Y.: Survei IoT healthcare device. Jurnal Sistem Cerdas **3**(2), 153–164 (2020). https://doi.org/10.37396/jsc.v3i2.55
20. Syagnik (Sy) Banerjee, Hemphill, T., Longstreet, P.: Wearable devices and healthcare: data sharing and privacy. Inf. Soc. **34**(1), 49–57 (2018). https://doi.org/10.1080/01972243.2017.1391912
21. Wiberg, M.: Addressing IoT: Towards material-centered interaction design. In: Kurosu, M. (ed.) HCI 2018. LNCS, vol. 10901, pp. 198–207. Springer, Cham (2018). https://doi.org/10.1007/978-3-319-91238-7_17
22. Yen, P.Y., Bakken, S.: Review of health information technology usability study methodologies. J. Am. Med. Inform. Assoc. **19**(3), 413–422 (2011). https://doi.org/10.1136/amiajnl-2010-000020
23. Yu, H., Zhou, Z.: Optimization of IoT-based artificial intelligence assisted telemedicine health analysis system. IEEE Access **9**, 85034–85048 (2021). https://doi.org/10.1109/ACCESS.2021.3088262

Guidelines for Practicing Responsible Innovation in HPC: A Sociotechnical Approach

Elaine M. Raybourn[1(✉)] and Killian Muollo[1,2]

[1] Sandia National Laboratories, Albuquerque, NM 87185, USA
{emraybo,kmuollo}@sandia.gov
[2] University of Central Florida, Orlando, FL 32816, USA

Abstract. While significant investments have been made in the exploration of ethics in computation, recent advances in high performance computing (HPC) and artificial intelligence (AI) have reignited a discussion for more responsible and ethical computing with respect to the design and development of pervasive sociotechnical systems within the context of existing and evolving societal norms and cultures. The ubiquity of HPC in everyday life presents complex sociotechnical challenges for all who seek to practice responsible computing and ethical technological innovation. The present paper provides guidelines which scientists, researchers, educators, and practitioners alike, can employ to become more aware of one's personal values system that may unconsciously shape one's approach to computation and ethics.

Keywords: ethics · responsible computing · sociotechnical systems

1 Introduction

High performance computing (HPC), or supercomputing, describes computation capable of rapidly performing complex calculations by functioning above a petaFLOP (computing speed equal to one million (10^{15}) floating-point operations per second). In layman's terms HPC is one million times faster than computing possible on our best gaming laptops, desktops, or servers. HPC performs complex calculations at very high speeds, processing data on hundreds or thousands of clusters of networked servers, called nodes, which work together in parallel. HPC is known for processing software codes, algorithms, and large multi-dimensional data sets for various domains including but not limited to energy, climate, healthcare, economic and financial services, and defense. High performance computing as an international community of agencies, national laboratories, academia, and industry has been on the forefront of many scientific insights and advances in technology such as artificial intelligence (AI), modeling and simulation, genomics, and quantum computing. Today even more supercomputing power is coming online with new exascale computers such as Frontier, located at Oak Ridge National Laboratory. Frontier leverages an ecosystem of new software technologies, scientific applications, and hardware developed by The United States Department of Energy (DOE) and National Nuclear Security Administration (NNSA) Exascale Computing Project (ECP) [31]. Exascale computing is a new class of high-performance computing systems whose power is measured in exaFLOPS, or computing speed equal to one billion calculations per second, and are one thousand times more powerful than today's petaFLOPS machines. Frontier currently functions at 1102 petaFLOPS, or 1.102 exaFLOPS. Exascale computing will further enable solving incredibly complex research problems, such as simulating the human brain, predicting space weather, cracking encryption codes, advancing medical research, and modeling the Earth's climate and the global economy [27].

While supercomputing applications require the specialized computational and networking hardware to work through very large data, such as a model of the global atmosphere, the more broad category of HPC encompasses many newer applications made feasible by the larger data capacities and ability to spread serial processing across many nodes simultaneously. Cloud infrastructures often offer some HPC-optimized resources for rent enabling many to access large-scale computer capabilities for a tiny fraction of the cost of building and operating a dedicated data center. HPC provides the data management, storage, and performance optimization that is necessary for pervasive smart environments and ecosytems. Therefore whether we are scrolling through social media posts on our mobile devices, sharing photos with our family in the cloud, remotely manipulating our smart home applications from afar, streaming live events, or engaging in video calls with colleagues, we are leveraging HPC. Today's cloud-based HPC has become mainstream in that it supports tasks accessed by non-scientists as well as consumers— strengthening its foothold as a key technology capability behind our daily interactions with pervasive and ubiquitous computing applications or ecosystems that enable and influence everything from how we learn and grow to how we live [10].

Given the pervasiveness of HPC + AI and the likelihood that future technological innovation will have intended as well as unintended impact on societies, we believe scientists, researchers, educators, and practitioners have opportunities to hone the practice of ethical and responsible computing in the design and development of HPC for pervasive ecosystems. The present paper provides guidelines for practicing responsible HPC innovation derived from the domains of mathematics and social science. We introduce progress tracking cards (PTC) for use within projects or by individuals and teams to codify the practice of a sociotechnical approach which focuses on becoming more aware of one's personal values system, and understanding how ones' values may unconsciously shape one's approach to computation.

2   Ethical Considerations in HPC

Ethical considerations may be challenging but they can be both existential and epistemological opportunities to better understand humanity and its relationship to the knowledge it produces. Ethics need not be an intractable problem or a scary topic to be avoided. Ethical considerations are opportunities to question our assumptions about what is known, to recursively explore meaning, and to then act from a position of deep conviction. We believe it is far better to have a voice in shaping innovation than to avoid accountability. Below we present some of the more common ethical considerations presented by sociotechnical systems and smart ecosystems powered by HPC.

- **Bias and fairness:** HPC hardware and software ecosystems are increasingly utilized to develop machine learning algorithms, large language models, and other AI systems which may result in the transmission of bias from training data integrity, sampling, aggregation, data engineering, etc. For example, see [7,8].
- **Intellectual property:** Code that is generated by AI systems may use copyrighted open source software in training data which raises questions about authorship as well as unintentional violation of copyright and licenses [7,11].
- **Privacy and data security:** Large language models may introduce security vulnerabilities, or buggy and insecure code which can be detrimental to sensitive data analysis in critical domains such as medicine, finance, healthcare, etc. [13]. Additionally, language models may plagiarize texts containing personal, sensitive, or other forms of identifiable information [18] as well as fabricate information [33].
- **Environment:** Managing power and energy consumption without sacrificing performance and reliability remains a challenge of high performance computing facilities [35]. Of additional concern is the amount of water used to cool HPC data centers, especially when scarce.
- **Access and Governance:** While cloud-based computing is helping to democratize HPC, costs associated with use, security, and storage continue to marginalize organizations, industry, and educational institutions who cannot pay for HPC-as-a-Service. Finally, for many scientists who rely on HPC for their research, timely access to supercomputers also remains a top challenge [38].

3   Responsible Computing and Innovation

A number of organizations provide resources to assist the scientific community with applying ethical decision making toward more responsible computing and innovation. The ACM Code of Ethics and Professional Conduct [24] offers high-level guidelines that serve as a basis of ethical decision making within the computing community. Several data science codes and frameworks of ethics have also been identified in [30]. The National Institute of Standards and Technology (NIST) Risk Framework [23] is a risk management approach for developers and stakeholders of computation leveraging AI systems which advises that efforts not only align with existing standards and guidelines in their respective domains, but also investigate recent advancements in domains such as healthcare or transportation (for an example from transportation see [15]).

The NIST guidance, for example, indicates that risk management is much more involved than solely coding principles of ethics into AI systems or constraining AI systems to behave ethically. Addressing ethics in software development is more complex than introducing ethics into computation alone – it requires careful attention from the individuals creating computation because ethics is *social* [17]. Highlighting the social nature of ethics, a recent article appearing in ACM's Interactions [39] called for human-centered AI and offered nine actions that can be taken to foster collaboration between professionals from the domains of AI and HCI (human computer interaction); including designing an ethical approach to AI collaboratively, and training the next generation of AI developers and designers with a hybrid university course curriculum consisting of AI major + social science minor, or HCI + AI.

The inconsistency of ethics courses offered in university computer science curricula has led to recommendations for the inclusion of more ethics training as well as teaching political action as it applies to computing [20]. Additionally Saltz et al. [30] identified twelve key themes relevant to data science and ethics education, and the National Academy of Sciences (NAS) also echoed the call for universities, professional societies, and scientists to invest in transdisciplinary research that addresses innovation in a more holistic manner (e.g. social and behavioral science + ethical thinking + computing research), moving beyond discipline-specific approaches [22].

The NAS made eight recommendations for responsible research; among them addressing ethics and societal consequences together from the start of a project, integrating a program of ethics into research proposals, seeking out the advice of subject matter experts on topics usually studied in the social sciences, such as race, gender, justice, etc.; publicly sharing research artifacts and codes, and engaging often with the public on matters of social nuance. The NAS also identified qualitative data collection methods from the social and behavioral sciences that are instrumental in illuminating the "morally relevant actors, environments, and interactions in a sociotechnical system; ethical reasoning provides a calculus for understanding how to resolve competing moral tensions involving those actors, environments, and interactions" [22]. They further indicate:

> Together, these concepts and methods enable the development of pragmatic practices that can guide researchers in ways to carry out socially attuned computing research. It is important to note again that computer scientists cannot be expected to become expert ethicists and social scientists. Rather, responsible computing research requires that they collaborate with experts in other disciplines who can bring these important instruments to bear as computing research is designed and carried out [22].

In addition to enabling the development of pragmatic practices and collaboration among researchers across scientific domains, it is equally important to engage practitioners and non-academicians who can help situate real-world societal nuances within sociotechical approaches. The real world, interpreted uniquely by each individual and evolving over time, serves to reflexively challenge assumptions present in theoretical constructs [28]. In this way, a sociotechnical approach becomes an opportunity to interweave ethics more thoughtfully into ones' efforts toward responsible computing and technical innovation.

4   A Sociotechnical Approach

We have argued that as with any ubiquitous and influential technology, HPC scientists, researchers, educators, and practitioners should carefully consider the full impact of its influence and use within larger cultural and sociotechnical contexts, especially when considering the role of HPC in innovations such as smart cities, smart grids, driverless cars, large-scale data analytics and other "intelligent" and self-organizing systems [34]. We use the term *sociotechnical* in the present paper to express the authors' underlying theoretical perspective that society and technology are intertwined, influence each other, and that when innovating we should iteratively consider the social and cultural contexts of intended use as well as unintended consequences. According to the National Academy of Sciences [22]:

> A sociotechnical approach enables identifying, designing for, and tracking the benefits and risks that arise from introducing novel technologies into social worlds. It draws on social theories and social scientific methodologies, and empirical observations that enable the development of hypotheses about the ways people interact with the world around them.

We posit that a sociotechnical approach is a precursor to practicing responsible computing and innovation. That is to say, while "ethics provides tools for the moral evaluation of behaviors, institutions, and social structures and for dealing with choices among and conflicts between values" [22], before we can adequately address moral evaluations of institutions, social structures, etc., it is necessary to evaluate our *own* behaviors, assumptions, and biases. While early pioneers may have relied on a "moral compass" to intuitively guide engineering innovation [40], it would be wise to first become aware of and understand our *theoretical lens* by which the social world is experienced, so we can later better articulate the sociotechnical approach from which each of us operates. It is unfortunate that rather unwittingly our values, assumptions, and biases may make it into computational designs and development without mindful attention and reflection. We can begin to address our fallibility by incorporating a sociotechnical *mindset* into our workflows and processes. Maintaining a responsible approach to ethical computing can present a challenging, yet necessary and even rewarding, undertaking.

5   Guidelines for Practicing a Sociotechnical Approach

As discussed in earlier sections, while professional organizations are beginning to construct robust guidelines for ethical approaches in computing [16], ethics is still generally treated and taught as a discipline entirely separate from computer science [29]. According to Califf and Goodwin [4], such a mental division can lead computer science students—potential designers of future HPC and AI systems—to neglect the significance of ethics in their field. Furthermore, engineering education often presents a divide with respect to sociotechnical curricula [19].

So, how can ethical consideration become a daily habit in a scientific software team? How does an individual or group begin the dialog around ethical considerations? According to [3], "one of the key issues to address is how to represent and reason with social values, mathematically and computationally, without reducing them to base quantities." We can also combine social science methods with critical methods to more deeply explore intercultural communication and meaning [21]. In this way, developers of scientific software need not wade too far from their familiar discipline for guidance in maintaining responsible and ethical practices. Many of the seemingly-foreign tenets of a sociotechnical approach, especially the exercise of identifying, analyzing, and minimizing bias, find analogs in the mathematical logic that already lays the foundations of HPC and AI. So while logic may regularly be used to identify bias in software and mathematical proofs, we can also sharpen our perspective-taking skills by applying what we know to the identification and mitigation of social bias.

5.1   Leveraging Familiar Parallels in Mathematics

Understanding the nuances of ethics might seem daunting to many scientific software developers, but the practice of upholding the logic of mathematics and computer science is far less so. Not only does nearly every algorithm have its roots in a mathematical proof, but any developer coming from a computer science or software engineering background has almost certainly been exposed to mathematical logic in their training or education. While other science, technology, and engineering fields relate to mathematics largely in terms of numeric computation, computer science is unique in that it overlaps with mathematics largely in the area of logical reasoning [2]. Therefore, by likening the process of maintaining responsible ethical habits based on a sociotechnical approach to well-studied mathematical practices, we can provide a first step toward responsible and ethical computing that is more accessible to the people actually doing that computing.

It is well documented that AI can reflect the explicit—or, more often, implicit—biases of its creators [20]. For example, Celi et al. [5] found that their AI-driven review of clinical papers disproportionately favored research from high-income countries authored by men. They concluded that their training dataset was inherently skewed by the nature of the system it originated from; in order for the resulting tool to be useful, they affirmed the importance of understanding the context of application, given that these inherent biases exist and cannot be avoided. This exemplifies one of the core aspects of the sociotechnical approach to ethics espoused in the present paper, that every agent and environment brings with it a lens from which it is perceived that must be acknowledged and examined in order to minimize adverse consequences in research and development.

Similarly, the end results of any mathematical endeavor rely heavily on the assumptions made by researchers at the beginning of their work. For example, it is well known that behaviors of mathematical systems and tests vary wildly based on initial conditions, and in most cases this effect cannot be avoided entirely but only minimized [9]. Furthermore, when it comes time to apply these theories in practical situations like meteorological forecasting, analyses that take such initial condition sensitivity into account have been measured to be more accurate in comparison to empirical observations (e.g. see [25]).

This is all to say that the social science practice of not only acknowledging but actively analyzing and curtailing inherent biases is already a skill that anyone in a mathematically-based field should also be familiar with. Instead of thinking of a sociotechnical approach to responsible, ethical computing as an entirely new discipline to understand, or one that is largely the sole responsibility of social scientists and ethicists, scientific software developers can draw on their existing logical patterns to critically analyze the tools they use and create. In particular, the process of mathematical modeling—that is, the process of tackling real-world problems through the formulation, analysis, and interpretation of mathematical systems [32]—provides an algorithmic approach to many of the sociotechnical considerations necessary for developing and honing an ethical lens.

5.2   Mindset: Analogy from Mathematical Modeling

The process of constructing a mathematical model provides a very direct analogy to examining bias, as assumptions not only affect end results but quite literally dictate the nature of the system being modeled [32]. In model construction, the first step after identifying a real-life problem is often to explicitly enumerate all assumptions of the model [1]. These can range from simple statements of fact, like "the population consists of N individuals," to intuitive observations of real-world phenomena, like "the disease will spread faster the more individuals become afflicted." Listing these out is vital, since each assumption will necessarily correspond to some mathematical equivalent; for example, the latter assumption in the previous sentence is common in susceptible-infectious-recovered (SIR) epidemiological models and motivates the inclusion of mass action principles in the core equations of the model [37].

The act of defining assumptions as plainly as possible *before* considering any analysis helps ensure proper scope and minimize confounding variables. But modeling, like software development, is an iterative process; it is not sufficient to settle on a plan once and adhere to it without recurrent investigation. All potential assumptions need to constantly be evaluated in the context of their application. Aarts [1] visualizes such a workflow, as illustrated in Fig. 1 below. With the iterative cycle of this process denoted by dashed arrows, we can see very clearly just how much work must go into formulation and constant reevaluation of a model before it ever sees actual application.

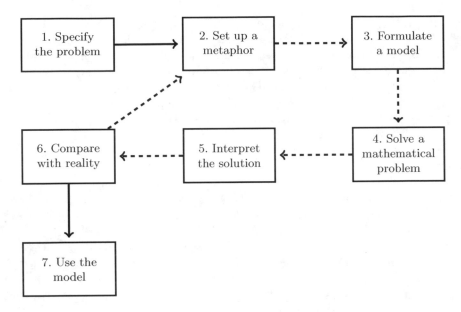

Fig. 1. Mathematical modeling workflow described by Aarts [1].

Contextualizing this framework in terms of a sociotechnical approach to software development, we can replace "model" with "project" (boxes 3 and 7) and "mathematical" with "computational" (box 4) to easily construct an analog. In step 1, before we even enter the iterative cycle of project development, we can begin to discuss and document the important ethical considerations and sociotechnical assumptions that could lead to biases, security vulnerabilities, and other ethical concerns later on. Then, as we work through the more traditional development in steps 2–6, we maintain awareness of these concerns in order to safeguard against unintentional ethical missteps. Finally, we make sure to continually compare the outputs and results of our tools with what we expect to produce, again keeping in mind our assumptions and the inherent biases present in our own viewpoints, our environment, and any input data we use. This thought process is one that is utilized in social sciences. While we can get through a lot of this process on our own, during this process it is advisable when possible to collaborate with social scientists, ethicists, and the public.

5.3   Tracking Benefits and Risks

As we have discussed in previous sections, the NAS includes in their definition of a sociotechnical approach the "tracking of benefits and risks that arise from novel technologies" [22]. So we must not only *apply* practices and habits that facilitate responsible computing, but *document* them, as well as our progress in maintaining them. To achieve this end, we turn to existing Productivity and Sustainability Improvement Planning (PSIP) tools. The PSIP toolkit [26] is comprised of publicly-available resources provided by the Interoperable Design of Extreme-Scale Applications Software (IDEAS) Productivity Project [36] which aims to refine computer science engineering practices in terms of productivity, sustainability, and overall quality [6]. In particular, we focus on their development of Progress Tracking Cards (PTCs). These are compact documents created for a specific project with a specific goal in mind, which provide explicitly itemized "stages" toward attaining said goal [14]. It is an important distinction to note that PTCs are *not* checklists; instead of listing isolated tasks that can individually contribute to some larger, unstated objective, PTCs describe incremental and measurable phases of implementation toward a single goal from a high-level perspective. For this very reason, we propose that PTCs make an ideal tool for responsible computing, as the NAS specifically mentions the shortcomings of "ethical checklists" [22]:

> Indeed, no simple checklist could suffice for determining if research is responsible; there is no mechanical procedure that can spare researchers from having to think about the values they embed in their research and the trade-offs they make in doing so.

We also chose to use PTCs for their focus on open-source sharing. In particular, the PSIP toolkit supports a PTC catalog [12], which is a public GitHub repository that development teams can use to observe others' existing PTCs as well as upload their own. In encouraging such collaboration, the use of PTCs allows teams that otherwise may not interact to share lessons learned and, in doing so, foster a community of responsible and ethical practice in computing.

To construct a PTC, we begin by defining our "target" and "user story." The former is fairly self-explanatory: a "target" is the specific goal that a PTC aims to facilitate achieving. As indicated by the subject of this paper, we construct a target as follows:

Target: Ensure that a scientific software development team is practicing responsible innovation and ethical computing to the highest reasonable standard, in line with a sociotechnical mindset.

Next, we define an appropriate "user story," which is a first-person statement following the template, "As a [role], I want [desire], so that [impact]" [26]. User stories may be inspired by software engineering use cases. Adopting the persona of a member of a scientific software development team, we construct the following user story:

User story: As a developer of scientific software, I want to understand, analyze, and, if necessary, mitigate the potential ethical implications and repercussions of my work. In doing so, I intend for the projects my team works on to accomplish what we intend them to, as well as to contribute to our society in a constructive manner.

Finally, we can use these abstract goals to construct an actual PTC. We will visualize this as a table with numbered stages accompanied by descriptions of what it means to exist in that stage. These descriptions should be written in the past tense to indicate that they represent the end state of a goal that will have been achieved upon arriving at that stage. The lowest stage will always begin at 0, and then increment to a number typically between 3 and 5, depending on how the stages are constructed and divided [14]. Figure 2 below compiles the principles and strategies discussed in this paper into a 5-stage PTC.

Stage	Description
0	Ethical considerations are not addressed at any point in the development process.
1	Ethical concerns have been communicated by individual developers in weekly meetings as problems have been identified.
2	Developers have implemented a plan for some level of formal analysis with regard to ethical concerns.
3	Team members have collaborated to discuss ethical considerations during development and have executed their plans. Testing and verification processes that address and measure ethical concerns have been developed and applied alongside the project.
4	Team members have collaborated to formally document ethical concerns, testing, and analyses both before and throughout development. Testing and verification processes have been designed with these concerns in mind and have been continually applied throughout the project's lifecycle. The team has shared lessons learned with the public.

Fig. 2. Proposed PTC for employing a sociotechnical approach for working toward responsible computing.

6   Conclusion

Understanding the nuances of ethics might seem daunting, but the actual practice of a sociotechnical approach does not have to be. Developers of scientific software can look to their familiar disciplines for guidance in maintaining responsible and ethical practices. Many of the seemingly-foreign tenets of a sociotechnical approach that are familiar to social scientists, especially the exercise of identifying, analyzing, and minimizing bias, find analogs in the mathematical logic that lay the foundations of HPC and AI. This logic can be applied to developing a mindset that questions existing assumptions and seeks to mitigate social bias.

Scientists, researchers, educators, and practitioners alike have opportunities to hone the practice of ethical and responsible computing in the design and development of HPC for pervasive smart ecosystems. The present paper provided guidelines for practicing responsible HPC and innovation. We introduced progress tracking cards (PTC) for use within projects or by individuals and teams to codify the practice of a sociotechnical approach. By focusing on becoming more aware of our own personal values system, and understanding how our values may unconsciously shape our approaches to computation we can practice more responsible innovation.

Finally, ethical considerations may be challenging but they can be both existential and epistemological opportunities to better understand humanity and its relationship to the knowledge it produces. Ethics need not be an intractable problem or a scary topic to be avoided. Ethical considerations are opportunities to question our assumptions about what is known, to recursively explore meaning, and to then act from a position of deep conviction. We believe it is far better to have a voice in shaping innovation than to avoid accountability.

Acknowledgements. This article has been authored by an employee of National Technology and Engineering Solutions of Sandia, LLC under Contract No. DE-NA0003525 with the U.S. Department of Energy (DOE). The employee owns all right, title and interest in and to the article and is solely responsible for its contents. The United States Government retains and the publisher, by accepting the article for publication, acknowledges that the United States Government retains a non-exclusive, paid-up, irrevocable, worldwide license to publish or reproduce the published form of this article or allow others to do so, for United States Government purposes. The DOE will provide public access to these results of federally sponsored research in accordance with the DOE Public Access Plan https://www.energy.gov/downloads/doe-public-access-plan.

References

1. Aarts, A.C.T.: Methodology of mathematical modeling [lecture notes], January 2010. https://www.win.tue.nl/iadan/model/modelB/Methodology_Mathematical_Modeling_MI_2010.pdf
2. Baldwin, D., Walker, H.M., Henderson, P.B.: The roles of mathematics in computer science. ACM Inroads **4**(4), 74–80 (2013). https://doi.org/10.1145/2537753.2537777
3. Bellman, K., et al.: Socially-sensitive systems design: Exploring social potential. IEEE Technol. Soc. Mag. **36**(3), 72–80 (2017). https://doi.org/10.1109/MTS.2017.2728727
4. Califf, M.E., Goodwin, M.: Effective incorporation of ethics into courses that focus on programming. SIGCSE Bull. **37**(1), 347–351 (2005). https://doi.org/10.1145/1047124.1047464
5. Celi, L.A., et al.: Sources of bias in artificial intelligence that perpetuate healthcare disparities – a global review. PLOS Digit. Health **1**(3) (2022). https://doi.org/10.1371/journal.pdig.0000022
6. BSSw Community: Productivity and Sustainability Improvement Planning (PSIP), January 2020. https://bssw.io/blog_posts/productivity-and-sustainability-improvement-planning-psip. Accessed 22 Feb 2023
7. Davis, T., Rajamanickam, S.: Ethical concerns of code generation through artificial intelligence. SIAM News **55**(10) (2022)
8. Delobelle, P., Tokpo, E.K., Calders, T., Berendt, B.: Measuring fairness with biased rulers: a survey on quantifying biases in pretrained language models (2021). https://arxiv.org/abs/2112.07447, https://doi.org/10.48550/ARXIV.2112.07447

9. Elliott, G., Müller, U.K.: Minimizing the impact of the initial condition on testing for unit roots. J. Econometrics **135**(1), 285–310 (2006). https://www.sciencedirect.com/science/article/pii/S0304407605001740, https://doi.org/10.1016/j.jeconom.2005.07.024

10. Gentzsch, W.: Towards ubiquitous HPC - passing HPC into the hands of every engineer and scientist. HPC Wire, 7 January 2016. https://www.hpcwire.com/2016/01/07/towards-ubiquitous-hpc/

11. Gewirtz, D.: I asked chatGPT to write a Wordpress plugin I needed. It did it in less than 5 minutes. ZDNET, February 2023. https://www.zdnet.com/article/i-asked-chatgpt-to-write-a-wordpress-plugin-i-needed-it-did-it-in-less-than-5-minutes/

12. Gonsiorowski, E., et al.: PSIP progress tracking card catalog [GitHub repository]. https://github.com/bssw-psip/ptc-catalog. Accessed 22 Feb 2023

13. Hammond, P., Ahmad, B., Tan, B., Dolan-Gavitt, B., Karri, R.: Asleep at the keyboard? Assessing the security of GitHub copilot's code contributions. arxiv:2108.09293, December 2021. https://arxiv.org/pdf/2108.09293.pdf

14. Heroux, M.A., et al.: Lightweight software process improvement using Productivity and Sustainability Improvement Planning (PSIP). Tools and Techniques for High Performance Computing (2020). https://www.springerprofessional.de/en/lightweight-software-process-improvement-using-productivity-and-/17832686

15. Hess, D.J., et al.: A comparative, sociotechnical design perspective on responsible innovation: multidisciplinary research and education on digitized energy and automated vehicles. J. Respons. Innov. (2021). https://par.nsf.gov/biblio/10296932, https://doi.org/10.1080/23299460.2021.1975377

16. Hind, M.: IBM factsheets further advances trust in AI, July 2020. https://www.ibm.com/blogs/research/2020/07/aifactsheets/

17. Johnson, D.G., Verdicchio, M.: Ethical AI is not about AI. Commun. ACM **66**(2), 32–34 (2023). https://doi.org/10.1145/3576932

18. Lee, J., Le, T., Chen, J., Lee, D.: Do language models plagiarize? In: Proceedings of the ACM Web Conference 2023 (WWW'23) Austin, TX, USA. Association for Computing Machinery, New York (2023). https://pike.psu.edu/publications/www23.pdf

19. Leydens, J.A., Johnson, K., Claussen, S., Blacklock, J., Moskal, B.M., Cordova, O: Measuring change over time in sociotechnical thinking: a survey/validation model for sociotechnical habits of mind. In: 2018 ASEE Annual Conference and Exposition, Salt Lake City, Utah, June 2018. ASEE Conferences (2018)

20. Moore, J.: Towards a more representative politics in the ethics of computer science. In: Proceedings of the 2020 Conference on Fairness, Accountability, and Transparency, FAT* '20, pp. 414–424. Association for Computing Machinery, New York (2020). https://doi.org/10.1145/3351095.3372854

21. Oetzel, J., Pant, S., Rao, N.: Methods for intercultural communication research. Communication (2016). https://oxfordre.com/communication/display/10.1093/acrefore/9780190228613.001.0001/acrefore-9780190228613-e-202

22. National Academies of Sciences Engineering and Medicine. Fostering Responsible Computing Research: Foundations and Practices. The National Academies Press, Washington, DC (2022). https://doi.org/10.17226/26507

23. National Institute of Standards and Technology. Artificial Intelligence Risk Management Framework, January 2023. https://doi.org/10.6028/NIST.AI.100-1

24. ACM Committee on Professional Ethics. ACM code of ethics and professional conduct (2018). https://www.acm.org/code-of-ethics

25. Rabier, F., Klinker, E., Courtier, P., Hollingsworth, A.: Sensitivity of forecast errors to initial conditions. Q. J. Roy. Meteorol. Soc. **122**(529), 121–150 (1996). https://doi.org/10.1002/qj.49712252906
26. Raybourn, E.M., et al.: PSIP toolkit: a lightweight process for incremental software process improvement, June 2021. https://www.osti.gov/biblio/1872186, https://doi.org/10.2172/1872186
27. Raybourn, E.M., Moulton, J.D., Hungerford, A.: Scaling productivity and innovation on the path to exascale with a "Team of Teams" approach. In: Nah, F.F.-H., Siau, K. (eds.) HCII 2019. LNCS, vol. 11589, pp. 408–421. Springer, Cham (2019). https://doi.org/10.1007/978-3-030-22338-0_33
28. Rigolot, C.: Transdisciplinarity as a discipline and a way of being: complementarities and creative tensions. Human. Soc. Sci. Commun. **7** (2020). https://doi.org/10.1057/s41599-020-00598-5
29. Saltz, J., et al.: Integrating ethics within machine learning courses. ACM Trans. Comput. Educ. **19**(4) (2019). https://doi.org/10.1145/3341164
30. Saltz, J.S., Dewar, N.I., Heckman, R.: Key concepts for a data science ethics curriculum. In: Proceedings of the 49th ACM Technical Symposium on Computer Science Education, SIGCSE '18, pp. 952–957. Association for Computing Machinery, New York (2018). https://doi.org/10.1145/3159450.3159483
31. Scoles, S.: New exascale supercomputer can do a quintillion calculations a second. Sci. Am. (2023). https://www.scientificamerican.com/article/new-exascale-supercomputer-can-do-a-quintillion-calculations-a-second/
32. Seino, T., Clarkson, P.C., Downton, A., Gronn, D., Horne, M.: Understanding the role of assumptions in mathematical modeling: analysis of lessons with emphasis on 'the awareness of assumptions'. Build. Connect. Theory Res. Pract. 664–671 (2005)
33. Shankland, S.: Computing guru criticizes chatGPT AI tech for making things up, February 2023. https://www.cnet.com/tech/computing/computing-guru-criticizes-chatgpt-ai-tech-for-making-things-up/
34. Steghofer, J.-P., Diaconescu, A., Marsh, S., Pitt, J.: The next generation of socio-technical systems: realizing the potential, protecting the value [introduction]. IEEE Technol. Soc. Mag. **36**(3), 46–47 (2017). https://doi.org/10.1109/MTS.2017.2728726
35. Sukhija, N., Bautista, E., Butz, D., Whitney, C.: Towards anomaly detection for monitoring power consumption in HPC facilities. In: Proceedings of the 14th International Conference on Management of Digital EcoSystems, MEDES '22, pp. 1–8. Association for Computing Machinery, New York (2022). https://doi.org/10.1145/3508397.3564826
36. IDEAS-ECP Team and Collaborators. Advancing scientific productivity through better scientific software: developer productivity and software sustainability report, January 2020. https://www.exascaleproject.org/wp-content/uploads/2020/01/IDEAS-ECP.Report.v1.0.pdf
37. Wilson, E.B., Worcester, J.: The law of mass action in epidemiology. Proc. Natl. Acad. Sci. **31**(1), 24–34 (1945). https://doi.org/10.1073/pnas.31.1.24
38. Scientific Computing World: HPC researchers rank 'availability of resources' as their primary challenge (2020). https://www.scientific-computing.com/news/hpc-researchers-rank-availability-resources-their-primary-challenge/

39. Xu, W., Dainoff, M.: Enabling human-centered AI: a new junction and shared journey between AI and HCI communities. Interactions, January–February 2023. https://interactions.acm.org/archive/view/january-february-2023/enabling-human-centered-ai-a-new-junction-and-shared-journey-between-ai-and-hci-communities

40. Zachary, G.P.: The hidden logic of ethical innovation, February 2022. https://techonomy.com/the-hidden-logic-of-ethical-innovation/

Experience Design for Multi-device Sharing Based on 3C Framework

Kun Wang[✉], Bilan Huang, Lin Ding, Hanxu Bu, Ying Ge, and Tingting Gu

Samsung Electronics R&D Center, Yuhuatai District, Nanjing, Jiangsu, China
{kun777.wang,bilan.huang,lynn.ding}@samsung.com

Abstract. With the development of current technology, intelligent interaction scenarios based on multi-device collaboration are becoming more and more abundant, and users in multiple devices have increasingly clearly formed a demand for device collaboration service experience. At the same time, as a basic scenario in a multi-device experience, sharing behavior has a crucial impact on the overall experience. Therefore, it is meaningful to re-examine the multi-device experience design method in the current environment based on the original design theory, and to establish a suitable multi-device sharing experience design method according to the universal user needs.

This paper conducts an in-depth theoretical analysis of the typical 3C framework of multi-device experience design theory, including the description of multi-device consistency, continuity and complementarity, but this theory can no longer fully explain the current increasingly complex multi-device experience scenarios. And lack of specific design principles. Therefore, through the sharing scene of multi-device experience, this paper proposes more detailed design principles in the classic 3C framework to guide the design of multi-device sharing scene. The specific method is: (1) Summarize several design principles based on the 3C framework through literature review and share the analysis of competing products/services (2) Review and verify these design principles by convening 30 experts (3) Modify the design principles to obtain the final design principles based on expert comments.

This research provides a method to guide designers in the design of multi-device sharing experience. From the perspective of typical sharing behavior characteristics, this method provides more detailed guidance for different types of sharing experience. The final guideline not only enriches the theoretical value and influence of the 3C framework, but also provides a structured problem-solving thinking in user-oriented product experience design, enriching the theoretical research methods of experience design.

Keywords: Sharing experience · Multi-device experience design · 3C framework

1 Background

We are already in the era of experience relying on multi-device interaction, and multi-device interaction that can be seen everywhere constitutes the interactive system of the current society. Through multi-device interaction, we can arrange all aspects of our lives. The design of smart scenarios based on multi-device systems needs to be further developed, and users in the deep smart ecological environment have increasingly clearly formed a demand for device system experience. Therefore, it is meaningful to examine the multi-device experience design method in the current environment, and to establish a suitable intelligent multi-device interaction scene design method according to the universal user needs.

The research on multi-device interactive experience has gone through a long process of development. In the early days of personal computing devices, a single device was the main area of concern for researchers and practitioners. Later, in his book "The computer for the 21st century", Mark Weiser (1991s) mentioned the vision of future device interaction, where people can interact with content through multiple computing devices of different shapes and sizes [1]. This idea inspired researchers to explore from a single device to a multi-device field. For example, Rekimoto, in the late 1990s, studied interaction techniques that went beyond the device boundaries of multiple laptops and displayed on a desktop/wall surface (Rekimoto 1997; Rekimoto and Saitoh 1999) [2].

At the same time, the market has launched many products with cross-device interaction capabilities, which provide new ways to perform daily tasks (Lyytinen and Yoo 2002) [3], for example, people can not only send and receive emails, but also send Their schedules, tasks, and contacts were synced with their PCs—common today, but at the time represented a major leap forward. Today, the most popular devices are replaced by PCs, smartphones, tablets, and TVs to smart speakers, smart watches, and augmented (AR) or virtual reality (VR) devices (GlobalWebIndex 2020) [4]. Many tasks span multiple devices (Dearman and Pierce 2008) [5], and people use multiple devices simultaneously and switch between them to complete a single task (Brudy et al. 2019) [6]. However, there are also some technical challenges in multi-device interactive experience, especially in sharing information and keeping it consistent across multiple devices (Dong et al. 2016) [7]. For example, commercial solutions are often limited to devices within a specific manufacturer's ecosystem (e.g., Apple), and there are few open standards that support the integration of multiple devices (Brudy et al., 2019) [6]. Therefore, current trends indicate that researchers and practitioners can no longer consider PCs, smartphones, or any other devices as independent platforms, but need to understand and design usage patterns across multiple devices (Levin 2014) [8].

In 2014, Michal Levin, a senior user experience designer at Google, was inspired by the multi-device interaction report investigated by Presence in 2011. In the book "Multi-device Experience Design: Product Development Model in the Internet of Things Era" [8], a new theoretical framework that can distinguish different behavior modes is proposed, namely the 3C framework: consistency, continuity and complementarity. Among them, consistency is the basis of multi-device interaction, which means that the core user experience elements such as the same content and functions are reproduced in multiple devices, and only adaptive adjustments are made between different devices; continuity reflects multi-device interaction. The flow of experience in the platform emphasizes the degree of cohesion of user operation flows in different usage scenarios; complementarity focuses on the scenario where multiple devices work together to achieve the same behavioral goal. In the specific design now, the 3C framework is not a simple choice, but needs to be combined according to different situations to guide the design.

On this basis, Gartner (2019) [9] proposed the concept of multi-experience in its 2020 technology trend report, and then, a large number of researchers explored MUX, including how to understand MUX and how to use it in Design under the concept of MUX (Ulrich Gnewuch • Marcel Ruoff • Christian Peukert • Alexander Maedche, 2021) [10], they summarize the path to realize MUX into three, path 1: Leveraging Multiple Devices, such as Mobile Banking Apps, Augmented and Virtual Reality in E-Commerce, etc.; path 2: Leveraging Multiple Modalities, such as From Smart Speakers to Smart Displays; and Path 3: Combining Multiple Devices and Multiple Modalities, such as Multiexperience in Enterprise Resource Planning (ERP) Systems. Luis Martín Sánchez-Adame, Sonia Mendoza et al. (2019) [11] proposed a set of consistency principles through in-depth research on the consistency principles in the study "Towards a Set of Design Guidelines for Multi-device Experience" Guidelines, as a means of building multi-device application interface designs. Li Yingzhu (2018) [12], a professor of the Multimedia Department of Zhongyun University, showed in "A Study on Continuity of User Experience in Multi-device Environment" that familiarity, consistency, and relevance have a significant impact on the continuity dimension of user experience. Dimitrios Raptis, Jesper Kjeldskov, and Mikael B. Skov (2016) [13] present challenges in six themes of privacy, appropriation in their study "Continuity in Multi-Device Interaction: An Online Study" based on the analysis of online forum comments, customization, awareness, exclusion, and troubleshooting in relation to continuous interaction across devices.

In addition, Gu Lili of Xi'an Polytechnic University and others proposed a card-based design method for multi-device experience in their research [14]. Henrik Sørensen, Dimitrios Raptis, Jesper Kjeldskov, and Mikael B. Skov (2014) [15] innovatively proposed the 4C framework in the study "Principles of Interaction in Digital Ecosystem Ecosystems". The 4C framework specifically explains the interaction that occurs in the digital ecosystem, providing new insights into existing frameworks and theories, incorporating understanding of existing digital ecosystems, and generating ideas and discussions when designing new ecosystems. Through the expansion of theoretical research above, the design methods in the field of multi-device interaction have been greatly enriched. However, there is still a lack of more detailed research content for the specific guidance methods of the 3C framework in specific scenarios.

In addition to research in the field of theory and methods, many researchers have also conducted in-depth explorations in combination with specific device applications in the experience scenarios related to multi-device interaction. Henrik Sørensen and Jesper Kjeldskov (2012) [16] provided a music playback interface design for multi-device interaction in their research. The interface design based on distributed interaction emphatically reflects the scene characteristics of multi-device interaction; Marta E. Cecchinato, Anna L. Cox and Jon Bird (2017) [17] studied the daily use of smart watches to understand the added value and challenges of being connected on the wrist and proposed improvements to smart watch experience design in multi-device tasking method. Khalid Majrashi et al. (2018) [18] studied the cross-device experience design in the mobile user interface starting from the continuity characteristics in the 3C framework, and emphasized that consistency has certain value in achieving continuous experience; Khalid Majrashi et al. (2017) [19] summarized some interoperability issues during multi-device interaction by studying the body posture of mobile users during cross-device interaction. Additionally, Khalid Majrashi, Margaret Hamilton, Alexandra L. Uitdenbogerd, and Shiroq Al-Megren (2021), in their study Cross-Device User Interactive Behavioral Patterns, involved 16 students and identified six major cross-device User Interaction Behavior Patterns: Visual Memory, Habit, Prospective Memory, Distributed Achievement, Instant Recovery, Spatial Memory, with suggestions on how to align designs with identified user behavior patterns [20]. The above studies have studied the characteristics of multi-device scenarios from the perspective of devices and users, but there is currently a lack of relevant research on multi-device sharing experience design.

Generally speaking, although the existing research on multi-device experience can guide the general direction of multi-device experience design, the design principles tend to explore the content from an overall perspective, lacking targeted research on specific scenarios, and the best in multi-device scenarios. There are few systematic research results in the common field of shared experience.

Therefore, this paper focuses on discussing and researching how to supplement the principles of the 3C framework in multi-device experience design. The issues to be discussed in this paper are as follows:

1. What are the specific design principles based on the 3C framework in a multi-device scenario?
2. What characteristics or combinations of characteristics do these specific principles manifest in shared experiences?
3. From the perspective of user needs, what is the design strategy for sharing experience?

2   Related Work

In order to obtain answers to the above questions, this paper not only conducts an in-depth analysis of the original 3C framework theory, but also explores the specific behavior of sharing experience. After sorting out the existing research results, the cross-device experience in under the current conditions, the second-level guidelines based on the 3C design framework. However, the experience scenarios involved in this guideline are often universal experiences, and no specific design principles or guidance are proposed for specific experience scenarios. Therefore, the thesis needs to explore the multi-device design principles of shared experience through targeted research. To this end, it is necessary to clarify the specific scope and objects of the shared experience studied.

Through the research of mobile phones on the existing competing products on the market, the paper explores the characteristics of the target object of the research, and selects typical scenes for in-depth research through feature summary.

First, the researchers collected mainstream services and products on the market that involve multi-device sharing experience, and analyzed them through the case study method. In the end, a total of 24 research cases were collected, including mainstream brands such as Apple, Huawei, Xiaomi, Vivo, etc., and niche brands such as Pipizhilian, iVCam, etc.

Secondly, based on the analysis of these cases, the researchers defined the definition of multi-device sharing experience discussed in this paper, which is "a behavior of transferring a target object from one device to another or several devices". In addition, sharing scenarios are classified based on the two dimensions of timeliness and participation of experience (see Fig. 1):

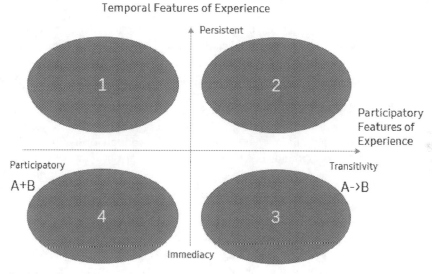

Fig. 1. According to the continuity of the device's sharing behavior and the way of transmitting content during the process of multi-device interaction, the sharing behavior is classified in two dimensions

According to the different types of sharing behaviors defined above, the researchers obtained the following three types of sharing scenarios by combining the characteristics of competing products obtained by classification in various fields:

Area 1 (Persistent-participation type sharing): In this type of sharing behavior scenario, the object of device sharing is the persistently generated information flow, and it is the process of switching from a single device to a multi-device scenario.

Area 2 (Persistent -transfer sharing): In the scenario of this type of sharing behavior, the object of device sharing is the persistently generated information flow, and the information or content is a one-way flow from one device to other devices.

Area 3 (immediacy- transfer sharing): In the scenario of this type of sharing behavior, the object of device sharing is fixed content/information, and it is a one-way flow from one device to other devices.

Area 4 (immediacy- participation type sharing): In this scope, researchers have not found any eligible competing services, and there are certain contradictions in the performance of this type of service in the two feature dimensions, so the content of this area Will not be covered by dissertation research.

3 Method

For how to obtain design guidelines, the paper formulates the following research path:

First of all, through the literature research method, the relevant literature of the existing multi-device experience scene is researched, So as to obtain the key words of experience feeling; then, combined with the structural theory of the 3C framework, the obtained keywords are classified to form a preliminary design principle.

The general process of the literature research method includes five basic links, which are: proposing a topic or hypothesis, research design, collecting literature, sorting out literature, and conducting a literature review. The proposed topic or hypothesis of the literature method refers to the idea of analyzing and sorting out relevant literature or reclassifying research based on existing theories, facts and needs. According to the subject of the research, the goal of the current literature research is to obtain the characteristic points of multi-device experience. Therefore, to integrate the existing research, the research design must first establish the research goal. The content of the hypothesis is designed as a specific, operable and repeatable literature research activity, which can solve special problems and have certain significance. [21].

After that, collect typical multi-device service cases on the market, analyze the characteristics of typical sharing experiences in products based on user use cases, and classify sharing behaviors according to the combination of behavioral characteristics. At the same time, the classified behavior types are intersected with the 3C theoretical framework, so as to get the guidance of the design method under the specific sharing experience.

Multi-case study method: under the guidance of theoretical sampling principles, two or more cases are compared or analyzed to identify the similarity or heterogeneity of the analyzed case units. In order to realize the theory construction. Compared with single-case analysis, the results of multi-case analysis are more universal. [22, 23].

Finally, experts are invited to evaluate the design principles based on literature and competing products. The specific method is: use the existing design principles as the basis, design different scenarios as the basis of experiential interviews, let the experts experience different types of sharing scenarios, score these principles, and use semi-structured interviews to understand the experts' opinions on Comments on these principles are used to confirm the final feasible design guidelines.

The overall research path is as follows (see Fig. 2):

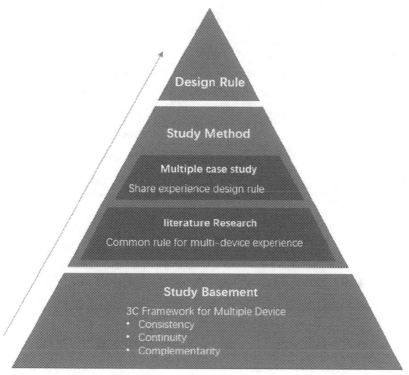

Fig. 2. The pyramid-shaped thinking map explains the final output of the research and the basic research content required for each step of the results

4   Study Result

According to the research path mentioned above, the researchers carry out specific methods, from literature research, competing product/case research and expert evaluation, to finally obtain feasible design principles.

4.1   Literature Research on 3C Framework in Multi-device Experience

According to the content of literature research, this paper divides literature research into three main stages, including literature collection, literature analysis and key information summary. The specific research structure is shown in the figure below (Fig. 3):

According to the above research methods, the paper collected nearly 50 existing research results in the field of multi-device, from which a total of 10 valuable documents were screened out, and the results are as follows (Table 1):

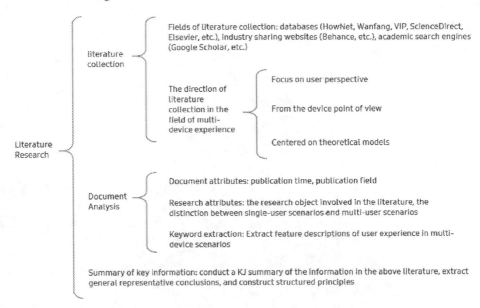

Fig. 3. Thinking frame of literature research

Table 1. Feature keywords from literature research

Current Studies	Feature Keywords	Belongs to 3C
Inter-Usability of Multi-Device Systems – A Conceptual Framework (2005) [24]	interoperability	consistency
	consistency	consistency
	transparency	continuity
	adaptability	continuity
Cross-platform service user experience: a field study and an initial framework (2010) [25]	similarity	consistency
Cross-Device Taxonomy: Survey, Opportunities and Challenges of Interactions Spanning Across Multiple Devices (2019) [6]	transitional	continuity
	transitivity (reachability)	continuity
	cognitive load	complementarity
	coordination ability	complementarity
Towards a Set of Design Guidelines for Multi-device Experience (2019) [26]	multimodality	complementarity
	traceability	continuity
	availability	consistency

(continued)

Table 1. (*continued*)

Current Studies	Feature Keywords	Belongs to 3C
A Study on Continuity of User Experience in Multi-device Environment (2018) [12]	visual (sensory) memory	consistency
	structural difference	consistency
The Ubiquitous Device Transition Experience of the Mobile User (2017) [19]	consistency	consistency
	fluency	continuity
	recognition	consistency
	learnability	consistency
	compatibility	complementarity
Multiple User Interfaces: Why Consistency is Not Everything, and Seamless Task Migration is Key (2006) [27]	seamless migration	continuity
Multi experience (2014) [8]	multimodal	complementarity
	multiple (perceptual) channels	complementarity
	multi-sensory matching	complementarity
An Empirical Evaluation of Asymmetric Synchronous Collaboration Combining Immersive and Non-Immersive Interfaces Within the Context of Immersive Analytics (2022) [28]	collaboration	complementarity
Cross-Platform Usability Model Evaluation (2022) [29]	seamless transition	continuity

According to the results of the preliminary arrangement above, the paper reintegrates the results from the theoretical dimension of the 3C framework to obtain the detailed rules of the specific experience design guidelines, as shown in the following Table 2:

Table 2. Feature keywords for 3C structure

3C Structure	Feature Keywords
Consistency	Interoperability, availability, sensory memory, structural difference, recognition, learnability, similarity
Continuity	Transparency, adaptability, transitional, transitivity (reachability), fluency, seamless migration/transition, traceability
Complementarity	cognitive load, coordination ability, multimodality, compatibility, multiple (perceptual) channels, multi-sensory matching, collaboration

Based on this table, the researchers analyzed and screened the collected indicator system again, and adjusted or deleted the places where there was a large repetition in the secondary indicators or the level of information description was inconsistent with the requirements of the design principles. According to the in-depth analysis of the data, there is an overlap between the description in the project "structural difference" and " recognition ", and the definition of the latter can be extended to cover the former, therefore, "structural difference" is not considered in the design In the principle, to prevent unreasonable resource allocation in the later guidance process; similarly, "sensory memory" and "learnability" are also covered by "recognition" and "similarity", so they are also deleted Minus. In addition, such as "transparency" and "adaptability" can be collectively referred to as "adaptability", " transitional ", "seamless transition" and " transitivity " describe the connection state of task flow; The concept of complementarity also has a lot of repetition. Through the integration of concepts, two different secondary indicators are sorted out from the two aspects of hardware and efficiency, namely "hardware compatibility" and "multi-device collaboration".

4.2 Competitors Research on Cross-Device Sharing Experience

In this part, the thesis summarizes three types of sharing behaviors based on the previous exploration and research on sharing behaviors, and takes them as the scope of the research, from which typical experience scenarios are selected for in-depth analysis, for example, in the continuous-participation category, the researchers deeply studied the classified cases and summarized the key information of the cases, taking the case of Continuity Camera as an example:

Case scenario: Apple provided details about its new Continuity Camera feature, which enables users to use their iPhone as a webcam. The best part is, you just hold your iPhone close to your Mac and it will automatically connect

Scene conditions: Both devices must be signed in to the same Apple ID. You can connect via cable, but if connecting wirelessly, both devices must have Wi-Fi and Bluetooth turned on

Summarize the key features and their descriptions:
Seamless: During the sharing process, the device can naturally judge the user's intention and actively complete the sharing, saving user behavior

Based on the same analysis method, the paper also extracts the same keywords for all cases of the other two categories. The final analysis results obtained are as follows Table 3:

Table 3. Feature keywords from cases

Categories of Sharing	Feature Keyword	Typical Case
Continuous-Participatory sharing	Fluency	Information synchronization: Apple "relay"; Experience Sharing: Apple Simulcast Sharing
	Convenience, quickness, simplification	
	Diversity	
Continuous-Transfer sharing	Synchronous	Ability to lend: Continuity Camera, Huawei magic link; Screen Sharing: Share your screen
	Fluency	
	Convenience, quickness, simplification	
Instant-Transfer sharing	Integration	Content delivery: airdrop
	Seamless	
	Fast, immediacy	
	Ecological	

The above characteristics describe the targeted experience performance of each sharing behavior under different categories, and the performance of the characteristics can in turn guide the characteristic tendency of experience design. Therefore, the paper takes three types of typical sharing experience as the object of follow-up research, ensuring the comprehensiveness of the research on sharing experience, and refining the measurement methods of each indicator in sharing experience.

4.3   3C Design Principles for Sharing Experiences Across Devices

Combining the results of current literature research and the characteristic description of sharing experience in competing product research, researchers can combine the two to obtain a more comprehensive multi-device experience design principle that meets the sharing behavior experience.

The content in the literature research covers common multi-device design principles and represents a general experience. However, in the analysis of competing products for sharing behaviors, since the research scenarios are more specific, the scope of sharing behaviors is clearly defined. Therefore, compare the characteristics summarized in the competing products with those in the literature, remove the repeated experience descriptions in the two, and form a design principle that conforms to the multi-device sharing experience, as Table 4 shows:

Table 4. Design principle according 3C framework

3C Framework	Design Principle	Detail Index Description
Consistency	Wholeness	A single device can reflect the service characteristics of the overall system, and the experience difference between using multiple devices at the same time and using a single device alone is small
	Availability	Depending on the user's level of expertise, they should be able to use the system at a basic or more advanced level with no further learning costs
	Identification	Interface elements on different devices in the same system environment show consistent style characteristics, and users can recognize and perform cross-device behavior operations without deliberate memory
	Similarity	Content and elements maintain similar or identical rendering across devices
Continuity	Adaptability	The same content supports multi-device interaction, and adapts based on device characteristics while ensuring normal task flow
	Transitivity	Connection matching (manual/automatic) across devices is natural and does not cause user confusion
	Fluency	The flow of content is fast and natural, and does not require redundant operations by users. And users clearly know what they can do after the transfer is completed
	Synchronization	During the transfer process, the content will be displayed synchronously on the sending device and the target receiving device, or the progress of the behavior process will be displayed synchronously on different ports
Complementarity	Compatibility	Fewer errors when streaming content across multiple devices
	Collaboration	The degree of improvement in the completion efficiency of the same task after other devices are added

4.4 Expert Evaluation

According to literature research and research on competing products, the thesis obtained the design principle of multi-device sharing experience with theoretical guiding value, but the objective evaluation of this principle needs to pass professional verification and approval to ensure the objective value of the design principle and feasibility. Therefore, the specific purpose of this expert evaluation is to allow experts to feel and experience the operation of fixed cross-device sharing scenes, understand the scene objects targeted by the design principles, and hope that experts can combine some of their experience and expectations in the field of multi-device, to evaluate the given principles and methods of cross-device sharing experience design, in order to improve and revise the 3C framework design guidelines in the paper.

Preparation of Expert Evaluation. The paper verifies the objective value of the existing design framework through expert evaluation, and hopes to refine the guiding significance of the system through expert evaluation, making the conclusion more feasible. Therefore, the researchers invited experts with certain experience in the field of multi-device design and service development, and provided reference material background and actual device environment as the basis for analysis and evaluation. Afterwards, the experts evaluate the suitability of the detailed standards of the existing design principles. The result is an instructive design guide.

First of all, regarding the selection and invitation of experts, according to the purpose of the research, it is necessary to invite people with professional backgrounds to participate in the standard evaluation work. Therefore, it is necessary to clearly define the scope and conditions of experts to ensure that the results are reasonable. Based on the requirements for professional experience, the paper decides to define the identity of an expert as follows:

Condition 1. An engineer or designer with a mid-level or above title

Condition 2. Engineers or designers who have been engaged in cross-device services and related fields for more than 2 years

Therefore, according to the specific conditions, the researchers invited a total of 30 professionals, including development engineers, experience designers, and product architects in the field of TV services, mobile device services, and cross-device services, to conduct communication and interviews. Get their multi-angle professional value evaluation of existing design principles in cross-device fields. The expert composition of this evaluation is as follows Fig. 4 Shown:

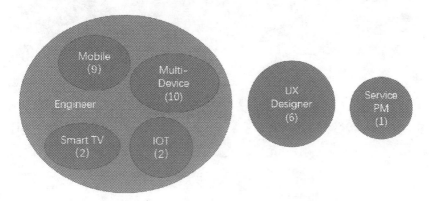

Fig. 4. Expert invited structure for this estimation

Conduction for Expert Evaluation. Regarding the link of evaluation design, the thesis refers to the method of expert evaluation and follows five specific principles to ensure the rationality of evaluation: ① Letter inquiry. Repeatedly seek expert advice by means of communication. ② Multidirectional. The survey respondents are distributed in different professional fields, and they can learn the opinions of various experts on the same issue. ③ Anonymous. Survey respondents can learn the opinions of other experts through the organization of survey organizers. But they don't know who the other is. The specific stage of the evaluation avoids the introduction and communication links of experts, which helps them express their independent opinions. ④ Repeatedly. Repeated verification is carried out in a controlled manner, so that the scattered opinions gradually tend to be consistent, so as to exert collective wisdom. In the specific evaluation, after three groups of repeated expert verification, the independence of each group of conclusions is guaranteed, and the evaluation conclusions of the experts are verified each other. ⑤ Focus. Statistical methods are used to gather the opinions of all survey respondents, and the individual judgments of each expert are reflected in the final collective opinions as much as possible [30, 31].

Based on the above principles, the implementation process of the expert evaluation link in this paper is as follows: First, the experts were consulted with the experts through emails. Since there are some obscure terminology in the design principles, the investigators conducted an offline interview with the experts. Specific concepts are communicated to ensure the validity of the assessment results. As Fig. 5 Shown is a specific communication environment.

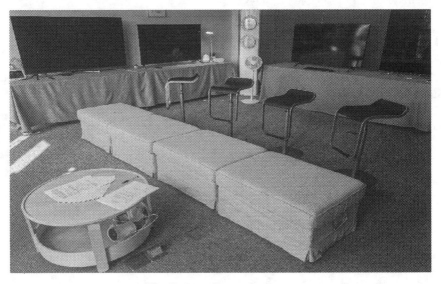

Fig. 5. Interview environment.

Secondly, organize focus groups to conduct offline interviews with experts, a total of 3 groups with 10 people in each group. In each group, the researchers first describe the research purpose and relevant professional vocabulary to the experts; then, they show the experts three different sharing scenarios through video, so that the experts can better understand and understand the objects to be evaluated. The three scenarios are:

Scenario 1 (continuous-participatory sharing): All devices participating in the sharing behavior, both the receiver and the sender, continue to participate in the content, and the sharing behavior is bidirectional and interactive. Apple Shareplay is one of the typical services;

Scenario 2 (continuous-transfer sharing): The sharing behavior between devices is a directional and continuous content and information sharing, and the sharing behavior is a one-way flow. Among them, the performance of Huawei Changlian service in such scenarios is more prominent;

Scenario 3 (instant-transfer sharing): the sharing behavior between devices is completed instantly, and the content is a fixed one-way flow. Typical cases include airdrop for file transfer, Xiaomi mutual transfer, etc.

Finally, according to the design principles obtained in the research, the meaning of the second-level principles was conveyed to the experts, and the experts were required to independently complete the evaluation of the importance of the second-level indicators under the first-level indicators of the 3C framework. In some cases, experts are again invited to give appropriate reasons for the evaluation results given by themselves, so as to facilitate subsequent rational adjustments to specific projects.

Analysis of the Results from Expert Evaluation. The researchers used the mean value and the coefficient of variation to analyze the degree of experts' recognition of the indicators. The larger the mean value, the more experts agree with the index; the smaller the value of the coefficient of variation (CV), the more consistent the opinions of experts, and $Cv < 0.25$ is a good index [31]. The specific finishing results are shown in the following Table 5:

Table 5. Evaluation result (Special score has been marked)

3C Framework	Design Principle	Expert Rating mean (μ)	Expert Rating Standard Deviation (σ)	Cv= σ/μ
Consistency	Wholeness	4	0.966	0.242
	Availability	4.1	0.831	0.203
	Identification	4.267	0.998	0.234
	Similarity	3.800	0.909	0.239
Continuity	Adaptability	4.3	0.690	0.161
	Transitivity	4.367	0.875	0.200
	Fluency	4.6	0.663	0.144
	Synchronization	4.167	0.898	0.215
Complementar ity	Compatibility	4.234	1.023	0.242
	Collaboration	3.900	1.012	0.259

It can be seen from the table that the average value of 8 indicators is above 4.0 (average upper limit 5.0), indicating that experts recognize this indicator; Indicators need to be discussed again. The CVs of the nine indicators are above 0.25, indicating that the experts have relatively consistent opinions on the indicators; the Cv of the indicator "collaboration" is greater than 0.25, indicating that there are large differences of opinion. Therefore, the researchers conducted in-depth exploration and analysis on the results of this part.

- For Similarity: Mean 3.8, Cv 0.239. It shows that the experts have relatively unanimous opinions on this indicator and express their disapproval. Some experts mentioned that "the description in similarity, content and elements maintain a similar presentation on different devices, and the interface elements mentioned in recognition show consistent style characteristics. The concept is basically the same, and the scope covered by the latter is wider". Therefore, based on the opinions of experts, the researchers removed this option;
- For Collaboration: the average score is 3.9, but the Cv is 0.259, indicating that experts disagree on this indicator. An in-depth analysis of expert comments that gave low evaluations in this option found that some experts disagreed with this option because the type and quantity of equipment referred to in the option "other equipment" were different. Clear, there is a misunderstanding. Therefore, from the perspective of scene experience, the researchers supplemented and refined the description of "collaboration" and modified it to "collaboration: the efficiency of completing the same task is improved after other different types of devices are added."

Finally, according to the evaluation of experts, the researchers obtained revisions and confirmations for the current shared experience design guidelines, which improved the guiding value of the guidelines from the aspects of objectivity and professionalism.

5   Conclusion

Through the collection and summary of the existing research results, the paper obtains the experience design features concerned in the field of multi-device experience design, and classifies them according to the description of consistency, continuity and complementarity, and obtains the general 3C framework experience design rules; Afterwards, through the research of competing products and user feedback, the detailed description of the characteristics in the sharing experience will be concretely implemented, and the measurement direction and general standards of each characteristic will be established; Finally, through the evaluation of the theoretical standards obtained by experts in different fields, the design guidelines are revised to strengthen the objectivity and authority of the guidelines in terms of theoretical guidance, and better become the principles of subsequent design, as shown in the following Table 6 As shown, the final theory provides detailed guidelines for sharing experience from the three aspects of consistency, continuity and complementarity.

According to this guideline, when designing cross-device shared experiences, experience designers can reasonably allocate design resources in order to ensure a better user experience to the greatest extent while resources are available.

Table 6. Sharing design principle based on 3C

3C Framework	Design Principle	Detail Index Description
Consistency	Wholeness	A single device can reflect the service characteristics of the overall system, and the experience difference between using multiple devices at the same time and using a single device alone is small
	Availability	Depending on the user's level of expertise, they should be able to use the system at a basic or more advanced level with no further learning costs
	Identification	Interface elements on different devices in the same system environment show consistent style characteristics, and users can recognize and perform cross-device behavior operations without deliberate memory
Continuity	Adaptability	The same content supports multi-device interaction, and adapts based on device characteristics while ensuring normal task flow
	Transitivity	Connection matching (manual/automatic) across devices is natural and does not cause user confusion
	Fluency	The flow of content is fast and natural, and does not require redundant operations by users. And users clearly know what they can do after the transfer is completed
	Synchronization	During the transfer process, the content will be displayed synchronously on the sending device and the target receiving device, or the progress of the behavior process will be displayed synchronously on different ports
Complementarity	Compatibility	Fewer errors when streaming content across multiple devices
	Collaboration	The efficiency of completing the same task is improved after other **different types of equipment** are added

6 Discussion

In the specific research field, this paper collects and summarizes the current feature descriptions for multi-device experience in the existing research through the method of literature research, classifies the results according to the content of the 3C framework, and clarifies the secondary indicators of the theory. Refining their specific definitions based on existing research; afterwards, cross-analyze the shared experience characteristics and multi-device experience in competing product research, and obtain 3C design guidelines for multi-device shared experience. At the same time, in order to ensure the feasibility of the conclusions obtained in the research, the paper conducts a supplementary evaluation of the conclusions through expert evaluation, and adjusts the final research conclusions according to the evaluation results of experts to make them more valuable and objective.

At the same time, in the research process, the thesis adopts the method of combining literature research and case study, and obtains research conclusions in specific fields from the general research results; Considering the theoretical basis of the research, the follow-up can add more exploration of new research methods to the current conclusions, so as to obtain more innovative conclusions and better endow the research results with time-sensitive value.

In general, this paper summarizes and obtains a systematic design method from general conclusions by combining various research methods, and improves the reliability and value of the method through expert evaluation, providing a reference for the research of design methods and theories. Which enriches the achievements in the research field of multi-device experience design, and provides a reference for innovative research ideas.

References

1. Weiser, M.: The computer for the 21st century]. ACM SIGMOBILE Mob. Comput. Commun. Rev. **3**(3), 3–11 (1999)
2. Rekimoto, J., Saitoh, M.: Augmented surfaces: a spatially continuous work space for hybrid computing environments. In: Proceedings of the SIGCHI conference on Human Factors in Computing Systems, pp. 378–385 (1999)
3. Lyytinen, K., Yoo, Y.: Ubiquitous computing. Commun. ACM **45**(12), 63–96 (2002)
4. Droesch, B.: Influencers more likely to inspire gen zer and millennial purchases. Insider Intell. (2020)
5. Dearman, D., Pierce, J.S.: It's on my other computer! computing with multiple devices. In: Proceedings of the SIGCHI Conference on Human Factors in Computing Systems, pp. 767–776 (2008)
6. Brudy, F., Holz, C., Rädle, R., et al.: Cross-device taxonomy: survey, opportunities and challenges of interactions spanning across multiple devices. In: Proceedings of the 2019 CHI Conference on Human Factors in Computing Systems, pp. 1–28 (2019)
7. Dong, C., Loy, C.C., Tang, X.: Accelerating the super-resolution convolutional neural network. In: Leibe, B., Matas, J., Sebe, N., Welling, M. (eds.) ECCV 2016. LNCS, vol. 9906, pp. 391–407. Springer, Cham (2016). https://doi.org/10.1007/978-3-319-46475-6_25
8. Levin, M.: Designing Multi-device Experiences: An Ecosystem Approach to User Experiences Across Devices. O'Reilly Media, Inc. (2014)
9. Jiao, P., Alavi, A.H.: Artificial intelligence in seismology: advent, performance and future trends. Geosci. Front. **11**(3), 739–744 (2020)
10. Eng, B.I.S.: Ulrich Gnewuch• Marcel Ruoff• Christian Peukert• Alexander Maedche
11. Gómez, M.H., Luis, S.P.: Libertad y orden en la acción social: una relectura de las aportaciones de Parsons. Revista de estudios políticos **116**, 145–166 (2002)
12. Lee, Y.J.: A study on continuity of user experience in multi-device environment. J. Digit. Converg. **16**(11), 495–500 (2018)
13. Bruun, A., Raptis, D., Kjeldskov, J., et al.: Measuring the coolness of interactive products: the COOL questionnaire. Behav. Inf. Technol. **35**(3), 233–249 (2016)
14. 顾丽丽, 张敏言, 姬文浩. 跨设备的用户体验设计. 艺术科技, **29**(3), 97–97 (2016)
15. Sørensen, H., Raptis, D., Kjeldskov, J., et al.: The 4C framework: principles of interaction in digital ecosystems. In: Proceedings of the 2014 ACM International Joint Conference on Pervasive and Ubiquitous Computing, pp. 87–97 (2014)

16. Sørensen, H., Kjeldskov, J.: The interaction space of a multi-device, multi-user music experience. In: Proceedings of the 7th Nordic Conference on Human-Computer Interaction: Making Sense Through Design, pp. 504–513 (2012)

17. Cecchinato, M.E., Cox, A.L., Bird, J.: Always on (line)? User experience of smartwatches and their role within multi-device ecologies. In: Proceedings of the 2017 CHI Conference on Human Factors in Computing Systems, pp. 3557–3568 (2017)

18. Majrashi, K.: User need and experience of Hajj mobile and ubiquitous systems: designing for the largest religious annual gathering. Cogent Eng. 5(1), 1480303 (2018)

19. Majrashi, K., Hamilton, M., Uitdenbogerd, A.L.: The ubiquitous device transition experience of the mobile user. In: Proceedings of the 14th EAI International Conference on Mobile and Ubiquitous Systems: Computing, Networking and Services, pp. 537–538 (2017)

20. Majrashi, K., Hamilton, M., Uitdenbogerd, A.L., et al.: Cross-device user interactive behavioural patterns (2021)

21. 孙海法, 朱莹楚. 案例研究法的理论与应用. 科学管理研究, 22(1), 116–120 (2004)

22. 苏敬勤, 李召敏. 案例研究方法的运用模式及其关键指标 (2011)

23. Stake, R.E.: Multiple Case Study Analysis. Guilford Press (2013)

24. Denis, C., Karsenty, L.: Inter-usability of multi-device systems: a conceptual framework. Multiple user interfaces: cross-platform applications and context-aware interfaces, pp. 373–384 (2004)

25. Wäljas, M., Segerståhl, K., Väänänen-Vainio-Mattila, K., et al.: Cross-platform service user experience: a field study and an initial framework. In: Proceedings of the 12th International Conference on Human Computer Interaction with Mobile Devices and Services, pp. 219–228 (2010)

26. Sánchez-Adame, L.M., Mendoza, S., Meneses Viveros, A., Rodríguez, J.: Towards a set of design guidelines for multi-device experience. In: Kurosu, M. (ed.) HCII 2019. LNCS, vol. 11566, pp. 210–223. Springer, Cham (2019). https://doi.org/10.1007/978-3-030-22646-6_15

27. Pyla, P.S., Tungare, M., Pérez-Quinones, M.: Multiple user interfaces: why consistency is not everything, and seamless task migration is key. In: Proceedings of the CHI 2006 Workshop on the Many Faces of Consistency in Cross-Platform Design (2006)

28. Reski, N., Alissandrakis, A., Kerren, A.: An empirical evaluation of asymmetric synchronous collaboration combining immersive and non-immersive interfaces within the context of immersive analytics. Front. Virtual Real. 2, 1–29 (2022)

29. Majrashi, K., Hamilton, M., Uitdenbogerd, A.L., et al.: Cross-platform usability model evaluation. Multimodal Technol. Interact. 4(4), 80 (2020)

30. 罗子明. 消费者心理学 (第二版) : 清华大学出版社, 2002 年7月: 293

31. 徐蔼婷. 德尔菲法的应用及其难点. 中国统计, 2006(9)

A Systematic and Innovative Six-in-One Evaluation Framework to Drive the Development of Future Hidden Champions

Dayou Wu[1]([⊠]), Guochao Peng[2]([⊠]), Yiwan Ai[1]([⊠]), Huan Li[2]([⊠]), Shaolan Li[2]([⊠]), and Yating Peng[2]([⊠])

[1] Diginova Ltd., Guangzhou, China
[2] Sun Yat-Sen University, Guangzhou, China
penggch@mail.sysu.edu.cn, lishlan3@mail2.sysu.edu.cn

Abstract. Nowadays, the global market is becoming increasingly competitive and enterprises around the world are facing more development challenges. At the same time, balancing economic development needs and environmental issues continues to attract ever greater attention. Taking into account multi-view factors, we propose a systematic and innovative six-in-one evaluation framework consisting of SRDI, "manufacturing individual champions", "hidden champions", ESG, digitalization and MOCA indicators. This six-in-one evaluation framework can not only help enterprises plan their own path to grow into a global enterprise with high-quality products and services remaining high competitiveness, but also help countries seize a leading position in the global industrial chain and achieve sustainable development.

Keywords: six-in-one evaluation · hidden champions · SRDI · ESG · digital transformation · MOCA

1 Introduction and Background

Standards generally refer to something established by authority, custom or general consensus as a model, example or point of reference, which is the fruit of human civilization's progress, the technical basis for economic and social activities, and the bridge for world interconnection. With the deepening development of economic globalization and the acceleration of the new round of technological revolution and industrial reform, standards have become a key element in the profound restructuring of the global innovation map and industrial layout [1]. The important role of standardization in promoting economic and trade exchanges, supporting industrial development, promoting scientific and technological progress, and regulating social governance has been increasingly highlighted. At a time of unprecedented competition in science and technology, international standards are not only the "access card" to the world market, the "common language" for economic and social activities, but also an important arena for international discourse. Being a leader in standards is an important symbol of a country's commitment to high-quality development and high-quality competition [2].

In light of such international trends, standardization has been elevated to a strategic level in the overall development of the Communist Party of China and the country. At the same time, it is worth noting that a quality reform is necessary for China's manufacturing industry to enter the middle and high-end of the global value chain. To realize such a quality reform, the first step is to improve the standards and evaluation system for the Chinese manufacturing sector.

In terms of content, the national policy shows a high level of attention to the issues of SRDI (Specialized, Refinement, Differential and Innovation), digitization and ESG, which will be interpreted later [3]. For example, the 2022 Government Work Report states that China will strive to promote specialized and innovative enterprises that produce new and unique products (SRDI enterprises), and provide them with more support in terms of funding, personnel and the development of business incubation platforms [4]. China aims to nurture 1 million innovative medium-sized enterprises (SMEs), 100,000 SRDI enterprises, and 10,000 "little giants" from 2021 to 2025 as part of an ambitious plan to boost the vitality of SMEs in its sprawling industrial economy [5]. The concept of "little giants" refers to best specialized enterprises that specialize in niche sectors, have high market shares and are highly innovative. These "little giants" are similar to "hidden champions", a term coined by German author Hermann Simon to describe the small, highly specialized world market leaders in Germany [6]. The issues of SRDI, digitization and ESG are closely related and inextricably linked to the development of future leading companies.

The focus of this paper is to address the era call of how to enable enterprises to position and plan their own path to gradually develop into SRDI enterprises, "little giants" and then "hidden champions" in a set of systematic standards, as well as deepen digitalization and achieve ESG outcomes in the process, so as to help Chinese enterprises stand and lead in the times and maintain sustainable competitiveness in uncertainty. From an international perspective, this paper is also an important point of reference and guidance for other companies worldwide that are in a similar situation and have growth aspirations. Based on this focus, we propose a systematic and innovative six-in-one evaluation framework to promote the development of future hidden champions, which consists of SRDI, "manufacturing individual champions", "hidden champions", ESG, digitalization and MOCA indicators. The rest of this paper will provide an in-depth description and explanation of this proposed framework.

2 Overview of the Six-in-One Evaluation Framework

In simple terms, the six-in-one evaluation framework aims to establish a systematic and practical indicator system by combining the standards of SRDI, "manufacturing individual champions", "hidden champions", ESG, digitalization, and MOCA to serve as a benchmark for internationalization and digitalization.

As a whole, the six-in-one evaluation framework gives enterprises a full view of their life cycle which they go through from inception to liquidation [7], enabling them to see their current situation. A business grows and ages in the same way that humans beings do: when it is young, it has great flexibility but weak control force. As it ages, with the wealth of experience and knowledge accumulated, control force increases but flexibility decreases. Basically, companies may go through a growth phase (slow and rapid growth stage, stability stage) and a decline phase (slow and fast decline stage, crisis stage) over time [7]. Based on the enterprise life cycle theory, companies need to maintain a balance in their development and be reborn when necessary to always remain young and prosperous [8]. On the on hand, the six-in-one evaluation framework with various integrated indicators helps companies understand their specific conditions such as the SWOT(strengths, weaknesses, opportunities and threats) dimension [9], monitor critical points in the possible decline phase of the company, and determine whether they are out of the development pipeline. On the other hand, enterprises can conduct further discussion about enterprise development strategies to create a second curve of growth [10] based on the combination of MOCA, ESG and digital indicators, so that they can continue to maintain the momentum of innovation and growth.

The brief definitions and values of each of the six evaluation standards are summarized in Table 1 below, with the specific meaning and indicators discussed in more detail in later sections.

Table 1. Overview of the six-in-one evaluation framework

Standards	Interpretation	Value
SRDI enterprises	The SRDI refers to specialized, refinement, differential and innovation, which is a major project implemented by China to guide SMEs to take the path of specialization, refinement, differentiation and innovation, enhance independent innovation capability and core competitiveness, and continuously improve the quality and level of SME development. And SRDI enterprises refers to specialized and sophisticated enterprises that produce new and unique products [11]	In any given chain in China, there are many dynamic small players involved. Leading through SRDI indicators will help enterprises achieve technological breakthroughs, innovation and upgrades, and enhance their core competitiveness
Manufacturing Individual Champions	Manufacturing individual champions refer to enterprises that have focused on specific product segments of the manufacturing market for a long time, with internationally leading production technology or process, and the market share of a single product is among the world or domestic leaders [12]	Through the application of manufacturing individual champion indicators, enterprises will be guided with a clear growth path, thus helping China to transform from a large manufacturing country into a strong manufacturing country, speed up the optimization of industrial organization, break through key areas and enhance the competitiveness of the manufacturing industry

(*continued*)

Table 1. (*continued*)

Standards	Interpretation	Value
Hidden Champions	"Hidden Champions" is a term coined by German author Hermann Simon to describe SMEs that are highly specialized world market leaders with annual revenues of up to $50 billion and are hidden from public view [6]	The index traction of "hidden champions" will help enterprises strengthen their supporting and leading roles in the industrial chain and consolidate their market position. It will also help to promote the further development of China's various industrial segments to be strong in the globalized competition
ESG	The ESG evaluation system is a system of indicators around environmental(E), social(S) and governance(G). It is an emerging corporate evaluation standard that focuses on a company's environmental, social and governance performance rather than just its financial performance [13]	The ESG indicators introduced in this paper aim to help companies better identify and manage sustainability risks and opportunities related to financial performance, and help them navigate the path to IPO and move towards internationalization
Digitalization	Indicators related to digital transformation refer to a model that deals with the definition, creation, delivery and acquisition of value benefits of digital transformation. It is derived from the "Reference Model" for Digital Transformation Value Benefits of the Integration of "Informatization" and "Industrialization" published by the National Standardization Administration in 2022, which is the first national standard for digital transformation published in China	The introduction of a digital dimension provides scientific measurement and guidance for quality development, helping companies to gain a competitive advantage, maintain a dominant position and achieve sustainable growth
MOCA	The MOCA indicator is a unique Chinese aesthetic indicator innovatively proposed in this paper, which stands for Art Measurement, ergonomics Order, Complexity and Association, and it includes three aspects: ergonomics [14], fuzzy biology [15] and sensory association [16]	Focusing on the culture of Chinese characteristics in the Second Axial age, it integrates traditional ideas such as Confucianism and Taoism, and combines traditional Chinese aesthetic concepts to help companies achieve innovation excellence, user intimacy and operational excellence from three parts: ergonomics, fuzzy biology and sensory association

3 Indicators Derived from Manufacturing Champions

3.1 The Importance of SRDI in China

As mentioned in Table 2, the enterprises featured by "specialized, refinement, differential and innovation" are called SRDI enterprises. And the SRDI is expressed in many aspects of enterprises management. To be more specific, specialized mainly refers to firms provide specialized production or services, which means that the firms have specialized technologies and provide a small number but high quantity productions and services. The refinement mainly refers to refined management. The differential refers to productions or services of enterprises having their own characteristics in appearance or function. The innovation presents in productions, management and technologies [17].

Nowadays, as the Sino-US trade friction and the COVID-19 pandemic, the uncertainties in the world have increased and China is facing complex and volatile international environment. In addition, SMEs play a critical role in accelerating innovations, promoting employment and advancing economic development. In order to promote the development of SMEs, China has proposed the specialized, refined, different and innovative development path to SMEs of the manufacturing industry.

The SRDI SMEs is backbone force in SEMs, which always focus on one link of industrial chains. Therefore, promoting development of the SRDI SMEs is helpful for improving the stability of supply and industrial chains and reducing the interference of external environment changes on economic operation. At the same time, it can give more core technologies and services to the value chain, which is conducive to value chain upgrading and economic resilience enhancing of China.

3.2 The Importance of Individual Manufacturing Champions in China

The individual manufacturing champions have two common characteristics: the first is specialization, which means that enterprises must focus on related fields for a long time. The second is champions, which requires enterprises to have champion market position and technical strength in the production subdivision field [18].

The individual manufacturing champions are the next stage of the SRDI enterprises and have more advanced technologies, management, services and products. As a result, the individual manufacturing champions can help companies understand their specific conditions and development stage. What's more, the individual manufacturing champions are beneficial to achieving technical breakthroughs, which can support transforming China from a manufacturer of quantity to one of quality. In addition, the technological advantages of individual manufacturing champions enterprises can increase the international competitiveness and occupy a leading position in the global industrial chain, so as to enhance the global market position of China in the world.

3.3 The Importance of Hidden Champions in Germany

The characteristics of hidden champions (HCs) as follows: 1) they possess a large share of the global market with fast growth based on export. 2) they possess source technology that their rivals cannot imitate and they lead a great deal of innovation. 3) they keep high return on investment and sound equity capital rate. 4) they aspire to be market leaders in global niche markets. 5) they continue efforts to maintain highest levels of operational efficiency in process and functions. 6) they have a unique style of management and corporate culture [19].

Our study builds the evaluation indicators of hidden champions of China through study common characteristics in German, which has a lot of advantages. First, HCs focus on narrowly markets and provide high-quality products. And they expand internationally to increase sales and achieve scale economies. Therefore, the HCs in China is expected to grow into globally competitive businesses. Second, the hidden champions encourage enterprises to engage in innovation and pursue innovation-driven development, which can improve the strategic scientific and technological strength of China. Third, becoming hidden champions means that the enterprises have market leadership and has allowed them to utilize and strengthen their resources and competences at a global level, enabling them to focus on specialized, high-technology products and services instead of price competition, which helps China achieve high-quality economic development.

3.4 Aligning the Indicators of SRDI, Individual Manufacturing Champions and Hidden Champions

The company cannot achieve business growth without organizational support. Ram Charan, the famous management consulting masters in the world, used to six analyze The Amazon Management System deeply from six aspects which are business model; talent management; innovation engine; digital transformation; organizational culture; and strategic decision [20]. The six modules can reveal an enterprise's organizational framework deeply and comprehensively, which is also suitable for six-in-one evaluation framework in our research. As a result, we used the six modules as first-order index in our evaluation framework. The indicators we build are as follows:

Table 2. Overview of aligned indicators

Primary indicator	Interpretation	Secondary indicators
Business Model	A complete business model may include descriptions of organizational governance, structures and capabilities, partners, the target market, the value proposition, who is creating and capturing value, the value chain, as well as which activities will be conducted by the focal firm, by partners, or through arm's length transactions, as well as revenue and cost structures [21]	Customer service
		Product quality
		Product value chain depth
		Market leadership
		Cash flow management
Talent Management	Although the conceptual boundary of talent management has a degree of debate, there are practices activities of it include recruiting, selection, development, and career and succession management [22, 23]	Talent structure
		Employee stability
		Talent cultivating mechanism
Innovation Engine	The innovation can be expressed in many aspects of companies, and in our research, we only consider the technological innovation	Innovation input
		Innovation output
		Innovation utility
Digital Transformation	Digital transformation can be defined as a change in how a firm employs digital technologies, to develop a new digital business model that helps to create and appropriate more value for the firm. And it involves changes in strategy, organization, information technology, supply chains and marketing [24, 34]	Digital strategy
		Digital enabling production
		Digital enabling operations
		Digital enabling product/service innovation
		Digital business model innovation

(*continued*)

Table 2. (*continued*)

Primary indicator	Interpretation	Secondary indicators
Organizational Culture	Organizational culture is defined as shared assumptions, values, and norms. it is a source of sustained competitive advantage and empirical research shows that it is a key factor to organizational effectiveness. In our study, we use Denison organizational culture framework to build indicators, which identified and validated four dimensions of organizational culture that are conducive to organizational effectiveness: adaptability, consistency, involvement, and mission [25]	Involvement
		Consistency
		Adaptability
		Mission completion
Strategic Decision	A strategy can broadly be understood as a description, plan or process for how to move from the current situation to a desired future state. We focus on the process of strategic decision making to build secondary indicators [21]	Strategic insight
		Strategy implementation
		Strategic evaluation

4 Indicators Derived from ESG and SASB

4.1 The Inclusion of ESG and SASB

Under the tide of "dual carbon" strategy, ESG has become an important global consensus concept, which emphasizes that companies should not only focus on financial performance, but also measure corporate value from environmental, social and governance perspectives, so that their performance in fulfilling social responsibility can be quantified, compared and continuously improved [26]. China has entered a new stage of development and is focusing on how to achieve green development, high-quality development and sustainable development, whether at the national level, the social level or the level of market participants. It is worth mentioning that in 2021, the State-owned Assets Supervision and Administration Commission of the State Council (SASAC) has included ESG as a key task to promote the fulfillment of corporate social responsibility. More importantly, in October 2022, China's 20th National Congress Report clearly states that "We should accelerate green development transformation, promote environmental pollution prevention and control, enhance ecosystem diversity, stability and sustainability, and actively and steadily promote carbon peaking and carbon neutrality" [27].

As most SRDI companies will face the listing evaluation and go international with development, corporate ESG governance, as an important part of listing disclosure information and a hot topic of domestic and international attention, needs to be incorporated into the corporate development framework as early as possible [28, 29]. For the disclosure of ESG information, organizations around the world have developed various standards for economic entities to follow. The main disclosure standards currently in the marketplace include GRI, ISO26000, SASB, CDP and IIRC, each with its own focus [30]. Among these organizations, the Sustainability Accounting Standards Board (SASB) is an independent, non-profit organization dedicated to defining accounting standards to harmonize ESG measurement. This paper's six-in-one evaluation framework ultimately adopts the SASB standards for ESG indicators. This is because the SASB standards are broadly applicable to both listed and non-listed companies, and the SASB standards focus on ESG issues that have a practical impact on corporate finance [31]. It is not only applicable to investors managing different types of assets, such as equities or bonds, but also helps specialized companies better identify and manage sustainability risks or opportunities related to financial performance, and helps companies bridge the gap between going public and going international.

4.2 Indicators Derived from ESG and SASB

As noted above, the emphasis on sustainability in the SASB standards is primarily from a business perspective, through the regulation of business behaviors and activities to improve enterprises' ability to create long-term value. Specifically, the sustainability dimensions of the SASB standards included in this paper are divided into five: the environment, human capital, social capital, business model and innovation, and leadership and governance. According to the SASB standard reports for 77 industries published by the SASB Foundation, 30 relevant sustainability topics can be identified from these five sustainability dimensions, each of which can be listed with its specific definition and measurement metrics in the corresponding industry SASB Standards [32, 33]. It is worthwhile for companies in various segments to think about their key issues at a very early stage, based on their own specific characteristics, and to include the corresponding indicators in their corporate governance disclosures (Table 3).

Table 3. Overview of aligned indicators

Primary indicator	Interpretation	Secondary indicators
Environment	This dimension as a primary indicator includes environmental impacts, either through the use of non-renewable natural resources as inputs to production factors or through harmful emissions to the environment, which may affect the company's financial position or results of operations [32]	Water & wastewater management
		GHG emissions
		Air quality
		Energy management
		Waste & hazardous materials management
		Biodiversity impacts
		Fuel management
Social Capital	This dimension deals with the expectation that a company will contribute to society in order to gain social license to operate. It deals with the management of relationships with key external parties (e.g. customers, local communities, the public and government) [32]	Human rights & community relations
		Customer welfare
		Data security and customer privacy
		Access and affordability
		Fair marketing and advertising
		Fair disclosure and labeling
Human Capital	This dimension focuses on managing a company's human resources (employees and individual contractors) as a key asset for achieving long-term value. It includes issues that affect employee productivity, management of labor-management relations, management of employee health and safety, and the ability to create a culture of safety [32]	Labor relations
		Fair labor practices
		Diversity and inclusion
		Employee health, safety, and wellbeing
		Compensation and benefits
		Recruitment, development, and retention

(*continued*)

Table 3. (*continued*)

Primary indicator	Interpretation	Secondary indicators
Business Model & Innovation	This dimension is primarily concerned with the influence of innovation and business models. The company's value creation process involves the integration of environmental, human and social issues, including resource recovery and other innovations in the production process; and product innovation, including efficiency and responsibility in the design, use phase and product handling [32]	Lifecycle impacts of products and services
		Environmental and social impacts on assets and operations
		Product packaging
		Product quality and safety
Leadership & Governance	This dimension deals with issues inherent in managing business models or common practices in the industry. Its importance lies in the fact that these issues can clash with the interests of stakeholder groups and even create potential liability, restrictions, or revocation of operating licenses [32]	Systemic risk management
		Accident and safety management
		Business ethics and transparency of payments
		Competitive behavior
		Regulatory capture and political influence
		Materials sourcing
		Supply chain management

5   Indicators Associated with Digital Transformation

The development of digital technologies has reshaped business models in various industries over the past decades and countless firms express a need for digital transformation. So it is important to take digital transformation into consideration for the six-in-one evaluation framework. In addition, China has recently launched a new national standard [34], which provides very comprehensive guidance to justify the value of digital transformation in enterprises. This national standard has been used to guide the development of digital transformation indicators in our proposed framework, as shown in Table 2 above.

6 Driving Corporate Innovation with MOCA Indicators

6.1 The Origin of MOCA

Professor Jaspers has a very famous proposition – "the age of the axis". In his "The Origin and Goal of History" published in 1949, he mentioned that the period from 800 BC to 200 BC was the "axial age" of human civilization, which was a major breakthrough in the spirit of human civilization. In the axial age, great spiritual mentors emerged in all civilizations - Confucius and Lao zi in China, Socrates and Plato in ancient Greece, Jewish prophets in Israel, Sakyamuni in India and so on. The ideological principles they put forward have shaped different cultural traditions, and have affected human life deeply [35].

Nowadays, with the accelerated development of global integration and the deepening of political, economic, cultural and other exchanges, people are entering a new era. Ewert Cousins proposed to call the era that people are entering the second axial age. Now the "second axial age" has quietly dawned. The second axial age can be seen as the awakening of spirituality, which is different from the experience corresponding to sensibility and the science corresponding to rationality. Spirituality corresponds to philosophy and art. As the development represented by scientific knowledge gradually reached its peak, it also began to fall into the dilemma of development. The emergence of spirituality as the leading role is not only the result of the development of rational science, but also the inevitable choice to solve the inherent weaknesses and limitations of rationality.

Therefore, in the process of entering the second axial age, people should pay more attention to the role of aesthetics and philosophy in design, production and operation process [36]. The aesthetic ideology contained in Chinese traditional culture provides guidance for organizations to better adapt to the changes and challenges of the second axial age. As we are about to enter the second axial age, while looking forward to the future, we should also learn the essence of traditional aesthetic thoughts, and consider the guidance of the classical thoughts of the first axial age to the current development.

The traditional Chinese thought of "people-oriented" has triggered people's thinking about the "human" factor in industrial processes. With the development of artificial intelligence and other technologies, more and more work that originally were finished by people has been replaced by machines. Because of the efficiency and convenience of the machine, the human factor has begun to be ignored by some enterprises. Confucius emphasize "harmony", that is, human should be the first place. Under the guidance of this thought, we should pay more attention to the role of people in the second axial age. Ergonomic design put forward that the whole process of products should better reflect humanistic care, both for customers and employees of enterprises. Human are the most dynamic factor that cannot be ignored in the process of industrial design and production [37]. The concept of "people-oriented" reflects concern for human beings, and the application of ergonomics makes the concept of "people-oriented" come into being.

The "Tao follows nature" of Taoism encourages the application of bionic design in industrial processes. Laozi, an ancient Chinese philosopher, put forward in the Tao Te Ching that "beauty lies in the Tao", and the essence of the Tao lies in nature, which is to tell people that they should be good at discovering the regulations contained in nature, and apply the aesthetics contained in it to all aspects of daily life. The viewpoint of "Tao follows nature" and "the unity of man and nature" can also be applied to modern industrial design and production [38]. At present, with the improvement of consumption level, people are no longer satisfied with the practical functions of products, and products need to bring more added value to consumers. Fuzzy biology reflects the traditional idea of "unity of nature and man". Some bionic research achievements of scientists have entered people's lives through the re-creation of industrial designers, constantly satisfying people's material and spiritual pursuits, and reflecting the design integration of nature and human, design and science, design and technology. Luigi Corrani also said: "The foundation of design should come from the truth presented by life born in nature" [39]. Mercedes-Benz has made great achievements in the field of bionics. Its products embody the ingenious concept of bionics everywhere from structure to appearance, helping Mercedes-Benz stand out in the homogeneous automobile industry. There are many similar excellent enterprises. The application of fuzzy biology and bionics, which embodies the concept of "Tao follows nature" in industrial design, has improved the beauty, complexity and fineness of products, and helped the innovative integration of product design.

Aesthetic design is also reflected in the exchange of senses and emotions. Liezi mentioned that "the heart condenses and the form interprets". Liang Qichao defined the value of beauty as interesting, which contains the changes of human psychology caused by sensory association. Applying synaesthesia to product design helps to enhance the relevance and consistency of user experience [16]. Through the design of all-around emotional contact points in user service scenarios, we can convey consistent emotions to users, and then complete the connection of user experience design [40]. This also reflects the "people-oriented" idea, that is, paying attention to the user's internal feelings and emotional experience in the process of using the product.

Is Chinese traditional culture compatible with science and technology? How can Chinese philosophy theory reinvigorate through traditional Chinese thinking, so that Chinese civilization can better benefit mankind? MOCA indicator gives an answer to these questions. Based on the characteristics of the second axial age and the excellent traditional Chinese philosophy, we can find that ergonomics, fuzzy biology and sensory association play important roles in guiding the current organization to adapt to the development of the times. Although there are many other ideas in Chinese traditional culture that can be used to guide people's actions in the second axial age, this paper selects the three most representative aspects to construct MOCA indicators. M represents the art measurement, O represents the order of ergonomics, C is complexity, and represents the fuzzy biology and bionics. A stands for association, which corresponds to synaesthesia. The primary and secondary indicators of MOCA will be introduced in detail in Sect. 6.2.

6.2 MOCA Innovation Indicators

MOCA indicators proposed in this paper correspond to ergonomics order, fuzzy biology and sensory association. The indicators under the three parts will be described below (Table 4).

Table 4. Overview of MOCA indicators

Primary indicator	Interpretation	Secondary indicator
Ergonomics Order	Throughout the whole process of product design, production and final user experience, ergonomics is widely used	Ergonomics order in product
		Ergonomic order in office environment
		Ergonomic order in factory
		Ergonomics order in organization
Fuzzy Biology & Bionic	With the rapid development of life, machinery, materials, information and other sciences, the research and application of fuzzy biology and bionics have received more and more attention. It is necessary to learn from the shape, structure, texture and other characteristics of certain organisms and combine them with the actual functions of the product	Bionic elements
		Value discovery of biological features
		Rationality of the combination of bionic objects and product
		Associativity
		Sustainability of design
Sensory Association	People have five senses, namely vision, hearing, smell, taste and touch. Synaesthesia is a measure of the degree to which users feel shifting or multi-sensory superposition when using the product	Adhere to customer-centered idea
		Focus on the whole process of experience design
		Overall vision of synaesthesia design
		Interest brought by synaesthesia design

First, the ergonomics order part of MOCA. In terms of product design process, consider the physiological and psychological characteristics of users. In terms of the office design process, consider how to create a comfortable office environment. And many scholars have paid attention to the application of ergonomic principles in creating a safe and healthy working environment. In terms of factory design process, consider the possible problems in human-computer interaction. It is required that the physiological characteristics parameters of workers can still be within the appropriate range under the influence of machinery, equipment, environment and other factors. In addition, people's psychological and cognitive characteristics will also affect their work. So the factory should try to use clear signs and colors as instructions, and make good use of VR and AR and other virtual reality technologies to reduce the cognitive pressure of employees. In terms of organizational structure design process, consider how to maximize the innovation ability of people. In short, ergonomics order focuses on how to optimize human health, safety and comfort under the interaction of human, machine and environment, so as to improve work efficiency.

Second, the bionic and fuzzy biology part of MOCA. Bionic design needs to have clear bionic elements, including bionic concepts, bionic objects and bionic ideas. It is an indispensable step to clarify the elements of bionics and pave the way for the follow-up work. What's more, in the process of bionic design, we should pay more attention to the value discovery of biological features, that is, extract specific biological features from the bionic objects and modify them, so as to better integrate the biological features with the technological products.

Third, the sensory association part of MOCA. In this part, we need to focus on people's sensory and its influence to people's psychology. AI emotion prediction technology, which has received more attention in recent years, can help products better perceive, recognize and understand human emotions, and can make intelligent and sensitive responses to human emotions. In addition, although the body is embedded in the cultural environment, the culture contained in the product should be understandable, and the best emotional experience brought by synaesthesia should be felt by people without corresponding cultural background. Synaesthesia brings rich sensory association, breaking the barrier between users and brands, thus creating a connection. Consumers meet self-identity from the brand, which triggers user resonance and increases the familiarity of products and brands.

With the advent of the second axial age, using MOCA, organizations can better apply the ideological core of Chinese traditional culture to the process of enterprise product design, production, promotion and other processes, and achieve multi-dimensional high-quality development. What's more, according to the "second curve" theory mentioned above, enterprises need to create their second curve if they want to maintain sustained growth in this complex environment. MOCA indicators emphasize the application of ergonomics order, synaesthesia and fuzzy biology in the development of enterprises, and help them continue to carry out subversive innovation, better adapt to the second axial age, and bring them more possibilities.

7   Conclusion

For the rapid and stable internationalization of enterprises, this paper proposes a six-in-one evaluation framework that takes "Hidden Champions" as the first standard, aligns the manufacturing individual champions and SRDI standards from left to right, complemented by the control of ESG points, digital measurements and the guidance of MOCA innovation indicators to facilitate enterprises' growth in a practical way.

This six-in-one evaluation framework has far-reaching implications for companies and countries in the world. For the country, it can promote the building of a strong country and international convergence. As stated in the previous sections, many countries such as China is in an important period of high-quality transformation and development. Supporting the creation of new models and new industrial forms is conducive to promoting the upgrading of the manufacturing industry and providing strong support for the construction of a strong manufacturing country. Also, it will help them build an integrated indicator system to enhance international influence and discourse.

For enterprises, on the one hand, it helps them clarify their current development status and transformation challenges by deeply locating their development advantages and disadvantages. Through the clarification of a series of important indicators, it will help them improve their innovation capability, enhance their market competitiveness and fully stimulate their development vitality. On the other hand, it provides optimization guidance for enterprises' high-quality development, helps them transform into specialized and refined development, and lays the foundation for them to accelerate technological innovation and sustainable development. This has universal applicability to international companies. In particular, the introduction of digitalization, ESG and MOCA innovation indicators will help companies around the world to have a more complete view to seek the second growth curve.

In conclusion, this paper outlines the conceptual origin, specific formation process, and general demonstration of the six-in-one evaluation framework. As a next step, field visits to companies and applications will be conducted accordingly to collect further feedback data and to optimize the framework. Through this approach, an integrated, international, practice-based leading six-in-one evaluation framework will be completed and presented.

Acknowledgement. This research was supported by a grant funded by the National Natural Science Foundation of China (No.: 71974215).

References

1. Brunsson, N., Bengt, J.: A world of standards (2002)
2. Mattli, W., Büthe, T.: Setting international standards: technological rationality or primacy of power? World Polit. **56**(1), 1–42 (2003)
3. Asian Development Bank. The 14th five-year plan of the People's Republic of China—fostering high-quality development (2021). https://www.adb.org/sites/default/files/publication/705886/14th-five-year-plan-high-quality-development-prc.pdf. Accessed 31 Jan 2023
4. 2022 Government Work Report. https://english.www.gov.cn/2022special/govtworkrepo rt2022. Accessed 20 Jan 2023
5. The Ministry of Industry and Information Technology. Proposal of the Central Committee of the Chinese Communist Party on Drawing Up the 14th Five-Year Plan for National Economic and Social Development and Long-Range Objectives for 2030 (2021). https://cset.georgetown.edu/publication/proposal-of-the-central-committee-of-the-chinese-com munist-party-on-drawing-up-the-14th-five-year-plan-for-national-economic-and-social-dev elopment-and-long-range-objectives-for-2030/. Accessed 20 Jan 2023
6. Simon, H.: Hidden Champions of the Twenty-First Century: Success Strategies of Unknown World Market Leaders. Springer, New York (2009). https://doi.org/10.1007/978-0-387-981 47-5
7. Koval, V., Prymush, Y., Popova, V.: The influence of the enterprise life cycle on the efficiency of investment. Baltic J. Econ. Stud. **3**(5) (2017)
8. Yue, W., Hanxiong, W., Wang, W.H.: Analysis of enterprise development strategies based on the features of different stages in enterprise life cycle. In: Proceedings of the 8th International Conference on Innovation and Management, pp. 802–806. Kitakyushu, Japan (2011)
9. GURL, Emet: SWOT analysis: a theoretical review (2017)
10. Morrison, J.I.: The Second Curve: Managing the Velocity of Change. Ballantine Books (1996)

11. Chen, L., Peng, C.: Research on the growth path of domestic small and medium-sized enterprises from "specialized, refined, different and innovative" to "hidden champions." Southwest Finance **11**, 29–42 (2022). (in Chinese)
12. The Ministry of Industry and Information Technology. Implementation Plan of Special Action for Cultivating and Enhancing Individual Champion Enterprises in Manufacturing Industry. https://wap.miit.gov.cn/jgsj/zfs/qypy/art/2020/art_c61cdc1f38b3424aaf3d9c54086b05ce.html. Accessed 31 Jan 2023. (in Chinese)
13. EBA Report on Management and Supervision of ESG Risks for Credit Institutions and Investment Firms. https://www.eba.europa.eu/sites/default/documents/fifiles/document_library/Publications/Reports/2021/1015656/EBA%20Report%20on%20ESG%20risks%20management%20and%20supervision.pdf. Accessed 31 Jan 2023
14. Lefer, D., Buckland, G., Evans, H.: They made America: from the steam engine to the search engine: two centuries of innovators, Hachette, UK (2009)
15. Sun, J., Dai, Z.: The current situation and future of bionics. J. Biophys. (02),109–115 (2007). (in Chinese)
16. Sun, N., Fan, S.: The application of synaesthesia in experience design. Lit. Art Contending (06), 191–193 (2016). (in Chinese)
17. Liu, C., Mei, Q.: Study on the development of "special, elaborative, characteristic and innovative" road based on small and micro-sized enterprised **35**(05), 126–130 (2015). (in Chinese)
18. The portrait and selection of individual manufacturing champions – a new series of studies on SRDI. https://pdf.dfcfw.com/pdf/H3_AP202208091577022676_1.pdf?1660047012000.pdf. Accessed 20 Jan 2023
19. Lee, S.S., Chung, Y.K.: A study on development strategy of Korean hidden champion firm: focus on SWOT/AHP technique utilizing the competitiveness index. J. Int. Entrep. **16**(4), 547–575 (2018). https://doi.org/10.1007/s10843-018-0234-7
20. Charan, R., Yang, Y.: Bezos' Digital Empire. China Machine Press, Beijing (2020)
21. Dahan, N.M., Doh, J.P., Oetzel, J., Yaziji, M.: Corporate-NGO collaboration: co-creating new business models for developing markets. Long Range Plann. **43**(2–3), 326–342 (2010)
22. Collings, D.G., Mellahi, K.: Strategic talent management: a review and research agenda. Hum. Resourc. Manag. Rev. **19**(4), 304–313 (2009)
23. Lewis, R.E., Heckman, R.J.: Talent management: a critical review. Hum. Resourc. Manag. Rev. **16**(2), 139–154 (2006)
24. Verhoef, P.C., et al.: Digital transformation: a multidisciplinary reflection and research agenda. J. Bus. Res. **122**, 889–901 (2021)
25. Zheng, W., Yang, B., McLean, G.N.: Linking organizational culture, structure, strategy, and organizational effectiveness: mediating role of knowledge management. J. Bus. Res. **63**(7), 763–771 (2010)
26. Li, T.T., Wang, K., Sueyoshi, T., Wang, D.D.: ESG: research progress and future prospects. Sustainability **13**, 11663 (2021)
27. Jinping, X.: Hold high the great banner of socialism with Chinese characteristics and strive in unity to build a modern socialist country in all respects. In: Delivered at the 20th National Congress of the Communist Party of China, October 2022
28. Berthelot, S., Coulmont, M., Serret, V.: Do investors value sustainability reports? A Canadian study. Corp. Soc. Respons. Environ. Manag. **19**(6), 355–363 (2012)
29. Deng, X., Cheng, X.: Can ESG indices improve the enterprises' stock market performance?—an empirical study from China. Sustainability **11**(17), 4765 (2019)
30. Ortas, E., Álvarez, I., Garayar, A.: The environmental, social, governance, and financial performance effects on companies that adopt the United Nations Global Compact. Sustainability **7**(2), 1932–1956 (2015)

31. Busco, C., Consolandi, C., Eccles, R.G., Sofra, E.: A preliminary analysis of SASB reporting: disclosure topics, financial relevance, and the financial intensity of ESG materiality. J. Appl. Corp. Financ. **32**(2), 117–125 (2020)
32. Comment, Record of Public. "Conceptual Framework" (2013)
33. SASB.   https://www.sasb.org/implementation-primer/understanding-sasb-standards/. Accessed 22 Jan 2023
34. China Standardization Administration. Integration of informatization and industrialization—Digital transformation—Reference model for value and effectiveness (2022). http:// c.gb688.cn/bzgk/gb/showGb?type=online&hcno=35DEEC978F95393E59B1541FA80 11571. Accessed 22 Jan 2023
35. Zhang, C.: Recreation of Chinese Philosophy from the Perspective of the New Axial Age. Anhui: China University of Science and Technology (2017). (in Chinese)
36. Li, X.: On the source of Chinese thought of jaspers' "Axial age" concept. Mod. Philos. (06), 86–96 (2008)
37. Wang, B., Xue, Y., Yan, J., et al.: Human-oriented intelligent manufacturing: concept, technology and application. China Eng. Sci. (04), 139–146 (2020)
38. Xu, J.: The natural meaning of taoism is meaningful – the plastic art of bionic architecture. Furniture Interior Décor. **03**, 80–81 (2009)
39. Zhou, B.: Bionic design and application in industrial design. Packag. Eng. **01**, 151–153 (2008)
40. Siskszntmihalyi, M.: Flow: The Psychology of Optimal Experience. Harper Perennial Modern Classics, New York (2008)

Untapped Potential of Participatory Design - Citizen Centered Social Data Utilization for Smart Cities

Mika Yasuoka[1]([⊠]) [iD], Tomomi Miyata[2], Momoko Nakatani[2], and Yuki Taoka[2]

[1] Roskilde University, Roskilde, Denmark
mikaj@ruc.dk
[2] Tokyo Institute of Technology, Tokyo, Japan

Abstract. Our society has shifted to digital society, where generates tremendous amount of city activity data or *Social Data*. This potentially rich city resource has attracted attentions of diverse city players, and often described as "the new oil". Accumulated social data could potentially open to create better society, generate competitive industries, and improve citizen's well-being. However, majority of societies do not know how to utilize them for future cities, yet. Challenges to social data utilization are profound. Not only technical and political challenges are there also privacy and ethical challenges. Considering these social challenges, we explored potentials of social data utilization through a series of participatory design workshops. In the workshops, participants collected their own social data and used them for collective concerns. Through the case, we found an interesting potential solution of social data utilization for designing future city, by combining concepts of data donation and citizen as co-designer. Because the combination of data donation and citizens as co-designers could provide one of the optimal solutions for utilizing social data the most without violating the data ownership. By participating in the design process, the data owner can reuse their own donated data for their own purposes, holding a right to control and interpret in the design process. This article, by introducing a smart city workshop case, proposes and discuss a potential of data donation and participatory design, which could be one way to promote social data utilization for the greater good.

Keywords: Participatory Design · Data Donation · Social Data · CoDesign · CoDesigner

1 Introduction

Our society has shifted to digital society, where generates tremendous amount of city activity data. Some leading digital nations such as Denmark has already accumulated national, geographical, citizens data in cities (hereafter social data) since 70s. The amount of social data has continuously grown, accelerated with a global trend of digital transformation and automation of data collection. This potentially rich city resource has attracted a lot of attentions of diverse city related players such as politicians, city planners, industries, and most importantly people who live in the city. Social data has been described as "the new oil" [1], thus we have observed elevated expectations to our social data. With accumulated social data, we believe that possibilities will widely open to create better society, generate competitive industries, and improve citizen's well-being [2].

Despite the rich accumulation of social data and increased expectations, majority of societies and players in societies do not know how to utilize them for designing better future cities, yet. The unprocessed raw data taken from city activities and human behavior are often cumbersome to collect, refine, cleanse and re-organize. In many cases, not only it is time consuming to lean raw data, but it is also difficult to understand such raw data for ordinary decision makers in city offices or ordinary citizens as data owners with limited data science knowledge.

Previous research and practice have kept showing difficulty of utilizing social data. For example, the city of Copenhagen, Denmark established a novel data marketplace called City Data Exchange for selling and purchasing collected social data. The project unfortunately halted in two years due to a lack of attractive use cases and profitable business models [3]. Similarly, limited research has been conducted to utilize sensor data taken from city and personal activities despite high expectations of sensor data utilizations [4]. Data Driven Design (DDD) reported most social data came from Twitter posts or online SNS comments. This indicates, as a matter of fact, sensor and wearable data, which are regarded as "the new oil" has not been explored enough [5].

Challenges of social data utilization are profound. Not only technical challenges such as cleansing data process and visualization technique matching the purpose [4], there are also human, political, societal as well as ethical challenges. The questions frequently asked in this context are the ownership of the generated data ("Who own the data generated in cities") and authenticity of data ("Who maintain and guarantee data as genuine"). The latest European law, The General Data Protection Regulation (GDPR), requires respecting data ownership and providing an appropriate control to the data owner such as the right to data portability, and ownership of their own data. But how about other regions of the world? Even in Europe, from the point of date, personal data should be considered and dealt to fulfil its compliance even for societal benefit realization. Then, how can we harness the value of the new oil?

2   A Case

2.1   Background

Considering the challenges of social data mentioned above, we explore potentials of social data utilization in relation to city activities through a series of participatory design workshops. The base setting of the workshops was organized at Future Living Lab (https://www.futurelivinglab.org/).

Future Living Lab is a two year's research collaboration among telecom company, NTT Techno Cross, Roskilde University (Denmark) and Tokyo Institute of Technology (Japan). The lab aims at staging future way of living in 2030 through collective design process with city dwellers. Starting January 2022, the lab has provided collaborative design stages for co-creation through collective conceptualization, discussion, reflection, and makings towards wicked societal challenges. In the first project year 2022, the lab conducted three projects, and each project has focused theme such as 1) future dietary practice in city, 2) happiness at work, and 3) raising kids together with local community (See Table 1). The choice of project themes is made based on three main criteria; closely related to everyday life, geographically rooted, and recognized as societal challenge in our society.

Each project consists of four consecutive workshops, and each workshop has a unique topic and an objective. Briefly explains, the first workshop is to understand the current social situation through objective data such as statistics and subjective stories. The second workshop is designed so that participants would consider and discuss social data utilization. For example, participants discuss what kind of social data could be useful to understand, improve and create new design in cities. In the third workshop, participants were requested to bring their own original social data for collective use. The fourth workshop were used to elaborate their social data related social innovation ideas proposed in the third workshop. Each workshop roughly speaking, lasts three hours with, approximately 20 participants, consisting of university students, professors, industry professionals, and NPOs. Some participants participated all four workshops or several times while there were a few who participated once.

Table 1. The overall schedule of the three projects in 2022.

Projects	1st Workshop	2nd Workshop	3rd Workshop	4th Workshop
Future dietary practice	March	May	July	August
Happiness at work	October	December	January	March, 2023 (expected)
Raising kids	September	Early Nov	Late Nov	December

2.2 The Food Project

In this article, we introduce a project about the future dietary practice in city (hereafter, food project) as a case. The food project had workshops in March, May, July, and August as shown in Table 1. Participants were 23 total, consisting of participants with diversity of profession, age and gender. In the project, the four teams with 4–6 members were formulated, and they worked together spanning 6 months.

Table 2 introduces an overall workshop structure. The first workshop utilized varied data in city and city life, which were available as open data such as data from an institution of statistics or research centers. In addition, the workshop organizers (authors) crated reference data for discussion based on interview materials. Based on the knowledge the participants acquired in the first workshop, in the second workshop participants identified a societal challenge to tackle through discussion among the team members. The participants discussed and developed their ideas towards an existing challenge regarding food in our society and discussed ideas about potentially valuable social data they could generate or collect on daily life. In the third workshops, participants developed their ideas further based on the collected their own social data taken from their everyday city activities. In the fourth workshop, each team developed their ideas and created visible and tangible outputs based on their own idea.

Table 2. The workshop structure.

Workshop Number	Purpose and Activities
1st	**Understand**. With open data, participants learn and receive knowledge on a designated topic and domain
2nd	**Ideate and create**. Identify a societal challenge to tackle through discussion among the team members. Based on the knowledge acquired in the first workshop, participants create a concept for social challenge. Participants discuss ideas about potentially valuable social data they could generate or collect personally, for understanding and solve the challenge
3rd	**Iterate and create**. Participants developed their ideas further based on the collected own social data taken from their everyday city activities
4th	**Propose a solution**. Each team developed their ideas and created visible and tangible outputs based on their own idea

As previously mentioned, one workshop last approximately three hours. One workshop could often be structured with introduction, data sharing, ideation, discussion, presentation, and conclusion. Below Table 4 is one example from the third workshop of the food project.

Table 3. A workshop structure.

Schedule	Duration	Purpose and Activities
00:00–00:40	40 min	**Introduction.** Introduction of the workshop and participants self-introduction, and reflection of the previous workshop
00:40–01:10	30 min	**Data sharing.** Sharing, reading, and reflecting data
01:10–02:10	60 min	**Ideation.** Choose and develop an idea
02:10–02:25	15 min	**BREAK**
02:25–02:45	20 min	**Presentation** Team presentation
02:45–03:00	15 min	**Conclusion.** Each team developed their ideas and created visible and tangible outputs based on their own idea

2.3   Presented Social Data

Social Data were used in the first and third workshops as design materials for the workshop activity, although the other two workshops also utilized social data, indirectly to some extent. Before introducing details of the social data utilized in the first and third workshops, let us briefly clarify how social data was dealt in the second and fourth workshops. In the second workshop, the workshop participants discussed what kind of social data could be collected for the third workshop, and in the fourth workshop, the participants developed service and product idea based on the particular social data brought to the third workshop.

To begin with, in the first workshop, the workshop organizers prepared three different kinds of social data. First data is statistical data (Fig. 1), which consists of 11 pages of data visualization with summary texts taken from different sources and themes. All collected data were relevant to the theme "food in our future". For example, data in the sheet #3 introduce eating style, with four figures, graphs and short texts, and the data in the sheet #3 informs the number of people living alone in 2010 through 2022 and consequently showed eating alone have been increased. The sheet #11 describes a global trend of vegan's food intake. It also introduces a tendency of different vegan styles in the world.

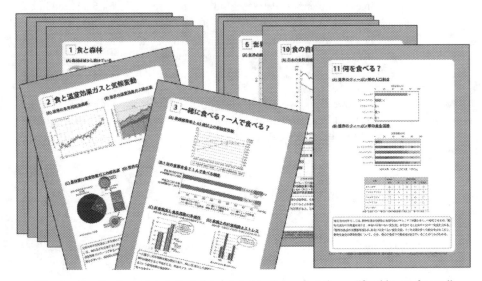

Fig. 1. A collection of statistical data related to the project theme "food in our future."

The second data is six short videos, which the speaker told own story on food from own perspective (Fig. 2). Each video length slightly varies from 30 s to 1 min. Six speakers are consisted of four women and two men, and age ranging from 14 to 51 years old and the topic introduced in the short talks varies from own dietary custom to the global trend. For example, 14 years old *Julia* talked about vegetarian and plant-based food, which she believes important shift to take concerning about our future food intake, both for nature and human health. *William*, a university student, mentioned opportunity and possibilities of insect food as key future protein source.

The third prepared data is from Human library. We borrowed a concept of human library, which is defined as "an event that gets strangers talking openly and directly with each other about prejudice [6]". In our workshop, one person who are knowledgeable

Fig. 2. A list of six video speakers. The story with theme "food in our future" is introduced.

about the future food participated as online subject, so that the workshop participants could ask questions to the professional person on "food in the future" in real time.

In the third workshop, the participants prepared social data on "food" by themselves in relation to their everyday activities and brought them to their workshop table. In the second workshop, each team discussed what kind of data could be interesting to collect and each member collected their social data individually during approximately one month. The four teams considered, prepared, and collected different social data based on the discussions on the second workshop. The below Table 4 shows an overview of the collected social data of the four teams.

Table 4. Collected Social Data.

Team #	Collected Data	Data Attribute
Team 1	Private food intake	Log data
Team 2	Shopping records	Log data
	Electronics usage	Sensor data
Team 3	Shopping records	Log data
	Plant/Vegetation growth records	Log Data
	Food waste	Sensor data
Team 4	Electronics usage	Sensor data

The collected social data was unique in itself. Roughly explained, Team 1 collected a list of private food intake as log data (Fig. 3). For example, one participant brought a collection of ready-made food box, snacks, and energy bars, while another brought a collection of restaurant food. Team 2 collected electronic sensor data in addition to the food shopping records. For example, one sensor owner collected multiple data in the private room (Fig. 4) from temperature, usage of refrigerator, human traffic volume. Although they are very simple data, to some extent, data can easily disclose the data owners' lifestyle.

Fig. 3. An example of log data of food intake. Log data from two participants

3   How the Social Data Were Processed in the Workshops

The collected data for a month by the workshop participants were brought and used at the third workshop. This section identifies and elaborates how the social data were collected before the workshop, shared, and processed during the workshop, and finally regarded and reflected in the end of the workshop.

3.1   Before the Workshop

Before the workshop, the workshop organizers explained the purpose of the workshops and participants were agreed to the data collection such as recording voice and taking pictures. The further usage of collected data during the project period were agreed limited to research purpose.

3.2   During the Workshop

During the workshops, participants were requested to collect social data by themselves. Participants' social data were collected often in a shared cloud depository, in this case,

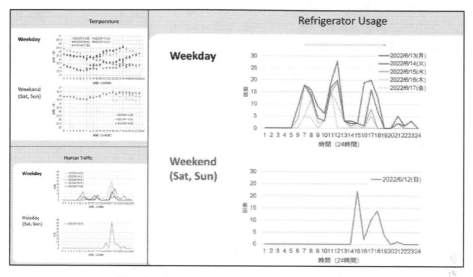

Fig. 4. An example of sensor data representation

Dropbox or Google Drive among team members, where all group members could see who and when the data was uploaded. Social data were shared and viewed both in digital and physical formats. Some data are printed out in paper and put on the workshop table so that everyone can touch, shuffle, and point out to others.

The collected social data was used as design materials for creating new design solutions during the workshops, aiming at improving well-being on *food in future* for city dwellers. Social data were mainly used during data sharing and ideation phase of the third workshop shown in Table 3.

3.3 End of the Workshop

In the end of the workshop, the social data were left to the workshop depository. The original data owners would not take them back so that it became a shared material for workshop participants and the organizers as we agreed in the beginning. In the end of the workshop, social data were mainly used by the organizers analysis and academic work.

4 Discussion

Through the food project, we found an interesting potential of social data utilization for designing future city. We would like to discuss two unique elements: they are 1) data donation and 2) citizen as co-designer. Although the two elements are independent possibilities, they are, at the same time, complementary to each other. By deploying the two concepts at the same time, the utility of data would increase for the "greater good" in society.

4.1 Data Donation

The workshop participants were surprisingly willing to share their personal data as data owners. The shared data are their vital data, trash data and dietary data, to name a few. Some data could be categorized as sensitive data according to GDPR as data can easily identify personal way of living and sensitive routine. However, it was not a concern of GDPR at the workshop as data was provided by the participants, the owner of the data approved to use their data for the scientific purpose. This action can be interpreted as social data donation of the data owner.

Data donation [7] is defined as an approach to data collection enabled by recent political directives such as GDPR. The data donation makes the owner actively consent to transfer their data to the activity reconstructing its data context. Such frameworks for utilizing personal data have been studied for decades. Epstein et al. [8] investigated opportunities of collecting and sharing personal data and introduced the lived informatics model of personal informatics. During the corona pandemic, data donation in wider scale was testified as well. For example, the Robert Koch Institute in Germany developed the Corona Data Donation App, with which donors could share data from fitness trackers and smartwatches to understand the spread of COVID-19 [9]. Similar trial was conducted by the COVID-RED project, the Julius Center in The Netherlands, where Donors could provide collected data from wearable devices [10]. Studies to date suggests that not only Corona Pandemic crises [9, 10], but also during times of crisis in general such as natural hazards or violence attack [11, 12], citizens were more likely to share data physically and emotionally, to achieve a greater good of society. Thus, their donation were initiated by collective or principlism, rather than other motivations such as egoism or altruism reasons [13].

The increase in successful cases of data donation might raise hope that the use of social data will become easier and flourished. However, at the same time, the lack of understanding how the donated data were used and how the data were useful has also raised concerns persistently around the data donation related actions. Consequently, the importance of a concept citizens as co-designer, discussed in the next section, could become a complementary pair of the data donation.

Similar concept to data donation, information bank has also discussed recently as an entity to utilize social data. However, this approach is still considered as ambivalent solution of social data. First of all from GDPR perspective, the concept is still immature. And secondly as information bank mainly considers and discusses simplistic financial benefits of the data owner based on the egoism or altruism reasons [13], but not discuss wider societal benefits. As an organisation, information bank must collect, control, and manage large amount of personal data centrally, so that it still requires technical development and social considerations.

4.2 Citizens as Co-designer

Citizens as data owners acted as co-designers in the workshops by creating solutions collaboratively together with other participants. By participating in the design process, the data owner can reuse their own social data for their own purposes, holding a right to control and interpret in the design process. The owners showed a positive attitude to donate their own data and utilized them for designing solutions in the course of collective design activities. The co-designer opportunity of the data owner could easily enforce this positive data utilization cycle for societal good.

Previous research indicates that currently data owners have utilized their own personal data for reflecting their own behavior but not for designing and creating solutions of collective concerns (Fx. [4, 5, 8]). Data owners might be concerned about not knowing how their data is interpreted and used. Our data supports this view. If the owners have any control over their own data, they could willingly contribute with their social data.

5   Conclusion

This article, by introducing a workshop case, proposes and discuss a potential of data donation and participatory design, which could be one way to promote social data utilization for the greater good of our society.

References

1. The Economist: The wrold's most valuable resource is no linger oil, but data (2017)
2. Carvo, R.A., Peters, D.: Positive computing: technology for wellbeing and human potential (2014)
3. Minicipality of Copenhagen and Capital Region of Denmark: City data exchange - lessons learned from a public/private data collaobration (2018)
4. Kirk, A.: Data Visualisation: A Handbook for Data Driven Design. SAGE Publications Ltd. (2016)
5. Bertoni, A.: Data-driven design in concept development: systematic review and missed opportunities. In: Proceedings of the Design Society: DESIGN Conference, pp. 101–110. Cambridge University Press, Cambridge (2020)
6. Simon, N.: The participatory museum. Museum 2.0 (2010)
7. Bietz, M., Patrick, K., Bloss, C.: Data donation as a model for citizen science health research. Citiz. Sci. Theory Pract. **4**, 1–11 (2019). https://doi.org/10.5334/cstp.178
8. Epstein, D.A., Ping, A., Fogarty, J., Munson, S.A.: A lived informatics model of personal informatics. In: UbiComp 2015 Proceedings of the 2015 ACM International Joint Conference on Pervasive Ubiquitous Computing, pp. 731–742 (2015). https://doi.org/10.1145/2750858.2804250
9. Diethei, D., Niess, J.: Sharing heartbeats: Motivations of citizen scientists in times of crises. In: Proceedings of the Conference on Human Factors in Computing Systems (2021). https://doi.org/10.1145/3411764.3445665
10. Julius Center: About COVID-RED
11. Linlin Huang, Y., Starbird, K., Orand, M., Stanek, S.A., Pedersen, H.T.: Connected through crisis: Emotional proximity and the spread of misinformation online. In: CSCW 2015 - Proceedings of the 2015 ACM International Conference on Computer Supported Cooperative Work & Social Computing, pp. 969–980 (2015). https://doi.org/10.1145/2675133.2675202
12. Yasuoka, M.: Correlation with aspiration for change : a case study for restoration after natural disaster. In: Partiipatory Design Conference, pp. 1–4 (2012)
13. Daniel Batson, C., Ahmad, N., Tsang, J.A.: Four motives for community involvement. J. Soc. Issues **58**, 429–445 (2002). https://doi.org/10.1111/1540-4560.00269

User Experience in Intelligent Environments

Investigating the Psychological Impact of Emotion Visualization and Heart Rate Sharing in Online Communication

Riko Horikawa[1]($\boxtimes$), Tatsuo Nakajima[1], and Bruce Ferwerda[2]

[1] Department of Computer Science and Engineering, Waseda University, Tokyo, Japan
{riko.horikawa,tatsuo}@dcl.cs.waseda.ac.jp
[2] Department of Computer Science and Informatics, Jönköping University, Jönköping, Sweden
bruce.ferwerda@ju.se

Abstract. In recent years, the integration of physical and cyber spaces has rapidly progressed. Sensing data from various sources is increasingly being fed back into physical space, and there are increasing cases of sensing and utilizing human biosignal information and emotions as well. This study investigates the psychological effects of visualizing and sharing people's emotions and heart rate through two case studies. The first case study examines the psychological effects and usefulness of sharing others' emotion and heart rate by displaying them beside he or she in physical space using a prototype of an augmented reality application called "Emo-Space". The second case study proposes chat systems called "Emo-Circle" and "Heart-View" that allow for the visualization and sharing of emotions and heart rate and examines the effects of using the system on interpersonal relationships and self-awareness of emotions. We provide insights from the two case studies into that how such data of emotions and heart rate data indicating the physical and mental states of individuals can be applied to daily lives, including communication with others.

Keywords: Emotions · Heart Rate · Visualization · Social Media

1 Introduction

Currently in Japan, Society 5.0, a human-centered society that aims to solve social issues and create new value by integrating cyberspace and physical space, has been proposed as the desirable future society [1]. While a vast amount of information on people and objects is being sensed, there have been studies on how to visualize and provide such data in a way that is best suited to the situations and the individuals [2].

In recent years, with the spread of wearable devices such as Apple Watch[1], an increasing number of people are able to easily manage their health by checking health data and other information related to their personal daily physical conditions [3]. Furthermore, the scope of sensing is not limited to simply quantifiable information such as biosignals;

---

[1] https://www.apple.com/watch/.

N. A. Streitz and S. Konomi (Eds.): HCII 2023, LNCS 14036, pp. 169–184, 2023.
https://doi.org/10.1007/978-3-031-34668-2_12

recent developments also allow for the estimation of emotions and visualization of them as data through techniques such as estimating by heart rate [4], and text posts on social media [5]. These data on emotions and heart rate have mainly been used for monitoring an individual's situation [3]. However, there is potential for these techniques to be used as a means of understanding the situation of others and spaces, but the effects on relationships with others have not been fully examined. Therefore, we conducted two case studies to examine the psychological effects of visualizing and sharing emotions and heart rate in both physical and cyber spaces.

In the first case study, we created a prototype of an augmented reality (AR) application called *Emo-Space* to investigate how interactions and psychological effects are caused between people by visualizing individual emotions and heart rate in physical space. We conducted a participatory design workshop and participants discussed the system. In the second case study, we separated the effects of visualizing emotions and sharing heart rate to investigate them individually. We developed two chat systems, *Emo-Circle* and *Heart-View*, and investigate the effect on relationship with others in online communication.

From the results of these two case studies, we found that visualizing emotions and heart rate in online communication increases empathy toward others and enhances the ability to accurately read other people's emotions. It was especially shown that Emo-Circle was useful for self-awareness of one's own emotions, confirming that the system can be used in various use cases in the future. We believe that this research will serve as a reference for future experience design using emotions and heart rate data.

2   Related Work

2.1   Emotion Visualization Interface

Aoshima et al. proposed a framework for nonverbal communication using an interface that displays one's own and others' emotions using an emotion wheel. "Emotion Broadcasting Interface" and "Emotion Monitoring Interface" enable the intuitive transmission of one's own emotions and understanding of the distribution of emotions of others [6], but there has not been enough discussion on how the actual use of such an interface in online communication affects relationships with others and desirable use cases.

2.2   Use of Heart Rate as a Communication Cue

With the advancement of wearable technology, biological data such as heart rate can be easily measured on a daily basis, and attempts have been made to use it not only for personal monitoring but also for interpersonal communication. Liu et al. proposed an application that allows for the sharing of heart rate through text messages and showed that sharing heart rate with others in daily life can be used as a means of expressing emotions and communicating personal situations [7]. They also showed that providing heart rate information and visualization through graphs can increase empathy and familiarity in the perception of stigmatized group members [8]. The addition of auditory representations, such as heartbeats, in addition to visual representations increases emotional convergence [9].

Hassib et al. stated that the use of applications that display and explicitly transmit heart rate information between close friends and partners, either through asynchronous messaging or in real time, can support empathy and an implicit understanding of each other's emotional states and, in special cases, may arouse curiosity [10]. Although many use cases of heart rate-based communication have been proposed, they are limited to unilateral sharing with a partner or between pairs of acquaintances and sharing in social media and its effects on relationships with others have not been examined.

2.3 Construction of Good Interpersonal Relationships and Understanding of One's Own Feelings

Okada et al. noted that there are few psychoeducational programs to foster understanding of one's own feelings and propose deepening understanding of one's own feelings as an approach to constructing good interpersonal relationships [11]. Ikeda et al. proposed a method for deepening the understanding of one's own emotions by plotting self-rated emotions on Russell's circular model and then presenting the difference from the emotions analyzed from bioinformation [12]. However, the interface used their study does not have words that express emotions, and therefore, it is not appropriately designed for expressing emotions.

3 The First Case Study

In the first case study, we created a prototype of an AR application called Emo-Space to investigate the psychological effects by sharing personal situations with others by visualizing heartbeat information in public spaces. We conducted a participatory design workshop, surveyed participants' motivation for the experience and discussed the design of the system.

3.1 System Design

Emo-Space is a smartphone-based AR application, and Fig. 1 shows the initial prototype system in use. Emo-Space displays heart rate information (heart rate waveform) in AR so that it appears above a user's head when the smartphone is pointed at a specific person in the space the user is in. The aim is to enhance the sense of realism by overlaying heart rate information on the actual appearance of the target person in the physical space. When used in a public place, the user can set it to the mute mode, considering that the target person's heartbeat may be audible. In addition to the target person's profile information, Emo-Space also includes a function to let the user know that he or she has seen emotions through this service, a chat function, and a function to tell the user what he or she wants to talk about, allowing new communication to be established through this service. Additionally, detailed information indicating emotions estimated from the participant's heart rate is displayed at the bottom of the screen.

As shown in Fig. 2, we also developed a function called "Emo Map", which uses the collected emotion data of each person to provide a real-time view of the distribution of the persons' emotions in the space in which they are located. By color-coding the map

Fig. 1. An image of the initial prototype service in use

according to the type of emotion and plotting a circle on the museum map that reflects the magnitude of the person's heart rate, a new experience that allows a user to grasp his or her own and others' emotions spatially and intuitively is offered. A user can find people not by name, but in terms of what kind of emotions they have by using Emo Map. Emo-Space also implements a function to narrow down the emotions displayed on Emo Map to only those selected by a user and a function to suggest people who have emotions similar to his or her own. These functions allow a user to easily find people who have similar emotions and thoughts to him/herself and are expected to trigger new communication.

Fig. 2. A screenshot of Emo Map

3.2 Participatory Design Workshop

Participants. A participatory design workshop was held to discuss the current prototype design of Emo-Space. In this workshop, there were 5 participants aged between 21 and

22, including 4 males and one female. After explaining its motivation and objectives to the participants, we also discussed use cases where the service design and emotional sharing would be effective.

Discussion Topics. In this workshop, open discussions were held on the following five topics: (a) the difference between communication in physical space and cyber space, (b) the usability and desirable uses of the emotion analysis function, (c) opinions on visualizing one's own emotions and showing them to others and seeing others' emotions, (d) use cases where visualization of emotions and other personal situations is desirable, and (e) opinions on using the service and evaluation of the current prototype design.

3.3 Insights from Workshop

The discussions in the previous section revealed the type of communication that participants desire on a daily basis. Many participants noted the importance of sharing the atmosphere of the space when communicating, and while citing the convenience of online communication, they also expressed a desire to interact with others in a physical space. From this perspective, the survey confirmed that improving the quality of communication in physical spaces will continue to be important.

With regard to emotion, which was the most important factor in this study, the participants had little experience in using emotion analysis by AI and tended to be satisfied with the level of emotion ability that is within the range of human ability. Although the ability to analyze emotions beyond the range of human recognition is useful for individual mental health and self-awareness, the feeling of being watched without permission, as in the experience of using AR in this study, is likely to be a factor of resistance. Therefore, to add value to the emotion visualization experience, it is necessary to dispel the passive and negative image of "being watched by others".

On the other hand, the opinions on Emo Map focused on the great interest and desire to know emotions from the space in which the person is located, rather than the person itself, and showed that tying emotional data to places and objects that evoke emotions has the potential to significantly change our perception and communication experience in the physical space. In other words, simply linking emotion data to people and visualizing them does not create new communication; it is only when emotion data are shared with others via shared places and objects that the value of the experience is enhanced, such as new discoveries from the emotions of others.

In the future, it is necessary to examine the opportunities of Emo-Space that elicit users' active expression of emotions and enhance the value of experiences in physical spaces through visualization of emotions by considering shifting the target of emotional relationships from people to shared spaces and objects.

4 The Second Case Study

This study aimed to examine the psychological effects and usefulness of sharing personal situations with others by visualizing heartbeat information in public spaces. To conduct user evaluations, we developed two chat systems, Emo-Circle and Heart-View, which allow users to visualize emotions using Emo Map and share their heart rate information, respectively.

4.1 Research Questions

The following research questions have been set for this study:

- RQ1: How does the use of Emo-Circle and Heart-View affect relationships with others compared to text communication?
- RQ2: Does the use of Emo-Circle and Heart-View affect the self-awareness of emotions?
- RQ3: In what situations is the use of Emo-Circle and Heart-View most appropriate?

For RQ1, we will compare the changes in closeness, empathy, and other emotional items such as the ability to accurately read others' emotions, trust, and the desire to know others better, between text communication and the use of Emo-Circle and Heart-View. For RQ2, we will investigate the effects of Emo-Circle and Heart-View on the ability to "have a bird's-eye view" of one's emotions and the ability to "observe" changes in one's emotions based on the lower-order goals for enhancing emotional self-awareness proposed by Okada et al. [11].

4.2 System Design

System Overview. Three different chat systems intended to be used as a social platform were developed to investigate the above research questions. These include Normal-Chat, which allows users to share comments only, Emo-Circle, which visualizes the emotions of users when sharing comments using an Emo-Map, and Heart-View, which allows users to share comments along with their heart rate. The Unity[2] game engine, version 2021.3.15f1, was used to create these systems. The systems were built in WebGL format and were launched on a local server for the evaluation experiments. The participants used a MacBook Air to operate the chat systems.

Interface Design. The functions and interfaces of the three types of chat systems are described below.

Normal-Chat
Normal-Chatwas developed as an ordinary text communication chat system for comparison with the other two chat systems. It includes an input field at the bottom of the screen (as shown in Fig. 3), where users can type a comment and post it by clicking the "Post" button on the right side of the input field. Personal identifying information such as usernames and icons are also added to the comments. In this experiment, we displayed comments of fictional characters on the timeline at designated times as if others' comments were synchronized in real time.

Emo-Circle
Emo-Circle is a chat system that allows users to share comments and visualize emotions on Emo-Map. Emo-Map, shown in Fig. 4, is in the center of the screen and displays 8

---

[2] https://unity.com/.

Fig. 3. A screenshot of Normal-Chat

basic emotions in a circular layout based on Plutchik's Wheel of Emotions [13]. The design of Emo-Map is inspired by the "Emotion Live Interface" proposed by Aoshima et al [6]. In Emo-Map, each emotion word is written in both Chinese Characters and English. The Emo-Map's circle shows emotions that are weaker in the center and those that are stronger toward the outer edge.

To post a comment on Emo-Circle, first, you post an emotion pin on Emo-Map by clicking on the position on Emo-Map that represents your emotion. Then, you enter your comment in the input field on the right and click the "Post" button to complete the comment posting. After the comment is posted, you can check your comments and the colors of the emotion pins on the lower left of the screen. As shown in Fig. 5, as you use this chat, the emotion pins of yourself and others accumulate in Emo-Map.

As in Normal-Chat, we displayed emotion pins and comments of fictional characters on the timeline at designated times as if others' comments were synchronized in real time for the experimental reasons.

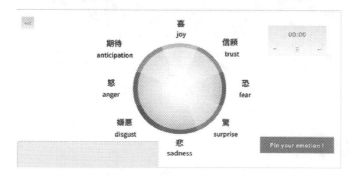

Fig. 4. An interface of Emo-Circle

Heart-View

Heart-View is a chat system that allows users to share their heart rate along with comments. As Fig. 6 shows, the latest and the maximum heart rate since using this system are displayed on the left side of the screen, while the average heart rate of all users

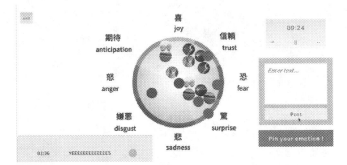

Fig. 5. A screenshot of Emo-Circle

in Heart-Chat is displayed on the right side. To post a comment, users can press the "Share your HR" button on the bottom left corner and enter a comment. The posted comments will be displayed in the center of the screen, and you can use the slider at the bottom of the screen to filter others' comments by the heart rate value associated with the comments as Fig. 7 shows. Fitbit Charge5[3] measured the heart rate per minute and transferred it to this chat system. As with the two previous systems, we displayed heart rate and comments of fictional characters on the timeline at designated times as if others' comments were synchronized in real time for the experimental reasons.

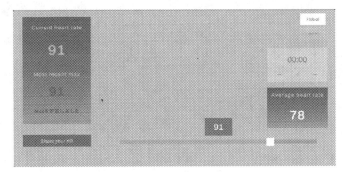

Fig. 6. An interface of Heart-View

4.3 Experiment

Participants. In this experiment, there were 16 participants aged between 21 and 25, including 12 males and 4 females. The experiment was conducted individually and face-to-face, one person at a time. Participants watched a movie while using the proposed chat systems. The movie was displayed on a dedicated monitor and listened to through headphones. Figure 8 shows the scene of the experiment.

---

[3] https://www.fitbit.com/global/jp/products/trackers/charge5.

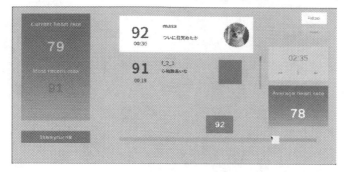

Fig. 7. A screenshot of Heart-View

Fig. 8. A scene of experiment

Scenario. In this experiment, we aimed to create a situation where it was easy to compare one's own and others' emotions and heart rate by providing a common topic and set the scenario as "chatting while watching the same movie online with multiple people." We used the movie "Yes Man" (2008), produced by Warner Brothers, for a 10-min viewing time for each chat system, considering the time constraint on participants. This condition was based on the study that revealed that short-term heart rate variations were measured in 5 min and comedy movies caused rapid changes in emotions [14]. Figure 9 shows the flow of the experiment.

Fig. 9. The flowchart of the experiment

Questionnaire Design. After using Emo-Circle and Heart-View, the participants were asked to complete a survey using a 5-point Likert scale or open-ended questions. Table 1 shows the questionnaire questions.

Table 1. Questionnaire Questions (Excerpt).

No.	Question	Answer Style
1	How did the following items (A. accuracy of reading others' emotions, B. intimacy, C. empathy, D. trust, E. desire to know others more deeply) change in comparison to Normal-Chat?	5-point Likert scale (1: Decreased - 3: Un changed - 5: Increased)
2	To what extent do you agree with the following statements? "I was able to get a bird's eye view of my emotions."	5-point Likert scale (1: Strongly Disagree - 5: Strongly Agree)
3	To what extent do you agree with the following statements? "I was able to observe changes in my emotions"	5-point Likert scale (1: Strongly Disagree - 5: Strongly Agree)
4	In which situations do you want to use the proposed chat systems?	Open-ended

4.4 Results

For all items on Heart-View presented hereafter, results were compared between people who wear wearable devices in daily lives and have experiences of monitoring their heart rate and those who do not. However, Mann-Whitney U test showed no significant differences in all items.

Changes in Emotions and Recognitions Toward Others. In this section, we present the results of the user evaluations of the impact of the proposed system on relationships with others. Specifically, we show the results of the question 1. As Fig. 10 and 11 show, the highest average score for Emo-Circle was "empathy" (4.19) and for Heart-View it was "Accuracy of reading others' emotions" (3.75).

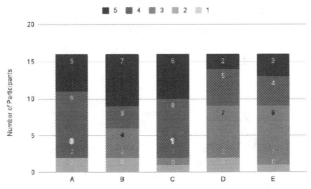

Fig. 10. The results of question 1 for Emo-Circle (A. accuracy of reading others' emotions, B. intimacy, C. empathy, D. trust, E. desire to know others more deeply)

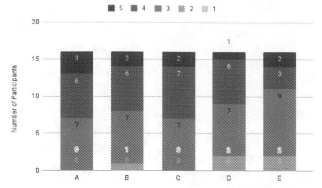

Fig. 11. The results of question 1 for Heart-View (A. accuracy of reading others' emotions, B. intimacy, C. empathy, D. trust, E. desire to know others more deeply)

Self-awareness of Emotions. This section presents the results of an evaluation of the impact of using the proposed system on the participants' ability to understand and observe their own emotions.

Impact on the Ability to Have a Bird's Eye View of Self-emotion. Figure 12 shows the results of the question 2 for Emo-Circle and Heart-View. The average scores for Emo-Circle and Heart-View were 3.94 and 3.31, respectively.

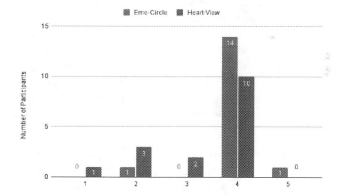

Fig. 12. The results of question 2 for Emo-Circle and Heart-View

Impact on Self-emotion Observation. Figure 13 shows the results of question 3 for Emo-Circle and Heart-View. The average scores for Emo-Circle and Heart-View were 4.31 and 3.38, respectively.

4.5   Discussion

Changes in Emotions and Recognitions Toward Others. The study evaluated the effects of visualizing emotions and sharing heart rate on relationships with others by

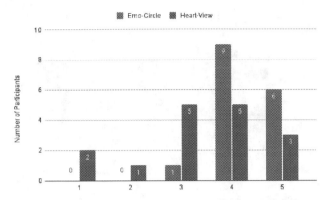

Fig. 13. The results of question 3 for Emo-Circle and Heart-View

comparing "Normal-Chat" that only shares comments with "Emo-Circle" and "Heart-View" in five areas: "ability to correctly read others' emotions," "closeness," "empathy," "trust," and "desire to know others more deeply."

Ability to Correctly Read Others' Emotions. Emo-Circle found that 14 participants responded that their ability to correctly read others' emotions had "increased or slightly increased" when compared to Normal-Chat. The visual representation of others' emotions on Emo-Map made it possible to more accurately recognize the emotions of the other person compared to just comments. However, if the comments associated with the emotion pins did not match the participant's expectations, it could cause a sense of discomfort with the location of the emotion pin and make it difficult to understand others' emotions. It would be necessary to examine how the results change when various people with different thoughts and values are used as participants and the chat system is used simultaneously by multiple people. Heart-View had the highest average scale value for this item. Judging from participants' comments, heart rate may be useful as a means of understanding others' true emotions and situations due to its objectivity and uncontrollable states.

Closeness. In Emo-Circle, the visual clarity of Emo-Map, which allows for easy understanding of others' emotions, effectively increased feelings of closeness. According to Iwawaki et al. [15], we are sensitive to common points with others, and thus the degree of commonality is quantified as closeness. In this experiment, participants likely felt closer to others who shared similar emotions as they perceived the distance on the Emo-Map between their own emotion pins and others' as psychological distance. In contrast, in Heart-View, as shown in Fig. 11, only two participants evaluated it as "increased" compared to Normal-Chat. Several participants commented that they could not determine if their emotions were in agreement based on heart rate alone. From the perspective of the relationship between commonality and closeness as pointed out by Iwawaki et al.

[15], it can be inferred that the lack of closeness was due to the inability to find common points with others based on heart rate alone.

Empathy. Emo-Circle had a significant positive impact on the participants' sense of empathy and closeness to others, as 14 out of the participants reported feeling "heightened" or "somewhat heightened" compared to normal chat. The use of Emo-Map, which allows users to easily find others with similar emotions and opinions, likely contributed to this increase in empathy. However, the effects of empathy may vary depending on the type of content used in the experiment. In this study, the content used was a comedy movie, which may have less conflict and fewer differing opinions, leading to less of a decrease in empathy. Further research is needed to examine how political or controversial topics may affect empathy. Additionally, there are different definitions of empathy, such as cognitive empathy and emotional empathy [16], so further examination is needed to determine which definition is being used. Heart-View also had a positive impact on participants' ability to understand the emotions of others, but it is unclear if the motivation to view others' heart rates is high enough to increase empathy. The results of this study also indicate that viewing others' heart rates alone may not be sufficient to increase empathy, as seen in previous studies by Liu et al.

Trust. In Emo-Circle, the participants became more aware of the existence of others by expressing their emotional pins on Emo-Map, and the fact that they had more clues that helped them to know others may have increased their sense of trust. In Heart-View, one participant stated that the heart rate is a numerical value that the participants themselves cannot control. Therefore, it is possible that the state in which such an uncontrollable value is shared with others may have increased the sense of trust, although the participants can easily adjust their appearance to others in online communication, but it must be said that the effect is limited from the evaluation results. There is a research that shows that it is important to use real names and to make appropriate comments to increase the sense of trust toward others online communications [17], such as on social media. This may be because all of the proposed chat systems were set up to be used anonymously. In addition, since trust in others is fostered through long-term interaction, it is possible that this experiment was not set up in a situation sufficient to increase trust. It is necessary to examine the influence of long-term use on the sense of trust in the future.

Desire to Know Others More Deeply. In Emo-Circle, it is possible that interest in others was enhanced by the fact that Emo-Map made it easier to compare the feelings of themselves and others. In Heart-View, some participants said that sharing heart rate information with others does not lead to motivation to watch others' heart rates unless there is a change in the values. The fact that the Heart-View interface was designed to make it difficult to check the changes in the heart rate of others may be one of the factors that prevented the participants from becoming more interested in others. It is possible that this item is affected by the way participants usually interact with others on social media, and it is necessary to conduct a survey on each participant's awareness when using social media and analyze changes for each participant.

Self-emotion Understanding. This research examines the impact of visualizing emotions and sharing heart rate on self-awareness, from the perspectives of "being able to overview one's own emotions" and "being able to observe changes in one's own emotions." The results show that in Emo-Circle, 15 participants answered that they "could overview their own emotions" and "could observe changes in their own emotions." However, in Heart-View, the percentages were approximately 60% and 50%, respectively. The study analyses the impact of each chat system on these aspects.

Impact on the Ability to Have a Bird's Eye View of Self-emotion. In Emo-Circle, several participants said that they were able to reflect on their own emotions by comparing them to the emotion's words on Emo-Map when they posted their emotion pins. The fact that participants input their own emotions themselves rather than relying on text information, contributed to a deeper understanding of their own emotions and thus to the overview of their own emotions. Additionally, as one participant said, "It was interesting to observe that people have completely different emotions in the same scene", it was likely to be easy to compare other people's emotions with one's own emotions on Emo-Map, which might have also contributed to having a bird's eye view of one's own emotions and broadening one's horizons. It could be that users place emotion pins carelessly without much consideration when it is only for their own record, but when they are exposed to other people, the consciousness of being seen might lead to more careful analysis of emotions, which is something that should be examined in the future.

In Heart-View, as several participants stated, heart rate was found to be less effective in evoking specific emotions. Only looking at one's own or others' heart rate did not lead to an overview of one's own emotions. As proposed by Ikeda [12], using a technique that estimates emotions based on heart rate and presenting not only heart rate but also the estimated emotions might have made it possible to realize the overview of one's own emotions.

Impact on Self-emotion Observation. It is found that Emo-Circle made it easy for participants to observe changes in their emotions from the comments of participants. However, the ability to observe changes in emotions may also be affected by factors such as the extent of interests for the movie having watched during the experiment and the intensity of daily emotional changes, which may vary depending on the participants' personalities. Therefore, the analysis based on the participants' level of interests and personalities would be necessary to observe changes in emotions.

The Heart-View tool, on the other hand, was found that to be less effective in evoking emotions. Several participants said that they had difficulties using heart rate to judge emotions and interpreting the heart rate. However, there is a limited connection between heart rate and emotional state. As almost of all participants stated, they considered a high heart rate as what indicates excitement statements regardless of whether the emotion is positive or negative. While heart rate may not be a precise indicator of subtle emotions, it can be used to determine if one is in an excited state by detecting sudden changes in heart rate, which motivated many participants to share and compare their current states with others.

Use Cases for the Proposed System
One participant stated that she would like to use Emo-Circle to record her own emotions, while another participant stated that she would like to save the changes in Emo-Map

state used while viewing a common work of art by several people and look back on it later. The value of using Emo-Map not only for communication scenes, but also for recording their own and others' emotions for later review, was also found. Regarding the experience of placing emotion pins on the emotion map, one participant stated that he was hesitant to place when other people's emotion pins had already been placed in the same emotional position as his. It became clear that the visual situation of oneself and others through the Emo-Map also had the effect of making people think about the emotional balance in the moment, even in online communication.

While half of the participants were reluctant to use Heart-View in the future, some pointed out that the heart rate is an objective value and that it is highly reliable. Therefore, by displaying the heart rate with subjective data such as emotion pins in Emo-Circle, there is a possibility that the sharing of the heart rate will affect the way people perceive others.

5 Conclusion

In this study, we investigated how the use of emotional visualization and shared heart rate in communication can affect relationships with others and support self-understanding, compared to text communication.

We conducted two case studies. In the first case study, we developed a prototype of an AR app called Emo-Space to investigate how interactions and psychological effects are created between people by visualizing individual emotions and heart rate in physical space. Then, we conducted a participatory design workshop and surveyed the participants about the design and motivation of the system.

In the second case study, we developed two systems. Emo-Circle for emotional visualization and Heart-View for shared heart rate and conducted user evaluations. The results showed that using Emo-Circle increased empathy toward others, while using Heart-View increased the ability to correctly read others' emotions. Emo-Circle was also useful for self-awareness of one's own emotions.

Emo-Circle and Heart-View were considered to be used as communication tools, however, it was shown that Emo-Circle can also be used as a diary to record one's emotions. Mitsui et al. proposed a lifelogging system that automatically records emotions by analyzing sentences posted on SNS [5]. Emo-Circle allows users to review not only their own emotions but also the emotions of others at the same time, which may be useful to reflect more clearly on the situation at that time. We would like to verify its usefulness as a means of recording emotions in the future. We would also like to examine what kind of psychological effects and interactions with others can be generated by linking emotion and heart rate data to various objects in the physical space.

References

1. Cabinet Office, Government of Japan. Society 5.0. https://www8.cao.go.jp/cstp/society5_0/. Accessed 9 Feb 2023
2. Nakajima, T., Lehdonvirta, V.: Designing motivation using persuasive ambient mirrors. Pers. Ubiquit. Comput. **17**, 107–126 (2013). https://doi.org/10.1007/s00779-011-0469-y

3. Rapp, A., Cena, F.: Personal informatics for everyday life: how users without prior self-tracking experience engage with personal data. Proc. Int. J. Hum. Comput. Stud. **94**, 1–17 (2016). https://doi.org/10.1016/j.ijhcs.2016.05.006

4. Tsunoda, K., Eguchi, K., Yoshida, K., Watanabe, T., Mizuno, S.: Estimating mood state change caused by contents viewing using heart beat and respiration: a study with Japanese comedy. IPSJ Techn. Rep. (Web) **2016**(CDS-16), 4, 1–8 (2016)

5. Mitsui, K., Ito, C., Nakanishi, Y., Hamakawa, R.: Emote: an emotional record life log system using SNS postings. (SNSの投稿を用いた感情記録ライフログシステムEmote) Res. Rep. Entertai. Comput. **2014-EC-32**(1), 1–6 (2014)

6. Aoshima, S., Aoki, U., Miyashita, Y.: Emotion live interface using emotion wheel. Techn. Rep. IPSJ **2010-HCI-139**(5), 1–7 (2010)

7. Liu, F., Dabbish, L., Kaufman, G.: Supporting social interactions with an expressive heart rate sharing application. In: Proceedings of the ACM on Interactive, Mobile, Wearable and Ubiquitous Technologies, vol. 1, pp. 1–26. ACM (2017). https://doi.org/10.1145/3130943

8. Liu, F., Kaufman, G., Dabbish, L.: The effect of expressive biosignals on empathy and closeness for a stigmatized group member. In: Proceedings of the ACM on Human-Computer Interaction, vol. 3, pp. 1–17. ACM (2019). https://doi.org/10.1145/3359303

9. Winters, R.M., Walker, B.N., Leslie, G.: Can you hear my heartbeat?: hearing an expressive biosignal elicits empathy. In: Proceedings of the 2021 CHI Conference on Human Factors in Computing Systems, pp. 1–13. ACM (2021). https://doi.org/10.1145/3411764.3445545

10. Hassib, M., Buschek, D., Wozniak, P.W., Alt, F.: Heartchat. In: Proceedings of the 2017 CHI Conference on Human Factors in Computing Systems, pp. 1–13. ACM (2017). https://doi.org/10.1145/3025453.3025758

11. Okada, K., Takano, M., Tsukahara, M.: Development of a psychological education program to deepen self-understanding of emotions: practicing in small groups with junior high school students who have a sense of discomfort in interpersonal relationships. (感情の自己理解を深めるための心理教育プログラムの開発—対人関係に苦手意識を持つ Sch. Ment. Health **18**(2), 132–146 (2015). https://doi.org/10.24503/jasmh.18.2_132

12. Ikeda, Y., et al.: Supporting awareness through visualization of emotions using physiological information. In: Proceedings of Interaction 2017, pp. 634–637 (2017)

13. Plutchik, R.: The emotions, pp. 109–112 (1991)

14. Murase, C., Kawamoto, R., Sugimoto, S.: Analysis of emotional changes and heart rate variability induced by audiovisual stimulation. (視聴覚刺激による情動の変化—心拍変動の分析) J. UOEH **26**(4), 461–471 (2004). https://doi.org/10.7888/juoeh.26.461

15. Iwawaki, H., Yano, E., Shinohara, K., Kato, S.: Modeling of personal sense of intimacy using common points of contents - campus community aid. Int. J. Affect. Eng. **8**(3), 659–665 (2009). https://doi.org/10.5057/jjske.8.659

16. Yamaguchi, R., Miyamoto, R.: Neural basis of cognitive empathy and emotional empathy through observation of others' expressions: study on adult women. (他者の表情観察を通した認知的共感と情動的共感の神経基盤—成人女性を対象として) Clin. Neurophysiol. **46**(6), 567–577 (2018). https://doi.org/10.11422/jscn.46.567

17. Ministry of Internal Affairs and Communications of Japan. Whitepaper on ICT Usage and Penetration Survey. https://www.soumu.go.jp/johotsusintokei/whitepaper/ja/h30/html/nd143210.html. Accessed 9 Feb 2023

Sustained Participation Motivation of Quantified Self for Personal Time Management

Huan Li[(⊠)], Yongxin Kong, and Guochao Peng

Sun Yat-sen University, Guangzhou, China
lihuan66@mail2.sysu.edu.cn

Abstract. The rapid development of mobile Internet promotes the rise of quantified-self. Time management is an important part of quantified-self. Users quantify their time and realize time management through using time management apps. Based on the unified theory of acceptance and use 2(UTAUT2) model, this paper constructs an influence mechanism model that affects sustained participation motivation of quantified self for personal time management. The results show that performance expectancy, effort expectancy, hedonic motivation and habit have significant positive effects on behavioral intention. Social influence, facilitating conditions and price value don't have significant effect on behavioral intention. The conclusion of this study offers opinions and suggestions for the interaction design and user time management and has practical reference significance for related enterprises to improve user stickiness.

Keywords: quantified self · sustained participation motivation · time management · UTAUT2

1 Introduction

As the popularity of smart phones and mobile Internet, the society is characterized by permanently online and permanently connected. It is much easier for people to get all kinds of fragmentary information, which makes people pay too much attention to mobile phones and harder to stay focused for long periods of time to do something else. As a result, people are looking for ways to correct this behavior and time management software comes into being. Nowadays, a lot of users choose to use time management apps to quantify time management, so as to increase productivity of work and take control of their lives. So the quantified self has permeated people's time management activity.

The quantified self is defined as the process by which individuals use quantified tools (i.e., smartwatches, body fat scales, and quantified applications) to monitor and collect data of their own bodies, states, and behaviors for self-reflection and self-knowledge acquisition [1]. The previous studies have shown that use of quantified self technologies (OSTs) increases self control and promotes positive behavioral changes by providing users within formation about themselves. However, it has been reported that around half of users discontinue using their OSTs several months after their purchase [2].

In the background described above, we are committed to research users' motivation for quantified self-sustained participation in personal time management. Specifically, our study answers the following questions:

How do people quantify themselves when they use time management apps for time management practices?
What factors influence people's sustained participation motivation in quantifying self by using time management apps?

The study contributes to enrich perspective for the research of quantifying self-sustaining participation motivation. What's more, the relevant research results can help guide the function optimization and service improvement of the OSTs. At the same time, it can help users better recover their focus time from the electronic screen.

2 Literature Review

The quantified self refers to the real-time measurement and recording of human-related data using a range of modern technological means, which was first introduced in 2007 by Kelly and Wolf. In a 2007 article in the magazine Wired, Kelly and Wolf proposed the concept of "quantified-self" to describe this behavior. Since then, there has been a vigorous quantified-self movement around the world, and scholars have begun to pay attention to this movement at the same time. The quantified self is mainly achieved through a series of hardware and software such as smart phones, wearable devices and accompanying applications, which constitute the empirical mode of people's understanding of themselves in an ordinary way and widely covered in health, education, social, work and other fields [3].

The research of quantified self has risen in multiple fields, such as health, physiology, finance, and so on. Hong uses in-depth interviews with self-trackers and grounded theory to analyze the connotation and dimension of consumers' quantified-self consciousness and it is divided into three dimensions: individual thinking, social projection, and data sensitivity [3].

Tracking and effectively managing personal time is one of the important dimensions of quantified self. As a result, time management software is widely used in the workplace and personal life, providing a set of digital solutions for individuals under the sense of time crunch. At present, the relevant research of quantified self in individual time management behavior mainly analyzes quantitative self-technology and personal media-oriented time management practices through qualitative research. From the perspective of time sociology, Cao et.al study how college students in China manage time with time tracking apps in the background of the COVID-19 times through the perspective of the sociology of time, so as to provide insight into the dichotomy of autonomy and out-of-control in the quantified self [4]. Liu Yixuan analyzed the self-control technologies such as quantified self and invitation monitoring in the time management app, and analyzed how users internalize the external truth into their own behavior style with the help of external new media technology, and further shaped themselves into a highly disciplined modern subject [5]. Based on the review of relevant literature, we find that few studies focused on quantitative self-sustaining engagement motivation for individual time management practices.

3 Theoretical Background and Research Model

3.1 Theoretical Background

In 2012, Viswanath et al. extends the unified theory of acceptance and use of technology (UTAUT) to study acceptance and use of technology in a consumer context, which called UTAUT2. The UTAUT2 incorporates three constructs into UTAUT: hedonic motivation, price value, and habit. Individual differences - namely, age, gender, and experience – are hypothesized to moderate the effects of these constructs on behavioral intention and technology [6].

According to UTAUT2, performance expectancy, effort expectancy, social influence, hedonic motivation, price value, and habit are theorized to influence behavioral intention to use a technology, while behavioral intention, facilitating conditions and habit determine technology use. Also, individual difference variables, namely age, gender, and experience are theorized to moderate various UTAUT2 relationships. The lighter lines in Fig. 1 show the UTAUT2 model [6].

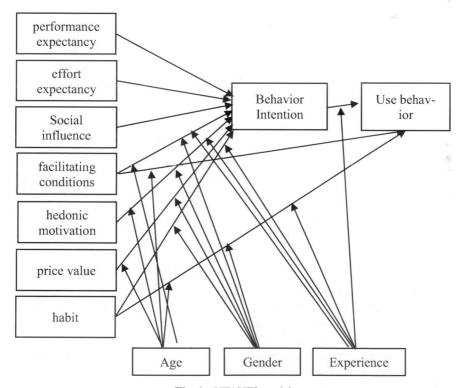

Fig. 1. UTAUT2 model

3.2 Research Model

In our research, we drop individual difference variables of the original UTAUT2 and only consider the influence of performance expectancy, effort expectancy, social influence, hedonic motivation, price value, and habit on behavioral intention to use a time management app (Fig. 2).

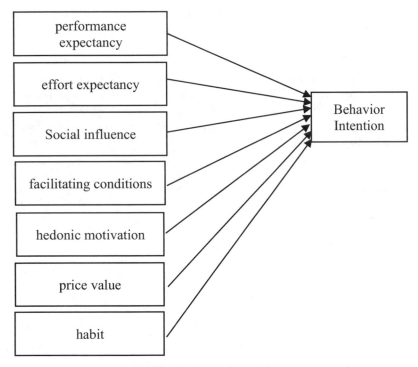

Fig. 2. Research model

3.3 Hypothesis Development

Performance Expectancy: The performance expectancy is defined as the degree to which using a technology will provide benefits to consumers in performing certain activities [6]. According to Compeau and Higgins [7], if people expect positive consequences in return for its use, they are intent to adopt new technology. Therefore, we hypothesize that if users are more likely to continue using time management apps if they think the use of time management apps will help improve their work and study performance. Thus,

H1: The performance expectancy has positive impact on intention of time manage-ment app's users.

Effort Expectancy: The effort expectancy is defined as the degree of ease associated with consumers' use of technology [6]. With the help of quantified tools to interfere with control and accurate rational behavior choices, users can promote their self-activities and decision-making efficiency [8]. As a result, if a time management apps are easy for users to use, their behavioral intention to use a time management app will increase. Thus, we hypothesize:

H2: The effort expectancy has positive impact on intention of time manage-ment app's users.

Social Influence: The social influence is defined as the extent to which consumers perceive that people who are important to them (e.g., family and friends) believe they should use a particular technology [6]. If people who are important for users think they should use time management apps, users will be influenced by them increase their intentions to use time management apps. Therefore, we hypothesize:

H3: The social influence has positive impact on intention of time management app's users.

Facilitating Conditions: The facilitating conditions refer to consumers' perceptions of the resources and support available to perform a behavior. A consumer who has access to a favorable set of facilitating conditions is more likely to have a higher intention to use a technology [6]. A consumer with a lower level of facilitating conditions will have lower intention to use technology. Thus, we hypothesize:

H4: The facilitating conditions have positive impact on intention of time management app's users.

Hedonic Motivation: The hedonic motivation is defined as the fun or pleasure derived from using a technology, and it has been shown to play an important role in determining technology acceptance [6]. If users get more pleasure when using time management apps, they will have more intention use time management apps. Thus, we hypothesize:

H5: the hedonic motivation has positive impact on intention of time management app's users.

Price Value: The price value is defined as consumers' cognitive tradeoff between the perceived benefits of the applications and the monetary cost for using them, which is positive when the benefits of using a technology are perceived to be greater than the monetary cost and such price value has a positive impact on intention [6]. Thus, we hypothesize:

H6: The price value has positive impact on intention of time management app's users.

Habit: There are at least two key distinctions between habit from different perspective. One distinction is referring to the habituation proposition as the habit/automaticity per-spective (HAP) and, another distinction is consistent with TPB as the instant activation perspective (IAP). Staying faithful to TPB, IAP assumes that repeated performance of a behavior can result in well-established attitudes and intentions that can be triggered by attitude objects or cues in the environment. Once activated, attitudes and intentions will automatically guide behavior without the need for conscious mental activities. The HAP assumes that repeated performance of a behavior produces habituation and behavior can be activated directly by stimulus cue. The key difference between the IAP and the HAP is whether conscious cognitive processing for the makeup of intention is involved between the stimulus and the action. 81). Habit is a learned out-come and only after a relatively long period of extensive practice can it be stored in long-term memory and override other behavior patterns. Habit will have strong effect on intention and use for users [6]. Thus, we hypothesize:

H7: The habit has positive impact on intention of time management app's users.

4   Research Design and Data Analysis

The scale used in this study was adapted from the measurement scale of UTAUT2 model. The variables involved in this study were all measured by 5-level Likert scale. We adapted the method of online questionnaire survey to collect survey data. A total of 241 questionnaires were recovered. And Our research subjects are users who is use the Forest app, so 62 invalid questionnaires were deleted. Finally, 179 valid questionnaires were recovered.

4.1   Descriptive Statistical Analysis

In the end, 179 valid questionnaires were collected in this study, and the respondents were specifically targeted at Forest APP users. The basic information is shown in Table 1. In this study, it is found that the time of most people use time management app is not long. Therefore, this study analyzes the influence factors of sustained participation motivation on the quantified-self in time management apps, which can provide reference for the development of time management apps.

Table 1. Descriptive statistics of samples

User characteristics	Distribution	Number	Accounted(100%)
Gender	Male	77	42%
	Female	102	58%
Education level	Junior college and below	1	0.5%
	Undergraduates	129	72%
	Master and above	49	27.5%

(continued)

Table 1. (*continued*)

User characteristics	Distribution	Number	Accounted(100%)
Time length of use	Under 1 year	72	46%
	1 to 2 year	58	26%
	2 to 3 year	40	16%
	Above 3 year	38	12%

4.2   Reliability and Validity Test

Tables 2, 3 and 4 present the measurement model results, including information about reliability, validity, correlations and factor load. The Cronbach's alpha value was .75 or greater, suggesting that the scales were reliable. According to the reliability analysis results in Table 2, the Cronbach's alpha value was 0.8717, 0.911, 0.8343, 0.8526,0.8375, 0.9272, 0.887, and 0.9535. All the coefficients were around 0.8 or above. As a result, it can be seen that the measurement scale has good reliability, and the questionnaire has passed the reliability test.

According to the Table 3, all factor load value were above 0.6, all the average variance extracted (AVE) values were above 0.5 and composite reliability (CR) were above 0.8, which indicates the measurement scale has good validity. What's more, all the average variance extracted (AVE) values were greater than related coefficients with other variables, which also indicates that the measurement scale has good validity.

Table 2. Reliability analysis results

Research variables	items	Corrected Item-Total Correlation	Cronbach's Alpha if Item Deleted	Cronbach's Alpha
performance expectancy	PE1	0.7007	0.8668	0.8717
	PE2	0.8183	0.7629	
	PE3	0.7483	0.8256	
effort expectancy	EE1	0.8308	0.8732	0.9111
	EE2	0.8142	0.8791	
	EE3	0.8048	0.8824	
	EE4	0.7482	0.9024	
social influence	SI1	0.5141	0.9089	0.8343
	SI2	0.7673	0.7009	
	SI3	0.7789	0.7005	

(*continued*)

Table 2. (*continued*)

Research variables	items	Corrected Item-Total Correlation	Cronbach's Alpha if Item Deleted	Cronbach's Alpha
facilitating conditions	FC1	0.7466	0.7905	0.8526
	FC2	0.7048	0.8100	
	FC3	0.6956	0.8116	
	FC4	0.6043	0.8390	
hedonic motivation	HM1	0.7360	0.7492	0.8375
	HM2	0.7579	0.7175	
	HM3	0.6265	0.8603	
price value	PV1	0.8305	0.9118	0.9272
	PV2	0.8898	0.8672	
	PV3	0.8478	0.9055	
habit	HT1	0.7386	0.8789	0.8870
	HT2	0.8389	0.7871	
	HT3	0.7633	0.8560	
behavioral intention	BI1	0.9030	0.9321	0.9535
	BI2	0.8880	0.9420	
	BI3	0.9181	0.9206	

Table 3. Analysis results

Research variables	CR	AVE	items	Factor load
performance expectancy lePara>	0.878	0.706	PE1	0.792***
			PE2	0.885***
			PE3	0.841***
effort expectancy	0.912	0.722	EE1	0.887***
			EE2	0.867***
			EE3	0.850***
			EE4	0.791***
social influence	0.858	0.676	SI1	0.600***
			SI2	0.887***
			SI3	0.939***

(*continued*)

Table 3. (*continued*)

Research variables	CR	AVE	items	Factor load
facilitating conditions	0.856	0.598	FC1	0.797***
			FC2	0.796***
			FC3	0.809***
			FC4	0.685***
hedonic motivation	0.850	0.654	HM1	0.796***
			HM2	0.858***
			HM3	0.770***
price value	0.931	0.818	PV1	0.870***
			PV2	0.941***
			PV3	0.901***
habit	0.866	0.686	HT1	0.941***
			HT2	0.810***
			HT3	0.719***
behavioral intention	0.954	0.875	BI1	0.942***
			BI2	0.913***
			BI3	0.950***

Note:
1. PE: Performance Expectancy; EE: Effort Expectancy; SI: Social Influence; FC: Facilitating Conditions; HM: Hedonic Motivation; PV: Price Value; Bl: Behavioral Intention.
2. $*p < 0.05$; $**p < 0.01$; $***p < 0.001$.

Table 4. Differential validity analysis

variables	average	standard deviation	PE	EE	SI	FC	HM	PV	HT	BI
PE	3.79	0.68	**0.84**							
EE	4.23	0.65	0.46*	**0.85**						
SI	3.04	0.76	0.50*	0.12*	**0.82**					
FC	3.91	0.69	0.45*	0.53*	0.38*	**0.77**				
HM	3.65	0.82	0.67*	0.41*	0.61*	0.57*	**0.81**			
PV	3.49	0.86	0.52*	0.30*	0.45*	0.44*	0.61*	**0.90**		
HT	2.72	0.97	0.42*	0.15*	0.50*	0.30*	0.61*	0.56*	**0.83**	
BI	3.48	1.02	0.51*	0.17*	0.54*	0.40*	0.69*	0.59*	0.69*	**0.94**

Note: PE: Performance Expectancy; EE: Effort Expectancy; SI: Social Influence; FC: Facilitating Conditions; HM: Hedonic Motivation; PV: Price Value; Bl: Behavioral Intention.

4.3 Structural Model

The table 5 present the fitting degree of the research model. The Chi-square to degree of freedom ratio (χ^2/df) was 1.87, the comparative fit index (CFI) value was 0.939, and root-mean-square error of approximation (RMSE) value was 0.070, which suggests that the fitting degree of the structural model was good (Table 6).

Table 5. Imitative effect analysis

indicators	r	Fitting value
χ^2/df	<5	1.87
CFI	>0.9	0.938
RMESA	<0.08	0.070

Table 6. Model summary

hypothesis	β	standard estimation	t value	Sig	Conclusion
H1: performance expectancy -> behavioral intention	0.148	0.093	1.52	0.065	Set up
H2: effort expectancy -> behavioral intention	0.159	0.073	2.2	0.028	Set up
H3: Social influence -> behavioral intention	0.02	0.076	0.27	0.7	Don't set up
H4: facilitating conditions -> behavioral intention	0.041	0.089	0.46	0.65	Don't set up
H5: hedonic motivation -> behavioral intention	0.317	0.179	1.77	0.077	Set up
H6: price value -> behavioral intention	0.086	0.072	1.2	0.231	Don't set up
H7:habit-> behavioral intention	0.48	0.10	4.79	0.00	Set up

The direct effects of the structural model are shown in Table 7. According to the data in table 7, performance expectancy, effort expectancy, hedonic motivation and habit have significant positive effects on behavioral intention (β = 0.148, 0.159, 0.317, 0.48, p < 0.1), assuming that H1, H2, H5 and H7 are supported. Social influence, facilitating conditions and price value had no significant effect on behavioral intention (β = 0.02, 0.041, 0.086, p > 0.1), indicating that H3, H4 and H6 were not supported.

Table 7. Hypothesis verification

hypothesis	Hypothesis context	Conclusion
H1	The performance expectancy has positive impact on intention of time management app's users	Set up
H2	The effort expectancy has positive impact on intention of time management app's users	Set up
H3	The social influence has positive impact on intention of time management app's users	Don't set up
H4	The facilitating conditions has positive impact on intention of time management app's users	Don't set up
H5	The hedonic motivation has positive impact on intention of time management app's users	Set up
H6	The price value has positive impact on intention of time management app's users	Don't set up
H7	The habit has positive impact on intention of time management app's users	Set up

5   Conclusion

The research results show that the stronger the performance expectancy of users in using time management apps, the stronger the intention of users to use them. The main goal of using time management apps for users is to improve the efficiency of work and study. But beyond that, users have other needs, such as receiving and processing information in a timely, which requires that the functional design of time management apps should be based on user needs and improve the service quality.

The study finds that the effort expectancy has a significant positive impact on users' intention to use time management apps, which reflects that the lower the difficulty of using time management apps, the higher their intention to use them. Therefore, it is worth thinking about how to design a time management apps with simple interface, easy operation and easy use for users.

The results show that hedonic motivation has a positive effect on users' intention. Innovation is "the degree to which a person accepts new ideas and makes innovative decisions independently"; Novelty seeking is the tendency of individuals to seek novel information or stimuli. Such innovation and pursuit of novelty can increase users' hedonic motivation to use products. Taking Forest APP as an example, it provides users with novel time management functions, which can plant users' study/work time into trees for visualization and be related to tree planting behaviors in real life. Users can get a greater sense of satisfaction and pleasure through using it, so as to increase their intention to use it. Therefore, for time management apps developers, they should pay attention to functional innovation and service innovation of apps, so as to improve user stickiness.

The research shows that habit has a positive influence on users' intention. When users use time management apps for a long time in study or work and form positive views on them, relevant behavioral awareness will be generated. Such intentions are stored in users' consciousness, which is easier to promote users' intention to use time management apps.

In our study, social influence, facilitating conditions and price value had no significant effect on behavioral intention. One possible reason for it is that the goal of users using time management apps is to achieve self-regulation, which is a self-driven behavior and less influenced by others. Therefore, the effect of social influence is not significant. In addition, this study takes the Forest APP as an example. The APP can buy the permanent use right at one time. When the user decides to buy it, the monetary cost is paid at one time, and the price value of subsequent users may not change significantly, so there is no obvious influence on the user's intention to use it. As far as the facilitating conditions are concerned, the use conditions of time management apps only require owning a mobile phone without too much support from resources, which can be satisfied for most users. Therefore, there is no significant impact on users' intention.

6   Deficiencies and Prospects

This study uses the service of the questionnaire star survey platform to collect sample data by issuing electronic questionnaires. The sample data are mostly concentrated in young college students, and the sample scope is not wide enough. Moreover, this study did not dynamically track the differences of perception used by the respondents in different time periods, so it could not effectively reflect the changing process of user behavior. Subsequent studies can focus on the effects of new interaction patterns on users' continuous use behavior. In addition, our research only studies the influencing factors from a large direction. In future studies, it can be analyzed one by one according to every variable.

Acknowledgement. This research was supported by a grant funded by the National Natural Science Foundation of China (No.: 71974215).

References

1. Choe, E.K., Lee, N.B., Lee, B., Pratt, W., Kientz, J.A.: Understanding quantified-selfers' practices in collecting and exploring personal data. In: Proceedings of the SIGCHI Conference on Human Factors in Computing Systems, pp. 1143–1152, April 2014
2. Suh, A.: Sustaining the use of quantified-self technology: a theoretical extension and empirical test. Asia Pac. J. Inf. Syst. **28**(2), 114–132 (2018)
3. Jin, H., Peng, Y., Chen, J., Park, S.T.: Research on the connotation and dimension of consumers' quantified-self consciousness. Sustainability **14**(3), 1504 (2022)
4. Cao, P., Fang, H.: 'Stay focused': the quantified self and mediated time management practices. Chin. J. Journal. Commun. **44**(03), 71–93 (2022). (in Chinese)
5. Liu, Y.: Quantitative self and invitation monitoring in time management APP. Media Forum **5**(03), 118–120(2022). (in Chinese)

6. Venkatesh, V., Thong, J.Y., Xu, X.: Consumer acceptance and use of information technology: extending the unified theory of acceptance and use of technology. MIS Q., 157–178 (2012)
7. Compeau, D.R., Higgins, C.A.: Application of social cognitive theory to training for computer skills. Inf. Syst. Res. **6**(2), 118–143 (1995)
8. Jin, H., Yan, J., Zhang, Y., Zhang, H.: Research on the influence mechanism of users' quantified-self immersive experience: on the convergence of mobile intelligence and wearable computing. Pers. Ubiquitous Comput., 1–12(2020)

Evaluating Students Experiences in VR Case-Studies of Information Systems Problem-Based Teaching

Junyang Li[1] , Guochao Peng[1(✉)] , Miguel Baptista Nunes[2] , Ning Zhang[3] ,
Jiazheng Liang[1], and Tingyu Luo[1]

[1] School of Information Management, Sun Yat-sen University, Guangzhou 510006, China
penggch@mail.sysu.edu.cn
[2] School of Internet of Things, Xi'an Jiaotong-Liverpool University Entrepreneur College,
Taicang, Suzhou 215400, China
[3] Research Center for Digital Publishing and Digital Humanities, Beijing Normal University,
Zhuhai 511449, China

Abstract. Information systems (IS) is inherently an applied research discipline. Therefore much of the teaching in IS uses problem-based approaches that are highly reliant on case-study analysis and discussion. One of the few drawbacks of using case-studies with undergraduate students, is their difficulty in relating to professional environments and contexts of which they completely lack experience of. Understanding professional work in real organizations is fundamental in much of IS thinking and development. This paper designed and developed a VR case-study application that allowed the virtual visit of an organization mentioned in a case-study. And then, we conducted an experiment evaluation of the whole application done with 30 students taking a bachelor degree in IS. Eventually, we discussed the results of this evaluation and provides recommendations for future development using this type of technology. This study proved to be very popular with students and enabled a more immersive and physical understanding of a complex professional environment as well as permitting visit of the different organizational spaces and interaction with non-person characters (NPCs) (managers and systems users) that are part of the case study.

Keywords: Information Systems Teaching · Problem Based Learning · Case-study learning · VR Environments

1 Introduction

Information Systems (IS) an academic discipline is seen to in a "perpetual and continuous social construction" [1], meaning that the field is in continuous evolution due to the constant changes in society, organisations and individuals combined to the revolutionary rate of Information and Communication Technologies (ICT). This poses serious continuity problems for teaching syllabus, applicability of theories and pedagogical approaches. Contrary to more theoretical natural science subjects or more traditional humanities fields that focus on the past, IS needs to link its pedagogical approaches according to the role and relevance of IS research to practice. IS as a discipline is at the intersection of knowledge of the properties of physical objects (ICT and nowadays the Internet of things (IOT) and knowledge of human behaviour [2].

As a discipline, these characteristics of information system are the same as those of other design disciplines (such as architecture or engineering). These disciplines also involve people and artificial products. The theory links the natural world, the social world and the artificial world of human architecture [2]. Teaching IS therefore become very complex as there is greater demand from student and businesses alike for state-of-the-art education in emerging ICT that will allow them to participate more effectively in an increasingly technology-based information society. The IS discipline is being called upon to address some of these educational needs, similarly to many other design disciplines such a Computer Science, Control Automation, Electronic Engineering, etc. However, the rapid speed of the development and change of information and communication technology makes educators have little time to reflect on these changes and emerging technologies, which creates the danger that education only focuses on tools or grammar and other issues, at the expense of basic principles or their meaningful applications [3]. Therefore, IS education faces a dilemma: between an objectivist perspective for teaching the basics of tools and syntax and a more pragmatic and socio-cultural pedagogical perspective that emphasizes principles and application of the technology [4].

A teaching approach that focus on tools and technologies, may be more comfortable to educators as it allows them to focus on what they know and have researched on for years. However, it compromises the longevity and applicability of the knowledge acquired. Obviously, it is not to let students equip the basic skills of using specific tools, but how to effectively learn and use these tools [5]. For instance, it is not important that we teach our students how to program in a specific language (Fortran, BASIC, Pascal, C, Visual Basic, C++, Java, Python, etc.), but how to learn the logic behind programming in general so that they can learn any new programming language that may emerge. Therefore, the teaching of IS needs to be applied and contextualised. This paper reports on the use of problem-based learning (PBL) using case-studies.

This type of approach is commonly used in IS teaching nowadays, mostly in modules on IS design and development. In most instances, case-studies are given to students in text format. However, these case-studies are not always easily understood by undergraduate students with no experience of work organisations and their respective contexts. This often poses cognitive overloads and barriers to student understandings that compound the difficulty of the subject matter. The paper therefore proposes a VR environment to better enable the understanding of real-world contexts.

One of the disadvantages of traditional VR is that the immersion is not too realistic and movement is done by jumping or moving through stick controller. This paper reports on the introduction a VR walker (also known as a VR treadmill) as an element to make movement within a VR environment more natural and ubiquitous. A fully immersive VR environments are often themselves rather artificial in term of movement and exploration of the environment itself, recurring to jumping from one point to another for instance. In order to diminish this often disorienting feature, we introduced a VR walker into the VR environment. This is we believe such a complex VR environment was created for

IS educational purposes. This paper describes the pedagogical and technical thinking behind the process of development of this VR educational environment.

2 Literature Review

2.1 Information Systems Teaching and Learning

Academic learning in Information Systems can be defined as a series of activities that promote acquisition of high-level knowledge [6]. However, both the nature of knowledge and the way this knowledge is to be acquired is changing due to the fast development of ICT and the Information Society we all live in [7]. Therefore, it must be assumed that academic learning in information systems is not only a passive process of acquiring inert and abstract facts and concepts. If learners do not know how to apply these facts and concepts in an appropriate environment, then these knowledge and concepts will be useless [8]. So academic learning in IS can be re-defined as the process of constructing knowledge and the development of reflexive awareness, where the individual is an active processor of information. Learning is the result of interaction with a rich learning environment and participation in real activities, social interactions and negotiations based on previous knowledge [9].

This demand for situational learning, social negotiation and multiple perspectives means that a variety of different learning strategies must be adopted to help learners build knowledge [10]. The adoption of these different strategies has created the need to develop real and rich learning. Grabinger and Dunlap [11] believe that this is necessary to promote learning in a real environment, and encourage learners to increase their sense of responsibility, initiative, decision-making ability, intentional learning and ownership of the learned knowledge. In the IS teaching and learning, these rich learning environments often take the form of case-studies. However, the environments by themselves are not a solution. These case studies need to be embedded within a wider pedagogical approach to teaching. Approaches such as inquiry-based learning and problem-based learning are commonly used to set holistic learning activities that to be explore authentic case studies, though realistic task capable of motivating and challenging the learner [12]. Therefore, our goal is to design such a real and rich learning environment to truly serve the well-designed learning activities, rather than define the structure and path of learning, which is the normal temptation of educational technicians [13]. In fact, the process of a perspective or understanding is very important. If all relevant information is specified in advance, it is impossible to carry out meaningful construction [14].

2.2 The Use of Case-Studies in IS Problem Based Learning

PBL is a learner-centred teaching method, which enables learners to investigate by applying theory to practice and using knowledge and skills to develop feasible solutions to clear problems [15]. Duch, Groh, and Allen [16] propose that PBL develops important transferable skills, such as the ability to: think critically; analyse and solve complex real-world problems; find, evaluate, and use appropriate learning resources; work cooperatively; demonstrate effective communication skills; and use content knowledge and intellectual skills to become continual learners. This approach is ideal to IS teaching and its applied nature as discussed above. Moreover, it is a fundamental tool in the teaching of IS analysis and design, an otherwise "very dry" and conceptually difficult subject to teach and engage undergraduate students [17].

In truth, it is common while teaching courses on IS. Especially "Systems Analysis and Design" course, to witness students' difficulties in incorporating what they have learned in theory into a real-life environments and problems [18]. The most common strategy to mitigate these problems in IS teaching is through the use of PBL based supported by case-studies, since these involve problem solving within a real life or work-related context [19]. The problem in the context of the case-study becomes the driving force for students to learn and apply complex modelling techniques [20]. The modelling skills that are the core for teaching course in Systems Analysis and Design and found so dull in theory, are learned by doing and through practice [21]. Additionally, the use of case studies within a PBL general framework enables the development of problem solving, critical and analysis skills and the opportunity to use reflection as part of learning [22]. The PBL application of case studies may also involve problem-based group projects in real life assigned to student teams, which provide appropriate environment and stimulation for learning and have a high retention rate [23] and the additional acquisition of social interaction, communication, negotiation and team-work skills [24]. However, the selection of the problems and case-study contexts is critical to the success of any PBL approach, as is the tutor ability to guide the learning process and conduct a thorough debriefing in the conclusion of the learning experience [15].

Case studies is a useful approach for students acquire applicable competence in professional career [25]. Avison, Fitzgerald and Powell [26] suggested using case studies approach to Information System research. Case studies allows teacher to bring real-world examples to the classroom, but teacher must develop teaching skills in the use of case studies method of teaching [27]. Students can identify, analyse and solve problems in cases. This way of learning can facilitate and improve students' ability of comprehensive use of knowledge and independent learning. Through searching and collecting information in the cases, students' enthusiasm for learning is easy to be aroused, and their desire for knowledge is also easy to be aroused and enter the state of learning. Baumgartner and Shankararaman [28] compared and evaluated four different models (Harvard-style, single piece, mini-story, student-centred) of using case studies in academic learning method for university-level computing educator. Most of students prefer have a single "base-line story" case study rather than several "mini-stories" case studies during the course because students want to explore in-depth of the case study [29].

2.3   Case-Studies Represented by VR Environments

The realism of problem-based learning brings the process elements of excitement, active participation and participation into it. It inspires greater motivation and obtains considerable satisfaction from verifiable and tangible results [23]. Traditional use of case studies in lectures are text-based, simplified, students cannot get interactive and immersive experience from the presentation of case studies, and case documents cannot easily be modified when it has been set out [30]. Teaching in virtual world has potential for multi-university collaboration and multi-disciplinary courses [31]. Tsai, Yu and Hsiao [32] designed an educational online game, which presented problem-based learning model for constructivist learning, students are given a series of game tasks from NPC and they need to solve it. Wagner [31] described a course "Virtual organizations and global teamwork" which requires student complete assignments demanded by a virtual organization inside Second Life, the experience of learning with virtual world is different from classroom learning, it is immersive and learning-by-doing, students can look at virtual presentation slides and complete assignment in the virtual world. There are some factors affect the experience of online application, such as configuration of PC, Bandwidth problems, software is free to download and use, but not free for what student want to do with software, some important feature maybe charged, and it is difficult to manage student in a virtual world meeting.

3   Research Structure Design

This study designs and develops a VR case-study application based on the case content, and uses it in undergraduate course lecture. Students in the course will participate in the evaluation of VR cases-study. We conduct this study in the following 4 steps (see Fig. 1): (1) VR case-study content creation, (2) VR case-study testing, (3) Implement VR case-study in the course, (4) Evaluation of VR case-study.

3.1   Design and Create a Case for VR Case-Study Application

VR case-study consisted of three components: content of case-study, VR environment, and system functions. We create a case-study based on a real case and using PBL theory to write scripts. The virtual environment should be as close as possible to the real environment where the case occurred. According to the case description, we used Unity3D to create a VR environment that conforms to the case scenario. In order to increase the user's immersion in the VR scene, we have added many functions to enable users to interact with things in the VR environment and improve their realism.

3.2   Test VR Case-Study Application

After completion of VR case-study application development, we conducted several tests, such as unit testing, integration testing and system testing in the lab, to ensure the usability of the application. Tests were done by 2 school staff, 2 PhD students and 1 master student who were teaching assistant of the course, and 2 undergraduate students who took the course in the previous academic year.

3.3   Implement VR Case-Study in IS Course

In past teaching activities, students would receive case-study scripts from lecturer in the course, case is in form of printed paper version and electronic version. But in this research, they could also have a VR case-study as an alternative learning material. Student are advised to form a group of 3 or 4. And then students were freely to enter VR case-study and get case information from NPCs.

3.4 Evaluate Feasibility of VR Case-Study Application

During experiments, student would experience a set of VR devices such as VR headset, VR handling controller and VR walker machine. After experienced the VR case-study, every student was invited to fill a questionnaire. And then we collected questionnaire and analyze it to find students' opinions of VR case-study.

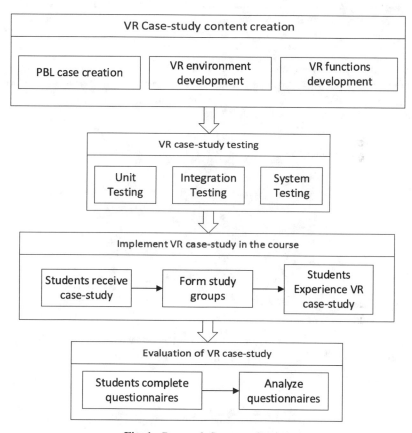

Fig. 1. Research Structure Design

4 The VR Case-Study Environment Development

This study focuses on the undergraduate elective course "Information System Modelling" within the "Information Management and Information System" major offered by the School of Information Management, Sun Yat-sen University as an example. The case provided in the class is based on a real business case, and the teaching content is designed accordingly. The learning goal of students is to use the information system model to design an information system for a wood factory that can meet the information needs of its various departments. Students need to analyse the work functions and needs of each department, and put forward a comprehensive information system design for the factory using information systems analysis and design theories.

The VR case-study was run using one desktop computer which running with CPU i7-9700 @ 3.00 GHz, 16 GB RAM, Nvidia GeForce RTX 1070. A full kit set of HTC Vive Pro headset with Vive Wireless Adapter. A VR Walker machine in the lab space. And A 60-in. LCD display. The computer and the LCD display are connected through HDMI cable. When the VR factory application is running on the computer, we can see the view that the participants are currently seeing in the VR environment from the LCD display.

We designed and developed a VR case-study application for students to learning the case. We built a virtual factory in the virtual environment, including offices, warehouses, manufacturing workshops, stacking yards, parking area, etc. of all departments (see Fig. 2).

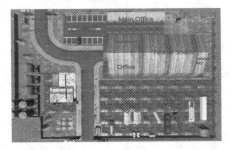

Fig. 2. Aerial view of the VR Factory Environment.

The application was built in Unity3D within the use of SteamVR plugin and Unity UI Toolkit. We changed the default handling input settings of HTC Vive Pro controller to fit our application (see Fig. 3).

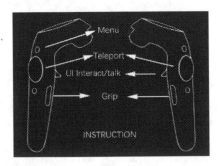

Fig. 3. The HTC Vive Controller and handling input settings used in VR Factory

Students can use the teleport function or VR walker machine to move in the VR environment. There are many NPCs in the VR factory, and each NPC is the employee of a certain department in the factory. Students can go to the NPC's office to communicate with them. There will be dialogue subtitles on the top of the NPC's head for students to see and listen. Through the dialogue with NPC, students can obtain the information and content in the learning case. On the desk of each office, there will be a map of the factory and the corresponding NPC dialogue content, which students can grip it on hand to read for reference (see Fig. 4).

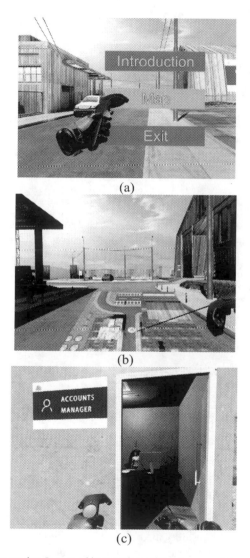

(a)

(b)

(c)

Fig. 4. Presentation Image of interaction with (a) menu, (b) map, (c) NPC

Interact with Ground: In the unity, we created a panel in virtual environment as ground, and add a script component to the panel with custom teleport area. The script allows VR walker and controller can interact with ground so that user can move in VR environment.

Interact with NPCs: NPCs were assigned to the corresponding department office according to the description in the case content and the job position of the person. When students enter the office, NPC will wave to students and say greetings. Students can talk with NPC through the interactive button of the handling controller. During the dialogue with NPC, NPC will always face the player. We also used the method of manual recording to dub the NPC's conversation content. Students can listen and watch the information provided by NPC.

Interact with Map: Map shows the location of each area of the factory. Students can pick up the map on the table and check it at any time.

Interact with Paper: There is a table in front of each NPC, on which there is a paper case of the NPC's conversation content. Same as the map, students can pick up the paper to view the case content at any time.

5   Evaluation of the VR Case-Study Environment

We recruited 30 participants who were all undergraduate students from "Information System Modelling" undergraduate course. The VR factory case is arranged for students as a final coursework. In class, students will receive and read the case text in both paper and electronic versions. At the same time, students can also go to the VR laboratory to enter the VR case-study experience the VR factory. The specific experience design is shown in the Fig. 5:

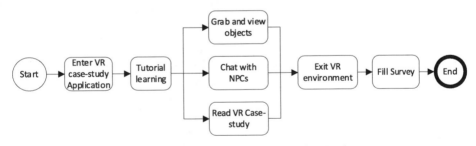

Fig. 5. VR Case-study Experiment Flow Design

After arriving at the VR laboratory, participants should step on the VR walker, put on the VR helmet after taking safety measures such as binding the safe belt, wait for the VR case-study application to load and start, and then begin to experience the VR factory. The whole experiment process takes 30 min. Participants can experience 20 min of VR case-study on the VR walker and spend 10 min filling the questionnaire (Table 1).

Table 1. Data to be captured from experiment survey

Data Category	Description of category	Data attempt to capture	Sources
Immersive Experience	The sense of immersion is related to the image processing and comprehension capability of VR technology	Accurate information	[33, 34]
		understand case	
		High resolution	
		Smooth display	
		Multimedia resources	
		High sound quality	
		Light, shadow, color, texture	
Interaction Experience	User's feeling of interacting with the virtual display of content, emphasizing on actionability	Clear instruction	[35, 36]
		Fast response	
		Accurate operation Easy to operate Easy to find NPC Easy to find content	
Physiological Experience	Act directly on the somatic body or are caused by psychological influences	Fun	[33, 34, 37]
		Comfortable	
		Exhaustion	
		Vertigo	
		Dull feeling	

Participants evaluations were collected after completed VR case-study experience. There are 30 questions include 3 open questions were asked in questionnaires. We scale the evaluation in three dimensions: ease of use, usefulness, immersive experience, interactive experience, and physiological experience. The first three questions are used to classify participants characteristics about age, gender and whether used VR before the experiment. Participants were ages between 18 and 21 years old (mean = 20, SD = 0.77). As shown in Table 2, the number of male and female is close, but there are significantly more people without VR experience than those who had experienced VR before.

Table 2. Characteristics of Participants

		Number	Percentage
Gender	Male	14	46.7%
	Female	16	53.3%
	Total	30	100%
Experienced VR before	Yes	11	36.7%
	No	19	63.3%
	Total	30	100%

The reliability scale test for each dimension and overall score are above 0.7, it means the factors had acceptable to good reliability (see Table3).

Table 3. The Reliability Test Result of Questionnaire

	Ease of Use	Usefulness	Immersive Experience	Interactive Experience	Physiological Experience	Overall
Cronbach α	0.747	0.726	0.862	0.841	0.819	0.798

The descriptive statistical analysis result for VR case-study experiment is shown in Table 4. Overall, the evaluation of each dimension is positive (mean >3). Usefulness had significant higher score (min = 3.00, mean = 4.16) in the experiment. There are big differences on the participants' opinions on Physiological experience (min = 1.00, max = 5.00, SD = 0.8). We can see that the values of physiological experience are quite spread out.

Table 4. Descriptive Statistics of questionnaires

	N	Min	Max	Mean	Std. Deviation
Ease of Use	30	2.00	5.00	3.7667	.67688
Usefulness	30	3.00	5.00	4.1667	.55450
Immersive Experience	30	2.00	5.00	3.9167	.76783
Interactive Experience	30	2.00	5.00	3.8067	.66537
Physiological Experience	30	1.00	5.00	3.6333	.83721

6   Discussion

Despite of the sample size of this experiment is relatively small, we still get many feedback and suggestions from open questions. Majority of test participants were generally satisfied with the VR case-study teaching application. We have made statistics and analysis on the features of VR case-study that students feel useful and useless (see Table 5).

Table 5. Students' Opinions on Usefulness

Usefulness	Classification	Details
Useful of VR case-study	Factory environment	1. Layout of facilities
		2. Position of staffs' office
		3. Presentation of factory scene
	Dialogue with NPCs	4. Responsibilities of different departments
		5. The way to obtain information from different department
		6. Understanding of factory operation process
Less useful of VR case-study	Places without functional features	1. Empty rooms
		2. Lack of introduction in some areas
		3. Some NPCs are not interactable
	Insufficient information in conversation	4. NPCs are not smart enough to ask random questions
		5. Some information is missing

The VR scene offers a convenient method for players to explore the internal environment of the lumberyard, understand the overall operational process, and learn about the workings of each department. This includes the presentation of the office area, the distribution of staff, and the placement of instruments and equipment. With the use of a VR walker, students can immerse themselves in the environment and interact with NPCs. This provides them with a deeper understanding of the nature of each position and the responsibilities required. Some respondents have reported difficulty in finding the location of department offices. To address this, we added some additional office rooms in the VR environment that were not included in the paper case-study. Interestingly, we received feedback from some respondents who found the inclusion of empty rooms to be meaningful. Similarly, we received comments about the limited usefulness of some un-interactable NPCs in providing information about the case-study. The dialogue texts of these NPCs are pre-designed, so respondents can only follow the dialogue as set by the application. However, some respondents have expressed a desire to ask questions more freely.

7   Conclusions

In summary, the aim of this paper was to propose a way of using VR technology to show case-study in undergraduate course teaching, and presents evaluation results of feasibility study after using VR case-study with 30 students. Participants rated the overall experience good comments. Generally, participants felt VR case-study is useful and easy to use. It provides strong immersive and aesthetic experience together with user-friendly interaction interface.

While the research is conducting, there are several limitations exist in the current work, we were only verifying the feasibility of VR case-study application according to the experience feedback of student from courses. In the future, students can be divided into two groups to carry out group comparison experiments. One group is using printed paper case-study, and the other is using VR case-study. Then we can evaluate and compare the influence of the two groups on learning with different types of case-study. For example, to evaluate learning interest, learning motivation and learning effect from two groups. At present, only one student can be allowed to enter the VR case-study at a time. In the future, the multi-player feature can be added to enable multiple students to enter at the same time and see each other in the VR environment. At the same time, it can also provide a collaborative opportunity for the coursework in a multi-person group.

References

1. Banville, C., Landry, M.: Can the field of MIS be disciplined? Commun. ACM **32**(1), 48–60 (1989). Author, F., Author, S.: Title of a Proceedings Paper. In: Editor, F., Editor, S. (eds.) CONFERENCE 2016, LNCS, vol. 9999, pp. 1–13. Springer, Heidelberg (2016)
2. Gregor, S., Jones, D.: The anatomy of a Design Theory. Association for Information Systems (2007)
3. Nilsen, H., Purao, S.: Balancing objectivist and constructivist pedagogies for teaching emerging technologies: evidence from a Scandinavian case study. J. Inf. Syst. Educ. **16**(3), 281 (2005)
4. Feyzi Behnagh, R., Yasrebi, S.: An examination of constructivist educational technologies: key affordances and conditions. Br. J. Edu. Technol. **51**(6), 1907–1919 (2020)
5. Albion, P.R.: Web 2.0 in teacher education: two imperatives for action. Comput. Sch. **25**(3–4), 181–198 (2008)
6. McPherson, M., Nunes, M.B.: The role of tutors as an integral part of online learning support. Eur. J. Open Distance E-Learn. **7**(1) (2004)
7. Fonseca, D., Conde, M.Á., García-Peñalvo, F.J.: Improving the information society skills: is knowledge accessible for all? Univ. Access Inf. Soc. **17**(2), 229–245 (2017)
8. Nunes, M.B., McPherson, M.: Constructivism vs. objectivism: where is difference for designers of e-learning environments? In: Proceedings 3rd IEEE International Conference on Advanced Technologies, pp. 496–500. IEEE, July 2003

9. Bonk, C.J., King, K.S.: Searching for learner-centered, constructivist, and sociocultural components of collaborative educational learning tools. In: Electronic Collaborators, pp. 61–86. Routledge (2012)
10. Duffys, T.M., Jonassen, D.H.: Constructivism: new implications for instructional technology. In: Constructivism and the Technology of Instruction, pp. 1–16. Routledge (2013)
11. Grabinger, R.S., Dunlap, J.C.: Rich environments for active learning: a definition. ALT-J. **3**(2), 5–34 (1995)
12. Prince, M.J., Felder, R.M.: Inductive teaching and learning methods: definitions, comparisons, and research bases. J. Eng. Educ. **95**(2), 123–138 (2006)
13. Blake, R.J.: Brave New Digital Classroom: Technology and Foreign Language Learning. Georgetown University Press (2013)
14. Duffy, T.M., Jonassen, D.H.: Constructivism and the Technology of Instruction: A Conversation. Routledge, Milton Park (2013)
15. Savery, J.R.: Overview of problem-based learning: definitions and distinctions. In: Essential Readings in Problem-Based Learning: Exploring and Extending the Legacy of Howard S. Barrows, vol. 9, no. 2, pp. 5–15 (2015)
16. Duch, B.J., Groh, S.E., Allen, D.E.: Why problem-based learning? A case study of institutional change in undergraduate education. Power Probl. Based Learn. **4**, 189–200 (2001)
17. Garfield, J.: Assessing theoretical concepts in systems analysis and design: a scaffolded case study approach (2017)
18. Gackowski, Z.J.: Case/real-life problem-based learning with information system projects. J. Inf. Technol. Educ. Res. **2**(1), 357–365 (2003)
19. Belt, S.T., Evans, E.H., McCreedy, T., Overton, T.L., Summerfield, S.: A problem based learning approach to analytical and applied chemistry. Univ. Chem. Educ. **6**(2), 65–72 (2002)
20. Savery, J.R., Duffy, T.M.: Problem based learning: an instructional model and its constructivist framework. Educ. Technol. **35**(5), 31–38 (1995)
21. Bider, I., Henkel, M., Kowalski, S., Perjons, E.: Simulating apprenticeship using multimedia in Higher Education: a case from the information systems field. Interact. Technol. Smart Educ. **12**(2), 137–154 (2015)
22. Blackburn, G.: A university's strategic adoption process of an PBL-aligned eLearning environment: an exploratory case study. Educ. Tech. Res. Dev. **65**(1), 147–176 (2017)
23. Gackowski, Z.J.: Case/real-life problem-based learning with information system projects. J. Inf. Technol. Educ. **2** (2003)
24. Humphreys, P., Lo, V., Chan, F., Duggan, G.: Developing transferable groupwork skills for engineering students. Int. J. Eng. Educ. **17**(1), 59–66 (2001)
25. Baumgartner, I., Shankararaman, V.: Actively linking learning outcomes and competencies to course design and delivery: experiences from an undergraduate Information Systems program in Singapore. In: 2013 IEEE Global Engineering Education Conference (EDUCON), pp. 238–246. IEEE, March 2013
26. Avison, D., Fitzgerald, G., Powell, P.: Reflections on information systems practice, education and research: 10 years of the information systems journal. Inf. Syst. J. **11**(1), 3–22 (2001)
27. Hackney, R., McMaster, T., Harris, A.: Using cases as a teaching tool an IS education. J. Inf. Syst. Educ. **14**(3), 229 (2003)
28. Baumgartner, I., Shankararaman, V.: Case studies in computing education: presentation, evaluation and assessment of four case study-based course design and delivery models. In: 2014 IEEE Frontiers in Education Conference (FIE) Proceedings, pp. 1–8. IEEE, October 2014
29. Baumgartner, I.: Case study methodology in technology-focused Information Systems courses: examining the students' perspective. In: Proceedings of 2013 IEEE International Conference on Teaching, Assessment and Learning for Engineering (TALE), pp. 223–226. IEEE, August 2013

30. Guy, E., Pemberton, L., Knight, J.: Rich cases: a framework for interactive case studies in Information Systems teaching. Eur. J. Open Distance E-Learn. **3**(2) (2000)
31. Wagner, C.: Teaching tip: learning experience with virtual worlds. J. Inf. Syst. Educ. **19**(3), 263 (2008)
32. Tsai, F.H., Yu, K.C., Hsiao, H.S.: Designing constructivist learning environment in online game. In: 2007 First IEEE International Workshop on Digital Game and Intelligent Toy Enhanced Learning (DIGITEL 2007), pp. 212–214. IEEE, March 2007
33. Tcha-Tokey, K., Loup-Escande, E., Christmann, O., Richir, S.: A questionnaire to measure the user experience in immersive virtual environments. In: Proceedings of the 2016 Virtual Reality International Conference, pp. 1–5, March 2016
34. Shin, D.: Empathy and embodied experience in virtual environment: to what extent can virtual reality stimulate empathy and embodied experience? Comput. Hum. Behav. **78**, 64–73 (2018)
35. Doumanis, I., Economou, D., Sim, G.R., Porter, S.: The impact of multimodal collaborative virtual environments on learning: a gamified online debate. Comput. Educ. **130**, 121–138 (2019)
36. Takatalo, J., Nyman, G., Laaksonen, L.: Components of human experience in virtual environments. Comput. Hum. Behav. **24**(1), 1–15 (2008)
37. Wiederhold, B.K., et al.: An investigation into physiological responses in virtual environments: an objective measurement of presence. Towards Cyberpsychol. Mind Cognit. Soc. Internet Age **2**, 175–183 (2001)

Assessing Lighting Experience Using Physiological Measures: A Review

Yingbo Luo and Hanling Zhang[✉]

School of Design, Hunan University, Changsha 410082, Hunan, China
{luoyingbo,jt_hlzhang}@hnu.edu.cn

Abstract. The lighting environment is essential to human health, productivity, and efficiency. Lighting experience can be defined as the user's psychological feelings and satisfaction in the lighting environment. With advances in technology, physiological measures methods are increasingly being used to measure and predict user status and to assess user experience. In particular, the lighting experience has been characterized using various physiological sensor data. We reviewed 22 related articles using physiological measures (heart, brain, blood pressure, skin, and ocular) to obtain relevant data. We introduce the basic principles of various physiological measures, the experimental methods, and the limitations of conducting lighting experience assessment and organize the relevant professional equipment and wearable devices used in the experimental process. Specific measures, devices and scale usage are shown graphically for comparison. This review aims to provide a reference for future related research and assist researchers in selecting measures to evaluate lighting experience.

Keywords: Lighting · Experience Assessment · Physiological Measures

Abbreviations

BP   Blood Pressure;
BR   Blink Rate;
BVP Blood Volume Pulse;
CCT Correlated Color Temperature;
ECG Electrocardiogram;
EDA Electrodermal Activity;
EEG Electroencephalogram;
EOG Electrooculogram;
FP   Fixation Point;
HF   High Frequency;
HR   Heart Rate;
HRV Heart Rate Variability;
LF   Low Frequency
PD   Pupil Diameter;
SC   Skin Conductance;
SCL Skin Conductance Level;
SCR Skin Conductance Response;
ST   Skin Temperature

N. A. Streitz and S. Konomi (Eds.): HCII 2023, LNCS 14036, pp. 213–228, 2023.
https://doi.org/10.1007/978-3-031-34668-2_15

1 Introduction

1.1 Background

The global economy has shifted from manufacturing to service and knowledge-based sectors with indoor office operations. At the same time, people are forced to study or work long hours at home due to the COVID-19 pandemic. Among the factors of the indoor home environment, lighting has a key impact on people's productivity and physical health [1], e.g., receiving too little or too much lighting leads to depressed mood or visual discomfort [2]; inappropriate lighting leads to an increase in musculoskeletal disorders [3], and so on. Consequently, there is a need to analyze the diversity of lighting needs and user experiences in the home office context and match the corresponding lighting design to achieve an efficient, rational, and comfortable office environment.

There are a variety of understandings of the definition and measures of lighting experience, mainly including visual comfort, fatigue, cognitive (brain) load, and emotion, all of which are important variables in understanding user experience [4]. Visual comfort is defined as no visual discomfort, that is, the visual features of the current environment do not interfere with the user's vision and activities. The primary indices evaluated include the amount of light (describing the physical quantity of light such as illumination), glare (too much light causes the user's visual performance to decrease), light uniformity (the uniform distribution of light in space), and light quality (the quality of light rendering color) [5] and so on. The fatigue level mainly includes the user's visual and brain fatigue in the lighting environment [6]. Cognitive load represents the amount of memory resources used while working. When the quantity and complexity limits of processable information are exceeded, cognitive overload occurs, task performance decreases, and the user experience suffers [7].

User experience evaluation is an essential step in lighting research and design to analyze user needs and improve product design. It is primarily divided into qualitative and quantitative methods of evaluation. Qualitative evaluation methods include subjective scales, questionnaires, interviews, and observations, which are subjective and biased due to the influence of user preferences, backgrounds, and other differences, and the research is time-consuming and costly; quantitative evaluation methods include the analysis of data such as usage logs of user products, and also include the methods based on physiological parameter measures. Compared to qualitative evaluation methods, physiological measures are more direct, realistic, objective visualization of users' feelings that are not influenced by other factors, and more scientific and credible [8]. Combining subjective evaluation with objective measures is more correct and promising [9]. In the field of lighting research, experimental methods of physiological measures are currently being used to evaluate user experience with the benefits of being scientific, efficient, independent of environmental factors, and effective. The purpose of this study is to provide a review of experimental research on lighting experience evaluation using physiological measures, specifically (i) the specifics of lighting experience evaluation; (ii) experimental settings and methods and equipment for physiological measures; and (iii) the advantages, disadvantages, and development trends of various methods.

1.2   Related Work and Limitations

A recent review of the lighting experience was conducted by Alice et al. [10], which provides a systematic review of studies evaluating visual quality and lighting perception using VR. Haneen et al. [11] provided a comprehensive review of user comfort studies of immersive virtual environments (IVE), including thermal comfort, acoustic comfort, etc., and lighting visual comfort. Nastaran et al. [12] provided a systematic review of field studies and laboratory experiments on daylight visual comfort, focusing on the parameters and thresholds of relevant comfort indicators. A review of physiological measures as an experimental methodological trend for evaluating user lighting experience is still lacking. Zahra et al. [13] reviewed light-induced ocular physiological and perceptual responses in an office environment, focusing on pupil size, eye movements, gaze direction, degree of eye-opening, and blink rate. In this review, we have expanded the range of measures considered and reviewed the equipment used for physiological measures, summarizing the limitations and experiences with the methods themselves. These measures are characterized by their representativeness in the published literature. We summarize the key findings of the review in tables that can be used to guide the experimental design or select measures for specific tasks to evaluate the lighting experience.

2   Methods

The Preferred Reporting Items for Systematic Reviews and Meta-Analyses (PRISMA) were used to guide the selection process [14]. We searched the Web of Science database core collection for full-text research articles published in peer-reviewed scientific conference proceedings or journals, with publication dates restricted to the period between 2017 and 2022 in English. Keywords searched included "smart home lighting," "smart lighting," "lighting," "lighting comfort," "visual comfort," "visual perception," "physiological measures," etc. The keyword combinations were filtered. To limit the number of relevant papers, we only considered experiments that used physiological measures to evaluate user lighting experience. We excluded articles that 1) did not specify instruments or devices used for relevant physiological measures; 2) introduced lighting designs, techniques, or inventions.

An initial search identified potentially relevant papers to the current research question. Secondly, titles and abstracts were screened against the selected inclusion and exclusion criteria. Thirdly, a snowballing procedure was conducted through the reference lists and citations of the selected papers to identify additional articles and select the appropriate ones to be added to the review list. Fourthly, the selected articles were screened in their entirety. Ultimately, 22 eligible articles were included in our data synthesis for the final review. 4 were full-text conference articles, and 18 were full-text journal articles. These 22 articles were published in 16 different conference proceedings or journals and focused primarily on evaluating the lighting experience using physiological measurements. As a reference supplement, the experimental environments of the selected papers were not limited to offices but also included gymnasiums, cockpits, tunnels, and other environments (see Table 1). Through analysis and organization, five key metrics were identified in this review: heart measures (HR, HRV derived from ECG), blood pressure (BP), brain measures (EEG), skin measures (SCR, SCL, ST, etc.), and ocular measures (eye movements, ocular physiological parameters, etc.) (see Table 2). The percentages of relevant physiological measures were 13 for heart measures, 11 for brain measures, 1 for blood pressure, 6 for skin measures, and 8 for ocular measures. Electrocardiogram (ECG) and electroencephalogram (EEG), as objective indicators of subjective sensory and cognitive tasks [15], have been widely used in studies of the relationship between physiological changes and the light environment.

Seventy-three percent of the included studies used a combination of physiological measures and subjective measures (see Table 3). This hints at a research trend to combine subjective and objective evaluation methods to understand the user lighting experience.

Table 1. The experimental environments in articles reviewed.

Domain	Reference	Number of articles
Indoor office/activity lighting	[6, 9, 15–28]	16
Drive lighting	[29, 30]	2
Daylight in gymnasium	[31]	1
VR lighting	[7]	1
Tunnel lighting	[32]	1
Indoor sleep lighting	[33]	1

Table 2. Representation of physiological measures across the literature.

Heart (13)	Brain (11)	BP (1)	Skin(6)	Ocular (8)	References	Number of articles
				✓	[7, 22, 23, 25, 28]	5
✓	✓				[15, 16, 26, 30]	4
✓			✓		[20, 27, 31]	3
✓			✓	✓	[19, 29]	2
	✓				[18, 24]	2
	✓				[9, 21]	2
✓	✓	✓			[33]	1
✓	✓		✓		[17]	1
✓					[32]	1
✓	✓			✓	[6]	1

Table 3. Studies which employ physiological measures and at least one subjective assessment.

Subjective assessment	Reference	Number of articles
NASA-TLX	[7, 18, 25]	3
Karolinska sleepiness scale (KSS)	[15, 26, 27]	3
Likert scale	[16, 19, 31]	3
Semantic differential scale	[15, 16]	2
NEO-PI-R personality scale	[19]	1
Visual perception questionnaire (ENISO, 2001)	[20]	1
De Boer Scale	[29]	1
PSQI (Pittsburgh Sleep Quality Index)	[33]	1
CES-D (Center for Epidemiological Survey, Depression Scale)	[33]	1
Visual Analogue Scale (VAS)	[26]	1
Other scales	[6, 9, 20, 21, 23–25, 27, 30]	9

3 Evidence for Physiological Measures

The basic principles and experimental approaches for each of the physiological measures considered in this review are described in detail below.

3.1 Heart Measures

During the literature search, measures of cardiac activity using ECG techniques were the most commonly used method (13 cases reported in this paper), and the indicators included HR and HRV, which reflect autonomic nervous system activities and are quantitative information on physical or mental fatigue, emotion, and workload [34]. Cardiac activity is analyzed in the time or frequency domain by collecting electrical signals from the heart. Time domain metrics are more straightforward, where HR is usually measured as the number of heartbeats per minute and as a beat-to-beat interval (IBI) metric traditionally measured in milliseconds, etc. The frequency domain approach defines ECG waves as distinct spectral components, such that the low-frequency portion (LF, 0.04–0.15 Hz) is mediated by the parasympathetic nervous system and sympathetic nerves, and the high-frequency portion (HF, 0.15–0.45 Hz) is mediated by the parasympathetic nervous system only [35], so the ratio of HF to LF: HF is used to identify the high and low boundaries. An increase in the HF value or a progressive decrease in ratios assumes that the user is more physiologically comfortable. In addition, studies have also used blood volume pulse (BVP) measures, and because blood volume varies with pulse and heart rate, HR and HRV features can be extracted from the BVP signal.

Kakitsuba et al. [16] identified users' boundary illumination levels by collecting data on ECG activity under lighting conditions while combining subjective scales for assessing luminance, glare, and comfort, and demonstrated that there were no significant differences in boundary illumination levels estimated based on psychological and physiological responses. Some researchers [6, 15, 17, 26, 27] evaluated users' work engagement performance, efficiency, and fatigue; they measured ECG activity using relevant equipment. The experimental results demonstrated that lighting levels (CCT and illuminance) impact work engagement, and the degree of impact varies from person to person, so it is necessary to develop lighting personalization models to improve work efficiency by adjusting lighting conditions.

In studies on visual comfort evaluation of lighting environments, Papinutto [19] used Empatica E4 wristbands to measure BVP, combined with eye-tracking and subjective scales. Chinazzo [20] studied the effects of light on user visual perception and temperature perception, and recorded BVP data by a photoelectric volumetric pulse (PPG) sensor for signal processing to obtain HR. Stanke [29] used the BIOPAC MP 36, a biosignal acquisition device commonly used in psychophysiological studies, to collect HRV data from drivers to evaluate their discomfort when perceiving glare from car headlights.

In addition, there are measures related to physiological fatigue: HRV of drivers in tunnel driving was measured to obtain relevant data indicators [32]. HR and BP data of users under different lighting conditions were measured to study the physiological and psychological effects of different lighting conditions on young people at bedtime [33].

In part of mood measures, Hassib [30] used the wearable device Polar H7 chest strap sensor to collect HR data to study the driver's emotional state and driving performance when faced with different ambient lighting in the vehicle.

3.2 Brain Activity

In this review, 11 studies used brain activity to study users' cognitive abilities and psychological changes, 2 of which used only brain activity measures alone, i.e., the typical human physiological signal-visual evoked potential PRVEP. Electroencephalography (EEG) is a method that reflects cortical physiological activity by recording electrical signals emitted by brain tissue in the skull and scalp and can reveal subtle changes in alertness, attention, and subtle changes in workload. Its advantages include the high temporal resolution of the EEG signal and the high-speed signal transmission, which allows for the real-time recording of physiological responses. In addition, EEG signals are considered as a direct indicator of cognitive state [36], which is influenced by both physiological and psychological effects and therefore contains more objective and comprehensive information. Therefore, obtaining the EEG representation pattern of the comfort of the light environment facilitates the judgment of the user's subjective satisfaction in a particular environment based on the objective physiological parameters of the EEG characteristic values.

The recording of EEG signals in experiments usually involves placing electrodes at locations on the user's scalp according to the international 10–20 system. The collected raw EEG signals are preprocessed and analyzed to obtain the results. The rhythmic waves, such as alpha-band waves (alpha; 8–13 Hz) and beta-band waves (beta; >13 Hz), can effectively reflect changes in fatigue and alertness[37]. For example, an increase in the percentage of alpha waves or a decrease in edge frequency assumes that the user becomes more comfortable physiologically [38, 39].

When studying users' visual comfort in lighting environments, in addition to ECG data, the researchers also used EEG values to monitor users' EEG continuously [16].

In assessing work engagement and performance, the Emotiv EPOC + EEG headset device was used to measure users' brain activity while performing cognitive tasks under different room lighting levels [17]. EEG data were collected to investigate the effects of illumination level and color temperature on brain load [18]. In addition to focusing on heart rate HR, a simple brain wave instrument was used to measure and record the tension or relaxation state of the users' brain waves [15, 21]. In addition to measuring HR and HRV, the device was used to collect EEG data in the light environment to analyze the effect of CCT and illumination on work performance [6, 26].

In terms of physiological fatigue assessment, in addition to measuring HR and BP, the EEG signals of users were also measured. EEG signal analysis showed that the alpha wave decreased in the resting state at all three color temperatures, indicating a low level of fatigue [33]. In part of mood measures, in addition to measuring HR, EEG data were collected and recorded using the Muse brain-sensing headband to analyze the driver's emotional state [6].

Pattern reversal visual evoked potential (PRVEP) is used as a clinical test in the medical field to record electrical activity in the stimulated occipital visual cortex, primarily through flash and image stimulation of the retina, and can be used to study human sensory function, neurological disorders, behavior, and psychological activity [40]. Researchers used medical EEG equipment to measure PRVEP and quantify human perception under changes in the lighting environment to determine the link between the environment and the subjective perception and objective responses [9]. Lu [21] used 10–20 system electrodes to measure PRVEP to study the effects of different lighting conditions on light comfort, visual fatigue, and work efficiency; Hu [24] used the same EEG measurement method to obtain the relationship of "environmental variables-subjective satisfaction-EEG eigenvalues" by combining subjective satisfaction evaluation and environmental variables.

3.3 Blood Pressure

Blood pressure (BP) is the pressure acting on the walls of blood vessels as it flows through. Used only once in the experimental study covered in this review as a measure, BP is primarily influenced by factors such as physical activity, stress, sleep, digestion, and time of day phases [41]. And it has been demonstrated that increased blood pressure is associated with increased task load and can be used to differentiate between work and rest periods: blood pressure is lowest at rest and highest during tasks that are subjectively perceived as more effortful [42].

The physiological and psychological effects of different lighting conditions on young people at bedtime were investigated [33]. HR, EEG, and BP were measured under different lighting conditions using a monitor, in which the diastolic and systolic BP would vary separately. It was found that young people were more likely to choose low CCT and neutral white light when they were relaxed.

3.4 Skin Measures

Among these studies, skin-related measures were used six times, including skin surface temperature and electrical activity (EDA) measures. ST reflects the state of the body's thermoregulatory system. EDA presents changes in electrical activity in endocrine sweat glands controlled by the sympathetic nervous system, which reflects the emotional state. GSR reflects emotional intensity information, and higher SC represents higher emotional arousal [43]. In related experiments, researchers often combine skin measures with other physiological measures and subjective scales to assess users' visual comfort in illuminated environments with reasonable accuracy. Researchers used skin surface temperature probes to measure the user's ST to obtain the user's level of thermal comfort under different lighting conditions [17]. They used an Empatica E4 wristband to record wrist ST, combined with physiological data such as wrist skin conductivity (SC), eye tracking, and BVP with subjective assessment scales to assess the user's visual comfort in illuminated environments. The experimental results showed that the method could reasonably predict user behavior categories [19]. An innovative hybrid experimental method combining thermal and visual stimuli from real and VR environments was used to study the effect of the interaction of light color and temperature on users' subjective perception and physiological responses [20]. ST, HR, EDA [tonic skin conductance level (SCL) and numbers of skin conductance responses (nSCR)], etc., were measured in the experiments combined with subjective evaluations. The conclusions showed that daylight color significantly affected thermal perception, and orange daylight in VR environments resulted in warmer thermal perception at comfortable temperatures.

3.5 Ocular Measures

Eye-related measurements have been used a total of eight times in the study, including ocular physiological parameters and ocular behavioral action recordings. According to a relevant existing review, Hamedani et al. [13] summarized all physiological responses related to glare and visual discomfort in the current study, including absolute or relative pupil diameter, eye movement velocity, blink rate, etc., where pupil size instability (PUI) is one of the symptoms of visual discomfort. Researchers have measured the physiological characteristics of eyes to obtain the effects of lighting [22]. Among them, ocular physiological parameters such as ciliary muscle accommodation (ACC) and lens higher order aberration (HOA) represent the perceived degree of visual fatigue, and pupil size is a manifestation of adaptation to lighting conditions. In addition, eye movements such as blink parameters are visual fatigue indicators, and gaze duration represents reading performance. In those studies [6, 19, 25], in addition to other physiological data, eye-tracking glasses were used to record eye movements (e.g., sweep, blink and gaze counts and durations) to evaluate user visual comfort. The study [23] combined physiological measurements, visual performance, photometry, and subjective assessments to measure the effects of lighting conditions on visual comfort and task performance. Including mean pupil diameter (PD), pupil disorder index (PUI), blink rate (BR), blink amplitude (BA), fixation eye gaze rate (FR) and frequency duration (FD), and combined visual performance (CVP) (reaction time and accuracy also represent characteristics of visual performance measures), it is the first study to bring together a wide range of objective, subjective, and photometric measures. Similarly, the study [28] examined ocular physiological characteristics, motor behavior, and task performance responses under different lighting conditions in an office with daylight as the primary light source. Additional data included ocular convergence (EC) and combined reading performance (CRP), which are also critical to the overall performance and productivity assessment of office workers at their workstations.

The experiment [7] used a commercially available HTC Vivo Pro Eye headset to collect pupil dilation data in millimeters and excluded invalid data such as blinks, demonstrating that the function of assessing cognitive load under lighting conditions can be achieved using a commercially available VR headset with eye-tracking capabilities.

4   Experimental Environments and Devices

The related experimental research environments include live lighting simulation, screen rendering-based, and VR environment lighting simulation. Among them, the live lighting simulation approach is mainly through building natural office environments or simulated laboratories, changing lighting conditions, and collecting users' physiological data and subjective scales, which can obtain reliable data in natural physical spaces. However, this method has high environmental requirements, including temperature, humidity, materials, etc. It is expensive and time-consuming to build the experimental environment, and daylight's effect must be considered for experiments in an authentic physical space. Screen rendering-based lighting simulation is more efficient, mainly through computer software rendering images for experiments. Still, users' immersion and experience feelings are limited: they can not experience the lighting design in a one-to-one ratio. Thus, immersive virtual environments (IVE) are becoming a research trend: building a virtual environment through VR allows users to realistically experience lighting design from a first-person perspective and interact with lighting cases, greatly enhancing the user's sense of presence and involvement. In existing studies [7, 20] investigated cognitive load assessment based on VR lighting environments in experiments. They demonstrated the achievability of VR combined with physiological measurements for lighting experience evaluation by measuring and analyzing the pupil size of users under scene lighting using an off-the-shelf VR headset with integrated oculomotor (Tables 4 and 5).

Table 4. The experimental setting used for lighting experience investigations using physiological measures: distribution.

Experimental setting	Reference	Number of articles
Laboratory simulation	[6, 9, 15–19, 21, 24–29, 33]	14
Real lighting environment	[22, 23, 28, 31, 32]	5
VR simulation	[7, 20]	2
Screen render simulation	[30]	1

Table 5. Studies using physiological measuring devices.

Device	Measure	Reference
DAQ terminal intercross	HRV	[16]
Optical Pulse Ear-Clip (Shimmer3 GSR)	HR	[17]
Empatica E4 wristband	BVP, IBI I HR (BVP)	[19, 20]
ErgoLAB wearable human physiology recorder	HR I ECG	[6, 31]
Xiaomi heartbeat bracelet	HR	[15]
BIOPAC MP 36	HRV	[29]
BIOPAC MP 150	HRV	[32]
PHOEBE PMS8310 monitor	HR	[33]
Polar H7	HR	[30]
Kendall H124SG	HR, HRV I HR	[26, 27]
EEG-1100, Nihon Kohden Co	EEG	[16]
Emotive EPOC+	EEG	[17]
EasyCAP	EEG	[18]
NDI-094C, Haishen	EEG	[9]
BIOPAC MP 150	EEG	[33]
Muse brain-sensing headband	EEG	[30]
Encephalon 131–03	EEG	[26]
ErgoLAB-EEG Cap	EEG	[6]
PHOEBE PMS8310 monitor	BP	[33]
Shimmer3 GSR + Unit, Temperature Probe	SCL, ST	[17]
Empatica E4 wristband	SC, ST I SCL, nSCR	[19, 20]
iButtons data loggers (DS1921H-F5, Maxim Integrated)	ST	[20]
ErgoLAB wearable human physiology recorder	SCR	[31]
BIOPAC MP 36	SCR	[29]
Kendall H124SG	SCL	[27]
SMI eye-tracking glasses 2.0	ETG	[19]
NIDEK AR-1S, NIDEK OPD Scan III, NIDEK AL Scan	ACC, HOAs, PS	[22]
Tobii Glasses	PD, PUI, BR, BA, FR, FD, CVP	[23]

(continued)

Table 5. (*continued*)

Device	Measure	Reference
HTC Vive Pro Eye headset	PS	[7]
BIOPAC MP 36	vEOG	[29]
Tobii X2-30 Eye Tracker	Eye blinks, Fixations, Saccades	[25]
Tobii Glasses2	PD, FP	[6]
Tobii Pro Eye Tracker	PD, PUI, BR, BA, FR, EC, CVP, CRP	[28]

5   Conclusions

Experimental studies that combined multiple physiological measurements accounted for the majority, with 12 of the articles covered in this review using two or more physiological measures. Those using only one physiological measure included five eye measures, four EEG activities, and one ECG activity. Table 6 provides a high-level summary of the relevant studies.

The disadvantages of using traditional medical devices to collect physiological data include cumbersome assembly, long use hours, inconvenience of mobility, etc. With the development of sensor technology, the devices used in physiological measure modalities are increasingly lightweight, efficient and accurate, inexpensive and comfortable [44], and some of these wearable devices can enable the collection and analysis of users without interfering with the user's task physiological data. Table 5 provides device usage for the relevant studies.

In addition, some researchers have presented pros and cons analyses of the devices used [17], when measured for work input, concluded that EEG headsets may not be practical enough in natural office environments. Wearing headphones may cause subjects discomfort (e.g., headaches) while performing tasks. In addition, data collection from EEG headsets requires subjects to remain stationary to avoid intensive artifacts, thus limiting user activity and preventing full simulation of behavior in real office scenarios.

This review begins by defining what is involved in evaluating lighting experience and demonstrates the growing empirical basis for using physiological measures. The basic principles and specific experimental approaches of various physiological measures and related equipment are the focus of this review, which concludes with a visualization of the research using a tabular format to facilitate comparisons and help other researchers refer to and select appropriate experimental approaches and physiological measures.

Due to the limitations of traditional subjective assessment, physiological measures have the advantages of being scientific, realistic, efficient, etc. Our findings suggest that combining physiological measures with a subjective assessment to evaluate users' lighting experience and determine reliable and effective lighting comfort zones has become a research trend, and related experimental studies are becoming more and more common. In addition, we found that because the construction of natural experimental environments is affected by factors such as space, temperature and humidity, and cost, lighting experimental research based on VR environments is rapidly developing, and high controllability, relatively low cost, and fast construction represent its advantages

Table 6. Summary of results of physiological measurements in relevant studies.

Device	Measure	Reference
Measuring the effect of color temperature and illuminance on work fatigue	HRV (LF, HF) EEG Ocular Measure	[6]
Measuring the effect of VR environmental lighting conditions on cognitive load	Ocular Measure	[7]
Measuring the correlation between subjective perception and physiological parameters under different illumination levels	EEG	[9]
Measuring the effect of color temperature and illuminance on work efficiency	HR EEG (Alpha, Beta)	[15]
Measuring gender differences in contrast comfort boundary illumination	HRV (LF, HF) EEG (Alpha, Beta)	[16]
Measuring the effect of illuminance on work engagement	HR EEG (Alpha) SCL, ST	[17]
Measuring the effect of color temperature and illuminance on mental load	EEG	[18]
Measuring the effect of illuminance on visual comfort	HR SCL, ST Ocular Measure	[19]
Measuring the effect of daylight color on visual perception	HR SCL, SCR	[20]
Measuring the effect of different illumination color temperature combinations on work efficiency and visual fatigue	EEG	[21]
Measure of the effect of illumination on physiological parameters of the eye	Ocular Measure	[22]
Measuring the effect of lighting conditions on visual comfort and task performance	Ocular Measure	[23]
Measuring the effect of illuminance on visual comfort	EEG	[24]
Measure the effect of color temperature and illuminance on visual comfort	Ocular Measure	[25]
Measuring the effect of color temperature on fatigue and work performance	HRV (LF, HF) EEG	[26]
Measuring the effect of color temperature on emotion and task performance	HRV (LF, HF) SCL	[27]
Measuring the effect of glare on visual comfort, work performance	Ocular Measure	[28]

(*continued*)

Table 6. (*continued*)

Device	Measure	Reference
Measuring the effect of automotive headlight illumination on visual comfort	HR SCR Ocular Measure	[29]
Measuring the effect of ambient light on mood in the car	HR EEG	[30]
Measuring the effect of daylight on visual comfort	HR SCR	[31]
Measuring the effect of tunnel lighting on physical load and mental load	HRV (LF, HF)	[32]
Measuring the effect of color temperature on the psychological and physiological effects of bedtime	HR EEG (Alpha) BP	[33]

for lighting experience assessment. However, further research is needed on the realism of VR lighting design and the resulting user-generated vertigo and discomfort [45]. Future research could combine VR headset devices with physiological measure devices such as eye tracking for lighting experience evaluation, which also has excellent research potential.

With the development of the global trend of home offices, people pay more and more attention to lighting comfort. The lighting experience of users in office situations has been studied in relevant experiments. It has been found that computer work fatigue is significantly affected by changes in different lighting environments [6], so it is necessary to conduct in-depth research on the lighting conditions of computer work environments to help reduce fatigue and thus improve work efficiency. There is also more research needed, for example, the lighting requirements of users in different task scenarios may be different. There needs to be more research in this area related to the evaluation model of user lighting experience in the home office context, which is what we will focus on in our subsequent study.

Acknowledgement. This work was supported by funds for the National Natural Science Foundation of Changsha (kq2202176), Key R&D Program of Hunan(2022SK2104), Leading plan for scientific and technological innovation of high-tech industries of Hunan (2022GK4010), National Key R&D Program of China (2021YFF0900600), the National Natural Science Foundation of China (61672222).

References

1. Gerhardsson, K.M., Laike, T.: User acceptance of a personalised home lighting system based on wearable technology. Appl. Ergon. **96**, 103480 (2021)

2. Baron, R.A., Rea, M.S., Daniels, S.G.: Effects of indoor lighting (illuminance and spectral distribution) on the performance of cognitive tasks and interpersonal behaviors: the potential mediating role of positive affect. Motiv. Emot. **16**, 1–33 (1992)
3. Garcia, M.-G., Aguiar, B., Bonilla, S., Yepez, N., Arauz, P.G., Martin, B.J.: Perceived physical discomfort and its associations with home office characteristics during the COVID-19 pandemic. Hum. Factors, 187208221110683 (2022)
4. Dandan, H., Ming, L., Luoxi, H., Yandan, L.: Applicability analysis of human health evaluation methods in light environment research. Zhaoming Gongcheng Xuebao, pp. 32–03 (2021)
5. Carlucci, S., Causone, F., De Rosa, F., Pagliano, L.: A review of indices for assessing visual comfort with a view to their use in optimization processes to support building integrated design. Renew. Sustain. Energy Rev. **47**, 1016–1033 (2015)
6. Fang, Y., et al.: A study of the effects of different indoor lighting environments on computer work fatigue. Int. J. Environ. Res. Public Health **19**, 6866 (2022)
7. Eckert, M., Habets, E.A.P., Rummukainen, O.S.: Cognitive load estimation based on pupillometry in virtual reality with uncontrolled scene lighting. In: 2021 13th In-ternational Conference on Quality of Multimedia Experience (QoMEX), Montreal, pp. 73–76. IEEE (2021)
8. Guan, H., Hu, S., Lu, M., He, M., Zhang, X., Liu, G.: Analysis of human electroencephalogram features in different indoor environments. Build. Environ. **186**, 107328 (2020)
9. Hu, S., He, M., Liu, G., Lu, M., Liang, P., Liu, F.: Correlation between the visual evoked potential and subjective perception at different illumination levels based on entropy analysis. Build. Environ. **194**, 107715 (2021)
10. Bellazzi, A., et al.: Virtual reality for assessing visual quality and lighting perception: a systematic review. Build. Environ. **209**, 108674 (2022)
11. Alamirah, H., Schweiker, M., Azar, E.: Immersive virtual environments for occupant comfort and adaptive behavior research – a comprehensive review of tools and applications. Build. Environ. **207**, 108396 (2022)
12. Shafavi, N.S., Zomorodian, Z.S., Tahsildoost, M., Javadi, M.: Occupants visual comfort assessments: a review of field studies and lab experiments. Sol. Energy **208**, 249–274 (2020)
13. Hamedani, Z., et al.: Visual discomfort and glare assessment in office environments: a review of light-induced physiological and perceptual responses. Build. Environ. **153**, 267–280 (2019)
14. Moher, D., Liberati, A., Tetzlaff, J., Altman, D.G., PRISMA Group: Preferred reporting items for systematic reviews and meta-analyses: the PRISMA statement. Ann. Intern. Med. **151**, 264–269, W64 (2009)
15. Chen, R., Tsai, M.-C., Tsay, Y.-S.: Effect of color temperature and illuminance on psychology, physiology, and productivity: an experimental study. Energies **15**, 4477 (2022)
16. Kakitsuba, N.: Comfortable indoor lighting conditions for LEDlights evaluated from psychological and physiological responses. Appl. Ergon. **82**, 102941 (2020)
17. Deng, M., Wang, X., Menassa, C.C.: Measurement and prediction of work engagement under different indoor lighting conditions using physiological sensing. Build. Environ. **203**, 108098 (2021)
18. Bao, J., Song, X., Li, Y., Bai, Y., Zhou, Q.: Effect of lighting illuminance and colour temperature on mental workload in an office setting. Sci. Rep. **11**, 15284 (2021)
19. Papinutto, M., Nembrini, J., Lalanne, D.: "Working in the dark?" Investigation of physiological and psychological indices and prediction of back-lit screen users' reactions to light dimming. Build. Environ. **186**, 107356 (2020)
20. Chinazzo, G., Chamilothori, K., Wienold, J., Andersen, M.: Temperature-color interaction: subjective indoor environmental perception and physiological responses in virtual reality. Hum. Factors **63**, 474–502 (2021)

21. Lu, M., Hu, S., Mao, Z., Liang, P., Xin, S., Guan, H.: Research on work efficiency and light comfort based on EEG evaluation method. Build. Environ. **183**, 107122 (2020)
22. Cai, J., et al.: The effect of light distribution of LED luminaire on human ocular physiological characteristics. IEEE Access **7**, 28478–28486 (2019)
23. Hamedani, Z., et al.: Lighting for work: a study of the relationships among dis-comfort glare, physiological responses and visual performance. Build. Environ. **167**, 106478 (2020)
24. Hu, S., et al.: Research on the light comfort characterization method based on visual evoked potential energy. Build. Environ. **197**, 107831 (2021)
25. Han, L., et al.: Desktop lighting for comfortable use of a computer screen. Work **68**, S209–S221 (2021)
26. Askaripoor, T., et al.: Non-image forming effects of light on brainwaves, autonomic nervous activity, fatigue, and performance. J. Circadian Rhythms **16**, 9 (2018)
27. Smolders, K.C., de Kort, Y.A.: Investigating daytime effects of correlated colour temperature on experiences, performance, and arousal. J. Environ. Psychol. **50**, 80–93 (2017)
28. Hamedani, Z., Solgi, E., Hine, T., Skates, H.: Revealing the relationships between luminous environment characteristics and physiological, ocular and performance measures: an experimental study. Build. Environ. **172**, 106702 (2020)
29. Stanke, L., Viktorová, L., Dominik, T.: Discomfort glare perception by drivers—establishing a link between subjective and psychophysiological assessment. Appl. Sci. **12**, 3847 (2022)
30. Hassib, M., Braun, M., Pfleging, B., Alt, F.: Detecting and influencing driver emotions using psycho-physiological sensors and ambient light. In: Lamas, D., Loizides, F., Nacke, L., Petrie, H., Winckler, M., Zaphiris, P. (eds.) INTERACT 2019. LNCS, vol. 11746, pp. 721–742. Springer, Cham (2019). https://doi.org/10.1007/978-3-030-29381-9_43
31. Shi, L., Zhang, Y., Wang, Z., Cheng, X., Yan, H.: Luminance parameter thresholds for user visual comfort under daylight conditions from subjective responses and physiological measurements in a gymnasium. Build. Environ. **205**, 108187 (2021)
32. Peng, L., Weng, J., Yang, Y., Wen, H.: Impact of light environment on driver's physiology and psychology in interior zone of long tunnel. Front Public Health **10**, 842750 (2022)
33. Weng, Z., Zhou, L., Wei, M., Lin, Y.: Psychological and physiological influences of CCTs on young people before sleep. In: 2017 14th China International Forum on Solid State Lighting: International Forum on Wide Bandgap Semiconductors China (SSLChina: IFWS), pp. 105–108 (2017)
34. Thielmann, B., Pohl, R., Böckelmann, I.: Heart rate variability as a strain indicator for psychological stress for emergency physicians during work and alert intervention: a systematic review. J. Occup. Med. Toxicol. **16**, 24 (2021)
35. Akselrod, S., Gordon, D., Ubel, F.A., Shannon, D.C., Berger, A.C., Cohen, R.J.: Power spectrum analysis of heart rate fluctuation: a quantitative probe of beat-to-beat cardiovascular control. Science **213**, 220–222 (1981)
36. Lindsley, D.B.: Psychological phenomena and the electroencephalogram. Electroencephalogr. Clin. Neurophysiol. **4**, 443–456 (1952)
37. Trejo, L.J., Kubitz, K., Rosipal, R., Kochavi, R.L., Montgomery, L.D.: EEG-based estimation and classification of mental fatigue. Psychology **6**, 572–589 (2015)
38. Ray, W.J., Cole, H.W.: EEG alpha activity reflects attentional demands, and beta activity reflects emotional and cognitive processes. Science **228**, 750–752 (1985)
39. Kostyunina, M.B., Kulikov, M.A.: Frequency characteristics of EEG spectra in the emotions. Neurosci Behav. Physiol. **26**, 340–343 (1996)
40. Holder, G.E.: Electrophysiological assessment of optic nerve disease. Eye **18**, 1133–1143 (2004)
41. Adams, C.E., Leverland, M.B.: Environmental and behavioral factors that can affect blood pressure. Nurse Pract. **10**(39–40), 49–50 (1985)

42. Veltman, J.A., Gaillard, A.W.K.: Physiological indices of workload in a simulated flight task. Biol. Psychol. **42**, 323–342 (1996)
43. Mansi, S.A., et al.: Measuring human physiological indices for thermal comfort assessment through wearable devices: a review. Measurement **183**, 109872 (2021)
44. Nixon, J., Charles, R.: Understanding the human performance envelope using electrophysiological measures from wearable technology. Cognit. Technol. Work **19**(4), 655–666 (2017). https://doi.org/10.1007/s10111-017-0431-5
45. Ma, J.H., Lee, J.K., Cha, S.H.: Effects of lighting CCT and illuminance on visual perception and task performance in immersive virtual environments. Build. Environ. **209**, 108678 (2022)

Advancing User Research in Naturalistic Gambling Environments Through Behaviour Tracking. A Pilot Study

Marco Mandolfo$^{(\boxtimes)}$ ⓘ, Debora Bettiga ⓘ, and Giuliano Noci ⓘ

Department of Management, Economics and Industrial Engineering, Politecnico di Milano, Via Lambruschini 4/B, 20156 Milan, Italy
{marco.mandolfo,debora.bettiga,giuliano.noci}@polimi.it

Abstract. User research has widely employed ethnography to gain insights into the player-gaming terminal interaction in naturalistic gambling settings. However, inconsistencies in operationalisation and a lack of rigour in research procedures have been identified as limitations. In this paper, we address these issues by first advocating for the use of behavioural recording technology to support user research. We present a set of quantitative metrics extracted from non-invasive techniques, including video and audio recordings, that capture facial expressions, paralinguistic cues, proxemics, kinesics, and interactive haptic behaviours. Next, we examine the expert evaluation process as a structured analysis framework, including the mapping of environmental variables, the transparent and reproducible operationalization of a research protocol, and the interpretation of data. A pilot study is presented to provide practical guidelines for conducting user research in natural gambling environments. Our findings contribute to user research methodologies and highlight the potential advantages of the proposed approach, including its applicability, ethical considerations, and reliability.

Keywords: Electronic gaming machine · User experience · Ethnography · Biometrics · Methodology

1 Introduction

User research has found numerous applications in naturalistic gambling settings by means of ethnography to study the interaction between the player and the gaming terminal [1–4]. Being characterized by its indirect engagement with study participants and non-manipulative analysis context, ethnographic research is widely recognized as a valuable technique for investigating user behaviour in gambling settings. Its non-intrusive nature makes it a suitable approach for studying complex and sensitive human behaviours, particularly in gambling contexts [5, 6]. The adoption of observational research in the study of electronic gaming machines (EGMs) has been demonstrated in several noteworthy cases [4, 7–9]. However, despite relying on similar methodological premises, these studies tend to vary in their operationalisation practices. For instance, Griffiths (1991) examined the behavioural characteristics and the social nature of arcade patrons

© The Author(s), under exclusive license to Springer Nature Switzerland AG 2023
N. A. Streitz and S. Konomi (Eds.): HCII 2023, LNCS 14036, pp. 229–245, 2023.
https://doi.org/10.1007/978-3-031-34668-2_16

through participant and non-participant observation gathering tape-recorded data and retrospective notes [8]. With a similar research objective, Fisher (1993) carried out an observational study with the researcher positioned as a cashier in the change box of an arcade [9]. Although divergent operationalisations do not represent an issue per se, the absence of shared practices may hamper cross-study comparability in user research. A lack of a common method may also hinder replicability and lead to fragmentation within the same field of research. Such a lack of consensus on methodological best practices has been repeatedly evidenced in previous studies. For instance, Parke and Griffiths (2008) and Griffiths (2011) argue that numerous studies track discrete bits of data ("units") while watching or chatting with the gamblers, either during or after the investigated action [10, 11]. Analogous arguments are advanced by Landon et al. (2017) who also posit that the pace of EGM spins poses an additional element of concern [6]. Indeed, fast-paced spins are accounted as a substantial barrier to the manual recording of every event and player response.

The present paper intends to address such methodological issues to advance user research in gambling settings. We focus on EGM naturalistic settings and develop a discussion based on two elements. First, we advance an argument in favour of behavioural recording technology to support user research in gambling environments. Behavioural recording implies low measurement invasiveness and provides quantitative metrics with higher granularity in terms of event timing. We discuss a set of techniques based on video recordings that gather behavioural data including facial expressions, paralinguistic cues, proxemics, kinesics, and interactive haptic behaviours. The second element involves the process of expert evaluation as the methodological procedure to frame a structured analysis. We examine the researcher as the figure that can anticipate problematics, expectations, and potential impacts on the user experience when it comes to interactions between the player and the gaming terminal. Next, we report a pilot study to illustrate a practical application of the approach described. Our discussion aims to contribute to the methodological debate concerning the process of data collection and analysis, thus answering current calls for advancing user experience research [10, 11]. From a theoretical perspective, we ground our argumentation on the ethnographic research cycle [12], circumscribing our attention to data collection and data analysis phases. Accordingly, we discuss an approach that may complement other qualitative observational techniques to support future user research in the gambling context.

2   Behaviour Analysis Applied to EGM

Applied behaviour observation shares notable features with the practice of ethnography [13]. This research approach has found many previous adoptions in gambling investigations in naturalistic settings [8, 9, 11]. Such a practice of behaviour observation follows a codified process, which encompasses a sequence of recursive steps starting with the formulation of research questions, followed by a data collection stage, data analysis, conclusion drawing and reporting, which are iteratively performed [12]. The specific phase of data collection involves the act of participant observation and the creation of an ethnographic record. Whereas the phase of data analysis relies on one or more techniques to delve into behavioural variables. These embrace an ample spectrum of variables linked to human behaviour [14]. Regarding EGM settings, we claim that a specific subset of responses can find a suitable application. The proposition of a subgroup of variables is motivated by the fast pace of EGM, which demands consonant high response speed. We identify accordingly four individual responses belonging to the spectrum of behaviours, which, at the same time, have found previous application in EGM research [6, 15]. These include facial expressions, paralinguistic cues, proxemics and kinesics, and interactive haptic behaviours performed during an interaction with the gaming terminal. These behavioural responses and their related metrics are discussed in the following.

2.1 Behavioural Metrics Related to Facial Expressions

Facial expressions as a means to convey information have been widely investigated in previous literature [14]. Different typologies of coding have been proposed and can be clustered into two main typologies, namely expert manual coding and data-driven analyses. Expert manual coding is traditionally performed by an expert during the post-processing of video recordings resorting to different reference standards, which have evolved over time. Today the recognised standards are based on the analysis of conjoint movements of individual facial muscles ("action units") and include the Facial Affect Scoring Technique [16], the Facial Action Coding System [17] or the Special Affect Coding System [18]. On the other hand, data-driven analyses rely on data collected either through surface electromyography, namely the recording and quantification of the electrical signal generated by facial muscular fibres [19], or real-time software analyses which are designed to automatically recognise facial landmarks and associate their movements to a discrete set of facial expression [20]. These, in turn, are linked to either discreet categories of emotions deemed universal to all individuals [21] or in terms of a bidimensional framework encompassing activation and pleasantness levels [22]. Comprehensively, the information provided from facial expressions allows inferring specific affective states of the individual and thus an assessment in terms of arousal and valence.

The assessment of affective states through facial expressions has found previous applications in ethnographic studies involving naturalistic videotaping. In a study aiming at investigating the congruency between subjective feelings and external assessment through behavioural responses, Scherer and Ceschi (2000) carried out an empirical study involving passengers waiting in vain for their luggage on conveyor belts in airports [23]. The authors performed video and audio recordings through a hidden camera placed on luggage carts to track images of the participants' faces and upper torso. Such videos were subsequently analysed to code facial expression cues according to the Facial Action Coding System and linked to enjoyment.

Previous studies employing facial expression analysis in the naturalistic gambling field are rare. However, distinctive work has been performed in controlled laboratory settings. For instance, electromyography was employed to study the facial reaction of gamblers on a simulated EGM [24]. The authors investigated the activity of facial muscles (i.e., Corrugator Supercilli and Zygomaticus Major) traditionally associated with the dimension of emotional valence to evaluate responses of gamblers to game events including wins, losses, and near-misses. Electromyography was further employed in a laboratory gambling task by Gentsch et al. (2015) who tracked facial muscular activity changes in conjunction with different simulated gambling outcomes [25]. As shown by both studies, the analysis of facial expression appears suited to assess individual responses to single-game events. This is due to the significant temporal reactivity related to the facial muscular activity (e.g., electromyographic changes can be observed in relation to a stimulus lasting 0.5 s [26]).

While the existing body of literature using facial expressions to study EGM gambling behaviours is seemingly limited to laboratory environments, previous evidence from other fields shows that this class of analysis is applicable also in dynamic contexts. Also because the gaming terminal is static, the body positions of the players are mostly bounded to a seated or a standing position facing the EGM screen. Accordingly, we hypothesise the possibility of video recording the player's facial activity to observe her facial expressions resulting from the appraisal of a given game event. The recorded facial activity may hence be analysed either through expert or automatic coding to infer discreet categories of emotions (e.g., anger, contempt, disgust, fear, happiness, sadness, and surprise) or information concerning the affective arousal and valence of the gambler. We conjecture that the recording activity may be performed unobtrusively throughout the whole game experience, where environmental conditions of lighting and participants' head orientation prove to be adequate to coding standards.

2.2 Behavioural Metrics Related to Paralinguistic Cues

Paralinguistic cues represent a second parameter for behaviour analyses. This category of analysis encompasses vocal cues such as pitch, fundamental frequency, voice intensity, and speech rate which are traditionally observed in conjunction with an external stimulus [27]. This behaviour analysis is grounded on the assumption that vocal behaviour acts as a marker of individual affective processes which, in turn, can be objectively assessed through expert coding [14]. To date, many coding schemes for paralinguistic phenomena have been proposed [28]. These articulate the paralinguistic cues according to different levels (i.e., physiological, phonatory-articulatory, and acoustic levels) and are either related to affective states such as frustration, annoyance, tiredness, or amusement classifiable either through discrete categories or a continuous level in terms of valence, arousal and potency [29, 30]. Paralinguistic cues share notable similarities with facial expressions. Indeed, the two sets of individual responses are characterised by a constrained physical structure that conveys information about the affective states of the observed individual. However, different from the study of facial expressions, the analysis of vocal expressions tends to be more effective over large distances and in dim lighting conditions.

In observational research, paralinguistic cues have been adopted to study either interactive episodes between two or more individuals or vocal expressions of singles. In interactive settings, these metrics have been widely used to examine marital functioning, where different investigations focused on the fundamental frequency during couple conflicts as a measure of emotional arousal. For instance, Weusthoff et al. (2013) employed continuous speech recordings of couples during problem discussions to analyse the nonverbal transmission of distress [31]. The same metric was employed to delve into affective responses of individuals interacting with a digital interface [32]. Based on the automatic inference of expressions in speech, the author extracted different features from utterances and brief vocalisations of single individuals in conjunction with triggered interactive events.

The tendency to attribute human-like characteristics to an EGM and hence talk is a recurring trait observed in gamblers [33]. Such a tendency has been evidenced already in early observational studies carried out in arcades [8], where vocalisations towards the gaming terminal were pointed out as either irrational or rational verbalisations. The former encompasses swearing or solicitations at the machine, whereas the latter includes utterances referring to game events such as wins or losses. In the gambling context, such gamblers' utterances were gathered through portable microphones, thus granting portability and minimising intrusiveness [34].

Taken together, previous studies underscore the possibility of investigating paralinguistic cues in gambling venues. Quantitative investigations may not just delve into complete verbalisation but also examine utterances and brief vocalisations elicited during the interaction between the player and the gaming terminal. Paralinguistic cues such as the fundamental frequency of an audio signal or the vocal intensity provide quantitative metrics to infer states of psychological arousal in conjunction with specific game events (e.g., wins, losses, bonus game activations, etc.). This argumentation is specifically supported by the high temporal accuracy of paralinguistic expressions, that is the existence of a limited time lag between the recognition of a stimulus and the individual reaction [35]. At the same time, the adoption of paralinguistic cues should be evaluated in relation to the presence of crowds or external noise which may impair behavioural recordings.

2.3 Behavioural Metrics Related to Proxemics and Kinesics

Proxemics and kinesics represent a further class of nonverbal cues where individual behaviour is exercised to convey information. Proxemics embrace individual perception and structuring of interpersonal and environmental space, whereas kinesics refers to the actions of the human body, head, and limbs [14]. Unlike facial expressions, it should be noted that few body movements are expected to have invariant meaning within or across cultures [36]. Second, like verbal communication, the notion of intention is not uniquely defined. Accordingly, situational and volitional aspects should be considered when dealing with proxemics and kinesics.

Contrary to facial expressions and paralinguistic cues, which display a robust connection to specific affective states, proxemics and kinesics alone do not convey clear-cut affective content. However, their analysis is intended to accent or emphasise information regarding the intensity of the affective state and perceptions of decoders in terms of individual engagement or psychological stress [37]. More specifically, investigations analysing proxemics (i.e., body positions) of healthy participants are traditionally carried out in interactional settings, where two or more individuals interrelate or where a single individual interacts with an environment [38]. Common measures of proxemics include the distance or the frontal body orientation and are traditionally labelled through expert coding [39]. On the other hand, the analysis of kinesics (i.e., body actions) is centred on discrete actions performed by body units. These include the movements of the trunk, arms, and legs in terms of leaning, orientation, or rotation changes. For instance, investigations focused on the trunk code and its movements in terms of leaning forward or backward [27] or concerning its orientation as the degree to which an encoder's frontal body surface faces another encoder [40].

Proxemics and kinesics are well-established factors in observational research. Posture is often recognised as a modality for expressing engagement during interactions with devices, where postural behaviours coding may be performed either automatically or through expert observation to infer states of engagement from leaning forward or backward trunk movements [41]. These observational techniques are also applied in gambling venues. Braun and Giroux (1989) recorded adolescents' use of personal space in arcades, while Landon et al. (2017) report the tendency of patrons to look around or show frustration through abrupt movements such as during spin button hit [6, 42]. The vigour and moving frequency of limbs and the physical energy employed in pushing the spin button represented further observed variables in previous research as expressions of motor excitability during simulated or actual EGM gambling behaviours [8].

This evidence supports the adoption of behaviour analyses involving proxemics and kinesics in natural gambling environments. Applied studies may use such parameters to infer states of engagement from individual postural settings or pinpoint intense arousal from abrupt body moments. These metrics show a significant temporal accuracy since the expression of a physical action typically occurs following an external trigger. Hence, these behavioural metrics could conceivably be applied to spin-by-spin analyses. Furthermore, given the possibility to record body actions from distance, the related invasiveness or disturbance to the gambler is deemed significantly limited.

2.4 Behavioural Metrics Related to Interactive Haptic Behaviours

Interactive haptic behaviours refer to the relational aspects occurring between the individual, the object of investigation, and the environment. Interactive patterns provide information about the exploration processes in terms of sequences of actions and reactions to specific events or temporary halts. Such a variety of aspects is commonly codified through selective structural observation carried out along with the interaction development [43]. The study of interactive patterns between the observed person and a device has been often studied as a vehicle to convey information related to engagement or psychological stress, for instance occurring whenever an individual feels overwhelmed by the presented information [44].

Various interactive patterns are often investigated during the use of EGMs. For instance, relevant factors include the bet size, the cash-out frequency, the spin button hit frequency, the total time of play, the insertion of money, the change of betting lines, the access of player information, and the use of automatic betting [6, 15, 34]. Individual reactions are often evaluated in conjunction with specific outcomes. Besides wins and losses, these include bonus games, as in-game features activated when specific symbols are lined in a winning combination, near-misses, as unsuccessful outcomes proximal to the jackpot or a win, or losses disguised as wins, as outcomes where the cashed-in amount results lower than the bet amount [45].

The tracking of the sequence of interactive actions represents a well-rooted practice in observational research in naturalistic gambling environments. Though, the tracing of spin-by-spin activity might represent a hindrance to the researcher [6]. To solve this issue, we claim that video recording technology may support the researcher to gather observational material. The placement of a rear camera pointing to the screen of the EGM can record the gambling activity at a distance without constituting a means of hindrance or disturbance to the player. The recording of the whole screen activity has two significant advantages for observational research. First, the gambling activity may be coded in retrospect, either manually or automatically. Manual coding may involve significant effort but can be suited to small sample sizes. On the other hand, automatic coding allows the processing of larger sets of observations in the face of adequate model training. An example of automatic coding of EGM gambling events is advanced by Mandolfo et al. (2019), who tracked gamblers' bets and game events through screen capture and an optical character recognition algorithm [46]. Once trained the recognition algorithm on the screen area related to the wallet, the algorithm was able to detect changes in credit during the spin button hit and automatically detect wins and losses.

The second advantage related to the use of ambient cameras is to allow the observer to better mingle in the gambling venue without resorting to continuous manual coding. Indeed, manual coding may represent an element of disturbance not only for the observed gambler but may attract the attention of further patrons, thus influencing the context of analysis. Overall, the adoption of ambient recording instruments for video and audio grants low invasiveness and provides quantitative metrics with higher time accuracy. The four behavioural variables previously discussed are summarised in Table 1.

3   The Role of the Expert Evaluation

Ethnographic research carried out in gambling venues typically aims at understanding the experience of the gambler during the interaction with the gaming terminal by mapping the reactions of the gambler. Such mapping activity requires a description of the solution and identification of the main interaction flows it enables. The expert evaluation deals with this mapping activity performed by researchers, who provide inputs for the creation of observation protocols and data processing guides, which further contribute to the evaluation of the gambling experience. The researcher has the role to anticipate problems, expectations, and potential impacts on the gambling experiences when it comes to the interplay between the gambler and the gaming terminal. To this end, the investigator can prefigure the scenarios of use, expressing a critical evaluation of contextual variables and their influence on gambling behaviour. The expert plays multiple roles in structuring observational research. First, a preliminary activity is represented by the description of a system in terms of tasks and paths of users, flows of activities, and processes. In these terms, expert evaluation grounds its roots in user research and heuristic evaluation [43]. Second, the expert is involved in the definition of a research protocol. The expert should identify an observation protocol targeted at specific research questions. This should create an environment supporting the natural behaviour of the observed gamblers. The study protocol should ensure homogeneous test conditions for all the participants involved and it should be robust with respect to the variety of possible behaviours. Furthermore, it should include the definition of the unit of analysis (e.g., gambler's behaviours to predefined game outcomes), which ought to allow comparability

Table 1. Behavioural variables for observational research in naturalistic gambling environments.

Behavioural variable	Description	Information provided	Metrics
Facial expressions	Momentary facial movements as vehicles for information about affective states	• Discreet categories of emotions (e.g., anger, contempt, disgust, fear, happiness, sadness, and surprise) • Affective arousal and valence	• Expert or automatic coding based on action units' conjoint movements • Electric activity of facial muscles
Paralinguistic cues	Qualities of speech devoid of the actual verbal content	• Discreet categories of emotions (e.g., anger, happiness, sadness, and surprise) • Affective arousal, valence, and potency	• Fundamental frequency • Voice intensity • Vocal pitch • Speech rate
Proxemics and kinesics	Structuring of interpersonal and environmental space and actions of the body	• Accent or emphasise the intensity of engagement or psychological stress	• Physical distance between the participant and the object • Frontal body orientation • Truck leaning • Limbs abrupt movements
Interactive haptic behaviours	Relational aspects occurring between the individual, the object of investigation and the environment	• Psychological processes related to engagement and psychological stress	• Sequences of actions (e.g., spin button hit frequency, change of betting lines or size, cash-out frequency) • Temporary halts

with previous studies addressing a similar research question. The observation protocol should also ensure each participant's autonomy and set the data collection process to allow efficient and effective processing of information. Third, the expert has the role of the interpreter. To understand complex behaviour phenomena, the expert should triangulate data sources or theoretical perspectives to quantify the observed behaviours and provide inferences on common behavioural patterns among the different observations [47]. In particular, pattern matching involves the identification of similarities, sequences, correspondences or causation between events. The process of data interpretation should also ensure an emphasis on the presence of biases within the study design or confounding as alternative explanations of the results.

4 Applied Pilot Study

We report in the following a pilot study to illustrate a practical application of the approach described. In line with our discourse, we focus on the methodological aspects concerning research structuring, observation setting, data processing and result interpretation. We centred our study on the behavioural responses in conjunction with different EGM outcomes and select the individual as a unit of analysis. The described research was supported by one of the leading authorised gambling companies in Italy, as part of a research project delving into the behavioural manifestations of EGM players and investigating phenomena connected to the onset of problematic relationships with gambling activities. The procedures of this study were approved by the ethical committee of the university institution to which the authors refer.

4.1 Methodological Considerations Concerning Research Structuring

We structured our observational procedure intending to limit external biases related to the day and time of the investigation, the influence of the location, and the potential payroll day. Accordingly, the study involved four observation sessions, each lasting four hours. The observations were carried out in four different slot halls located in a major Italian city, with two sites belonging to central districts of the city and two located in a suburban area. Two sessions were carried out on weekdays during night openings, while two rounds of observations were undertaken during the morning opening hours. To control for bias related to the payroll day, the observation sessions took place on different monthly dates. Acknowledged the potential experimental barrier of player-specific factors [48], the pilot study involved non-participant behavioural recordings of single players.

4.2 Methodological Considerations Concerning the Observation Set

The observation set was structured to limit noise in the process of data collection. Potential sources of noise were deemed related to the typology of graphic interface, game features as well as ambient lighting, external sounds, and observation angles. To limit ambiguity related to the gaming terminal, each participant was invited to play on a single five-reel stand-alone slot machine chosen as the analysed stimulus in each slot hall. The selection of the specific EGM was advised by the slot hall owner on the criterion of the most used five-reel slot machine in the previous month. Before the research deployment, a preliminary inspection of each slot hall was performed during closing hours to describe the environment in terms of gamblers' paths as well as to map the possible interaction flows occurring between the gambler and the chosen gaming terminals. The selected EGMs were characterised by five fixed paylines and included free spins as bonus features activated when specific symbols were lined in a winning combination. Each terminal allowed a minimum bet of € 0.25 per spin and a maximum of € 1.00. The maximum payout of the EGM was €100.00. During the game session, the participant was observed at an adequate distance by the research team to avoid interference with the game. Overall, the behavioural recordings involved 19 adult voluntary players with a male prevalence and an estimated age range of 19–60. Each volunteer played with their own money and did not receive any sort of incentive to participate.

As concerns the observation technology, two high frame rate micro-cameras were employed to record the activity of the players. One was attached to the chosen EGM at head high in front of the player. Such a device included a mechanism for adjusting the recording angle and was employed to gather facial recordings as well as the vocal expressions of the participant. The EGM screen backlight provided suitable lighting conditions to detect the subject's facial landmarks. The second camera was attached to the wall behind the player to record the whole body of the participant and the game events displayed on the gaming terminal. The positioning of the instruments was done in such a way as to ensure that the second camera had a complete view of the EGM screen, as shown in Fig. 1.

Fig. 1. Illustrative observation setting employed. Ambient cameras are circled in red. (Color figure online)

4.3   Selected Measures and Data Processing

We analysed recursive behavioural variables of the player during the interaction with the EGM and the surrounding environment. These included the analysis of facial expressions, paralinguistic cues, proxemics and kinesics, and interactive haptic behaviours, as previously outlined. Facial expressions were extracted from frontal camera recordings and analysed through Noldus FaceReader 7. The analysis was carried out during the game session and data were extracted when the conditions in terms of lighting and participants' head orientation satisfied the General Face Model minimum requirements for detection. To control for individual differences in baseline facial expression, facial expressions were analysed after a face model calibration for each participant considering a resting state face frame recorded at the beginning of the game session. Facial states were analysed employing General Face Model with smoothening classifications through Noldus FaceReader analysis software, which implements the Facial Action Coding System to extract seven basic facial expressions [21]. The software analyses and assigns to each frame of the recording an estimation of the intensity of facial expression of the extracted emotions a score ranging from 0 (minimum) to 1 (maximum). Each facial expression was tallied as relevant if it was detected in a latency window of 3 s from the considered stimulus onset and the signal assumed a value above 0.1. The length of the latency window was set equal to the average lapse of time between consecutive spin button hits.

The analysis of paralinguistic cues involved the extraction of the fundamental frequency (f0) of each utterance in conjunction with all the recorded game events as a measure of arousal. f0 range was obtained from the audio signal extracted from the frontal camera after a bandpass filtering (high pass = 75 Hz; low pass = 300 Hz) to cut off potential external noise [49]. f0 range was calculated for each gambler as the difference between the individual minimum and maximum f0 values, generated by analysing audio recordings. Behavioural responses were classified based on the emergence of recurring vocal patterns in conjunction with specific game events.

Body proxemics was evaluated with respect to a single axis between the player and the gaming device and compared to the anatomical standard position, observed before the onset of the gaming session. Such information was manually coded and extracted from the second camera. Posture shifts were tallied and coded according to whole-body posture units and body action units in line with the Body Action and Posture Coding System [39]. Accordingly, players were reported with a leant back, forward, or neutral posture if at the occurrence of specific game events displayed a recurring tendency of the whole body to move or lean forward relative to the anatomical standard position.

Lastly, interactive haptic behaviours focused on the analysis of hit frequencies. These were tracked from the video recordings and measured as the time interval in seconds between two consecutive spin button clicks. It was observed that the pressing vigour depended significantly on the pressing style, where players tended to alternate spin button hits either with the fingers or with the palm of the hand. The recurring behavioural variables were scrutinized in conjunction with five events, namely (i) a simple loss, (ii) a win, (iii) a repetitive loss, as the series of at least ten consecutive losses during back-to-back spins; (iv) a near-miss, as and (v) a bonus game activation. Such game events were manually coded from the video recordings gathered from the rear camera and synchronised with information recorded from the frontal camera.

4.4 Data Analysis and Result Interpretation

The collected observations were analysed to highlight recurring behavioural patterns. Recurring patterns were intended as behaviours that show affinity in terms of similarities, frequencies, and sequences. The affinity was assessed across the four behavioural variables during post-processing data analysis through pattern matching carried out by two researchers. Given the limited sample size, the analysis followed a qualitative stance. The triangulation process required the comparison of (i) the main facial expression coded, (ii) the individual f0 extracted, (iii) the category of assumed posture, and (iv) the specific hit frequency. All the metrics were compared in conjunction with each game outcome, independently from the length of the gaming session. Two examples of patterns for the same game session of 39 spins are reported in the following. Figure 2 shows the pattern of hit frequency combined with posture coding, while Fig. 3 displays the pattern of hit frequency combined with the dominant facial expression coded.

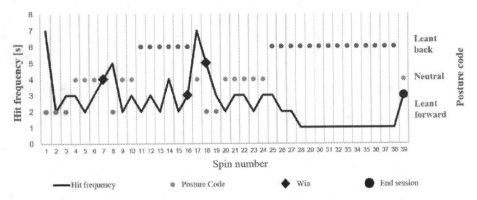

Fig. 2. Illustrative pattern of hit frequency combined with posture coding.

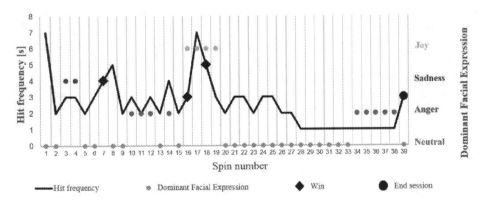

Fig. 3. Illustrative pattern of hit frequency combined with dominant facial expression.

Overall, results showed that two of the five analysed game events triggered recursive responses, namely behaviours showing similarities with a significant frequency in conjunction with the same game event. Specifically, repetitive losses and bonus game activations elicited distinct recurring patterns. In response to repetitive losses, notable behavioural patterns included at least one of the following behaviours: a change in the player proxemics characterised by a tendency to lean the body forward towards the slot machine, an intensification of the button hit frequency, or an increase in negative valence facial expressions (i.e., contempt, anger, and disgust). Concurrently with bonus game activations, we observed a propensity to lean the upper body forward towards the slot machine and a variation of the verbal behaviour towards a higher frequency.

Overall, none of the four behavioural variables resulted significantly dominant, underscoring the complexity of the studied behaviour. However, the continuous spin-to-spin behavioural tracking across four dimensions allowed the detection of multivariate patterns. Accordingly, though observed in a limited sample, the results support the argument that multimodal analyses are likely to enrich observational studies.

5 Discussion and Conclusions

The interest in the manners in which people gamble is sparked by several parties. First, the growing emergence of gambling as a societal issue in the public domain has fuelled arguments on its societal consequences [50]. Second, behavioural research focusing on the causes of addictive activities such as EGM gambling and the structural features of the EGM game experience, that act as a reinforcement of the gambling activity, has attracted the attention of social researchers [51]. Furthermore, the recognition of gambling as a rather mainstream recreational activity shed interest in the role of social factors [52]. In the present paper, we discussed how current ethnographic research in gambling venues might be enriched by using a set of behavioural measures and relying on expert evaluation. The discussed metrics are gathered from non-invasive measurement techniques based on video and audio recording and a subsequent structured coding process, which can be automatised recurring to algorithms for facial landmarks recognition, vocal spectrum analysis or optical recognition of game events. The low invasiveness of the measures results central in order not to denature the context of analysis. We claim that the adoption of such recording technology may help to complement current ethnographic research by observing player-specific responses to spin-to-spin analyses otherwise barely unachievable by the traditional observer.

The illustrative case study contributes to user research in gambling venues. We demonstrated the feasibility of performing unobtrusive behavioural recording that analyses multiple behavioural manifestations (i.e., facial expressions, paralinguistic cues, proxemics and kinesics, and interactive haptic behaviours). The introduction of behaviour tracking through video cameras would enable scaling up observations beyond the traditional sample sizes [4, 9], due to the possible data gathering on multiple gaming terminals concurrently. Relying on multiple data sources gathered automatically, would also support the ethnographer in systematically identifying aspects of the situation under study that have been excluded from first-hand observation. Thus, limiting possible sources of acknowledged biases in the ethnographic practice [53]. Social scientists can potentially use real-time behaviour tracking to investigate gamblers' behaviours. For instance, future user research might be carried out in naturalistic gambling venues to draft planimetric maps of these premises and show how the disposition of gaming terminals might affect gamblers' behaviours. Also, researchers can potentially use behaviour tracking to explore how interactive patterns emerge not only between the user and the EGM but also among different patrons. Future research might investigate how social dynamics reinforce or deter specific gambling behaviours.

However, we underscore that the technology placement should respect rigorous protocols. Video recordings require adequate lighting conditions to allow satisfactory data quality to be input into models for facial expression analysis. This should be ensured both in terms of frontal and lateral lighting in order not to create artificial shadows on the gambler's face or body. At the same time, an adequate distance between the recording device and the body of the subject is suggested to ensure reliable accuracy in facial landmark detection. Video recording should also respect definite recording angles in order not to cause erroneous visual perspectives. Similarly, audio recordings should ensure satisfactory quality in terms of loudness, sharpness, fluctuation strength and cut-out disturbing echoes.

To carry out preliminary activities according to a structured procedure, we further have underscored the role of expert evaluation. A structured research process encompasses multiple steps in observational research including the preliminary inspection and the mapping of both the environment and the gaming terminal. In these terms, preliminary research activities involve the understanding of potential biases affecting the observation protocol or the presence of confounding. Furthermore, the expert has the role to conceive and operationalise a study protocol to guide and govern the conduction of the observations. A study protocol directs the execution of a study to help ensure the validity of the final study results. Moreover, it should allow transparency in the methodological steps adopted to grant the observations' future reproducibility and replicability, thus potentially increasing and validity of the observed outcomes.

Lastly, our discussion proposed a descriptive pilot study. This was aimed at presenting a set of methodological aspects concerning research structuring, observation setting, data processing and results interpretation. We emphasise how the structuring of the observation setting in terms of preliminary analysis, instrumentation employed, and choice of behavioural metrics. Second, we have shown that multimodal analyses are likely to enrich observational studies. Specifically, user research in naturalistic gambling environments may benefit from higher objectivity associated with the observed phenomena through a rigorous process of continuous data collection. At the same time, we underscore how the researcher should embody the role of the interpreter, namely triangulating punctual data to translate them into knowledge to support practical applications. We stress that observational research has the potential to uncover contextualised data, often inaccessible through different approaches. In so doing, the outcome of observational studies should be employed to empower the same user, who is the object of the study, whenever behavioural phenomena appear to be connected to the onset of problematic relationships with gambling activities.

References

1. Dickerson, M.G.: FI schedules and persistence at gambling in the UK betting office. J. Appl. Behav. Anal. **12**, 315–323 (1979)
2. Aasved, M.J., Schaefer, J.M.: "Minnesota slots": an observational study of pull tab gambling. J. Gambl. Stud. **11**, 311–341 (1995)
3. Fong, L.H.N., So, A.S.I., Law, R.: Betting decision under break-streak pattern: evidence from casino gaming. J. Gambl. Stud. **32**(1), 171–185 (2015). https://doi.org/10.1007/s10899-015-9550-1

4. Delfabbro, P., Osborn, A., Nevile, M., Skelt, L., McMillan, J.: Identifying Problem Gamblers in Gambling Venues (2007)
5. Lincoln, Y.S.: Naturalistic Inquiry. In: Ritzer, G. (ed.) The Blackwell Encyclopedia of Sociology. John Wiley & Sons, Ltd (2007)
6. Landon, J., Du Preez, K.P., Bellringer, M., Abbott, M., Roberts, A.: On the feasibility of in-venue observations of electronic gaming machine gamblers and game characteristics. J. Gambl. Issues. 183–198 (2017)
7. Atkinson, P., Coffey, A., Delamont, S., Lofland, J., Lofland, L.: Handbook of ethnography. SAGE Publications (2001)
8. Griffiths, M.D.: The observational study of adolescent gambling in UK amusement arcades. J. Community Appl. Soc. Psychol. **1**, 309–320 (1991)
9. Fisher, S.: The pull of the fruit machine: a sociological typology of young players. Sociol. Rev. **41**, 446–474 (1993)
10. Parke, J., Griffiths, M.: Participant and non-participant observation in gambling environments. Enquire. **1**, 1–14 (2008)
11. Griffiths, M.D.: A typology of UK slot machine gamblers: a longitudinal observational and interview study. Int. J. Ment. Health Addict. **9**, 606–626 (2011)
12. Spradley, J.: Participant observation. Waveland Press (1980)
13. Mason, J.: Qualitative researching. SAGE Publications (2017)
14. Harrigan, J., Rosenthal, R., Scherer, K.: The New Handbook of Methods in Nonverbal Behavior Research. Oxford University Press (2008)
15. Rockloff, M.J., Hing, N.: The Impact of Jackpots on EGM Gambling Behavior: A Review. J. Gambl. Stud. **29**(4), 775–790 (2012). https://doi.org/10.1007/s10899-012-9336-7
16. Ekman, P., Friesen, W., Tomkins, S.: Facial affect scoring technique: a first validity study. Semiotica **3**, 37–58 (1971)
17. Ekman, P., Friesen, W.V: Facial Action Coding Systems. Consulting Psychologists Press. (1978)
18. Gottman, J., Krokoff, L.: Marital interaction and satisfaction: a longitudinal view. J. Consult. Clin. Psychol. **57**, 47–52 (1989)
19. Weyers, P., Mühlberger, A., Hefele, C., Pauli, P.: Electromyographic responses to static and dynamic avatar emotional facial expressions. Psychophysiology **43**, 450–453 (2006)
20. Roesch, E.B., Tamarit, L., Reveret, L., Grandjean, D., Sander, D., Scherer, K.R.: FACSGen: a tool to synthesize emotional facial expressions through systematic manipulation of facial action units. J. Nonverbal Behav. **35**, 1–16 (2011)
21. Ekman, P.: An argument for basic emotions. Cogn. Emot. **6**, 169–200 (1992)
22. Feldman Barrett, L., Russell, J.: Independence and bipolarity in the structure of current affect. J. Pers. Soc. Psychol. **74**, 967–984 (1998)
23. Scherer, K.R., Ceschi, G.: Criteria for emotion recognition from verbal and nonverbal expression: Studying baggage loss in the airport. Personal. Soc. Psychol. Bull. **26**, 327–339 (2000)
24. Sharman, S., Clark, L.: Mixed emotions to near-miss outcomes: a psychophysiological study with facial electromyography. J. Gambl. Stud. **32**(3), 823–834 (2015). https://doi.org/10.1007/s10899-015-9578-2
25. Gentsch, K., Grandjean, D., Scherer, K.R.: of Facial Muscle Movements in a Gambling Task : Evidence for the Component Process Model of Emotion. PLoS ONE. 1–31 (2015)
26. Codispoti, M., Bradley, M.M., Lang, P.J.: Affective reactions to briefly presented pictures. Psychophysiology **38**, 474–478 (2001)
27. Mehrabian, A.: Inference of attitudes from the posture, orientation, and distance of a communicator. J. Consult. Clin. Psychol. **32**, 296–308 (1968)
28. Poyatos, F.: Man beyond words: Theory and methodology of nonverbal communication. Monograph No. 15. Eric (1976)

29. Hopkins, C., Ratley, R., Benincasa, D., Grieco, J.: Evaluation of Voice Stress Analysis Technology. In: Proceedings of the 38th Hawaii International Conference on System Sciences. IEEE. pp. 20b-20b (2005)

30. Pereira, C.: Dimensions of emotional meaning in speech. In: Proceedings of the ISCA Workshop on Speech and Emotion, pp. 25–28 (2000)

31. Weusthoff, S., Baucom, B.R., Hahlweg, K.: Fundamental frequency during couple conflict: An analysis of physiological, behavioral, and sex-linked information encoded in vocal expression. J. Fam. Psychol. **27**, 212–220 (2013)

32. Shikler, T.S.: Multi-modal analysis of human computer interaction using automatic inference of aural expressions in speech. In: IEEE International Conference on Systems, Man and Cybernetics. pp. 404–410 (2008)

33. Kim, S., Mcgill, A.L.: Gaming with Mr. Slot or gaming the slot machine? Power, anthropomorphism, and risk perception. J. Consum. Res. **38**, 94–107 (2011)

34. Griffiths, M.D.: The role of cognitive bias and skill in fruit machine gambling. Br. J. Psychol. **85**, 351–369 (1994)

35. Scherer, K.R., Oshinsky, J.S.: Cue utilization in emotion attribution from auditory stimuli. Motiv. Emot. **1**, 331–346 (1977)

36. Hayduk, L.: Personal space: where we now stand. Psychol. Bull. **94**, 293–335 (1983)

37. Boomer, D., Dittmann, A.P.: Speech rate, filled pause, and body movement in interviews. J. Nerv. Ment. Dis. **139**, 324–327 (1964)

38. Altman, I., Wohlwill, J.F.: Personal Space: Advances in Theory and Research. In: Altman, I., Wohlwill, J. (eds.) Human Behavior and Environment, pp. 181–259. Springer, Boston, MA (1977)

39. Dael, N., Mortillaro, M., Scherer, K.R.: The Body Action and Posture coding system (BAP): development and reliability. J. Nonverbal Behav. **36**, 97–121 (2012)

40. Gifford, R.: projected interpersonal distance and orientation choices: personality, sex, and social situation. Soc. Psychol. Q. **45**, 145 (1982)

41. BianchiBerthouze, N.: Understanding the role of body movement in player engagement. Hum.-Comput. Interact. **28**, 40–75 (2013)

42. Braun, C.M.J., Giroux, J.: Arcade video games: proxemic, cognitive and content analyses. J. Leis. Res. **21**, 92–105 (1989)

43. Nielsen, J.: Heuristic evaluation. In: Nielsen, J. and Mack, R. (eds.) Usability Inspection Methods. pp. 25–62. John Wiley & Sons (1994)

44. Shneiderman, B., Plaisant, C., Cohen, M., Jacobs, S., Elmqvist, N., Diakopoulos, N.: Designing the user interface: strategies for effective human-computer interaction. Pearson Education (2016)

45. Dixon, M.J., Harrigan, K.A., Sandhu, R., Collins, K., Fugelsang, J.A.: Losses disguised as wins in modern multi-line video slot machines. Addiction **105**, 1819–1824 (2010)

46. Mandolfo, M., Bettiga, D., Lolatto, R., Reali, P.: Would you bet on your physiological response? An analysis of the physiological and behavioral characteristics of online electronic gaming machines players. In: NeuroPsychoEconomics Conference, p. 28 (2019)

47. Mandolfo, M., Pavlovic, M., Pillan, M., Lamberti, L.: Ambient UX Research: User Experience Investigation Through Multimodal Quadrangulation. In: Streitz, N., Konomi, S. (eds.) HCII 2020. LNCS, vol. 12203, pp. 305–321. Springer, Cham (2020). https://doi.org/10.1007/978-3-030-50344-4_22

48. Parke, J., Griffiths, M.: Slot machine gamblers — why are they so hard to study? J. Gambl. Issues. **6**, 1–11 (2002)

49. Owren, M.J., Bachorowski, J.A.: Measuring vocal acoustics. In: Coan, J. and Allen, J. (eds.) The Handbook of Emotion Elicitation and Assessment. pp. 239–266. Oxford University Press (2007)

50. Markham, F., Young, M.: "Big Gambling": the rise of the global industry-state gambling complex. Addict. Res. Theory. **23**, 1–4 (2015)
51. James, R.J.E., Tunney, R.J.: The need for a behavioural analysis of behavioural addictions. Clin. Psychol. Rev. **52**, 69–76 (2017)
52. Neighbors, C., Lostutter, T.W., Cronce, J.M., Larimer, M.E.: Exploring college student gambling motivation. J. Gambl. Stud. **18**, 361–370 (2002)
53. Duneier, M.: How not to lie with ethnography. Sociol. Methodol. **41**, 1–11 (2011). https://doi.org/10.1111/j.1467-9531.2011.01249.x

Using the Experience Sampling Method to Find the Pattern of Individual Quality of Life Perceptions

Tomoyo Sasao[1]([✉]) [iD], Mitsuharu Tai[2], Kei Suzuki[2], Shin'ichi Warisawa[1] [iD], and Atsushi Deguchi[1] [iD]

[1] The University of Tokyo, Bunkyo-Ku, Hongo 7-3-1, Tokyo, Japan
sasao@edu.k.u-tokyo.ac.jp
[2] Hitachi, Ltd., Chiyoda-Ku, Marunouchi 1-6-6, Tokyo, Japan

Abstract. In recent years, with the spread of smart cities, which comprehensively tackle the social experimentation and implementation of new technologies, countries worldwide are emphasizing the importance of development focusing on the well-being and quality of life (QoL) of citizens. One issue is that provider-driven projects in smart cities often need to push development forward in the minimum amount of time. If a project is carried out without fully determining whether the community and its citizens really need them, and if dialog with citizens is neglected, it is unlikely that useful services would be created. Therefore, to make human-centered improvements, we need a method to grasp whether the experiences of existing urban service and urban space help increase people's QoL as well as the characteristics of people whose QoL increases versus those whose QoL does not. Therefore, this research aims to develop a tool named ActiveQoL-ESM for measuring the satisfaction of each daily activity based on the experience sampling method (ESM), a classical method for continuously collecting personal subjective data that significantly change dynamically during daily life. Moreover, we propose a method for evaluating urban service and spatial experiences and for analyzing how to improve these experiences from the data gathered through the ESM. Through an experiment using ActiveQoL-ESM, we find suitable evaluation methods for capturing individual QoL perceptions. We show it is possible that the methods could help clarify the meaning of the word "citizens," not only from the attribute and personality data collected from the preliminary questionnaire but also from the contextual data gathered from Fitbit and smartphones.

Keywords: human behavior · lifestyle · daily life · experience sampling method · quality of life · citizen sensing · smart city measures · urban evaluation

1 Introduction

In recent years, with the spread of smart cities, which comprehensively tackle the social experimentation and implementation of new technologies, countries worldwide are emphasizing the importance of development focusing on the well-being and quality

© The Author(s), under exclusive license to Springer Nature Switzerland AG 2023
N. A. Streitz and S. Konomi (Eds.): HCII 2023, LNCS 14036, pp. 246–264, 2023.
https://doi.org/10.1007/978-3-031-34668-2_17

of life (QoL) of citizens [1, 2]. One issue is that provider-driven projects in smart cities often need to push development forward in the minimum amount of time. If a project is carried out without fully determining whether the community and its citizens really need it, and if dialog with citizens is neglected, useful services are unlikely to be created. Therefore, to make human-centered improvements, we need a method to grasp whether the experiences of existing urban service and urban space help increase people's QoL and to understand the characteristics of people whose QoL increases versus those whose QoL does not.

How should we define citizens' well-being and QoL? The Cambridge Dictionary defines QoL as "the level of satisfaction and comfort that a person or group enjoys" [3]. Satisfaction and comfort in this context are subjective feelings; therefore, they are highly likely to change depending on the various contexts of one's daily life and condition. In addition, different factors increase satisfaction depending on an individual's personality and lifestyle preferences.

However, at present, questionnaires are the only way to measure people's QoL and understand the state of a city; such surveys must be conducted once every few years at great cost by governments and public administrations. Therefore, it is difficult to grasp how the QoL of citizens changes as a result of smart city projects, which can change drastically in a short period of time.

This research aims to develop a tool named ActiveQoL-ESM for measuring the satisfaction of each daily activity based on the experience sampling method (ESM), a classical method for continuously collecting personal subjective data that significantly change dynamically during daily life [4]. Moreover, through experiments and analysis using real data, we propose two different types of methods for evaluating urban service and spatial experiences and analyzing how to improve these experiences from the data gathered through the ESM.

Section 2 presents a literature review, in which we summarize the conventional participatory urban evaluation methods and research on the ESM utilized in this system. In Sect. 3, we introduce the QoL sampling system (ActiveQoL-ESM) and the methods for evaluating cities based on the data collected. In Sect. 4, we describe initial experiments using this system. In Sect. 5, we discuss the results. Section 6 concludes.

2 Related Works

2.1 Participatory Urban Evaluation

There are several works measuring satisfaction of life, QoL, and happiness for urban evaluation. Urban Audit [5] was offered as a set of indexes for QoL-based-urban evaluation. These indexes, developed by DG-REGIO and Eurostat, are constructed from 336 indexes extracted from statistical city data in 25 categories in nine fields. The Better Life Index [6], developed by the OECD, measures the richness and happiness of life in each country and is reported openly. This compares 38 countries in 11 areas of life that are important to people and related to QoL. QoL in European cities [7] is an annual survey issued by EU that compares indexes between European cities from a QoL perspective.

Similar evaluations have been attempted in Japan. The Arakawa Gross Happiness (GAH) [8] index, developed by Arakawa Ward and the Research Institute for Local government by Arakawa City, extracts 39 indicators in six fields through a questionnaire to calculate happiness sensitivity. Furthermore, Arakawa Ward has picked up issues from the evaluation results and formulated priority measures. The Liveable Well-Being City Index (LWCI) [9] was developed by Smart City Institute-Japan in collaboration with the Royal Melbourne Institute of Technology as a Japanese version of the "Liveability Indicator" used for urban policy in Melbourne, Australia[10]. This index is estimated based on questionnaires and statistical data. There are five sub-indexes (our proposed assessment set called ActiveQoL is included). Each sub-index is selected based on the perspectives of the individual mind (happiness and relationships between people), human behavior (satisfaction of life activities and the impression of the city from the perspective of behavior), and the urban environment (ease of living based on objective data). In this way, the LWCI is a comprehensive urban evaluation index that incorporates the research results of a wide range of universities and companies.

The indicators listed here can be classified into objective evaluations based on numerical data, such as statistical values, subjective evaluations based on questionnaires to residents, or a combination thereof. For example, objective evaluation is the number of hospitals per population, and the corresponding subjective evaluation is based on the results of a questionnaire to residents. Subjective evaluation of such environmental assets and services is called subjective evaluation of external factors. Meanwhile, subjective evaluation of a person's inner life, such as whether there is anxiety about health, is called subjective evaluation of internal factors. QoL and happiness are essentially based on subjective evaluation of internal factors but, for example, the GAH mainly consists of subjective evaluation of external factors and includes subjective evaluation of some internal factors. These classifications and the positioning of some indicators mentioned above are summarized in Fig. 1.

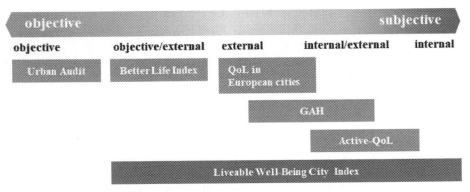

Fig. 1. QoL indicators for urban assessments

The works listed above are those that collect information by questionnaire or include this, but there are also some precedents for collecting information from data using IT. MIT sought to quantitively evaluate area. Evaluators choose one of two photos of Street View of areas by selecting that which is preferable, safer, easier to live in, etc. Then, they tried to score the area in a database from the these chosen answers. The Foundation for the International Cities with Arts, Culture, and Soft Infrastructures (FIACS) developed the area-qualia-index [11]. This measures urban development activities, including artistic and cultural aspects, and derives values from trend information of Twitter and human-flow data of residents and visitors.

All these indexes are strong candidates for an urban evaluation method, but there is still no way to capture the ever-changing consciousness of satisfaction that residents feel in daily life.

2.2 Experience Sampling Method

The ESM has been widely conducted in social science research after developing in 1970's [12]. This method is a survey in which subjects who lead daily lives are measured several times a day over several days, either at a fixed time or at random times. In this method, the subjects are not affected by extraordinary environments such as the laboratory, and are suitable for capturing the non-biased state in daily life. Moreover, the thoughts, judgments, emotions, and actions of the subject can be obtained immediately on site, and thus, recall bias can be minimized.

The disadvantage of this method is the large cost in terms of both labor and money. Initially, the laborious procedure of carrying and recording self-recorded recording paper was used, and then, according to the development of technology, it became standard practice within the ESM to have data collection functions installed on portable devices, lent to each subject, so that they could notice the time to provide answers [13].

Recently, a way to use smartphones has emerged. Since the smartphone owned by the survey respondent can be used to notify the time and collect data, it became possible to conduct the experiment at a lower cost. In addition, by enhancing the smartphone applications, the ESM can be implemented without programming skills. There are several application services of the ESM provided openly [14–17].

These methods have been developed mainly in the social sciences, especially in psy-chological research, and the application service mentioned above is also a specification for it. Meanwhile, the idea of using the ESM for urban evaluation is not yet mainstream, and methods for analyzing data and utilizing it for urban evaluation have not yet been fully studied.

3 ActiveQoL

We develop ActiveQoL, a system that combines an ESM-based LINE application, Google Maps timeline, and Fitbit, to enable low-impact sampling of the following data: location, biometric data (e.g., heart rate), and types of daily activities for evaluating their satisfaction levels in smart cities. In this chapter, we first describe the design concept and system configuration of ActiveQoL. Then, we present two methods devised for diagnosing urban conditions from a person-centered perspective.

3.1 Design Concept

We define "ActiveQoL" as an evaluation method of QoL to continuously improve smart cities in terms of residents' QoL. The QoL here is not the mid-to or long-term QoL that is expected to be captured by questionnaires, such as the level of happiness when reflecting on one's life [1] or the level of life satisfaction looking back on two weeks used in the WHOQOL index [2], and so on. QoL in ActiveQoL is a measurement of satisfaction with the quality of activities per activity unit that constitutes a day, which is an even shorter span of time so that it can be evaluated in relation to various places and services in the city.

To collect satisfaction with the quality of these activities, basically, participants will require direct input (e.g., 5-point rating) for each actual daily life activity through the experiment term using the ESM. However, because this method requires a large burden on the participants and is not feasible for long-term experiments, in the future, we plan to estimate the level of their satisfaction by using the information on their attributes and preferences and data on the context of each situation captured from their smartphones and wearable devices. If this estimation can be implemented with high accuracy, it will be possible to diagnose cities from long-term data on people through automatic sensing by smartphones and wearables, without putting a large burden on participants in the experiment. However, since this study focuses on the purpose of exploring how location-based satisfaction can be used to diagnose urban conditions, it does not cover the estimation of satisfaction.

3.2 System Configuration

The ActiveQoL measurement tools are described below.

1. ActiveQoL-ESM: A system for collecting details of activities and satisfaction levels using the smartphone messaging application LINE.
2. Pre-questionnaire: An online questionnaire constructed using the online questionnaire service, Qualtrics CoreXM [18] to learn about personal attributes and preferences. The data are used to analyze how much satisfaction differs depending on these characteristics.
3. Google Maps - Timeline Function: Participants record their travel history during the experiment period on their smartphones using Google Maps' Timeline service for smartphones, and after anonymization, contribute the data to the project.
4. Fitbit Sense: a wearable activity meter, distributed to participants, will be used to collect anonymized biometric data such as heart rate and the number of steps walked.

The basic components are 1 and 2, with 3 and 4 added for the purpose of augmenting and analyzing information on activity content and location. In particular, this study discusses the analytical possibilities that can be extended by combining the data of 3. In addition, 3 and 4 were included to collect data to enable future estimation of activity satisfaction from smartphone and wearable sensor data without using 1.

The system configuration of ActiveQoL-ESM is described below. Smartphone penetration in Japan is almost 90% among those aged under 60 years and nearly 70% among those in their 60s. Anyone can participate, and the ability to be notified of incoming signals allows people to correctly hear what is going on at any given moment. Messaging applications are also used by many people, and there is no particular need to learn how to use them.

To take advantage of these features, we consider an ESM system for smartphones with the following four functions.

- Send questions periodically. Questions are timed out before the next question is sent to have the most recent question answered.
- Multiple questions are sent consecutively at a time. This is called a series of questions; as soon as one question is answered, the next question is sent.
- Answers are made by tapping on a single choice. The maximum number of choices should be one screenful.
- From the perspective of ActiveQoL, the following five questions should be the basic form of a series of questions.

a. What was the activity (that was being performed immediately before the answer)?
b. How was the activity? Answer on a 5-point scale from positive (satisfying, enjoyable, inspiring, etc.) to negative (unsatisfying, unpleasant, boring, etc.).
c. How long did you perform the activity?
d. With whom did you perform the activity?
e. Where did you perform the activity?

LINE provides not only the basic functionality for one-on-one or group chats among multiple people but also an API for companies to distribute advertisements and create chatbots. Using this API, we developed a system that can send questions at specified times and collect responses(see Fig. 2). The function for sending questions is designed to be highly flexible. Different questions and options can be set for each target person, and a different time can be set for each target person. The system can also set a timeout period for each question, and if the timeout period is exceeded, the system will not accept responses to that question, thereby sampling the experience at a specific time. The system is written in Google Spreadsheet and AppScript. First, the questions and options to be sent are registered in the spreadsheet, and a timer is set for the sending timing when the activation is triggered. The questions to be sent are processed in the order of their question IDs. After the transmission process, a notification of the question is sent to the LINE registered as a participant in the experiment. To prevent a large number of notifications sent to a single participant at one time, the system is set up to not send the next question until a response is submitted by the participant or until a time-out occurs.

To register participants, simply register ActiveQoL-ESM as a friend on LINE app. Once registered as a friend, the LINE user ID is registered as the registrant's ID in the registrant list on the system, but the individual's name and other personally identifiable information are not registered. To send questions, this registrant ID is used to register the questions and options to be sent in a spreadsheet.

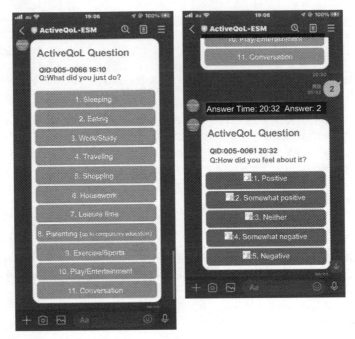

Fig. 2. Screen interface of ActiveQoL-ESM based on LINE app.

3.3   Evaluation Methods

In the initial stage of smart cities, services for many types of users (citizens) will undergo pilot tests with the aim of creating a city where no one is left behind to enhance their well-being. For example, there are services for the elderly to keep healthy, community building targeting parents of young children, environmental learning kits for children, and self-driving buses. It is important not only to capture the level of satisfaction but also to analyze the data so as to measure whether the well-being of people living in a smart city is appropriately enhanced through projects and to plan improvements to improve services and, hence, cities. In this study, we propose two analysis methods that focus on the features of the pattern of individual QoL perceptions for improvements in cities and projects.

Satisfaction-Based Method. First, we use decision tree methodology [19] with the objective variable as activity satisfaction to analyze the factors that lead to higher and lower activity satisfaction based on the data collected in the experiment. Decision tree methodology is one of the most widely used data classification methods in the medical and marketing fields. For the tree growth method, we will select CHi-squared Automatic Interaction Detector (CHAID), an automatic detection algorithm for interaction based on the chi-square test. Since CHAID repeats division by the combination of variables with the highest chi-square value, the variables closer to the parent node have a stronger correlation with activity satisfaction. We think this characteristic helps identify factors that have a large impact on activity satisfaction based on the placement of variables in the tree. We have 35 candidate explanatory variables. We seek to use the basic attributes of the participants in the experiment, personality characteristics, such as extroversion/introversion, and monetary sense of value, as collected from the pre-questionnaire. Variables related to the context of the activities actually performed include information collected from the ActiveQoL-ESM, such as what, where, with whom, and for how long, the time the notification was responded to, the time the person woke up that day, and the time they went to sleep the day before. In addition, information on whether they are at home or at work, which has become possible to obtain by linking to Google Maps timeline data, is used. Furthermore, by linking the ActiveQoL-ESM data with the pre-survey, the following data are generated: how much they like to do the activity (activity preference), under what conditions (where, with whom, how long) they like to do the activity, whether the conditions of the activity match their preferences for the actual conditions of the activity, and so on. To select explanatory variables, we first pick variables that correlate with activity satisfaction for activity X, which is the objective variable. Therefore, we set the case only for activity X responses and perform a chi-square test for each of the 35 variables listed above, and then extract the variables that are significant at $p < .005$. Next, to account for multicollinearity, we calculate the variance inflation factor (VIF) and finally select variables so that the VIF is less than 5.

Preference-Based Method. To examine urban improvements tailored according to people's characteristics, this method categorizes participants according to their activity preferences and activity satisfaction levels, and identifies the characteristics of each group (e.g., see Fig. 2). Why do we focus on activity preferences to categorize participants? We believe that activity preferences are an essential factor in deciding whose issues are prioritized for city improvement. In general, if you prefer to do activity X, you will tend to be highly satisfied with doing it, and if you dislike doing it, you will tend to be less satisfied with doing it. However, if the satisfaction level does not increase despite liking activity X, it is more likely that there is a problem with the environment of the activity or the context in which it is taking place in particular. Since smart cities are better at solving latent problems in these environments and situations than in the characteristics of the persons themselves, we consider that categorizing participants by their activity preferences is effective. Specifically, to improve services in a smart city, as shown in Table 1, we suggest dividing the respondents into three groups, A to C, and paying particular attention to Group B, which is considered to be particularly effective in improving services in a smart city. Group A comprises those who are highly satisfied with Activity X and do not consider that improvement is needed at this stage. Group C comprises those who are less satisfied with Activity X, but the reason is likely that they dislike doing Activity X, which makes it difficult to connect it to urban improvement as a smart city. Finally, Group B, which is the focus of this study, comprises those who like Activity X but have low satisfaction with it. There is high potential to increase their satisfaction by improving the quality of the urban environment.

Table 1. 3×4 types of people and three groups (A–C) for improvement of a smart city service for the preference-based method.

		No experience doing it	Activity Satisfaction "Exercise/Sports"		
			Negative (low satisfaction)	Neutral	Positive (high satisfaction)
Activity Preference "Exercise/Sports"	Like	B. "Prefer to do that activity but not satisfied with it." ⇒ QoL tends to be low, but there are opportunities to increase QoL.			A. "Likes and satisfied with doing that activity." ⇒ QoL is probably high.
	Neutral				
	Dislike	C. "Dislikes and is not satisfied with doing that activity." ⇒ QoL will almost certainly be lower and difficult to improve their QoL because we cannot force what they don't like to do.			

4 Field Test for the ActiveQoL Analysis Methods

4.1 Experiment Conditions

To test the two urban evaluation methods in practice and examine their effectiveness, we conducted a small-scale field experiment using ActiveQoL-ESM. We recruited participants for this experiment who could cooperate under the following conditions:

- Carry their own smartphone (required), and a wearable device (optional) and charge them daily for 28 days with setting the mode to record sensor data.
- Continue responding to the ActiveQoL-ESM (participants were not forced to respond to all notifications; they could respond to notifications when they noticed them and were ready to respond).
- Turn on the Google Maps timeline function at all times to automatically collect location data, and manually label their home on the Google Maps app.
- Provide all data collected through the experiment to us anonymously.

Because the experiment was in the early stages, we called for participants among researchers and students of our laboratories at The University of Tokyo and employees of Hitachi, Ltd. With which we were in a joint research project.

The experiment was conducted for 28 days, from December 1 to 28, 2022, with an incentive fee of 20,000 yen; 27 participants were recruited. Among them, there were 13 people who opted to utilize the Fitbit Sense wearable device. A breakdown of the participants is shown in Table 2.

Table 2. Breakdown of participants (gender, age, occupation).

	Age					Occupation				Total
	20s	30s	40s	50s	60s	University Researcher	Graduate Student	Employee (Research)	Employee (Other)	
Male	9	3	2	2	2	2	10	5	1	18
Female	7	1	1	0	0	3	3	3	0	9
Total	16	4	3	2	2	5	13	8	1	27

First, we provided experiment guidance on how to operate ActiveQoL-ESM and the other systems and to perform the initial setup. A preliminary questionnaire was conducted to clarify the participants' personal attributes and personality characteristics as well as their preferences for 14 activities and their conditions.

ActiveQoL-ESM sent a set of questions seven times a day, every 2 h from 7:30 to 19:30 during the experimental period. Each set of questions consists of six basic questions: the activity being performed now, its context (with whom, where, how long), and the level of mood for the activity on a 5-point scale (positive to negative). Furthermore, for the first set of questions of the day, we added three questions about when the participants went to bed the day before, when they woke up in the morning, and whether they slept well. The last question of the day was their level of satisfaction with the day on a 5-point scale.

A post-experiment questionnaire was conducted, asking about the usability, concerns about providing personal data, and impressions of participating in the experiment. We used the System Usability Scale (SUS), a simple and widely used instrument for evaluating various systems[20].

The experiment program was approved in advance by The University of Tokyo's Ethics Review Committee.

4.2 Results

We first present the basic performance of the ActiveQoL-ESM from quantitative data from the logs of the experiment and qualitative results from the post-experiment questionnaire. We also present the characteristics of the participants' satisfaction with the activity (rated on a 5-point scale of their moods during each activity).

As for the trial of the two analytical methods, satisfaction-based and preference-based, we present the results focusing on "work" and "study/learning," where the participants spent most of their time in the activities in this study.

Basic Performance of ActiveQoL-ESM. During the experiment, 5292 sets of questions were sent out, and 3833 of them (72.4%) were responded to. Individual differences in response rates were also found to be significant. For example, the response rate of those who responded the most was 97.4%, while the response rate of those who responded the least was 27.6%. A comparison by the time of day when notifications were sent shows the lowest response rate at 7:30 a.m., the first time of the day (444 responses, 58.7%), and the highest response rate at 11:30 a.m. (590 responses, 78.0%). The response rate tended to gradually decrease as the days passed and fell below 70% in the final week. 27 The average perceived usability of ActiveQoL-ESM was 63, which is below to the average SUS score (68). Only eight participants (30%) rated above 68, indicating that the system still remains difficult to use. From the open-ended comments in the post-experiment questionnaire, several comments pointed out similar usability issues, such as "I feel inconvenienced that it takes 2–3 min to respond to a set of questions," "The workload is too large and reduces QoL," and "The usability of the system is not enough for ordinary people with ordinary IT literacy." Meanwhile, there were also positive comments, such as "I felt I got a new bird's eye view of my life" through the process of responding to the sets of questions and checking location information in the experiment, "If feedback on the results and the analysis is returned to the participants, it will motivate me to continue to the experiment," and "It will be interesting to know how my data are analyzed." Furthermore, we asked how many days respondents would be able to cooperate without pay for an experiment using the current prototype in the post-experiment questionnaire; 9 (33%) replied less than 1 week, and 11 (40%) replied 1–2 weeks, indicating that 1 week was a realistic level of cooperation for free.

Activity Satisfaction. The mean of the 5-point scale (1: negative, 3: neutral, 5: positive) for the participants' mood during each activity in the responses of the ActiveQoL-ESM was 3.54 with a standard deviation of 1.02. The distribution of participants' mood for each activity is shown in Fig. 3. We regard the mood of the participants for each activity as their at-the-moment satisfaction with the activity, and use it as an indicator to refer to in order to improve smart city policies. Although the number of negative (1,2) responses seems small in the total responses, it is clear that negative moods occur with a non-negligible probability in some activities. For example, work, with the largest number of responses, has more than 27% negative moods, followed by transport (18.6%), study/learning (12.0%), rest (9.3%), sleep (9.2%), and household chores (8.8%). In addition, to improve the wellbeing of people living in a smart city, it is important to try to minimize not only negative but also neutral mood factors. Since the percentage of neutral mood in each activity tends to be different from that of negative mood, it seems we should consider different strategies for urban improvement (see Table 3).

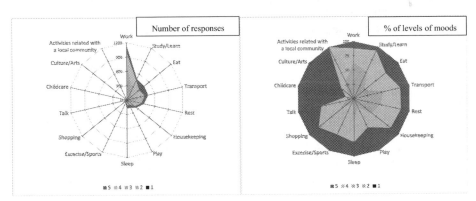

Fig. 3. Radar charts showing the percentage of 5 mood levels for each activity. The left side figure shows the number of activity responses to the ActiveQoL-ESM, and the right side figure shows its percentage.

Testing Analysis Methods. Hereafter, to test and compare the three analysis methods to find the pattern of individual QoL perceptions, we focused on work (1143 responses) and study/learning, (485 responses) the activities that the participants spend most of their time and respond to the ActiveQoL-ESM in large numbers. Since about half of the participants in this study were graduate students, and for them, academic work is

Table 3. Activities for which priority attention should be given for urban improvement.

Activities for which it is critical to address reducing negative moods (number of responses, % of total; >5%)		Activities for which it is critical to address reducing neutral moods (number of responses, % of total; >5%)	
Work	(310, 27.2%)	Study/Learning	(198, 40.8%)
Transport	(85, 18.6%)	Rest	(140, 38.4%)
Study/Learning	(58, 12.0%)	Work	(403, 35.4%)
Rest	(34, 9.3%)	Transport	(156, 34.1%)
Sleep	(16, 9.2%)	Activities related to local commu-	(2, 33.3%)
Household chores	(22, 8.8%)	nity	(77, 30.8%)
		Household chores	(18, 28.6%)
		Shopping	(48, 27.7%)
		Sleep	(98, 21.1%)
		Eat	(6, 14.6%)
		Talk	(25, 14.0%)
		Play	(3, 13.6%)
		Culture/Arts	(4, 6.0%)
		Exercise/Sports	

their lifework as well as work in the working people, work and study/learning data were combined for these analyses.

Satisfaction-Based. Figure 4 shows the results of the decision tree methodology, narrowed down to the ActiveQoL-ESM responses for work and study/learning and using satisfaction with these activities as the objective variables. We used IBM SPSS Statistics ver.29.0.0.0 for the analysis and Exhaustive CHAID for the tree growth method. The values defining the maximum depth of the tree were set to standard settings; the maximum number of CHAID levels: 3, the minimum number of output cases: 100 parent nodes and 50 child nodes.

The results of the 5-point scale for mood (interpreted as satisfaction) while working or studying were 40% Strong Positive + Positive, 37% Neutral, and 23% Negative + Strong Negative. First, occupation was taken as the variable with the strongest correlation with activity satisfaction in the tree. It would be a reasonable result we think since company employees, university researchers, and graduate students each perform very different tasks. Looking at the entire tree, we observe that university researchers and graduate students are relatively satisfied with their work, while company employees tend to be less satisfied. Next, under occupation, physical/psychological concerns in performing work/study are addressed in the case of graduate students and company employees. Graduate students tended to be more satisfied with higher levels of the concerns and were especially satisfied when they were working alone or with family friends. By contrast, company employees tended to be less satisfied when they were experiencing physical or psychological concerns. In particular, people who are more socially active tended to have lower levels of satisfaction. When there are no physical/psychological concerns, women tend to be more satisfied than men. In contrast to the other participants, university and college researchers have optimistic/pessimistic as a variable representing personal characteristics. While those who are more optimistic tend to be more satisfied,

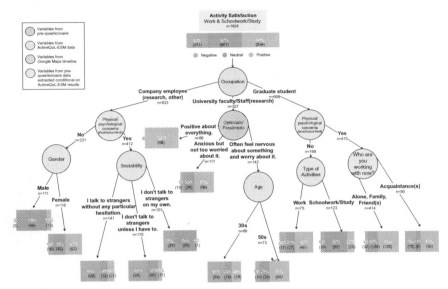

Fig. 4. Decision tree mapping based on activity types "Work" and "Schoolwork/Study" (the relative risk: 0.378, the standard error: 0.012).

a group of participants aged in their 30s who are more pessimistic appear to be less satisfied.

Preference-Based. Table 4 shows the number of ActiveQoL-ESM responses in each of the nine cells by crossing activity satisfaction (three levels) for work and study combined and their activity preferences (three levels). The area marked by the yellow line represents group A, which already has a high level of satisfaction without taking any action, as shown in Subsect. 3.2. The area marked with a blue line denotes group C, which has a low level of satisfaction but dislikes the activity, and thus, requires a different approach to improve it than a smart city does. The area marked in red represents group B, which is considered the most applicable target for smart city improvement. To characterize each group, we conducted a chi-square test using 35 candidate explanatory variables and extracted variables for which significant relations were found. In addition, we examined which items showed significant differences by percentages of residuals analysis. Table 5 shows the variables with significant relationships for each group, focusing only on items with significant positive residuals to make the characteristics clearer. The results show that Group B includes a specific age group and occupation: company employees in their 40s (research). Furthermore, as a factor behind the low level of work satisfaction, although they like their work, from the result that they had a higher challenging mindset than the other groups, but a lower level of day satisfaction, we can assume that there might have been an occurrence that made a big gap between their feelings and the actual situation that day. In addition, since a specific location was extracted as an explanatory variable, we can hypothesize that it might be possible to improve the extracted work environment as one of the strategies.

Table 4. Preference-based categorization based on the number of ActiveQoL-ESM responses for the activities of work and study/learning (groups marked in red that should be prioritized for consideration of smart city solutions).

			Activity Satisfaction			
			Negative 1~2	Nutral 3	Positive 4~5	Total
Activity Preference	Like	3.7~5.0	B 113	135	295	543
	Nutral	2.4~3.6	195	426 A	324	945
	Dislike	1.0~2.3	C 60	40	37	137
	Total		368	601	656	1625

5   Discussion

5.1   Importance and Challenges of Measuring Satisfaction with Each Activity

The important role of city planners and administrators is to allocate the limited budget to important categories and formulate strategies in order of priority. If they could know the quantity of activities being performed and the quality of the activities (satisfaction), it would be important information for prioritizing what to improve in the city. From the breakdown of the responses to the ActiveQoL-ESM for the experiment we conducted (Fig. 3), it was possible to visualize the distribution of the number of activities observed and the level of activity satisfaction for each of the activities. For example, for work, it can be seen that while the frequency is overwhelmingly higher than for the other activities, the percentage of those who are highly satisfied is less than half, which is less than for the other activities. As in this example, it is possible to approach QoL improvement for a large number of people by focusing on activities that have a large number of people engaged but few people with high satisfaction levels. In addition, niche activities with low frequency generally tend to be put off for improvement. However, by using ActiveQoL, it will be possible to find activities with a small frequency but with satisfaction issues (e.g., transportation, rest, housework in this case), shed light on issues contained in niche activities, and consider individualized solutions in an inclusive approach.

Meanwhile, one of the challenges in recording activities using the ESM is a problem of recording bias, as some activities are easy to record and some are difficult. For example, it should be noted that some activities that are extremely difficult to respond to cannot be recorded, such as activities that are easy to respond to (e.g., desk work) while activities that are difficult to respond to might not be recorded (e.g., face-to-face work with customers), or activities that are short in duration might not be recorded (e.g., greeting neighbors) while activities that are long in duration could be recorded (e.g., work). In the future, we hope that smartphones and wearable devices will be able to provide highly accurate estimates of the activities being performed. However, since it is difficult to achieve it immediately, for the time being, we think it is important to organize in advance all the activities that are difficult to be recorded by the ESM, so that those who conduct the analysis will understand them without neglecting them.

Table 5. Variables with significant correlation detected by chi-square analysis for Groups A–C. As a result of residual analysis, items with positive values out of the standard errors (1.96 or more) with significant differences are shown together with their values. In this table, only those with phi coefficients of 0.2 or higher (i.e., those that have a correlation with Groups A–C) are shown.

Correlation	Candidate variable	Group A N=656	Group B N=113	Group C N=100
Strong Relation	Age $\chi^2(8, N=869) = 346.026$, $p<0.001, \varphi=0.631$	~20s (+6.8) 30s (+4.8) 60s (+2.1)	40s (+11.4)	50s (+14.6)
	Occupation $\chi^2(6, N=869) = 305.856$, $p<0.001, \varphi=0.5.93$	Graduate student (+8.2) University faculty/Staff (+6.7)	Company employee (Research) (+9.3)	Company employee (Research) (+8.5) Company employee (Other) (+10.0)
	Challenge mind $\chi^2(8, N=869) = 291.205$, $p<0.001, \varphi=0.579$	Rather proactive in tackling (+7.2) Rather reluctant (+4.2)	Proactive in tackling anything (+11.0)	Neither (+12.9)
	Satisfaction with the day $\chi^2(8, N=794) = 229.355$, $p<0.001, \varphi=0.537$	Slightly positive (+5.2) Positive (+7.1)	Negative (+6.5) Slightly negative (+10.6)	Neutral (+2.3) Slightly negative (+3.2)
	Waking time $\chi^2(14, N=579) = 111.179$, $p<0.001, \varphi=0.438$	7:30–8:00 (+2.0) 8:00–8:30 (+2.1) After 8:30 (+2.9)	-6:00 (+3.9) 6:00–6:30 (+2.4)	6:30–7:00 (+3.3) 7:00–7:30 (+7.7)
	Which office you are at? $\chi^2(10, N=869) = 166.117$, $p<0.001, \varphi=0.437$	Kashiwa Campus, The University of Tokyo (+4.2)	Hitachi Office, Hitachi, Ltd. (+12.1)	Except workplaces (+3.2)
	Outdoors/Indoors $\chi^2(8, N=869) = 151.229$, $p<0.001, \varphi=0.417$	Definitely prefer being outdoors (+2.1) Prefer staying indoors (+5.6) Definitely prefer staying indoors (+4.2)	Prefer both (+9.5)	Prefer being outdoors (+7.3)
Weak Relation	Gender $\chi^2(2, N=869) = 106.342$, $p<0.001, \varphi=0.350$	Female (+10.1)	Male (+5.5)	Male (+7.9)
	Sociability $\chi^2(6, N=869) = 102.521$, $p<0.001, \varphi=0.343$	2 (+4.2)	3 (+8.8)	2 (+3.6)
	Family $\chi^2(4, N=869) = 85.921$, $p<0.001, \varphi=0.314$	Living alone (+6.5)	Living with family (+4.0)	Living with non-family (+6.9)
	Physical and psychological concerns about the activities $\chi^2(2, N=869) = 82.673$, $p<0.001, \varphi=0.308$	No concerns (+8.9)	Concerns (+4.9)	Concerns (+6.9)
	Time went to sleep the day before $\chi^2(10, N=565) = 47.417$, $p<0.001, \varphi=0.290$		11:00p.m.– 0:00a.m. (+2.7)	10:00p.m.– 11:00p.m. (+5.3)
	Optimistic/Pessimistic $\chi^2(6, N=869) = 58.569$, $p<0.001, \varphi=0.260$	Positive about everything (+6.3)	I feel anxious but I don't worry too much (+3.0)	I feel anxious but I don't worry too much (+5.4)

In addition, depending on the charting technique for showing trends in activity satisfaction, it may appear that different issues are found in the graphs. In Fig. 3, the radar chart is created by the total number of the ESM responses for each activity, but this graph cannot account for bias in the number of responses among participants. For example, if a few people are engaged in a particular activity and highly satisfied with it, while others are not satisfied with the activity and quit immediately, their dissatisfaction may be overlooked because the number of the ESM responses is not large, even though there are a non-negligible number of people who are not satisfied with the activity. Therefore, it is important to not only simply look at the number of the ESM responses, but also to calculate the average of each person's activity satisfaction for a particular activity X, look at the distribution of the average, and devise an analysis that does not overlook the satisfaction level of those who are less frequently involved in the activity.

Furthermore, another problem with the ActiveQoL-ESM survey is that it is impossible to collect the level of satisfaction with activity X from those who have not performed activity X. In other words, it is not possible to include the activity satisfaction ratings of those who had done activity X before the experimental period, but quit doing the activity itself due to low satisfaction. Therefore, it is considered that a different survey approach, such as a web-based questionnaire, will be necessary for them.

5.2 Features of Satisfaction-Based and Preference-Based Analysis Methods

In this experiment, we test the satisfaction-based and preference-based analysis methods we designed, focusing on work and study/learning, and consider we were able to confirm that each method can extract some target personas and environmental conditions that need priority improvement. For example, in the satisfaction-based analysis shown in Fig. 4, we can clearly observe that those who are less satisfied with their work/study are predominantly company employees who have physical and psychological concerns. By type of occupation, satisfaction tends to be lower among the more pessimistic 30s university faculty/staff and among graduate students who indicated that they had physical/psychological concerns when they were engaged in activities with acquaintances. The preference-based analysis in Tables 4 and 5 also shows that Group B, who like the activity itself but have low satisfaction, is significantly different from Groups A and C. It can be considered that in Fig. 4, some of the company employees in the low satisfaction group are in Group B. If we can grasp the attributes of the targets who are in low satisfaction and the context of their activities to some extent, we can conduct in-depth surveys by interviewing the targets even if we cannot directly find the factors that lower their satisfaction level. In addition, it would be possible to consider strategies to deeply approach the factors that lower the level of satisfaction.

First, the decision tree method used in the satisfaction-based method is a white-box model that can explain why the output came out, and unlike the black-box models often seen in machine learning, it has high explanatory potential. We believe that utilizing such white-box models may be effective for people to draw concrete targets for strategy improvement. On a side note, one of the drawbacks of decision trees is the characteristic that a slight change in the data can significantly change the predicted results (large variance). To reduce this variance, ensemble learning with random forests recommended, but we did not conduct it in this experiment.

In preference-based analysis, meanwhile, is a method to classify targets in advance by intentionally focusing on the activity preference variable, since the type of strategy to be considered differs greatly depending on differences in activity preferences. By classifying targets in advance, it is possible to grasp the ratio of the number of people (Table 4) in advance, and the scale and priority of actions for each target can be easily estimated. It is also possible to grasp how the number of people has shifted before and after the launch of the action, making it easy to measure whether the action is appropriately effective or not. From the above, it is important to effectively use the two different types of analysis: the satisfaction-based approach is useful for finding people in need in an exploratory way, while the preference-based approach is useful for understanding the target population and characteristics of the proposed actions, and for evaluating their effectiveness.

5.3   Toward a Long-Term ESM Survey

In the satisfaction-based and preference-based analyses, besides personal attributes and personality, the data of responses to the ESM were also taken up as several highly influential variables (what activity the participants are doing, with whom they are doing the activity, satisfaction for the day, waking time, sleeping time, and location of the workplace). Thus, to measure people's satisfaction, we found it necessary to collect not only static data such as web surveys, but also dynamic data through ActiveQoL-ESM. Therefore, it will be essential to improve the usability of the ActiveQoL-ESM so that participants can tolerate its operation over a long period of time.

First, to reduce the number of input items each time, it would be good to be able to switch to automatic estimation for activity types and contexts that are manually inputted yet have high estimation accuracy based on sensor data. For example, in terms of activity types, activities such as traveling, sleeping, and exercising, which show significant changes in acceleration and biometric sensor data, already have high classification accuracy and are being used in commercial applications. However, for activities such as work, where there are large individual differences in motion, it is difficult to classify using all the data. However, for activities such as work, where there are large individual differences in motion, it is difficult to classify using all data, so we would like to achieve improved classification accuracy by using individual history and learning from it. There are also activities and contextual information that are difficult to estimate adequately with commodity devices such as smartphones and Fitbit. For example, some classifications, such as whether the person who is working with you right now is a friend or an acquaintance, are difficult for automatic classification and must continue to rely on human labor using ESMs.

Furthermore, as indicated by the results of the post-questionnaire to the ActiveQoL experiment participants, we obtained several responses suggesting that providing feedback to them on the results of their input to the ESM may be effective for their continued participation. According to a 2016 Harvard Business School experiment comparing the effectiveness of monitoring (the feeling of being watched by others) and incentives (rewards), the monitoring group that received regular reports from an external source was more likely to continue the habit than the group that received incentives [22]. It is likely that implementing a reporting function as well as incentives such as rewards would be an effective way to do so.

5.4 Limitation

In this study, we analyzed the results of the experiment using the ActiveQoL-ESM only for work + schoolwork and compared the analysis methods. It is difficult to say whether the results of this study are generalizable to all activities, since some activities may be difficult to analyze with the amount of data we collected.

6 Conclusion

We hypothesized that activity satisfaction could be a useful new indicator for improving the QoL of individuals living in smart cities, and developed the ActiveQoL-ESM to collect activity satisfaction from the daily lives of individuals. We also proposed two methods; satisfaction-based and preference-based to improve cities by analyzing activity satisfaction, and through experiments investigated the characteristics and differences between them. The results of both methods show that they can reveal patterns of individual QoL perceptions based on contextual data collected from smartphones, as well as attributes and personality. In particular, we found that the satisfaction-based method can be used to analyze the current status of a city, while the preference-based method can be used for the ex-post evaluation of urban measures.

Acknowledgments. . The authors would like to thank all participants of the experiment using ActiveQoL-ESM in the long term. Especially, we would like to thank Deguchi and Warisawa Laboratory, and Hitachi and U-Tokyo Lab for cooperating with recruiting participants. This work was supported by the Habitat Innovation Project of H-UTokyo Lab, which is an industry-academia joint project between Hitachi, Ltd. And The University of Tokyo.

References

1. Khayal, I.S., Farid, A.M.: Designing smart cities for citizen health & well-being. In: 2017 IEEE First Summer School on Smart Cities (S3C), pp. 120–125. IEEE (2017)
2. The WHOQOL Group: The Development of the World Health Organization Quality of Life Assessment Instrument (the WHOQOL). In: Orley, J., Kuyken, W. (eds.) Quality of Life Assessment: International Perspectives. Springer, Berlin, Heidelberg (1994). https://doi.org/10.1007/978-3-642-79123-9_4
3. Cambridge Dictionary. https://dictionary.cambridge.org/. Accessed 18 Mar 2023
4. Hektner, J.M., Schmidt, J.A., Csikszentmihalyi, M.: Experience sampling method: Measuring the quality of everyday life. Sage (2007)
5. European Commission: Urban Audit. https://ec.europa.eu/regional_policy/en/policy/themes/urban-development/audit/. Accessed 18 Mar 2023
6. OECD Better Life Index. https://www.oecdbetterlifeindex.org/. Accessed 18 Mar 2023
7. European Commission: Quality of life in European cities. https://ec.europa.eu/regional_policy/en/information/maps/quality_of_life. Accessed 18 Mar 2023

8. Gross Arakawa Happiness: GAH. https://rilac.or.jp/?page_id=307. Accessed 18 Mar 2023
9. Smart City Institute Japan Liveable Well-Being City Indicator. https://www.sci-japan.or.jp. Accessed 18 Mar 2023
10. The Australian Prevention Partnership Center: Liveability indicators. https://preventioncentre. org.au/wp-content/uploads/2021/10/03-Liveability-Indicators.pdf. Accessed 18 Mar 2023
11. Energy Lab: Area Quaria Indicator (in japanese), http://datastock.sub.jp/fiacs/area-qualia-ind ex20221014-1.pdf. Accessed 18 Mar 2023
12. Csikszentmihalyi, M., Larson, R., Prescott, S.: The ecology of adolescent activity and experience. J. Youth Adolesc. **6**(3), 281–294 (1977)
13. Barrett, L.F., Barrett, D.J.: An introduction to computerized experience sampling in psychology. Soc. Sci. Comput. Rev. **19**(2), 175–185 (2001)
14. mEMA-Sense. https://apps.apple.com/jp/app/mema-sense/id1457623580. Accessed 18 Mar 2023
15. Better Evaluation: MetricWire. https://www.betterevaluation.org/tools-resources/metricwire. Accessed 18 Mar 2023
16. Idealab: ESpecialy Me (in japanese). http://esm.life/howto. Accessed 18 Mar 2023
17. JESMA: Exkuma (in japanese). https://www.jesma.jp/exkuma. Accessed 18 Mar 2023
18. Qualtrics CoreEX. https://www.qualtrics.com/jp/core-xm/. Accessed 18 Mar 2023
19. Hastie, T.J., Tibshirani, R.J., Friedman, J.H.: The Elements of Statistical Learning: Data Mining Inference and Prediction. 2nd edn. Springer, New York (2009). https://doi.org/10. 1007/978-0-387-84858-7
20. Brooke, J.: SUS: A 'quick and dirty' usability scale. In: Jordan, P., Thomas, B., Weerdmeester, B. (eds.) Usability Evaluation in Industry, pp. 189–194. Taylor & Francis, London, UK (1996)
21. From, W.: SUS: a retrospective. J. Usability Stud. **8**(2), 29–40 (2013)
22. Hussam, R., Rabbani, A., Reggiani, G., Rigol, N.: Rational habit formation: experimental evidence from handwashing in India. Am. Econ. J. Appl. Econ. **14**(1), 1–41 (2022)

Mutual Recall Between Onomatopoeia and Motion Using Doll Play Corpus

Takuya Takahashi[1,2] and Yasuyuki Sumi[1(✉)]

[1] Future University Hakodate, Hakodate, Hokkaido 0418655, Japan
t-takahashi@sumilab.org, sumi@acm.org
[2] Presently, with GREE, Inc.,Tokyo, Japan

Abstract. Onomatopoeia is used to describe the state and degree of movement. Since onomatopoeia is a linguistic symbol, it is expected that many people will recall the same image corresponding to the onomatopoeia. Is this really true? In this paper, we focus on playing with dolls, collect onomatopoeia uttered during doll play, and construct a corpus of co-occurrence relations between onomatopoeia and doll movements. In order to verify the value of this corpus, we confirm the recall of movement from onomatopoeia and vice versa. As an application example based on this corpus, we also present a prototype of "onomatopoeia camera," a system that automatically adds onomatopoeia and comic-like expressions to subjects' movements.

Keywords: Onomatopoeia · Motion corpus · SAX · Onomatopoeia camera

1 Introduction

Onomatopoeia is commonly used in our daily conversations. For example, we Japanese use an onomatopoeia "teku teku" to describe the state of walking motion and use another onomatopoeia "sasa" to describe faster movement.

Onomatopoeia is often thought as childish words or words just for extra decoration. Onomatopoeia, however, has attractive characteristics that bridge between linguistic symbols and unfixed concepts associated with bodily movements, mental status, and surrounding situations. We believe the deeper understanding of onomatopoeia leads us to mutual understanding among people having diffent culture, and between people and robots.

To date, many books and dictionaries focusing on onomatopoeia have been published. However, it is not enough to gather and discuss onomatopoeia as linguistic information to approach the essence of the characteristics of onomatopoeia. In this paper, we build an onomatopoeia corpus by collecting motion data of subjects as well as uttered onomatopoeia at the same time in order to enable more data-driven discussion of onomatopoeia. This paper also shows our attempt to build a system which mutually recalls between motion and onomatopoeia based on the corpus.

N. A. Streitz and S. Konomi (Eds.): HCII 2023, LNCS 14036, pp. 265–280, 2023.
https://doi.org/10.1007/978-3-031-34668-2_18

It is practically difficult to collect onomatopoeia and surrounding data comprehensively in daily life. So, we chose doll play as a target where we collect data related on onomatopoeia because we can observe many onomatopoeia is uttered along with doll movements. We collected onomatopoeic utterances and corresponding doll motion during doll plays for building an onomatopoeia corpus.

This paper describes our attempt to collect doll's motion data recalled from various onomatopoeia. We build a corpus consisting of onomatopoeia and corresponding motion. We analyze the corpus on how motion associated with onomatopoeia converges or disperses depending on doll players. Secondly, we show the diversion of the corpus to recall suitable onomatopoeia from various motion measured in other domains such as human actions and robot behaviors. Lastly, we also show applications based on the corpus, e.g., a prototyped system called "onomatopoeia camera", that automatically adds onomatopoeia and comic-like expressions to a photo according to the motion of the subject in the photo.

2   Related Work

There has been attempts to evaluate onomatopoeia quantitatively [6,7]. In these work, onomatopoeia was represented by multiple vectors corresponding to human impressions. Another work presented a method that enables the estimation and depiction of onomatopoeia in computer generated animation based on physical parameters [2]. There were studies focus on the sounds recalled from onomatopoeia [8,10,11]. In the work utilizing the features of onomatopoeia, there was an attempt to propose a system that can present the user with a list of onomatopoeia specific to a restaurant they are interested in [5]. In another study, they produced an onomatopoeic learning support tool for Japanese learners [12].

Thus, analysis of onomatopoeia is often done by focusing on the impressions and sounds of words. We believe, however, that analysis of linguistic information alone is insufficient. Therefore, we construct a corpus consisting of onomatopoeia and motion. We also propose a system for recalling onomatopoeia using the corpus. We observe what kind of onomatopoeia the proposed system recalls from motion queries in various domains. We also analyze the relationship between onomatopoeia and motion.

3   Motion Corpus

3.1   Corpus Consisting of Onomatopoeia and Motion

In this work, we construct a corpus that enables mutual recall between onomatopoeia and doll motion. The configuration of the corpus is a collection of doll motion data expressed by participants for each onomatopoeia (Fig. 1). Each doll motion data is a position coordinate of three axes and a rotation value of three axes, and each value is obtained by extracting a motif in the doll movement.

This chapter describes the construction of the corpus and the clustering of doll motions in each onomatopoeia in the corpus.

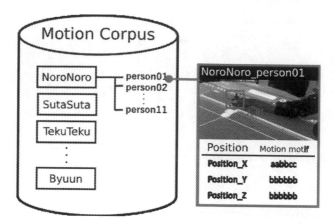

Fig. 1. Motion corpus consisting of onomatopoeia and corresponding motion of doll.

3.2 Data Collection of Doll Motion

As a situation setting for constructing the motion corpus, we focused on doll play in which onomatopoeia is likely to be uttered. Participants were presented with onomatopoeic words as shown in Fig. 2 and asked to express the movements evoked by the onomatopoeic words with a doll. We collected doll movements and onomatopoeias as label data. The participants were 11 male university students. The onomatopoeia presented to participants was 21 words, and they expressed doll movements three times at each onomatopoeic word. As a result, a total of 693 doll movements were collected.

The doll movement is time-series data consisting of three dimensional position coordinates and rotation values. We measured doll movements using optical motion capture system (OptiTrack system with eight cameras). The doll movements are defined as the X-axis for the front direction of the doll, the Y-axis for the vertical direction, and the Z-axis for the horizontal direction. The rotation of these three axes is Roll, Yow, and Pitch.

We used 21 onomatopoeic words that we had previously observed in playing with dolls (Table 1). In the doll play, each of the three participants held one doll and were asked to play with it freely on the table, which was recorded on video. From the video recordings of the doll play, we extracted the onomatopoeia frequently uttered by participants. We also added some onomatopoeic words from a Japanese onomatopoeia dictionary that are similar to the onomatopoeia collected in the doll play.

3.3 Extracting Motion Motif Using SAX

The range of movement of the collected dolls varied widely from participant to participant. For example, some people exaggerated the doll's walking movement, while others expressed it in a modest manner. It is not possible to quantify the

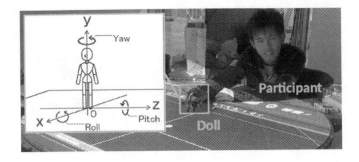

Fig. 2. Collecting motion data of doll movement associated by given onomatopoeia.

Table 1. Onomatopoeia prepared to build our corpus.

onomatopoeia expressing walking and running						
Noro Noro	Ta Ta Ta	Teku Teku	Da Da Da	Toko Toko	Dota Dota	Suta Suta
onomatopoeia expressing jumping and flying						
Pyon	Pyoon	Byon	Byoon	Hyuun	Pyuun	Byuun
onomatopoeia expressing collision						
Doon	Doka	Dosun	Poyon	Kotsun	Gotsun	Zudon

intrinsic proximity between the doll movements generated by multiple participants if the physical quantities related to the doll movements are used as they are. Therefore, to be able to handle the qualitative proximity of each doll movement, we extracted the movement motifs from the doll movements and converted them into string representations.

We used Symbolic Aggregate Approximation (SAX) as a method to extract motion motifs from doll movements. SAX is one of the methods proposed by Lin et al. [9] for compressing time-series data, which converts the time-series data into character strings. Therefore, it is possible to use converted character strings to apply to pattern search and natural language processing for time-series data. In this study, the character string obtained by SAX is the automaton in one doll movement [1,3,4]. The procedure of SAX is shown below (Fig. 3).

1. Normalizing time-series data and divid into w equal sized frames. Mean value of the data falling within a frame is calculated.
2. Determining breakpoints that will produce equal sized areas under Gaussian curve. Set the character of each area.
3. Converting the mean value of each frame to a character.

The features of SAX include character string length(w) and character type(a) parameters after converting. We set the character string length to 20 and the

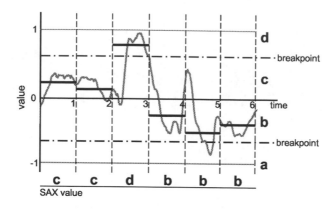

Fig. 3. String conversion of time-series data by SAX.

character kind 3 (w = 20, a = 3). We applied SAX to each of the three dimensional position coordinates and rotation values included in the obtained 693 doll movement data.

SAX converts data to relative values in order to normalize time-series data. We can compare with other data and measure the similarity between data, using the value converted to a character string at SAX. The threshold value for converting to a character string is automatically set to follow the normal distribution of the normalized time-series data. Therefore, SAX can mechanically convert unknown time-series data.

3.4   Cluster Analysis of Our Motion Corpus

We analyzed a hierarchical clustering of how the collected movements from doll play were grouped in each onomatopoeia in the motion corpus. Figure 4 on the left is a tree diagram obtained by hierarchical clustering, and the percentage of each class belonging to each onomatopoeia was calculated (right).

Most of the data for walking and running onomatopoeia were collected in C3. When these doll movements were checked, it was found that they were walking on the tabletop (Fig. 5). This indicates that the motions recalled from walking and running onomatopoeia are easy to unite independently of each other. From this, it was confirmed that the movements recalled by walking and running onomatopoeia are easily grouped into one class without depending on the person.

On the other hand, jumping and flying onomatopoeia tended to fall into the C1 and D classes, but were found to be dispersed in each class. The doll movements performed by the subject, which involved jumping and flying, were described by some as expressing a high mountain-shaped flight, while others as gliding horizontally with respect to the ground (Fig. 6). Therefore, it is considered that there was a difference in the vertical direction in the doll movement. From these results, it was confirmed that the motions recalled from the onomatopoeia that jumps and flies depend on people and belong to various classes.

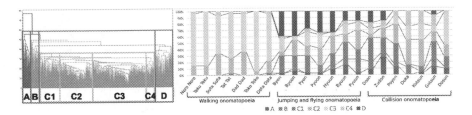

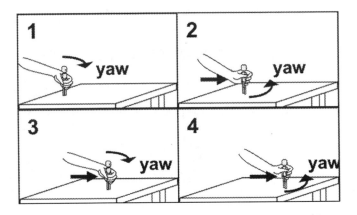

Fig. 4. Cluster analysis of doll motion data (left figure). Class distribution of motion data of each onomatopoeia (right figure).

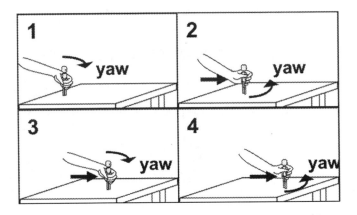

Fig. 5. An example of motion recalled from walking onomatopoeia.

Collision-type onomatopoeia tended to fall into the C1 and D classes but was found to be dispersed in each class. We confirmed the doll movements expressing the collision type onomatopoeia, various collision expressions were seen, such as colliding with something while walking or flying, falling down (Fig. 7). Therefore, it is considered that the difference between each motion data value was generated and distributed to each class. From these results, it was confirmed that the motions recalled from the collision type onomatopoeia tended to depend on each individual and belonged to each class.

4   Recalling Onomatopoeia from Motion

We prototyped a system that recalls onomatopoeia from arbitrary motion data. Figure 8 is an overview of the system.

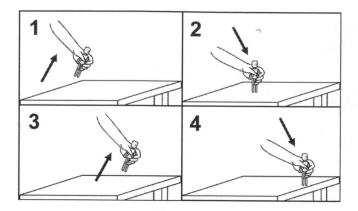

Fig. 6. An example of motion recalled from jumping and flying onomatopoeia.

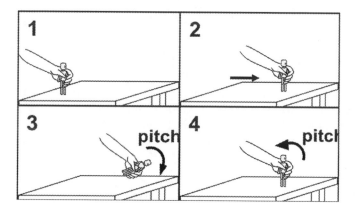

Fig. 7. An example of motion recalled from collision onomatopoeia.

4.1   Measuring Motion as Query

One of our goals is to recall onomatopoeia from movements in various domains. However, the range of motion as measured by the domain varies. For example, there are some ranges of motion such as doll play on a table and human physical movement. The information necessary for a motion query are three dimensional position coordinate and rotation. This section describes how to measure motion.

Doll movement in doll play or small robot motion are small range. For these domains, we used the motion capture system to measure the motion. We attached a few motion capture markers to a object of interest and created a rigid body. The position coordinate value and the rotation value of the created rigid body were measured. The motion capture system has high measurement accuracy of motion because it use many tracking camera. However, this system set up many cameras in a space. The measurable range of this system is small.

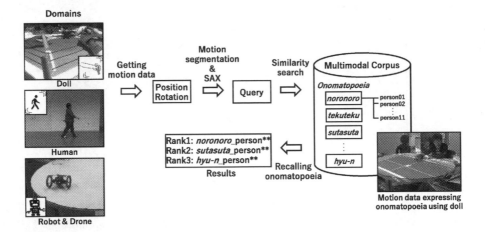

Fig. 8. Recalling onomatopoeia using our motion corpus.

The range of human activity related to walking and jumping movements is very large compared to playing with dolls. We used acceleration sensor and gyroscope sensor in this domain. We attached these sensors to a object and measured motion data. The position coordinate value and rotation value is obtained by integrating the obtained motion data. The measurable range using these sensors is big because these are easily mounted. However, the motion capture system has low measurement accuracy of motion.

4.2   Calculating Similarity Among Motions

The system performs a similarity search using motion data as the query. We used the Levenshtein distance as the method for similarity search. Levenshtein distance is a measure of the similarity between two strings. The distance is the number of deletions, insertions, and substitutions required to transform query characters into purpose characters. The greater the Levenshtein distance, the more different the characters are. This system calculate the Levenshtein distance between motifs of motion query extracted by SAX and each motion data in motion corpus. After performing the similarity search based on the motion, onomatopoeia of motion data with a shorter similarity distance is taken as the searching result.

5   Applying Doll Corpus into Other Domains

We observed that the proposed system recalls what kind of onomatopoeia from motion queries of various domains. We focused on doll play, small robot and human body movement in daily life as a domain. We confirm if motion dictionary have versatility through recalling onomatopoeia from multiple domains.

5.1   Within "Doll" Domain

Measurement of Doll Play. We observed that proposed system recalls what kind of onomatopoeia from doll motion in doll play (Fig. 9). Motion with high degree of freedom than motion corpus doll motion can be seen in doll play. In the case of same as motion corpus domain, we confirm that whatever proposed system can recall an onomatopoeia suitable for motion.

Three participants hold a doll and play with dolls on the table about five minutes. We prepared three types of dolls: hero, monster, and anthropomorphic tower. A projector displayed a wrestling stage on the table. We asked three participants to play with dolls freely. We measured the dolls motion using motion capture system.

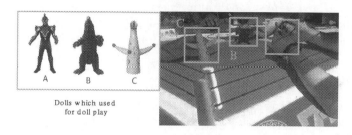

Fig. 9. Doll play: Playing with dolls on a table with a wrestling stage projected on it.

Recalling Onomatopoeia. As a result of onomatopoeia recalling from doll motion in doll play, walking motion recalled walking system onomatopoeia such as "*Suta Suta*" and "*Toko Toko*". Collision and overturning motion recalled collision system onomatopoeia such as "*kotsun*" and "*gotsun*". Motion queries in doll domain recalled onomatopoeia of a system suitable for motion.

5.2   Applying to "Robot" Domain

Measurement of Robot Motion. We observed that proposed system recalls what kind of onomatopoeia from robot motion (Fig. 10). We confirm that whether motion dictionary have versatility for motions other than the doll.

We used Jumping Sumo which is a toy drone as a robot. Jumping Sumo is a two wheels drone. This robot can be controlled by smartphone application. This drone has preset of motion and it can motion such as jumping and turning. We measured the preset motions using motion capture system.

Recalling Onomatopoeia. As a result of onomatopoeia recalling from robot motion, robot's rectilinear motion recalled walking system onomatopoeia such

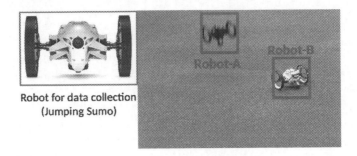

Fig. 10. Measuring robot motion.

as "*Ta Ta Ta*" and "*Toko Toko*". Jumping motion recalled jumping and flying system onomatopoeia such as "*Byoon*" and "*Hyuun*". Robot domain motion recalled onomatopoeia of a system suitable for motion.

5.3   Applying to "Human" Domain

Measurement of Human Body Movements. We observed that motion dictionary recalled what kind of onomatopoeia from human movement (Fig. 11). People can express the more exaggerated motion more than the body movement by using dolls. For example, by using doll we can express jumping higher and flying motion that human cannot do. However, we focus on motif of motion and compare these motions. In the motif of motions, walking and jumping are similar. Therefore, we assume that human body movement recalls onomatopoeia suitable for human movements.

We collected motion data that three participants attach the smartphone on the chest. We measured body movements using acceleration sensor and angular velocity sensor are mounted on a smartphone. We asked three participants to action three motions such as walking, running and skipping on a certain distance.

Fig. 11. Measuring human motion.

Recalling Onomatopoeia. As a result of onomatopoeia recalled from body movements in daily life, walking motion like walking and running recalled collision system onomatopoeia such as "*Kotsun*" and "*Doka*". Jumping motion like skipping recalled flying system onomatopoeia such as "*Byuun*" and "*Hyuun*". In the case of recalling onomatopoeia from human domain motion queries, some motion queries recalled onomatopoeia which are not suitable for system.

6   Discussion on Onomatopoeia Recalling

We observed that proposed system recalls what kind of onomatopoeia from motion queries of various domains using motion corpus. As a result, some motions such as doll, robot and human recalled suitable onomatopoeia. Jumping motion queries of these domains recalled jumping system onomatopoeia. We checked motif of the motion expressing jumping system onomatopoeia in motion corpus. The motif of these motion were characterized in the vertical direction (Table.2 and 3). These motif of vertical direction included several kinds of characters. It is conceivable that jumping and flying system onomatopoeia is likely to be recalled in jumping and flying motions because these motions are seen in the vertical direction motif.

Table 2. An example of position motif obtained from a robot's jumping motion.

Position	Motif
X	aaaaaaaabbbbbccccccc
Y	aaaaabccccccccbbaaaa
Z	bbbbbbbbbbbbbbbbbbbb

Table 3. An example of position motif obtained from a person's skipping motion.

Position	Motif
X	aaaaabbbbbbbbbbbccccc
Y	aaabccbaacccbabccbaa
Z	bbbbbbbbbbbbbbbbbbbb

We confirmed that the onomatopoeia of the collision system was recalled against the motion seen in the doll play. Participants were attacking and treading other dolls with his dolls. These motions recalled collision system onomatopoeia. These doll motions rotate in the middle of walking and flight operations, often colliding with the other dolls. The motif of these motion were characterized in the pitch rotation (Table 4). Collision system onomatopoeias are easy to be recalled for motion including pitch rotation. In one scene, walking motion of monster type doll recalled the collision system onomatopoeia. The monster type doll was attacked by another doll while walking in this scene. It was also seen that onomatopoeia recall combined with relationship with other doll motion was done. It was seen that there was difference in the motion motif representing the rotation values.

Table 4. An example of rotation motif obtained from a doll's collision motion.

Rotation	Motif
Roll	bbbbbbbbbbbbbbbbbbbb
Yaw	bbbbbbbbbbbbbbbbbbbb
Pitch	bbbbbbbbbbbabbccccccbb

On the other hand, walking motion of human could not recall walking system onomatopoeia. We compared the walking motion motif of human and doll. Humans move forward while maintaining their posture. The dolls were advancing while swaying alternately between left and right (Table 5). Also, There was a pattern that the doll was advancing while moving slightly up and down. It was seen from each motifs of walking motion that this doll motion affects the value of rotation value. People can express the more exaggerated or impossible motion more than the human motion by using dolls. For example, flying motions and collision motions. In onomatopoeia recall, the motion motif of three dimensional position and rotation were used for similarity search. However, It is conceivable that similarity search using all value quantities is not desirable because human do not much rotational motion. When recalling onomatopoeia in the human domain, we have to examine feature quantities used for similarity search.

Table 5. Comparing Yaw rotation motifs between walking motions of human and doll.

Motion actor	Yaw rotation motif
Human	bbbbbbbbbbbbbbbbbbbb
Doll	bbbcbcaccbbbbbbaaaab

7   Application Systems

7.1   Onomatopoeia Camera

We created an onomatopoeia camera that adds onomatopoeia following the movement of the subject in the camera and performs comic-like effects on photographs. A smartphone is attached to the subject's chest, and the acceleration value is acquired from the subject's smartphone by the shutter timing of the camera app created (Fig. 12). This application recall onomatopoeia displayed on the camera application using the motion corpus constructed from the obtained acceleration values (Fig. 13).

Fig. 12. Usage example of onomatopoeia camera.

We had several people experience this camera application and observed it. App users enjoyed seeing the onomatopoeia appearing in the first photo taken. Gradually, they thought about the patterns between onomatopoeic words and movements of humans and tried and errored what kind of onomatopoeia would be displayed. We think that users can learn cognitive science, such as what kind of onomatopoeia is recalled from human body movements, through camera applications.

This application can also manually input effect lines such as concentration lines, which are a type of manga expression, as shown in the photo on the right of the figure. By applying such comics effects to the photographed pictures, it is thought that the state at the time of photography can be conveyed clearly and expressively. Also, comics culture in Japan has been evaluated abroad, and we believe that the created applications will be useful for intercultural communication and onomatopoeic learning for non-native Japanese speakers.

7.2 Augmented Doll Play

This application measures a doll motion in doll play and recalls onomatopoeia from doll motion. The recalled onomatopoeia is displayed on the table (Fig. 14). We observed the situation of the players who played this AR system. The player tried what kind of onomatopoeia would be recalled for a certain motion. Other players looked at the onomatopoeia displayed on the table and moved

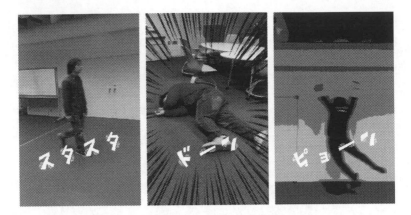

Fig. 13. Examples of onomatopoeia camera: The photo on the center has comic-like effect which is automatically added associated with the selected onomatopoeia. The photo on the right shows a monochrome effect.

the dolls. While the system recalled onomatopoeia from motion, the players recalled motion from onomatopoeia. We can learn motion and language from onomatopoeia. With this AR system, this language education for children or expansion of physical expression communication can be augmented.

Fig. 14. Projection of recalled onomatopoeia during doll play.

8   Conclusions

This paper showed our attempt to build a corpus consisting of onomatopoeia and corresponding motion of subjects. We built our corpus by choosing doll play as a target since we could observe various onomatopoeia.

We proposed a system which recalls onomatopoeia from doll's motion. We extracted motif from doll's motion data in order to abstractly represent the motion data associated with corresponding onomatopoeia. We confirmed if our system could successfully recalled corresponding onomatopoeia from motion queries across various domains. The result shows that the motion corpus associated with jumping and collision onomatopoeia of doll could be successfully diverted to both robot and human domains. Human walking motion, however, could not recall appropriate onomatopoeia associated with walking because the rotation values of them are quite different.

As application examples based on this corpus, we presented a prototype of "onomatopoeia camera", a system that automatically adds onomatopoeia and comic-like expressions to subjects' movements, and augmented doll play.

References

1. Canelas, A., Neves, R., Horta, N.: Multi-dimensional pattern discovery in financial time series using SAX-GA with extended robustness. In: Proceedings of the 15th Annual Conference Companion on Genetic and Evolutionary Computation (GECCO '13 Companion), pp. 179–180. ACM, NY, USA (2013). http://doi.acm.org/10.1145/2464576.2464664

2. Fukusato, T., Morishima, S.: Automatic depiction of onomatopoeia in animation considering physical phenomena. In: Proceedings of the Seventh International Conference on Motion in Games (MIG '14), pp. 161–169. ACM, NY, USA (2014). http://doi.acm.org/10.1145/2668064.2668096

3. Garg, Y., Poccia, S.R.: On the effectiveness of distance measures for similarity search in multi-variate sensory data: effectiveness of distance measures for similarity search. In: Proceedings of the 2017 ACM on International Conference on Multimedia Retrieval (ICMR '17), pp. 489–493. ACM, NY, USA (2017). http://doi.acm.org/10.1145/3078971.3079009

4. Gomes, E.F., Jorge, A.M., Azevedo, P.J.: Classifying heart sounds using multiresolution time series motifs: An exploratory study. In: Proceedings of the International C* Conference on Computer Science and Software Engineering (C3S2E '13), pp. 23–30. ACM, NY, USA (2013). http://doi.acm.org/10.1145/2494444.2494458

5. Kato, A., Fukazawa, Y., Sato, T., Mori, T.: Extraction of onomatopoeia used for foods from food reviews and its application to restaurant search. In: Proceedings of the 21st International Conference on World Wide Web (WWW '12 Companion), pp. 719–728. ACM, New York, NY, USA (2012). http://doi.acm.org/10.1145/2187980.2188192

6. Komatsu, T.: Quantifying Japanese Onomatopoeias: toward augmenting creative activities with onomatopoeias. In: Proceedings of the 3rd Augmented Human International Conference (AH '12), pp. 15:1–15:4. ACM, NY, USA (2012). http://doi.acm.org/10.1145/2160125.2160140

7. Komatsu, T.: Choreographing robot behaviors by means of Japanese onomatopoeias. In: Proceedings of the Tenth Annual ACM/IEEE International Conference on Human-Robot Interaction (HRI'15) Extended Abstracts, pp. 23–24. ACM, NY, USA (2015). http://doi.acm.org/10.1145/2701973.2702020

8. Kwon, S., Kim, L.H.: Sound sketching via voice. In: Proceedings of the 5th International Conference on Ubiquitous Information Management and Communication (ICUIMC '11), pp. 48:1–48:4. ACM, New York, NY, USA (2011). http://doi.acm.org/10.1145/1968613.1968672

9. Lin, J., Keogh, E., Lonardi, S., Chiu, B.: A symbolic representation of time series, with implications for streaming algorithms. In: Proceedings of the 8th ACM SIGMOD Workshop on Research Issues in Data Mining and Knowledge Discovery (DMKD '03), pp. 2–11. ACM, New York, NY, USA (2003). http://doi.acm.org/10.1145/882082.882086

10. Miyazaki, A., Tomimatsu, K.: Onomato Planets: physical computing of Japanese onomatopoeia. In: Proceedings of the 3rd International Conference on Tangible and Embedded Interaction (TEI '09), pp. 301–304. ACM, NY, USA (2009). http://doi.acm.org/10.1145/1517664.1517726

11. Oh, J., Kim, G.J.: Effect of accompanying onomatopoeia with sound feedback toward presence and user experience in virtual reality. In: Proceedings of the 24th ACM Symposium on Virtual Reality Software and Technology (VRST '18), pp. 81:1–81:2. ACM, New York, NY, USA (2018). http://doi.acm.org/10.1145/3281505.3283401

12. Yusuf, M., Asaga, C., Watanabe, C.: Onomatopeta!: developing a Japanese onomatopoeia learning-support system utilizing native speakers cooperation. In: Proceedings of the 2008 IEEE/WIC/ACM International Conference on Web Intelligence and Intelligent Agent Technology (WI-IAT '08) - Volume 03, pp. 173–177. IEEE Computer Society, Washington, DC, USA (2008). https://doi.org/10.1109/WIIAT.2008.300

Understanding Avoidance Behaviors of Users for Conversational AI

Siyuan Wu, Yatong Shu, Xinyue Yang, Zilin Huang, Xuzheng Zhang, Xiyin Chen, and Guochao Peng[(✉)]

School of Information Management, Sun Yat-Sen University, Guangzhou 510006, Guangdong, China
penggch@mail.sysu.edu.cn

Abstract. In order to provide better customer services to its rapidly growing users shopping online, retailers harness AI chatbots to solve issues around service provision and communication. This paper reports on an exploratory study that investigated obstacles and challenges affecting continuous engagement in conversational AI. 15 interviews were conducted to gather in-depth insights and diverse perspectives, and the qualitative data gathered was evaluated using a theme analysis technique. The findings revealed three types of avoidance behaviors as well as a collection of 14 critical hurdles associated to various technological, interactive, readable, psychological, and experiential components. Among them, psychological barriers were recognized as the most crucial. This challenge was triggered by a range of technological obstacles, user interaction obstacles, readability obstacles, individuals' experiential obstacles, and technological obstacles is the underlying causes of psychological, readable, and experiential obstacles.

Keywords: Avoidance behaviors · Factors of obstacles · Conversational AI

1 Introduction

As one of the most promising technologies in the service sector, AI chatbots are changing both marketing strategies and consumer behaviors [1]. Essentially, AI chatbot is a conversational agent that communicates with people using natural language and machine learning [2–4]. Due to their accessibility, immediacy, and low cost [5, 6], an increasing number of E-businesses harness AI chatbots to solve issues around service provision and communication [7], service failure such as product return and customer complaints [8] and trust recovery [9] by offering 24/7 customer care to customers. Juniper Research [10] highlighted that the increasing use of AI in the form of chatbots for customer service applications, where these deployments could realize annual savings of $439m globally by 2023, up from $7m in 2019. Despite such, consumers' continuous engagement and usage of AI chatbots, especially when encountering service failure and requiring product return, remains low nevertheless and, under certain circumstances, customers even deliberately eschew and oppose them.

N. A. Streitz and S. Konomi (Eds.): HCII 2023, LNCS 14036, pp. 281–294, 2023.
https://doi.org/10.1007/978-3-031-34668-2_19

A key challenge for Conversational AI is customer pushback from the demand side. Customers may be dissatisfied to Service of chatbot, such as respond inappropriately, dispose mechanistically, leading to a discrepancy between the user's real service experience and the user's expectations. That is, humans may create stereotypes that conversational AI technology cannot always really serve customers, humans often give superior online counseling services [6]. What's more, they may be feel horror and disgust to chatbot due to the uncanny valley feelings and algorithm aversion [3, 11]. Therefore, avoidance behavior of user has become one of the most significant challenges of conversational AI service providers. Considering this, it is crucial for promote customer self-service to explore why users avoid conversational AI and what form of avoidance they will take. Understanding the antecedents and forms of user avoidance can not only extend the growing literature on human-computer interaction in the service context but also help marketers and programmers to optimizing AI chatbot systems and technology. To investigate the challenges for consumers to continuously engage with AI chatbots, the study reported in this paper attempted to seek answers for three research questions:

RQ1: What are the forms of user avoidance to conversational AI?
RQ2: What obstacles are currently affecting user avoidance?
RQ3: How these obstacles may be interrelated and influence each other?

To achieve this aim, we conducted in-depth interviews with 15 participants in China. There are two main reasons that we selected China as our study context. Firstly, all members of the research group are situated in China, and it is convenient to approach participants. Secondly, China's online shopping apps (e.g., Taobao, JD.com, Pinduoduo) are developing rapidly, and AI chatbot technology is widely used in the field of e-commerce. In such a context, Chinese citizens have many opportunities to contact conversational AI. Meanwhile, they could encounter various challenges in using conversational AI due to the system design and information quality problems, which provides the great potential sample to study this phenomenon. China is thus an important area to understand the avoidance behavior toward AI chatbot.

2   Literature Review

To explore existing studies and literature related to the research topic, a systematic review was conducted. During this extensive review process, the researchers searched for adequate keywords (e.g., avoidance behavior, AI chatbot, conversational AI, and) in a number of databases (e.g., Web of Science, ScienceDirect, Google Scholar, ResearchGate, and ProQuest), and also tracked suitable citations in the retrieved articles. In this section, we first review relevant literature of conversational AI and avoidance behavior to contextualize our study.

Most existing studies about AI chatbot are based on the Computers as Social Actors (CASA) paradigm [12]. Usage toward AI chatbot has been a major focus of research across time [6, 13–15]. These studies report consumer distrust of AI chatbot and strong inclinations toward avoidance. Consumers perceive that AI chatbot fail to perform as well as human service and humans often give superior online counseling services [6]. In addition, AI chatbots primarily uses conversational cues (textual cues) to interact with the user and deliver information [12, 16]. Conversational cues change the user's perception and judgement of a communicator [17], resulting in the intention to use or avoid. According to several research, anthropomorphic dialogue design (e.g., self-disclosure, excuses, and thank you) might be off-putting to users since it does not accurately resemble human interaction [12]. In human-computer interaction (HCI), users' distrust of technology might affect how they intend to act [18], which could block job completion and hinder positive customer experiences.

Based on these consumer usage experience toward AI chatbot, avoidance is a likely consequence. However, prior studies on AI chatbot usage focus primarily on users' satisfaction, adoption, and continuance intention [7, 13, 14]; little research has been done to examine deliberate avoidance behavior. This behavior is referred to by Guo as a kind of passive usage behavior [19]. An individual's avoidance behavior can assume different forms, concerning reducing use, switching to alternative, or rejecting use [20].

Hence, an investigation on the characteristics and influencing factors of avoidance behaviors for AI chatbot that contributes to developing specific strategies for improvements (e.g., improved areas related to the development, implementation, and promotion) and engaging as many users as possible in using the chatbot to solve after-sales issues, is lacking in the literature. This research gap will be also addressed in this study.

3   Methodology

3.1   Inductive and Qualitative Approach

This study aims to investigate the forms and antecedents of avoidance behaviors when customer using conversational AI. Given the scarcity of existing literature on the phenomena studied this study adopts an exploratory and inductive approach.

We tend to gain insights into the behaviors of user in the process of avoidance that involve the changes of users' emotion and behaviors. In this study we selected qualitative approaches, using interviews, to capture the views, experiences, and/or motivations of individuals on their avoidance behaviors toward conversational AI, because this allows researchers to interact directly with the participants and seek the clarification for concerned matters [21]. In this way, we can have better chance to understand the changes of their cognition and emotion in the use process and gain insights into the mechanism of their avoidance behaviors, based on the perceptions and words of users used to describe their avoidance.

In the interviews, all participants were required to describe their experience and Inner feelings of using conversational AI. We thus referred to their description to determine their avoidance type.

3.2   Data Collection and Participants

The research adopted a two-stage interview: the first stage is open interview, and the second stage is semi-structured interview. Most qualitative studies start with open interviews to get a broad 'picture' of the research phenomenon [22]. First, we preliminarily explore the forms of avoidance behaviors of conversational AI and develop an initial explanation of the concepts to these forms by utilizing open interview. And then, we adopted semi-structured interview to exploring the antecedents of avoidance behaviors. There are no overall formal criteria is established to determine sample size [23], and data collection stops once the information richness occurs [22].

In the open interview, we recruited 4 participants for individual interview, since they have rich experience in using conversational AI and can clearly describe their usage and psychological process. The data analysis from this small sample size of the participants was sufficient for us to develop the outline of semi-structured interview and obtain a broad picture of users' avoidance behaviors. The second stage of 11 individual interviews were conducted in a semi-structured way. During this stage, individual interviews were used to improve the understanding of the antecedents of interviewees' avoidance behaviors of using conversational AI and their psychological cognition in the process that help us gain deeper insights into the changes of their attitudes and behaviors. As shown in Table 1, we interviewed a total of 15 users of conversational AI. The age of participants ranges from 18 to 32, and their education include undergraduate, master and PhD. With the researcher as interviewers, each interview lasted for 40 min to 1.5 h, and was digital recorded with consent obtained from the participants. The digital records were transcribed by the researchers, who also sent the transcripts to relevant participants for validation.

Table 1. Profile of participants.

ID	Gender	Age	Education	Frequency of chatbot usage
1	Male	27	PhD	Use it almost every day
2	Male	24	Master	Have tried it once or twice
3	Male	25	Master	Use it often
4	Male	21	Undergraduate	Use it sometimes
5	Female	20	Undergraduate	Use it sometimes
6	Male	32	PhD	Use it sometimes
7	Female	21	Undergraduate	Use it sometimes
8	Female	25	PhD	Use it often
9	Female	30	PhD	Use it sometimes
10	Male	29	Master	Use it almost every day
11	Female	18	Undergraduate	Use it often
12	Female	22	Undergraduate	Use it sometimes
13	Male	32	PhD	Use it sometimes
14	Female	20	Undergraduate	Use it sometimes
15	Male	30	PhD	Use it everyday

3.3   Data Analysis

The obtained qualitative data was analyzed by using a thematic analysis method. Thematic analysis is one of the predominant and effective techniques for analyzing qualitative data [24] and the identified themes emerge as important in describing a certain phenomenon [25]. Thematic analysis provides a set of systematic procedures that can generate codes and themes from qualitative data [26]. A code is a concise label that captures the meaning of a chunk of original data relevant to the research questions, while a theme is a pattern obtained through thematic extraction and is composed of a set of codes shared a central concept [27].

Table 2.   Summary of themes and key codes.

Main themes	Sub themes	Key codes
Technological obstacles	T1: Fail to recognize user patterns automatically	T1a: Difficult to identify consumer requests
		T1b: Difficult to identify scenarios
		T1c: Difficult to identify consumer needs
		T1d: Difficult to identify context
		T1e: Difficult to recognize user emotions
	T2: Technical defect of response	T2a: Incomplete corpus
		T2b: Irrelevant answers
		T2c: Respond inappropriately
		T2d: Repeated responses
		T2e: Grammatical mistakes
	T3: Lack of technical efficiency	T3a: Slow response
		T3b: Difficult to solve consumer problems
User interaction obstacles	I1: Usage complexity	I1a: Operation/process complexity
		I1b: Dialogue complexity
		I1c: Interface complexity
	I2: Usage difficulty	I2a: Difficult to operate
		I2b: Difficult to type
		I2c: Difficult to find the icon, interface, entry
	I3: Unreasonable Design/Settings	I3a: Use language of evasiveness, rote, pleasantry

(continued)

Table 2. (*continued*)

Main themes	Sub themes	Key codes
		I3b: No aging design
		I3c: Functionality redundancy
		I3d: Insufficient permissions of conversational AI
		I3e: Force users to use conversational AI
Readability obstacles	R1: Low readability	R1a: Long reply
		R1b: Large amounts of information
		R1c: Information irrelevance
		R1d: Information overload
	R2: Communication problems	R2a: Difficult to understand the information of reply
		R2b: Difficult to extract information
		R2c: Missing critical information
		R2d: Unsmooth communication
		R2e: Lack of emotional reassurance
Psychological obstacles	IDE1: thinking pattern/mindsets	IDE1a: Consider robots as tools
		IDE1b: Stereotypes
		IDE1c: Psychological resistance
	IDE2: Distrust	IDE2a: Distrusting belief
		IDE2b: Distrusting intentions
	IDE3: Needs/requirements	IDE3a: Needs to be served
		IDE3b: Needs to be valued or respected
		IDE3c: Needs to be understood
Experiential obstacles	E1: Bad experience	E1a: Waste time
		E1b: Inefficiency
		E1c: High Effort
		E1d: Low satisfaction
		E1e: Low expectation
	E2: Negative sentiment	E2a: Anxiety

(*continued*)

Table 2. (*continued*)

Main themes	Sub themes	Key codes
		E2b: Exhaustion
		E2c: Boredom
	E3: Intrinsic barriers	E3a: Cognitive load
		E3b: Social fatigue
		E3c: Social presence
		E3d: Value barriers
		E3e: Perceived differences
Avoidance behavior	A1: Reduce use	A1a: Forced use
		A1b: Try to use
		A1c: Information avoidance
	A2: Switch to alternative	A2a: Switch to Human
		A2b: Switch to another alternative
	A3: Resist to use	A3a: Denial/stop of service
		A3b: Reject repurchases
	A4: Avoidance tendency	A4a: Short-term avoidance
		A4b: Long-term avoidance

By following the guidelines given by Braun and Clarke [25] and the research steps by Peng and Nunes [28], the thematic analysis conducted consisted of several steps. First, the analysis process began by reading and proofreading transcripts with a view to becoming familiar with the data collected. The second step included an open coding process, from which a long list of codes was extracted from the dataset, as well as the corresponding quotes. We started the coding process with the data collected by the largest recorder and went through the process with other data obtained. The third step was concerned with rearranging and grouping the identified codes into 18 sub-themes and 6 themes, as summarized in Table 2. Through this step, the main categories of forms and antecedents affecting user avoidance behaviors started emerging, and the interrelations between the identified obstacles also became clear. The fourth step was to re-examine and reassure that all codes assigned to the themes and sub-themes followed a coherent pattern. Finally, all identified themes and sub-themes together with selected codes and quotations were related back to the research questions and served as the basis and evidence for reporting the findings in the following sections.

4   Findings and Discussion

Thematic analysis results included a classification of user avoidance behaviors for conversational AI as well as a set of critical barriers (total of 14) divided into five categories, namely technological obstacles (3), user interaction obstacles (3), readability obstacles (2), psychological obstacles (3), and experiential obstacles (3). Our findings show that, the types of avoidance behaviors for conversational AI can be divided into three group including reduce use, switch to alternative, resist to use, and users with avoidance behavior can be divided into long-term or short-term avoidance users.

4.1 Types of Avoidance Behaviors for Conversational AI

By the thematic analysis, we further conceptualized and classified users' avoidance behaviors for conversational AI into three group and seven presentation formats (as summarized in Table 3).

Table 3. Key concepts of avoidance behaviors of conversational AI users.

Avoidance behaviors	Key codes	Behaviors characteristics and performance
A1: Reduce use	A1a: Forced use	Passive to use, forced to communication, asking for help reluctantly
	A1b: Try to use	Trying to communicate and observe, reducing the frequency of inquiries
	A1c: Information avoidance	Ignoring some information sent by chatbot, reducing information exchange
A2: Switch to alternative	A2a: Switch to Human	Switching to manual service
	A2b: Switch to another alternative	Switching to other channels such as telephone service
A3: Resist to use	A3a: Denial/stop of service	Refusing or stopping inquiry services because of conversational AI
	A3b: Reject repurchases	Reject all services offered by the merchant and do not want to buy goods here due to conversational AI

As Wang (2021) shows that there are three categories about avoidance, concerning reducing use, switching to alternative, or rejecting use [20]. In the context of user avoidance behavior to AI chatbot, reduce use refers to a set of behaviors for users forced use, try to use, and information avoidance, the main characteristics of this category are users asking for help reluctantly, reducing the frequency of inquiries and ignoring some information sent by chatbot. The characteristics of switch to alternative are user switching to other channels such as human service online, telephone service. Resist to use refers to a set of behaviors for users' denial and stop service and reject repurchases due to AI chatbot. Moreover, and in light of the findings presented above, most users with avoidant behavior are inclined to long-term avoid, only few users are short-term avoid. In contrast, users of long-term avoidance assume forms of switch to alternative and resist to use, and they are less friendly and tolerant towards robots, which may be related to their psychological obstacles and experiential obstacles.

And what's interesting is the resist of use is not just a boycott of the chatbot service, but also denies all services offered by the merchant and do not want to buy products here anymore. That means the service quality of conversational AI not only affects users' avoidance behavior, but also directly affects users' purchase intention.

4.2   Crucial Factors Leading to User Avoidance Behavior for Conversational AI

As a result of the thematic analysis, it was found that technological obstacles, user interaction obstacles, readability obstacles, psychological obstacles, and experiential obstacles could all contribute to user avoidance of using AI chatbots.

Technological Obstacles
As confirmed by the users' interviewed, there are severe technical difficulties and challenges associated with the design and development of conversational AI.

The general feeling of the user is that conversational AI fails to recognize user patterns automatically. To be specific, it is extremely hard to identify consumer requests, scenarios, needs, and emotions when consumer asking for help: "Intelligent customer service currently cannot really very accurately identify what I want to express" (interview6) and "it may not be able to understand a particular situation or my request" (interview4). In addition, very often the AI cannot contact context that user input, "it can answer a single sentence of my question, but if it is a few more questions back and forth, even it has forgotten the context of the previous questions asked" (interview13) however, "the human service will not forget what I said before, they will string these words together and then make a comprehensive and integrated response" (interview14).

Moreover, technical defect of response and lack of efficient smart technology have been another long-lasting issue of conversional AI. For conversional AI, it is also a highly prioritized task for providers to accuracy of responses since it directly affect users' use feeling, "After talking a lot of nonsense still didn't get the answer I wanted, so I felt it wouldn't be as efficient as human service and a waste of my time" (Interview9). More importantly, conversational AI maybe reply irrelevant, repeated answer and have grammatical mistake "Every sentence it replies didn't feel very fluent either, or sometimes had grammatical problems" (interview9). More seriously, it cannot to solve problem that after-sale questions.

User Interaction Obstacles
User interaction obstacles were identified as a barrier that negatively influences user adoption of conversational AI. The usage complexity occurs as people find innovation to be difficult to grasp "complexity of idea" or to use "complexity of execution" [29]. The preliminary qualitative study revealed that some of the users might find the conversational AI complex/difficult to use. For example, "The interface looks very complicated, it has a lot of information tips or category templates, and then the activity templates, I think it is a bit complicated. And the elders think it's even more complicated, and I don't have a lot of patience to look at these anyway" (inreview9).

Furthermore, usage difficulty is also a form of interaction obstacles. Here, in this case, the qualitative study revealed that usage difficulty are the users difficult to operate, difficult to type and difficult to find the icon, interface, entry. For example, one of the respondents (interview11) remarked, "But like my parents they may still be more difficult to use, may not be familiar with this kind of cell phone shopping this kind of what, including sometimes return goods, exchange goods, typing this kind of operation". The most worrying thing is that the unreasonable design/settings, most interviewees mentioned the conversational AI using language of evasiveness, rote, pleasantry, and no aging design, witch result in bad experience of users. For example, "Its reply has the meaning of trying to pass the buck, and such words tend to anger me more" (Interview11) and "The elderly will feel more trouble, and its design interface is quite unfriendly to them, such as the use of cell phones, and then the icon is very small, they may not see, not easy to find" (interview8). In addition, users always be forced to use conversational AI and no one likes to be forced to use anything. "It's not that I chose AI service, but every time the merchant would hand it to me, and then I felt bad every time I used it" (interview7).

Readability Obstacles

Online communication in human-computer interaction (HCI) should convey not just service or operational information requested by the user, but information that can be read and understood. Existing literature reveals that the two most critical features of a conversation affecting the difficulty of comprehending information are dialog length and information content [30]. Our research shows that low readability and communication problems affect users' avoidance behaviors for conversational AI. Low readability means long reply, large amounts of information, information irrelevance, information overload. In reality, users already have very tight daily read tasks, and so may neither be willing nor able to afford additional read tasks: "If the chatbot sends me a bunch of messages and doesn't use them, it will definitely cause a drain on my time and cognitive load, with the result that I will avoid him" (Interview3). The communication problem means users difficult to understand the reply, extract information, and easy miss critical information: "I think I need to be more receptive to a response that is more understandable to me, a little difficult for me to understand if there is too much information" (interview10).

Psychological Obstacles

Although conversational AI providers have made substantial efforts to reassure intended collaborators and consumers, users still have strong avoidance intention. The analysis identified a further set of personal obstacles from a user's angle. Some of these barriers consist of thinking pattern/ mindsets, distrust, and needs/requirements. Most notably, most users did not seem to trust AI service. Distrust generally refers to the absence of trust or suspicion, or wariness, and is commonly viewed as a functional opposite of trust [31], and distrust was later extended to human relationships with non-human entities such as IT artifacts/technology [18, 32].

Like trust, distrust also comprises distrusting beliefs and intentions [31, 33]. Distrusting belief is defined as "the degree to which one believes, with feelings of relative certainty, that the other person or entity does not have characteristics beneficial to one" [31]. For example, interviewee 8 stated, "Negative experiences can make me chat with

AI service with a bias or distrust that I don't trust it to help me". While distrusting intentions refer to the trustor's unwillingness to depend on the other party [33]. Research confirms that d distrust thus alters/influences the trustor's behavior with the trustee [18]: "I would suspect that chatbot didn't help me to rush the logistics, so I would be suspicious of the it, and then would want to go to the human customer service for a verification" (Interview1).

Experiential Obstacles
Technical, interactive, and readable challenges on conversational AI design and development raises an essential experiential obstacle to user: "I encounter it every time, and then he seems to have a bad experience every time, causing me to have negative feelings" (interview7).

In fact, experiential obstacles may occur as after users use conversational AI, including bad experience, negative sentiment, and intrinsic barriers. Chatbots providers have been trying to improve the user's experience by various technical means, but they ignore the importance of users' past experience. For example, "It is possible that the next time I use it, I will substitute the negative emotions or negative experiences I had in my previous use and make a decision again" (Interview2) and "Because the kind of experience with conversational AI service in the past is not very helpful, so I feel that in the future may not be less likely to use it" (intereview8). Beyond bad experience, it was also identified that users had negative sentiment and intrinsic barriers with using conversational AI. The interviewed repetitively mentioned that "I get angry and anxious" (interview13) and "I will be annoyed, angry or irritated with speechless" (interview8) when they are using conversational AI. In fact, those negative sentiment are partially caused by intrinsic barriers, such as cognitive load, social fatigue, social presence, perceived differences, and value barriers of users.

It is worth mentioning that the concept of value barriers [34] is related to the concepts of perceived usefulness in the innovation diffusion literature [35]. In this case, the qualitative study indicated that users doubted the usefulness of conversational AI. For example, interviewee 8 stated, "I think AI service is a burden for me, and it has not helped me" and interviewee 4ststed, "I found it pretty much useless". According to the theoretical perspectives of IRT, the value barrier is one of the most important causes of user resistance [36].

5 Conclusions

This paper presents a range of critical obstacles affecting avoidance behaviors of users for conversational AI, by exploring and integrating the perspectives and insights of users with avoidant behavior. It can be concluded that, different users will present different forms of avoidance behavior. As such, our holistic set of findings derived from users who present different forms of avoidance is crucial to understand and potentially improve the status quo. Another important conclusion is that the identified a set of crucial obstacles affect avoidance behaviors of users and the identified obstacles are not just complicated but also interrelated. Specifically, the thematic analysis has led to the exploration of complicated inter-relationships between the identified obstacles as summarized in Fig. 1,

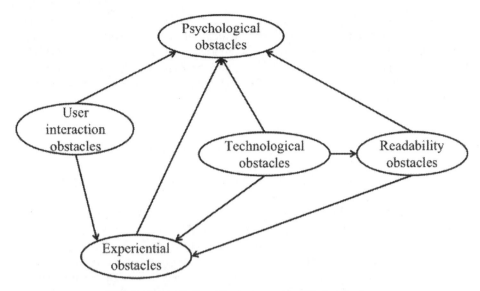

Fig. 1. Inter-relationships between identified obstacles.

which contributes to the literature in addressing the shortage of framework. From this network of inter-relationships, psychological obstacles emerged as the most problematic issue preventing continuous engagement in AI chatbot. As clearly shown in Table 2, this obstacle is attributed to a range of interactive, technological, readable, and experiential obstacles and technological obstacles is the underlying causes of psychological, readable, and experiential obstacles. Therefore, the study has notable practical implications for AI chatbots providers, especially for those who are considering the possibility of integrating AI chatbots into customer self-service systems [37]. It is with our research that we can provide guidance on the interaction and readability of AI chatbots, which will lead to an increase in user acceptance and maintain their use over time.

There are several limitations in this research. First, this study was conducted research setting of China. Therefore, our findings about identified obstacles and interrelationships amongst them may be mainly applicable to China and countries with similar condition. An interesting direction of future research is to validate and test these findings and propositions beyond the Chinese. Another, this research is qualitative research and utilized thematic analysis method to analyze the collected data. The data analysis thus is based on the understanding of the researchers towards the interview transcripts. Therefore, future studies can use the system logs or user reviews of the apps to analyze the users' avoidance behaviors and compare the results of this study, especially by using quantitative methods.

Acknowledgement. This research was supported by a grant funded by the National Natural Science Foundation of China (No.: 71974215).

References

1. Davenport, T., Guha, A., Grewal, D., Bressgott, T.: How artificial intelligence will change the future of marketing. J. Acad. Mark. Sci. **48**(1), 24–42 (2019). https://doi.org/10.1007/s11747-019-00696-0

2. Dale, E., Chall, J.S.: A formula for predicting readability: instructions. Educ. Res. Bull., 37–54 (1948)

3. Ciechanowski, L., Przegalinska, A., Magnuski, M., Gloor, P.: In the shades of the uncanny valley: an experimental study of human–chatbot interaction. Future Gener. Comput. Syst. **92**, 539–548 (2019)

4. Luo, X., Tong, S., Fang, Z., Qu, Z.: Frontiers: machines vs. humans: the impact of artificial intelligence chatbot disclosure on customer purchases. Mark. Sci. **38**(6), 937–947 (2019)

5. Przegalinska, A., Ciechanowski, L., Stroz, A., Gloor, P., Mazurek, G.: In bot we trust: a new methodology of chatbot performance measures. Bus. Horiz. **62**(6), 785–797 (2019)

6. Ashfaq, M., Yun, J., Yu, S., Loureiro, S.M.C.: I, Chatbot: modeling the determinants of users' satisfaction and continuance intention of AI-powered service agents. Telemat. Inform. **54**, 101473 (2020)

7. Huang, Y., Gursoy, D., Zhang, M., Nunkoo, R., Shi, S.: Interactivity in online chat: conversational cues and visual cues in the service recovery process. Int. J. Inf. Manag. **60**, 102360 (2021)

8. Rai, A.: Explainable AI: from black box to glass box. J. Acad. Mark. Sci. **48**(1), 137–141 (2020)

9. Toader, D.C., et al.: The effect of social presence and chatbot errors on trust. Sustainability **12**(1), 256 (2019)

10. Juniper Research. AI in retail. Segment analysis, vendor positioning & market forecasts 2019–2023. https://www.juniperresearch.com/researchstore/fintech-payments/ai-in-retail. Accessed June 2019

11. Dietvorst, B.J., Simmons, J.P., Massey, C.: Overcoming algorithm aversion: people will use imperfect algorithms if they can (even slightly) modify them. Manag. Sci. **64**(3), 1155–1170 (2018)

12. Feine, J., Gnewuch, U., Morana, S., Maedche, A.: A taxonomy of social cues for conversational agents. Int. J. Hum. Comput Stud. **132**, 138–161 (2019)

13. Laumer, S., Maier, C., Gubler, F.: Chatbot acceptance in healthcare: Explaining user adoption of conversational agents for disease diagnosis. In: Proceedings of the 27th European Conference on Information Systems (ECIS). AISeL (2019)

14. Pillai, R., Sivathanu, B.: Adoption of AI-based chatbots for hospitality and tourism. Int. J. Contemp. Hosp. Manag. (2020)

15. Munnukka, J., Talvitie-Lamberg, K., Maity, D.: Anthropomorphism and social presence in human–virtual service assistant interactions: the role of dialog length and attitudes. Comput. Hum. Behav., 107343 (2022)

16. Araujo, T.: Living up to the chatbot hype: the influence of anthropomorphic design cues and communicative agency framing on conversational agent and company perceptions. Comput. Hum. Behav. **85**, 183–189 (2018)

17. Hancock, J.T., Dunham, P.J.: Impression formation in computer-mediated communication revisited: an analysis of the breadth and intensity of impressions. Commun. Res. **28**(3), 325–347 (2001)

18. Chau, P.Y., Ho, S.Y., Ho, K.K., Yao, Y.: Examining the effects of malfunctioning personalized services on online users' distrust and behaviors. Decis. Support Syst. **56**, 180–191 (2013)

19. Guo, Y., Lu, Z., Kuang, H., Wang, C.: Information avoidance behavior on social network sites: information irrelevance, overload, and the moderating role of time pressure. Int. J. Inf. Manag. **52**, 102067 (2020)

20. Wang, T., Mai, X.T., Thai, T.D.H.: Approach or avoid? The dualistic effects of envy on social media users' behavioral intention. Int. J. Inf. Manag. **60**, 102374 (2021)
21. Alharbi, F., Atkins, A., Stanier, C.: Decision makers views of factors affecting cloud computing adoption in Saudi healthcare organisations. In: 2017 International Conference on Informatics, Health & Technology (ICIHT), pp. 1–8. IEEE (2017)
22. Moser, A., Korstjens, I.: Series: practical guidance to qualitative research. Part 3: sampling, data collection and analysis. Eur. J. Gen. Pract. **24**(1), 9–18 (2018)
23. Lopez, V., Whitehead, D.: Sampling data and data collection in qualitative research. Nurs. Midwifery Res. Methods Apprais. Evid. Based Pract. **123**, 140 (2013)
24. Xing, F., Peng, G., Zhang, B., Li, S., Liang, X.: Socio-technical barriers affecting large-scale deployment of AI-enabled wearable medical devices among the ageing population in China. Technol. Forecast. Soc. Change **166**, 120609 (2021)
25. Braun, V., Clarke, V.: Using thematic analysis in psychology. Qual. Res. Psychol. **3**(2), 77–101 (2006)
26. Nowell, L.S., Norris, J.M., White, D.E., Moules, N.J.: Thematic analysis: striving to meet the trustworthiness criteria. Int. J. Qual. Methods **16**(1), 1609406917733847 (2017)
27. Clarke, V., Braun, V., Hayfield, N.: Thematic analysis. Qual. Psychol. Pract. Guide Res. Methods, 222–248 (2015)
28. Peng, G.C., Nunes, M.B.: Exploring cultural impact on long-term utilization of enterprise systems. In: 43rd Hawaii International Conference on System Sciences, pp. 1–10. IEEE (2010)
29. Heidenreich, S., Spieth, P.: Why innovations fail—the case of passive and active innovation resistance. Int. J. Innov. Manag. **17**(05), 1350021 (2013)
30. Bailin, A., Grafstein, A.: The linguistic assumptions underlying readability formulae: a critique. Lang. Commun. **21**(3), 285–301 (2001)
31. McKnight, D.H., Chervany, N.: While trust is cool and collected, distrust is fiery and frenzied: a model of distrust concepts. In: AMCIS 2001 Proceedings, p. 171 (2010)
32. McKnight, D.H., Choudhury, V.: Distrust and trust in B2C e-commerce: do they differ? In: 8th International Conference on Electronic Commerce: The New E-Commerce: Innovations for Conquering Current Barriers, Obstacles and Limitations to Conducting Successful Business on the Internet, pp. 482–491 (2006)
33. McKnight, D.H., Kacmar, C.J., Choudhury, V.: Dispositional trust and distrust distinctions in predicting high-and low-risk internet expert advice site perceptions. E-Service **3**(2), 35–58 (2004)
34. Ram, S., Sheth, J.N.: Consumer resistance to innovations: the marketing problem and its solutions. J. Consum. Mark. **6**(2), 5–14 (1989)
35. Venkatesh, V., Morris, M.G., Davis, G.B., Davis, F.D.: User acceptance of information technology: toward a unified view. MIS Q., 425–478 (2003)
36. Talke, K., Heidenreich, S.: How to overcome pro-change bias: incorporating passive and active innovation resistance in innovation decision models. J. Prod. Innov. Manag. **31**(5), 894–907 (2014)
37. Gnewuch, U., Morana, S., Maedche, A.: Towards designing cooperative and social conversational agents for customer service. In: ICIS (2017)

How Remote-Controlled Avatars Are Accepted in Hybrid Workplace

Mika Yasuoka[1]([✉]) [iD], Tomomi Miyata[2], Momoko Nakatani[2], Yuki Taoka[2], and Nana Hamaguchi[3]

[1] Roskilde University, Roskilde, Denmark
`mikaj@ruc.dk`
[2] Tokyo Institute of Technology, Tokyo, Japan
[3] NTT Research, Tokyo, Japan

Abstract. Due to Covid-19 outbreak, more people in workforce started working from home. Especially, hybrid work style is widely accepted at workplace as more flexible and inclusive way. However, a challenge of the satellite side of hybrid meeting has also gradually recognized, namely being easily ignored by co-located participants. Regarding the issues that hinder the participation and collaboration of hybrid participants, only a limited study has been made with no clear solutions. Hypnotizing physical *embodiment* in hybrid work as one of the potential solutions for avoiding satellite participants being neglected in remote work environment, this work has implemented remote-controlled avatars as physical embodiment of a remote participant and investigated its impact on communication and collaboration in hybrid meetings. Our preliminary analysis of the field experiments indicated that the Avatar with physical embodiment increased satellite participant's social presence, and interestingly, the subjective satisfaction level of the satellite participant was significantly higher than the remote participation with typical meeting tools, such as Zoom. In this paper, two observed effects of avatars with physical embodiment on participating at remote work are discussed; firstly, acceptance of satellite participants through embodiment and, second, social presence and potential collaboration between AI and Human. Since the hybrid work is expected to increase further in our society, there are a lot of potentials for improvements to design better remote work environment through avatar as physical embodiment.

Keywords: Remote Work · Hybrid Work · Satellite Participant · Embodiment · Avatar

1 Introduction

Due to Covid-19 outbreak, more people in the workforce started working from home. This remote work became a daily practice at workplace. Since remote work has accepted as common practice as a part of the future work style after the pandemic, the potential of new working style is expanding drastically beyond our initial expectations. The remote work not only reduces travel time, improve work-life balance and flexibility, but also eliminates barriers for people with anxiety and disabilities who had limited opportunities

N. A. Streitz and S. Konomi (Eds.): HCII 2023, LNCS 14036, pp. 295–307, 2023.
https://doi.org/10.1007/978-3-031-34668-2_20

to participate in workplace previously [1]. Research on remote work after the pandemic has just begun, however, a shift of implementing a hybrid work model from traditional co-located work has already been observed as one of the prominent emerging phenomena even among the limited number of preliminary research. This shift has accelerated especially among leading digital societies, such as Denmark [2], where digital infrastructure of remote work has already stablished.

Hybrid work has potentials not only to limit some of the disadvantages of remote work [2], but also to increase diversity and inclusion [1] at work contexts. Hybrid work style, by providing workers freedom to choose a place to work, more flexible and inclusive emerging work style for many reasons. For families with small children, it is easy to accommodate to sudden illnesses. If workers are allowed to work at home several times a week, they will have more options where to live. Some wish to live in an area surrounded by nature, and others with their old parents in suburb cities, regardless of distance from their office.

Due to drastic technological progress of remote collaboration and communication tools such as Zoom, Teams, Slack, and Miro [3], and its upwards learning curves among people across nations through intensive mandate experience, people accumulated their skills and knowledge of remote work drastically. This created a unique global condition of equality of participation.

However, this participatory equality seems to be applied only when everyone is on remote condition. We have witnessed and gradually recognized a challenge of the satellite side of hybrid meeting, namely a challenge being easily ignored by co-located participants.

In hybrid work, a special consideration must be paid for equal participation because, it is extremely challenging to keep up social presence of the satellite participants in hybrid work settings. The more the co-located workers become concentrated and devoted to their work, the lower the social presence of the satellite participants in the team becomes, which undermine remote workers' participation at work. Regarding the issues that hinder the participation and collaboration of hybrid participants, only a limited study has been made with no clear solutions.

2   Preliminary Works: What We Found So Far

What is a key to support remote work? How can we resolve imbalance on the satellite side, especially in hybrid meetings? Based on the challenging agenda, we set our research question as follows: *How can the satellite participants in hybrid work avoid being neglected with the help of physical embodiment?*

At Future Living Lab (https://futurelivinglab.org/), a two year's research collaboration with a telecom company, NTT Techno Cross and two universities, Tokyo Institute of Technology and Roskilde University, a design project for future of remote work was initiated. Among distinct topics of inclusion and wellbeing on remote work, this research focuses the effect of physical *embodiment* [4] in hybrid work as one of the potential solutions for avoiding satellite participants being neglected in remote work environment. In this research, diverse styles of remote-controlled avatars are implemented as physical embodiment of remote participants and investigate its impact on communication and collaboration in hybrid meetings.

A research design of the experiment introduced in this paper was inspired by a series of small studies on hybrid work conducted over the past years by one of the authors. Before introducing the experiment in Sect. 3, the two previous studies, a literature review [2] and three-months field experiment [5], will be briefly introduced as a trajectory to the targeted study.

2.1 Prospects of Hybrid Work

One of the author's first study on hybrid work is a literature review conducted in 2020–2021 [2], which clarified understandings of advantages and disadvantages in remote work during the first year of the global Covid-19 outbreak, 2020. In 2020, many people around the world had experienced semi-forced remote work. Some people lived in countries such as the Netherlands and Denmark, where remote work has already moderately being introduced, while countries like Japan where the Internet installation rate is high, but the condition for remote work were immature. Note that the remote work settings in this context cover wide range from remote access to the corporate network or database (technical constraints) to practical agreements of working from home (social constraints).

The literature review, covering the first year of COVID-19 experience, handled 39 academic papers, which reveled advantages, and disadvantages of remote work. According to the study, the three most common advantages are 1) reduced travel time, 2) improved work-life balance, and 3) improved flexibility, while the disadvantages are 1) damaging mental health, 2) harming physical health, and 3) declining of work-relationships. One of the final remarks of the literature review presented a view that remote work would increase globally even after the pandemic and expected that many organizations would be preparing in implementing a hybrid work model as new normal. The preliminary conclusion of the work is that the hybrid model at workplace is promising as it expects to keep advantages and to limit some of the disadvantages of remote work.

This introduced preliminary view of the remote work in 2020 has also been supported by the most recent research from 2021 onwards. Rather than introducing complete remote work or returning to the pre-pandemic workstyle, more and more companies are shifting to hybrid work [6]. Some companies that haven't implemented remote work, have also explored possibilities of hybrid work environment [7, 8].

2.2 Potentials of Avatar

A three-month field experiment conducted in the spring of 2022 by one of the author's research group, indicated potentials of remote work from different angles. The experiment investigated effects of using avatars in business meetings between the managers and their co-workers [5]. This study explored effects of using digital avatar robots in virtual meeting environment, specifically, focusing on the perception of social presence and co-presence between workers and their managers. The experiment result indicated that in using digital avatar for the meetings, significant number of participants felt an improvement in social presence, co-presence, and overall virtual meeting experience.

The impact was greater especially to those who has a first meeting or has a meeting with persons from the higher corporate hierarchy. Our study suggested that remote work through digital avatar could be easier accepted and would increase social presence in remote work. Embodiment of the remote participants would facilitate collaboration due to its amplified social presence.

3 Experiment

3.1 Avatar at Hybrid Workshops

Most recently, authors have conducted a series of experiments on influence and acceptance of avatars in hybrid work context as a part of Future Living Lab. An ultimate purpose of the experiments is to conduct a test implementation, *living lab* [9] of embodied avatar and its social presence, to understand potentials of hybrid work supported by Avatar.

We conducted a successive four hybrid design workshops during March to August 2022. The number of participants of the workshops were five or six including one satellite participant, *Participant A*. The participants had diverse backgrounds such as university students, professionals at industries and non-profit organisations, and researchers. The participants were invited to the workshops through the authors' personal connections and advertisements put on the public space of authors' home university. Table 1 shows a formation of participants in each workshop session.

Duration of the workshops was approximately three hours each, and the participants received one design task to achieve in three hours, such as ideation and concept creation based on the workshop agenda. Typically, the workshop offers data set, paper templates, post-it and pens for working on specific ideation, creation, and discussion among group members.

Table 1. A formation of participants in each workshop session

Workshop# (Month)	Co-located Participants	Satellite Participant	Total Participants
1 (March)	5	1	6
2 (May)	4	1	5
3 (June)	4	1	5
4 (August)	4	1	5

While one member joined the workshops as a satellite participant, other participants were co-located and co-worked at workshop sites. The satellite *Participant A* joined the workshops through an embodied avatar, which *Participant A* controlled and spoke through. A remote avatar, *Avatar Bear*, with physical embodiment at co-located stage was presented as shown in Fig. 1. Avatar Bear can be interpreted as a substitute body of the satellite *Participant A* and equipped with fictitious AI functions. The AI functions were deployed based on the Wizard of Oz technique [6] mediated by a human operator, *Operator K* at the workshop site.

Fig. 1. Avatar Bear in Wizard of Oz method.

In order to test communicative and collaborative effects of Avatar Bear, diverse conditions of participation were designed (Table 2). Among four workshops, the first workshop used ordinary online meeting tool, *Zoom*, with a tablet screen, while the rest three sessions used the Avatar Bear. The Zoom in the first workshop was set up with a tablet on the movable table with wheels (Fig. 2) so that the remote participant's view can be easily adjusted with its display angle. Among three Avatar Bear sessions, a condition of the last session was slightly different from the two other sessions. In the second and third sessions, AI functions of the Avatar Bear was activated so that the Avatar Bear, by recognizing environment, conducted autonomous actions such as waving hands, nodding, and facing to the speakers without direct manipulation by the satellite *Participant A* from the distance. In Table 2 this setting is described as AI Avatar Bear *with Intelligence*, differentiating from *without automated behaviour* of the fourth session.

Table 2. Design of hybrid participation in four workshops

#	Avatar Participation
1	Zoom in the tablet set on the movable table with wheels
2	AI Avatar Bear with intelligence
3	AI Avatar Bear with intelligence
4	AI Avatar Bear without automated behavior

Fig. 2. Zoom in the tablet set on the movable table with wheels

On the other hand, in the fourth session, the Avatar Bear could act only when the satellite *Participant A* explicitly commanded actions. For this session, the three action buttons were prepared as shown in Table 3. The satellite *Participant A* send a command to the Avatar Bear and the commanded action was activated by Avatar Bear AI (*Operator K*) with a few second's delay.

Table 3. Three actions operated by the satellite *Participant A*.

#	Operation button	Meaning
1	I want to share	Preliminary operation for waiting to speak up
2	I have something to say	Waiting for the turn to speak
3	I feel neutral	Not moving, no need to get attention

3.2 Data Collection

To investigate the impact on communication and collaboration of AI Avatar Bear with embodiment, questionnaires were distributed to participants after the workshops. The collected answers were analyzed and qualitative interview as a semi-structured interview [10] was conducted within one week after the workshops, referring to the answers of the questionnaire.

Table 4. A brief overview of the questionnaire.

#	Questions	Measurement
1	Easy to talk to the Avatar Bear	7 Likert Scale
2	Easy to understand the Avatar Bear	7 Likert Scale
3	Easy to discuss with the Avatar Bear	7 Likert Scale
4	How did you think about an appearance of the Avatar Bear as a workshop member?	Open answer
5	How did you think about behavior of the Avatar Bear at the workshop?	Open answer
6	Feel free to leave your comments regarding the Avatar Bear	Open answer

The questionnaire consisted of six questions (see Table 4), which are to ask about impacts and impressions about AI Avatar Bear's workshop participation, satisfaction in communication and collaboration with the Avatar. The questionnaire was sent also to *Participant A*. In this case, *Participant A* answered about impacts and impressions about AI Avatar Bear's workshop participation, satisfaction in communication and collaboration with the co-located participants. All responses to question 1–3 were made on a 7-point Likert scale (from "1 strongly disagree" to "7 strongly agree"). The answers to the question four to six were open answers, which were later investigated in the in-depth interviews.

4 Preliminary Findings

The workshop participants were, as shown in Table 5, six, five, five and five each in total. A few participants joined four times consecutively, but overall members of the participants were different in every workshop. A satellite participant, *Participant A*, and *Operator K* were always the same person.

Table 5. Participants and their participation record.

Participants Name	W-1	W-2	W-3	W-4
Operator K	•	•	•	•
Participant A	•	•	•	•
Participant W	•	•	•	•
Participant I	•	•	•	•
Participant T	•	•		•
Participant H	•	•		
Participant F	•		•	
Participant Y			•	•
Total Participants	6	5	5	5

The original motivation of this study is to clarify whether the satellite participants in hybrid work can avoid being neglected with the help of physical embodiment. Specifically, the question was whether AI Avatar Bear with a physical embodiment would achieve participation, being recognized and accepted its presence by co-located participants in the work context. In this results section, a few noteworthy results related to recognition and acceptance of the Avatar Bear will be presented.

4.1 Recognition of Avatar Bear

The data from the questionnaires and the interviews clearly showed that the participants recognized and paid attentions to Avatar Bear during workshops. The co-located participants looked and turned to Avatar Bear, and frequently talked to the avatar.

First, let's review questions one to three. The first three questions direct and indirectly relates to the recognition of the Avatar Bear, which are 1) Easy to talk to the Avatar Bear, 2) Easy to understand the Avatar Bear, 3) Easy to discuss with the Avatar Bear. The overall average of the collected answers, for example, in the second session are 4.4, 2, 3, 4 respectively. An evaluation of the question 2 was relatively low, which were explained by a few interview comments as potentially solvable technical problem.

> The audio setup was important. It was hard to hear when the surroundings were noisy. I found it also difficult because of the time lag and not knowing what the Bear was watching. (Participant I)

Intriguingly, Participant A's view was somewhat different. In the interview, *Participant A* also made a remark that there were technical challenges such as voice volume setting and auto-mute setting. For example, auto-mute setting was a cause of prompt utterance not being heard on time and lost timing to speak. *Participant A* felt timely conversation as a team member, and any interventions of discussion among co-located discussion were difficult to make. As such, *Participant A* also expressed its dilemma that the Avatar was not always included to the discussion.

However, at the same time, the satellite *Participant A* recognized that the other participants were more attentive and occasionally approached or directed an eye on to the Avatar, comparing the past experiences as satellite participants. *Participant A* was confident that the Avatar Bear was recognized and accepted its presence by co-located participants, For example, the satellite *Participant A* commented;

> I kept having and increased feeling of participation in the workshop as other participants looked at and talked to me (*Participant A*).

Even though there were obvious discrepancies in communication, it seems the satellite *Participant A* externalised rather satisfied view as a satellite participant. Although this is a subjective view, the satellite participant at least felt highly likely to be listened and recognized by other co-located participants. Next, we will investigate further in this subjectivity aspect.

4.2 Participant Subjective Satisfaction

Both co-located participants and the satellite *Participant A* evaluated similarly with questions 1 and 3 of the questionnaires. Overall rating among participants including the satellite *Participant A* have not clearly changed overtime. However, the interview revealed that the satisfaction of the participants who continued to participate and *Participant A* are rather high in the 2nd and 3rd workshops.

According to subjective self-report in the interview, the satellite *Participant A*'s satisfaction is higher in the 2–4th workshops than in the first session. Furthermore, among 2nd to 4th workshops, *Participant A* is more satisfied in the 2nd and 3rd than the 4th workshop. In the last interview, *Participant A* reflected the 4th workshop as with extra burdens since every behaviour of Avatar had to be commanded all the time. What's worse was *Participant A* felt there was little feedback such as eye contacts from other participants, despite of the heavier burden than before. This experience hindered the Participant A's motivation of participation.

> I was too busy, giving commands and deciding Avatar Bear's next action without return of investment. I could not concentrate on discussion, which ended up not much participation at the workshop. (*Participant A*).

This subtle mood change of *Participant A* was not externalised in Likert scale nor not recognized by any other participants. However, *Participant A* affirmed that the 2nd and 3rd workshop were more satisfactory. *Participant A* reflected the 3rd workshop was most included and participated one.

4.3 Group Dynamics and Human Relations in the Workplace

Among the four workshops, Zoom was used in the 1st workshop, and Avatar Bear was used in the 2nd to 4th workshops. Avatar Bear was always a same stuffing bear, while the AI function specifications were, to iterate, changed in the 4th session, in which Avatar Bear's actions were substantially reduced compared to the 2nd and 3rd workshops. The specification change was made to increase a degree of freedom of the satellite *Participant A's decision*, and to improve overall satisfaction. This decision was made since the increase of the autonomous actions of the Avatar Bear was observed in the 2nd and 3rd workshops. Thus, the research design team evaluated that AI intervention was excessive. In order to improve its Avatar function, behavior buttons were introduced (See Table 3).

However, as a result, the satisfaction of the satellite *Participant A* was mitigated. Less movements of the Avatar Bear reduced Avatar Bear's social presence among the co-located participants. The co-located participants paid less attention to Avatar Bear overtime, and gradually Avatar Bear presence disappeared. This is at least how *Participant A* felt. The satellite *Participant A*'s view felt being ignored by co-located participants in spite of all the efforts of sending commands for better collaboration and participation.

> In all workshops, condition was same. Sometimes I couldn't hear co-located participants, and I couldn't see description of poit-it notes on the table. But this time, it was worse. I experienced that the Avatar was disappeared from the participants' consciousness. (Participants A)
>
> I kind of forgot the Avatar occasionally. Probably without movement of the Avatar, I was not sure if the remote participant was away from the desk or just to keep quiet. (Participants I)

From the co-located participants' point of view, it would be easier to talk or take actions to the Avatars, who are sure to present, while the co-located participants hardly dared to do so when the remote participant's presence was not guaranteed. It is not surprising that the co-located participants hardly take any affirmative actions toward the Avatar. The discussion would involve people in presence while remote participants without social presence are easily ignored from the co-located group discussion. This would be a natural reaction of group dynamics towards human relations in the workplace.

5   Discussion

It has hinted several potential effects of avatars with physical embodiment on participating at remote work, such as increasing satellite participant's social presence. Some of the most prominent preliminary findings are recognition of Avatar and the satellite participant, and subjective satisfaction among both co-locate and satellite participants and group dynamics towards human relations in the workplace.

Findings from our data indicates that small tuning of the Avatar Bear behavior settings might bring big differences in acceptance of the satellite participant, psychologically and practically. In this section, two aspects indicated by our preliminary findings are discussed.

5.1   Acceptance of Satellite Participant Through Embodiment and Social Presence

Our preliminary data showed the subjective satisfaction of the satellite *Participant A* as well as co-located participants were satisfactory in the 2nd to 4th workshops with the Avatar Bear than the 1st remote participation with a typical meeting tool, Zoom. Looking at this single result alone, an implication that embodiment can increase social presence and reduce the sense of exclusion of satellite participants seems to be valid or at least worth mentioning. Furthermore, since the overall subjective satisfaction of the participants has increased, it is tempting to conclude that the Avatar's social presence would contribute to include satellite participants in the hybrid work setting. However, our data also show that embodiment is not simply a matter of achieving social presence and inclusion of satellite participants.

Interestingly, throughout the four workshops, there were always a few occasions that co-located participants hardly showed clear recognition to the satellite participant's presence according to the interview of the satellite *Participant A*, meaning the satellite participant was not included to the discussion, simply being neglected. However interestingly, the subjective satisfaction level of the satellite *Participant A* was not correlated with the facts reported by the participants. The satisfaction of satellite *Participant A* was high in the 2nd to 4th workshops with Avatar Bear than the first remote participation with the typical meeting tool, Zoom, and this satisfaction was commented directly by the satellite *Participant A*.

In other words, having embodiment and achieving social presence might give a relative sense of participation of the remote participant, while the person can still be ignored occasionally. The satellite participant seems content, even sometimes ignored. This phenomenon leads us to hypothesize that what's more important for remote participants is to have a sense of physical participation through avatar, while being ignored or not is less matter. Also, it seems important for co-located participants to recognize a physical presence of all participants in the same place, even if they know that satellite participants behind Avatars are, in reality, located far away.

5.2   Collaboration Between AI and Human

The satellite *Participant A* was often unable to provide timely response due to slight network delays. Also, occasional troubles in understanding the situation of co-located site made the remote participant reaction delayed. This situation activated AI based automated decisions of Avatar Bear more frequently than originally planned. Thus, in the 2nd and 3rd workshops, more automated action of the avatar were activated independently and autonomously over time by Avatar Bear AI (*Operator K*), assuming the intentions and feelings of the satellite participant. To our surprise, our data hinted that the avatar in the 2nd and 3rd workshops was accepted better by all participants than the last workshop when the Avatar Bear acted entirely only by the satellite participant's commands. Comparing the second and third sessions with the fourth session, in the fourth session when the Avatar Bear's AI decisions were restricted, not only was the recognition of the other participants lowered, but the satisfaction of *Participants A* was also decreased.

As mentioned previously, the command function was implemented just before the 4th workshop. The research design team considered the Avatar Bear should have been controlled by the satellite *Participant A*. Thus, the team considered the unexpected autonomous action of the Avatar Bear should be terminated. As a result, the satisfaction of *Participant A* was damaged as mentioned before.

Previous research introduced and implemented automation of avatars [11, 12]. Ogawa et al. [8] implemented automated gesture function in their avatar so that avatars waves hands and nodding head while talking and listening to others.

Beyond predefined automated actions introduced by the previous research, our preliminary experiments indicate importance of active intelligent collaboration between AI and human. With current technology, it is still difficult for remote and satellite participants, to fully grasp local context and to follow conversation flow. Apart from technological challenges such as voice volumes or stable network connection, there exists challenges of human relations. Through tablet screen or avatar, it is still difficult to understand conversations and gestures from subtle body languages or tone of voices among co-located participants. The technological advancement made us possible to participate online work as closer to physical participation than ever, but online participation is not perfect enough to substitute with co-located participation. Our data indicated a potential of AI and human collaboration and co-creation under the current technological condition.

In our experiment, a human *Operator K* played a role of future AI using the Wizard of Oz method. Going beyond the currently implemented auto-generated Avatar actions such as waving and nodding, collaboration and co-creation between AI and human might open new stage of hybrid participation. The avatar has a potential not only automated remote support but also amplify potentials and capability of remote participants as well as improving overall quality of satellite participant social presence among co-located participants.

6 Conclusion and Implications

Satellite work is becoming an easier choice after Covid-19 at workplace, but we are also witnessed that the satellite side on remote work is unconsciously and unintentionally neglected and eliminated in hybrid meetings, which gives satellite workers' negative experience.

Our preliminary research indicates the satellite participants cannot avoid being neglected. However, AI Avatar bear with a physical embodiment helps providing social presence and occasionally achieve participation, being recognized, and accepted its presence by co-located participants. More notably, the satellite participant's satisfaction was higher than Zoom participation, especially when physical ability of satellite participant was amplified with the collaboration with AI functionalities of Avatar.

Based on the preliminary results introduced in this paper, we are currently exploring three potential research directions of our original research question; how can the satellite participants in hybrid work avoid being neglected with the help of physical embodiment?

One is to improve the quality of physical presence of avatars to provide the best hybrid work experience. In our experiment, we observed prompt collaboration between the remote operator as satellite participant and the Avatar Bear as AI mediated by human operator. The remote operator, *Participant A* and the Avatar Bear acted as one as if the Avatar possessed by human [7]. This collaboration amplified the satellite participant's capabilities and overall quality of satellite participant social presence. As exemplified in the experiment, we are interested in improving quality of interaction between satellite and co-located participants through establishing satellite participants and avatar collaboration. Currently, quite a few remote-controlled avatars have been starting to play active roles in our society. However, the existing usage of avatar is limited. In future, avatars can support remote operators by providing decision supports based on the on-site context judgment. This possibility of man-machine or human-avatar collaboration can extend human capability, which could result better acceptance and higher satisfaction of satellite participants in hybrid work.

Another possible direction is to increase and improve subjective satisfaction of collaborative work in hybrid environment as one of the indirect approaches to solve challenges of being neglected. Different from co-located work and remote work, in hybrid work, satellite participants tend to be less satisfied because less accepted by the co-located workers. We would like to work on such a challenge as to improve the satisfaction and fulfillments of not only one side of participants, but also both remote and co-located participants in hybrid work.

It is expected that the hybrid work will increase and widely accepted in our society. In such context, we imagine a role of avatar, physical embodiment as substitute of physical self, will increase drastically due to its physicality and social presence. Considering its high potential to deploy avatar as physical embodiment in hybrid work environment, further unsolved challenges will be identified – how remote-controlled avatars can support hybrid work and improve the overall work environment? How can avatar help be increasing worker satisfaction and wellbeing in hybrid work? We would like to contribute designing better remote work environment from such avatar-human collaboration perspectives.

Acknowledgments. This is a work based on the program, Future Living Lab, in collaboration with NTT Techno Cross and Tokyo Institute of Technology. Future Living Lab, funded by dLab challenge, Tokyo Institute of Technology.

References

1. Takeuchi, K., Yamazaki, Y., Yoshifuji, K.: Avatar work: telework for disabled people unable to go outside by using avatar robots "OriHime-D" and its verification. In: ACM/IEEE International Conference on Human-Robot Interaction, pp. 53–60 (2020). https://doi.org/10.1145/3371382.3380737
2. Rønnenkamp, C.: Working from Home in a COVID-19 World (2021)
3. Molla, R.: The pandemic was great for Zoom. What happens when there's a vaccine?
4. Jung, Y., Lee, K.M.: Effects of physical embodiment on social presence of social robots. Proc. Presence **2004**, 80–87 (2004)
5. Yasuoka, M., Zivko, M.: Effects of digital avatar robots on perceived social presence and co-presence in business meetings between the managers and their co-workers
6. Fayard, A.L., Weeks, J., Khan, M.: Designing the hybrid office. Harv. Bus. Rev. **2021**, 1–11 (2021)
7. Grzegorczyk, M., et al.: Blending the physical and virtual: a hybrid model for the future of work Standard-Nutzungsbedingungen: is a research assistant at Bruegel blending the physical and virtual: a hybrid model for the future of work. Bruegel Policy Contrib. (2021)
8. Bloom, N., Han, R., Liang, J.: How hybrid working from home works out (2023)
9. Yasuoka, M., Akasaka, F., Kimura, A., Ihara, M.: Living labs as a methodology for service design - an analysis based on cases and discussions from a systems approach viewpoint (2018). https://doi.org/10.21278/idc.2018.0350
10. Wood, L.E.: Semi-structured interviewing for user-centered design. Interactions **4**, 48–61 (1997)
11. Ogawa, K., Nishio, S., Koda, K., Balistreri, G., Watanabe, T., Ishiguro, H.: Exploring the natural reaction of young and aged person with Telenoid in a real world. J. Adv. Comput. Intell. Intell. Inform. **15**, 592–597 (2011). https://doi.org/10.20965/jaciii.2011.p0592
12. Tanaka, K., Nakanishi, H., Ishiguro, H.: Comparing video, avatar, and robot mediated communication: pros and cons of embodiment. In: Yuizono, T., Zurita, G., Baloian, N., Inoue, T., Ogata, H. (eds.) CollabTech 2014. CCIS, vol. 460, pp. 96–110. Springer, Heidelberg (2014). https://doi.org/10.1007/978-3-662-44651-5_9

Pervasive Data

Ethical Considerations of High Performance Computing Access for Pervasive Computing

Nathaniel Kremer-Herman$^{(\boxtimes)}$

Seattle University, Seattle, USA
nkh@seattleu.edu

Abstract. High performance computing makes many contemporary pervasive computing interactions possible such as increasingly accurate weather forecasts, market-scale financial services on demand, and big data analysis for highly personalized services. However, access to high performance computing resources is not necessarily equitable. Not everyone is uplifted by this computational power. Rather, high performance computing access can be seen as another aspect of the digital divide.

We acknowledge the ways in which equitable access to high performance computing resources has improved over time while also identifying potential threats to access of these resources. We provide considerations from the perspective of two popular ethical theories (contractarianism and utilitarianism) for reasoning about how these threats may be overcome or prevented from coming to pass. These perspectives can be extended to inform policy created by high performance computing providers.

Keywords: high performance computing access · computing ethics · digital divide · contractarianism · utilitarianism

1 Introduction

High performance computing (HPC) has increasingly accelerated research and improved the lives of HPC-connected society. HPC systems execute large scale applications with big datasets, running thousands or millions of concurrent computations, and spanning many processing nodes. Research applications exist across fields with high demand such as high energy physics, climate science, and medical research. Supercomputers, datacenters, and large compute clusters provide HPC resources which drive applications used by millions every day.

Beyond research, HPC makes many pervasive computing interactions possible. Climate and weather modeling, utilized by online weather services and smartphone apps, require large scale resources to compute trends and predict daily weather across the globe with increasing accuracy and granularity [12]. The modern, software-driven financial ecosystem relies upon *enormous* computational power to drive daily market activities from the personal (e.g. online

N. A. Streitz and S. Konomi (Eds.): HCII 2023, LNCS 14036, pp. 311–327, 2023.
https://doi.org/10.1007/978-3-031-34668-2_21

banking and financial portfolio management) to the societal (e.g. market trading and credit reporting) [5,18]. The rise in large scale machine learning [17] has also led to increased complexity across the board in web applications, requiring more resources to provide rapid, predictive, highly personalized web services [7] (from the seemingly trivial like email to complex social media systems). Cloud computing has vastly increased the amount of data people choose to store online, and businesses have created HPC applications to make use of this big data stored across datacenters worldwide.

Both the research and commercial arms of the HPC ecosystem have acted as a globalizing force as international collaboration is often a necessity to scale up applications to meet computational demand. Institutions without their own HPC resources may request a resource allocation on machines elsewhere to complete groundbreaking research. Multinational corporations use Internet scale services which span datacenters across continents. Companies provide this staggering infrastructure at significant construction and operating costs. However, just as HPC is a unifying avenue for the expansion of pervasive computing it has the potential to be used as a divisive geopolitical tool (wittingly or otherwise).

We discuss a few ethical considerations regarding equitable access to HPC resources. We demonstrate these issues are an extension of the concept of the digital divide, address progress made toward increasing HPC access, and identify threats to access such as geopolitical conflict. Given these concerns, we discuss two ethical theories (contractarianism and consequentialism) which provide insightful frameworks for crafting policy toward more equitable access to HPC resources worldwide.

2 Related Work

While there is not currently a significant, peer reviewed body of work on HPC access issues, much work has been done to understand societal access to computing at large (called the *digital divide*). The digital divide is multifaceted and global. It can be analyzed from the inequities introduced among socioeconomic classes [9], race and ethnicity [14], gender [6], rural and urban access [4], etc.

Those without proper access to computer technology (including personal computers, smartphones, and Internet access) are destined to fall behind those who have access leading to a lack of innovation in non-digital populations, increased inequality, and decreased participation in society [16]. HPC resource access issues exist as a subset of the digital divide. We focus on ethical issues associated with access to HPC for pervasive computing with impact on the general public regarding their access to innovations, to their social equality, and their participation in society as it is accelerated by ubiquitous computing.

Evidence for an HPC digital divide exists in work on increasing the adoption of HPC resources in underserved communities. The rise of affordable cloud resources has led to a sharp increase in adoption of cloud services worldwide, even in areas which have struggled to overcome the traditional digital divide [3]. This has allowed developers across the globe to collaborate on projects and for entrepreneurs to offer services which otherwise would have been impossible.

The pay-as-you-go model of many private cloud providers is beneficial for underserved communities and developing nations, however there are also significant issues which still exist [13]. There are additional costs beyond paying for computing time such as training a workforce to effectively interact with cloud environments. This can be particularly challenging for groups who have not had access to them ever before (especially outside of educational settings).

Compounding this lack of a trained workforce is also areas where there is no sustained *demand* for this body of knowledge in the workforce as has been noticed in some areas in Africa [1]. Dedicated efforts to build HPC capacity (i.e. increased knowledge and awareness in the workforce) across Africa have been met with promising results. One investigation into teaching HPC concepts in educational settings within developing nations defines some of the key challenges: lack of adequate facilities, lack of funding, lack of national infrastructure (e.g. Internet access and reliable electricity), and a delayed acquisition of resources [10]. Some of these challenges can be overcome with some ingenuity while others require lowering expectations of building a high-powered cluster in deference to teaching the fundamental theory of distributed systems (e.g. acquiring a small cluster of 5–10 previous generation, commodity machines). We proceed to discuss ethical issues with HPC access taking this related body of work as evidence that an HPC digital divide exists and currently creates a barrier to entry in some communities and nations which are difficult to transcend.

One ethical concern of high performance computing which has received considerable technical and social critique has been energy consumption. Powering large-scale systems like datacenters and supercomputers is an expensive task both financially and environmentally. The body of relevant work focuses on technical solutions toward increasing energy efficiency and reducing consumption of particularly onerous computations. It has been noted that energy consumption is one of the critical challenges in HPC [2] where advances in scheduling techniques and fast cleanup after job completion is critical in reducing energy overhead. One work surveys methods for modelling power consumption in datacenters at the software level such as virtual machine placement, migration, load balancing, and application-level energy consumption modeling [8]. Another work surveys software *and* physical causes of high energy use at datacenters [15]. They take into consideration the cooling budget for datacenters and the effect of server rack placement on energy usage.

Advances in the technical space toward energy-efficient HPC are also reflected in the ranking of the top 500 energy-efficient supercomputers in the Green 500 ranking which is tracked alongside the Top 500 ranking of supercomputers based on raw performance [11]. Data on both the Top 500 and Green 500 is collected and released every six months, showing the progress of pure performance and energy-conscious performance alike. Issues like energy consumption demonstrate that high performance computing incurs significant financial, environment, and social costs. We extend the umbrella of ethical concern in the HPC space by pivoting to an even more social-centric ethical issue: *access* to HPC resources.

3   The HPC Digital Divide

Using terminology noted previously regarding the digital divide [16], we assess the impact of an HPC digital divide from two perspectives: those *with* access to HPC systems and those *without*. We use innovation, equality, and participation in society as gauges for the effect HPC has on uplifting a community with access to HPC resources and/or the services made possible via these resources.

3.1   Innovation

Those *with* access to HPC resources and HPC-powered services are given more opportunities to innovate new, more advanced solutions to daily problems than those without access. More computational resources in terms of scale, speed, and heterogeneity provide a wider variety of options for entrepreneurs to host services for community benefit. Consumer-facing applications may be accelerated by offloading expensive computations onto HPC systems. Ubiquitous computing environments like smart cities, which produce enormous data, can have data stored within and analyzed on HPC resources.

Research and development are likewise accelerated. Groundbreaking industry research may be performed on a community's HPC resources, but if there are no provisions for open access those discoveries may remain proprietary and in the hands of that community rather than also benefiting those without access. While publicly funded projects increasingly require open access provisions for discoveries and data, this does not hold true for private enterprise.

Finally, those with HPC access benefit from cognitive offloading which can unburden people to focus on innovations rather than mundane daily tasks. Benefits such as cloud data storage accessible anywhere hosted in fault tolerant datacenters or artificial intelligence accelerated cognitive assistants which help plan calendars, shortcut communications with others, and personalize services by analyzing vast datasets are made uniquely possible via HPC. These kinds of services remove many logistical hurdles which, when out of the way, leaves more time for labor leading to innovation.

Those *without* access to HPC resources are likely to be left behind when it comes to innovation. As more applications pivot to cloud and HPC backends, those in communities without access to those infrastructures will be unable to scale their computations to the same degree as those with access. This means entrepreneurs in those communities will be unable to get some of the latest tools which make innovating easier. Less of their daily time will be offloaded onto HPC-enabled services. However, those without access may receive secondhand benefits from accelerated research and development by those with access so long as those discoveries and data are shared. This creates a dependency relationship between those with access and those without access, affecting the equality and effective societal participation of both groups.

3.2   Equality

Stratified access to HPC resources can lead to a gap in quality of life standards between those *with* access and those *without* it. Those who reap the benefits of HPC innovations will have access to a growing number of *de facto* standard methods of daily interaction and services. Advanced financial services, a growing number of consumer applications backed by HPC, multimedia subscription services provided via large scale computing, and nigh-infinite personal data storage are some of the key consumer benefits of HPC-enabled computing. As the ecosystem grows, those already inside will have access to cultural works and innovative services those without access cannot use. Those without access will be left behind, creating two classes of communities stratified by access to HPC resources and the services they enable.

An interesting aspect of this stratification to note is that there are likely subcommunities within the *in group* (i.e. those with HPC resource access). It is likely that both quality and quantity of access differs greatly within this group due to logistical constraints. Subcommunities are likely to be outpriced when compared to those who have significant capital (such as large corporations, government entities, and particularly wealthy individuals). Those who can afford to buy access to private HPC resources are provided more opportunities to start private ventures of their own (fueling an unequal access to innovative opportunities). Access to HPC resources alone does not guarantee equal access, equal benefits, nor equal outcomes for the in group. Rather, the degree of egalitarian outcomes for all those with access to HPC resources is likely linked to the degree of egalitarian policies which govern HPC infrastructure (who can stand up HPC resources and how) and access protocols (who can gain access to these resources, for how much money, for how long, etc.).

3.3   Participation in Society

Those *with* access to HPC-enabled services have greater participation in society than those *without*. This includes access to the most convenient methods of societal participation such as large-scale social media operations, HPC-driven news services, computerized voting and tabulation, etc. Those within the in group are granted lower barriers to entry in society as a consequence of their accelerated innovations and unequal access to services and resources.

Those *without* access may find the processes which allow them to participate in society phased out, replaced, or deprioritized in favor of new, HPC-enabled processes which they cannot access (or cannot afford to reliably access). When this happens, the opportunities for those without access to participate in society decrease or are potentially removed entirely. This process may be akin to companies and services transitioning from paper to electronic communications with customers or switching phone support to automated customer support systems. When these changes are made, certain communities and demographics are (likely unintentionally) excluded from participating as they no longer have the knowledge, resources, or capability to participate in the new processes.

3.4   Current Usage of HPC Resources

Table 1 shows the market segments using HPC systems in the Top 500 list from November 2022. Nearly half of all systems are used for private industry demonstrating the extent to which HPC can further expand the digital divide. It is also worth noting the relatively high academic usage. Whether the academic segment includes academic *research* or if that falls into the broader research category is undefined in the data. Regardless, HPC has applications for computationally accelerating the classroom experience as well.

Table 1. Top 500 Segments of System Share

Segment	Percentage
Industry	46.8%
Research	24.2%
Academic	17.4%
Government	05.8%
Vendor	03.4%
Other	02.4%

Table 2 breaks down more specifically the share of application areas on Top 500 systems from November 2022. A significant share of the applications have straightforward potential for user-facing interactions. Cloud services, IT services, weather and climate research, and information services are application areas which can serve as the backends powering pervasive interactions such as weather forecasting, automated customer support, and data analytics upon user datasets (such as organizational email, social media preferences, viewing history, etc.).

Table 2. Top 500 Application Area Share

Application Area	Percentage
Research	31.0%
Energy	10.3%
Cloud Services	10.3%
Benchmarking	10.3%
IT Services	10.3%
Software	06.9%
Weather and Climate	06.9%
Aerospace	03.4%
Services	03.4%
Information Service	03.4%
Not Specified	03.4%

3.5 Progress Toward Equitable HPC Access

There has been notable progress made toward making large-scale computing resources more accessible. Many privately funded resources provide access to highly scalable systems for a price far lower than the infrastructure costs a community or nation would need to set up a system on their own. Cities creating smart interfaces and digitizing their community experiences do not need to host solutions on their own. Companies and institutions needing to perform computationally expensive research do not need to spin up their own facilities.

The dramatic rise of cloud services is an example of increased access to HPC resources. Cloud and HPC resources provided by corporations like Amazon, Microsoft, Google, and IBM have allowed even relatively small organizations to host web content, perform data analytics, and provide third-party cloud services to their customers and users where before they would have little to no digital presence. The pay-as-you-go model for these services also provides the benefit of not requiring significant capital investment to get started which stands as a barrier to entry in starting up an on-premises HPC system.

In research and education spaces, there have been initiatives to increase equitable access to HPC systems. The US National Science Foundation XSEDE project and its followup ACCESS project, for example, provide free resource allocations to systems across the US for domestic student and faculty use in research and educational contexts. For higher education institutions with no local cluster and few funds to perform computations on a private cloud, programs like these are essential for keeping these institutions and their students from being left behind. The European Union has a similar program for the EuroHPC Joint Undertaking (EuroHPC JU) where any eligible European organization (from listed nations) can access resources for free for the purpose of research. Both public and private organizations can gain access no matter what kind of research they perform. The outcomes of any research on EuroHPC JU systems must be made public for open access, ensuring more equitable benefits from discoveries and innovations. Some other HPC facilities across the globe have posted access eligibility guidelines which allow members outside the host institution access to resources upon special authorization of director-level personnel.

3.6 Geographic Distribution of the Top 500

A noteworthy piece of evidence toward more equitable access to HPC resources is the increased proliferation of HPC systems on a global scale. Using data from the Top 500 supercomputers, we can see how the geographic distribution of these large systems has changed since the start of available Top 500 data in 1993. Figure 1 shows the geographic distribution in June 1993. The shaded nations represent those which have at least one supercomputer listed in the Top 500 ranking. The count of machines in each continent is found in Table 3.

There is a significant concentration of the top supercomputers in North America, Europe, and Asia. However, the tally is even more concentrated *within* these continents. The United States provided the overwhelming majority of North

Fig. 1. Geographic Distribution of Top 500 July 1993

America's supercomputers. Germany, France, and the United Kingdom make up the vast majority of Europe's supercomputing power. In Asia, Japan, Taiwan, and Hong Kong were the sole states with supercomputers in 1993. All of Oceania's top machines were hosted in Australia. Likewise, Brazil hosted all of South America's top machines.

Fig. 2. Geographic Distribution of Top 500 November 2022

Figure 2 shows the geographic distribution for November 2022. The data indicates a wider dispersion of Top 500 machines. While there is still a lot of concentration within wealthy nations in the global North, top machines have come from nations absent in the inaugural data (even a continent in the case of Africa). The concentration within continents is somewhat the same with the US making up the bulk of North America's top supercomputers. Japan and China comprise the vast majority of Asia's top machines. Within Europe, however, more nations are represented.

The changes in geographic distribution of the Top 500 over time are indicative of increased proliferation of HPC systems. This increased proliferation does not necessarily imply greater access to HPC services for the peoples of nations with Top 500 scoring machines, but there is likely to be a positive correlation between

Table 3. Count of Top 500 Supercomputers per Continent in 1993 and 2022

Region	1993	2022
Africa	0	1
Asia	113	218
Europe	134	131
North America	241	137
Oceania	10	5
South America	2	8

the two. We also note that the Top 500 data serves as a snapshot of the *most performant* HPC systems in the world. This is not indicative of the extent of proliferation of *all* HPC systems globally. We can consider this data a benchmark of resources a nation has put forth toward investing in HPC.

4   Additional Considerations for Equitable HPC Access

The HPC digital divide demonstrates how the benefits of high performance computing access can inequitably benefit communities with the most direct ties to HPC systems. More expansive and faster digital services, such as ubiquitous, cost-effective smart environments, broaden the ways these HPC-enabled communities participate in society and innovate. However, there are areas of concern for HPC which are not as readily apparent in the traditional digital divide.

4.1   Geopolitcal Conflict

HPC systems must be housed in large facilities. Often, these are government-funded laboratories. Access to the systems in these facilities may require open collaboration between nations. Research agreements between nations, such as EuroHPC JU noted previously, increase access to peoples from states without their own HPC resources (or perhaps with insufficient resources to drive future innovations). These agreements provide mutual benefit in that new research programs can flourish in nations without enough HPC resources while the nation providing resources typically benefits from results sharing. Other similar agreements based upon mutual benefit may exist outside of research.

However, there may be times when two nations come into conflict (or find themselves on opposing alliances in a separate conflict). In times of war, economic sanctions, or other international conflict, access provided between states may be rescinded. Continuing to provide HPC resources to citizens of an enemy state may constitute breaches of security or treaty agreements regardless of the intents of the *enemy actors* (who likely do not play an active, executive role in the geopolitics of their nation). Further, continued access may serve as a security issue should a well-intentioned actor from another nation become a victim themselves of a cyberattack thus compromising the security of the HPC system.

By rescinding access to HPC resources, one state may end up terminating critical services for another. This may be deliberate as an act of escalation or provocation. This may also be simply an unavoidable consequence of national security concerns. Regardless of intent, the termination of HPC-enabled services may sharply decrease the quality of life for some communities. These communities become part of the population *without* access to HPC resources and therefore lose the benefits toward innovation, equality, and participation in society they were previously afforded.

The politics *within* a nation which provides HPC resources to others may have similar effects. Internally, there may be concerns about funding priorities. Changing political landscapes may find funding and public support of HPC facilities supplanted with other policies and programs. Particularly volatile political landscapes (in the sense that political power changes hands frequently) are likely more susceptible to sudden changes in policy priorities and thus are more at risk of reneging on resource sharing agreements.

Private HPC enterprise is also affected by geopolitical conflict. Facilities located in a nation may cooperate with sanctions (voluntarily or by force) against another nation, rescinding access to their customers from that state. This is more complicated with multinational corporations which have HPC resources spread across the globe and rely upon this scale and availability to power their applications. The company will have to figure out the proper jurisdictions to determine which services or resources should be rescinded. There may also be conflicting jurisdictions where the requirements of one nation are more stringent (or differently strict) than another. Segments of the total set of resources and services may be disabled for some communities when nations come into conflict.

We note that geopolitical conflict need not be solely between nations. This issue can be generalized to politically-driven conflict between any two or more communities of arbitrary size such as two cities in the same administrative division or different neighborhoods in the same city. The core issue here is that there exists a group which has an inordinate amount of control over the access to HPC resources and services while other groups are dependent upon the openness of this other group to receive the benefits of these large scale systems.

4.2 Financial and Environmental Costs

It costs a lot of money to construct and operate an HPC facility, costing tens to hundreds of millions of US dollars to establish and millions to tens of millions to operate per year. The scales of these systems vary drastically, with the Top 500 supercomputer rankings for November 2022 having an average of 189,586 cores (with the top ten supercomputers averaging 409,807 cores). Some systems have *millions* of cores and require up to nearly 30,000 kW to operate. This staggering scale is infeasible for many communities to achieve and may be out of range for some nations seeking to cross the HPC digital divide and provide pervasive interactions for their citizens.

In addition to material costs (facilities construction, HPC system components, etc.), there is a significant human cost to running an HPC facility. There are numerous personnel costs to consider. From facilities logistics to technical support to in-house research staff, there may be tens to hundreds of employees working at a facility to keep it running as effectively as possible. Communities without a workforce possessing relevant technical skills may have to attract specialists from outside the community to work at the facility (at additional cost).

Being able to get the most computation per Watt has become more important as the world struggles with producing cost-effective renewable energy. Larger and larger HPC systems become an impracticality not only in terms of usage cost but also in terms of environmental costs. There are many efforts ongoing to address this. The Green 500 list of supercomputers ranks machines not in terms of raw performance but in energy efficiency. That being said, the energy demands of these systems are still quite high. For communities needing to expand their power delivery options to renewable energy sources, providing their own HPC services may take priority over adopting green energy or vice versa.

5   Two Ethical Perspectives on HPC Access

Considering the myriad issues surrounding HPC access, there needs to be a means of arriving at sensible, rational policies for HPC providers (whether public or private) to address these issues. We provide the perspectives of two popular ethical theories as guides for crafting ethical policies for HPC access. Noting the barriers to access mentioned previously, we use *contractarianism* and *consequentialism* to describe two possible frameworks to navigate the ethical issues of the HPC digital divide. It is important to note that there exist *many* viable ethical theories that should be considered. However, the two selected map readily onto legalistic and policy-based language commonly used in access agreements and service contracts.

5.1   Contractarianism

Contractarianism is an ethical theory which posits an act is ethical if it adheres to and is in service of one's social contracts. A social contract is an agreement between individuals to abide by a set of rules and principles which are meant to provide for the wellbeing of all participating in the contract. It is a fundamental pillar of modern society since governments are often enforcers of social contracts and the providers of a number of mutual benefits.

One may engage in both *implicit* and *explicit* social contracts. One does not choose to sign an agreement to adhere to the laws and norms of the country in which they are born, for example. This is an implicit social contract. However, if someone immigrates to another country they must fill out forms creating an explicit social contract between the state and the individual that they will obey the laws of that country. There are many implicit social contracts people engage in daily between friends, family, coworkers, and strangers. Explicit social contracts, often taking the form of codified rules for conduct and behavior, may be found in places like educational institutions and the workplace. Often, the most binding forms of social contracts are those made between individuals and a state as the state has the most power and influence to both enforce the social contract and to provide the most impact toward the wellbeing of its adherents.

An interesting facet of contractarianism not present in many ethical theories is the acknowledgement that society changes over time. Social priorities, such as social justice becoming more inclusive to marginalized groups, adapt to those participating in a social contract. In response to these changes, a social contract can be amended to include, for example, expanded rights and privileges for previously marginalized groups. Essentially, what is good for the wellbeing of a community may change such that the social contract no longer effectively promotes community welfare. The contract must be corrected to continue to be effective and worth upholding. Otherwise, it becomes meaningless.

Using contractarianism as a basis for HPC access provides a few underlying assumptions which should be reflected in policy. Primarily, access agreements (e.g. research agreements, pay-as-you-go contracts, etc.) should be mutually beneficial. The social contract made between those providing access and those gaining it should benefit both parties *and* promote the general welfare of all involved. Conditions upon which access relies should be explicitly stated, like eligibility rules and cases where access must be rescinded. To breach these conditions would lead to a breach in the social contract and lead to consequences for the breaching party. Finally, there should be explicit components of access agreements which encourage amendment over time and allow for mediation when conflict occurs. What we define as mutually beneficial and for the welfare of all involved is likely to change over time, so having policies which allow for meaningful discussion of outdated rules and mechanisms to change those rules are important.

We noted previously the benefits toward innovation those with access to HPC resources experience. Contractarianism-influenced policies support accelerating innovation. Its emphasis on promoting the welfare of all involved is important to consider. Policy may be formed to include those *without* access to HPC resources implicitly. Instituting contracts with results and data sharing provisions such as open access promotes mutual benefit for those directly involved in the contract (those with the resources and those gaining access) while also providing some benefit to those without access as a side effect since innovations are not kept proprietary. More access to the resources leads to more innovation globally.

Contractarianism can also be used to structure policies to address inequalities created by the HPC digital divide. Since social contracts change over time to adapt to changes in societal values, it stands to reason HPC access policies can be created in such a way that they can be readily amended. For example, the eligibility requirements for access to a system may be relaxed over time as more of the world becomes HPC-enabled. It is likely to become more important to societal welfare that more people gain access to HPC resources and services. This built-in flexibility to societal values makes contractarianism well-adapted to actively facilitate decreasing inequality in the HPC digital divide so long as society values furthering social justice. Should society no longer value this, however, the social contract may become static and leave out groups of people with no future way in.

Contractarianism also advocates for increased participation in society. As more services become HPC-enabled, a contractarian approach to addressing those affected by those services changing would be to craft policies to remedy this lost service. This may take the form of *proactively* onboarding those left behind with new technology (assuming this is financially and logistically feasible). Another contractarian approach would be to prevent the ceasing of alternative communication and participation methods outside of HPC-enabled services. By ensuring those without access retain viable means of participating in society, this approach also mollifies resulting increased inequality as well.

5.2 Consequentialism

Consequentialist ethical theories determine if an act is ethical based purely on its outcomes. Perhaps the most widely known consequentialist ethical theory is utilitarianism which emphasizes choosing to do those acts which maximize the most pleasure for the most people. Actions which are predicted to lead to more pain than pleasure (or said another way, would lead to more severe negative outcomes than positive ones) should be avoided. The classical version of utilitarianism is often called *act utilitarianism*. It requires the use of a pseudo-algorithm called the *felicific calculus* to quantify the degree of all positive and negative outcomes experienced by each person affected by an act. This calculus' output is the act which results in the highest net positive consequences.

In contrast, *rule utilitarianism* is a formulation which posits an act is ethical so long as it follows a general moral rule which, in most instances and in the long term, leads to the greatest good for the most people. This shortcuts the potentially tedious, time consuming, and mentally taxing process of working through the felicific calculus whenever one encounters an ethical dilemma. This somewhat relaxed definition of utilitarianism comes with an added benefit that its rule-based mechanism for decisionmaking is more similar to contractarianism than act utilitarianism. This makes a comparison of the ethical reasonings between contractarianism and utilitarianism more straightforward.

Utilitarian rules are considerations for what, generally, leads to the most positive outcomes for the most people. Considerations like promoting openness and avoiding arbitrary exclusion are key to closing of HPC digital divide. As a general rule, it is beneficial to be inclusive and to avoid policies which target specific demographics (such as members of certain communities) as one can readily imagine many situations where exclusionary practices cause significant harm. A rule utilitarian would follow (or devise new) rules which promote increased innovation, reducing inequality, and broadening participation in society via HPC access since addressing these issues would create more positive outcomes globally than either ignoring or exacerbating the issues.

A rule utilitarian may follow the maxim that it is generally beneficial to promote increased access to HPC resources to foster innovation. Since new technologies, research breakthroughs, and services made possible through HPC lead to global benefits, it stands that increased innovation due to greater accessibility leads to the most positive outcomes for the most people. However, innovations which are exclusionary should be avoided since it is generally detrimental to arbitrarily exclude communities from technological innovations.

Similarly, a rule utilitarian would argue that decreasing inequality by promoting increased HPC access would lead to global positive outcomes. As a rule in the utilitarian sense, decreasing social inequality generally leads to greater happiness than maintaining the status quo (or worse, actively *increasing* inequality). This can be extended to technological access issues as ubiquitous computing becomes more prevalent. Keeping access unequal is not beneficial since it robs entire communities of possible positive outcomes from HPC access such as new services, innovations, or social connections. This rescinding of benefits may lead not only to a stoppage of positive consequences but may also lead to future harm.

A maxim for increased participation in society for a rule utilitarian might be: realizing positive outcomes for communities relies upon greater participation in society. This is connected to increased openness and the goal of maximizing the population size who will likely experience the positive consequences of HPC access. Globally, society is more likely to experience positive outcomes when citizens can fully participate in society.

6   Discussion

Contractarianism and rule utilitarianism have some profound similarities. Both ethical theories emphasize performing actions which aim to produce the most good. The definition of good differs where contractarianism explicitly focuses on societal-level collective good whereas utilitarianism focuses on maximizing positive consequences of actions. Another noteworthy similarity is both theories' requiring consideration not just of self-interest but also the outcomes for others. In contractarianism, selfish gains are often sacrificed in order to promote greater societal wellbeing (such as theft being an act which breaks the social contract). For utilitarians, reasoning about an ethical dilemma requires acting as an impartial observer where one's own interests are not any more or less important than the interests of others.

However, there are some critical differences in how these two ethical theories arrive at the determination whether an act is ethical. Rule utilitarianism does not necessitate the input of others to determine rules. The theory posits that these rules follow reason and can be ascertained by anyone through contemplation. Social contracts, on the other hand, are made between individuals and between organizations. They require mutual benefit which, in turn, requires input from all involved parties to properly create the contract. This aspect of relational, reciprocity-based reasoning is absent in utilitarianism.

Another difference is the consideration of who is affected by actions. Rule utilitarianism concerns the consequences borne by everyone likely to be affected by an action while contractarianism is concerned with the rights, privileges, and outcomes for participants in the social contract. Those not engaged in a contract may be affected (perhaps indirectly) by choices made by contract adherents, though these people do not have consideration outlined in the contract. Such indirect impacts are accounted for in utilitarian thought, however.

At the organizational level, policy might be crafted to adhere to one particular ethical theory. Contractarianism matches well with legalistic language or when there are direct interactions between states and HPC resource providers. Rule utilitarianism is often communicated via commonsense maxims thus may be more approachable when litigious language is not needed. However, there are many other ethical theories to consider.

So long as an ethical theory provides a rational, consistent, verifiable method of determining the degree to which an act is ethical, it can be reliably used to craft policy. Rational theories posit an act is moral using clear reasoning. An ethical theory is consistent if it reliably produces the same determination of an act given identical (or nearly identical) circumstances. Someone can verify an ethical theory's determinations so long as one can work backward from the determination (e.g. an act is unethical) and clearly identify the mechanisms of the theory which led to the determination.

There are different foci depending on the chosen theory. Theories categorized as *virtue ethics* focus on striving to realize certain virtues in life (or within the mission of an organization). These virtues are moral characteristics we perceive as being demonstrated by the ideal person (a moral exemplar). Virtues such as prudence, courage, temperance, or justice are characteristics typically labeled as worthy of emulation. The theory of *deontology* focuses on adherence to absolute, universal moral laws which can be determined through reason. The various *relational ethics* focus on the material conditions and inequalities present between individuals and groups and often seek to address these inequalities. There are also other consequentialist ethical theories beyond utilitarianism to consider.

However, there are consequences to choosing *no* guiding ethical theory for determining policies. Without a guiding theory, there are no consistent, verifiable means of determining whether an act or policy is ethical. This would create a system ripe for abuse, misapplication, and changing whims as potentially disastrous decisions can be easily explained away without being held to account by the mechanisms of an ethical theory. Further, it becomes difficult to communicate to others any clear goals which transcend the personal beliefs of current leadership, current practices, or the majority rule of current membership. If the HPC digital divide is to be addressed, those making policy should be guided by clear, consistent, and rational ethical reasoning for why policies exist.

7   Conclusions

High performance computing resources deliver many pervasive interactions such as weather modeling, large-scale financial services, highly redundant data storage, and AI-enabled customer support systems. We have explored the potential outcomes of those with access to HPC systems and those without. In many ways, there exists an HPC digital divide between those *with* and those *without* access where innovation, equality, and participation in society are concerned. Additionally, geopolitics, finances, and environmental concerns exist in HPC where they may not exist in facets of the traditional digital divide.

We demonstrated how contractarianism and rule utilitarianism can be applied to reason about how to craft HPC access policies. While the reasoning may be different, both theories support an increased openness and lowering barriers to access for HPC systems as the most ethical path forward. Both emphasize working toward collective good which translates to increasing access in order to accelerate innovation, to decrease inequality, and to increase participation in society across all groups and communities. Without having a rational, consistent ethical framework as a guide for creating policies, the HPC digital divide is less likely to close. There are many ethical theories to guide the way.

References

1. Abiona, O., Onime, C., Cozzini, S., Hailemariam, S.: Capacity building for HPC infrastructure setup in Africa: the ICTP experience. In: 2011 IST-Africa Conference Proceedings, pp. 1–8 (2011)
2. Dutot, P.F., Georgiou, Y., Glesser, D., Lefevre, L., Poquet, M., Rais, I.: Towards energy budget control in HPC. In: 2017 17th IEEE/ACM International Symposium on Cluster, Cloud and Grid Computing (CCGRID), pp. 381–390. IEEE (2017)
3. Greengard, S.: Cloud computing and developing nations. Commun. ACM **53**(5), 18–20 (may 2010). https://doi.org/10.1145/1735223.1735232, https://doi-org.proxy.library.nd.edu/10.1145/1735223.1735232
4. Hollman, A.K., Obermier, T.R., Burger, P.R.: Rural measures: a quantitative study of the rural digital divide. J. Inf. Policy **11**(1), 176–201 (2021)
5. Hong, L., Zhong-hua, L., Xue-bin, C.: The applications and trends of high performance computing in finance. In: 2010 Ninth International Symposium on Distributed Computing and Applications to Business, Engineering and Science, pp. 193–197 (2010). https://doi.org/10.1109/DCABES.2010.45
6. Imhof, M., Vollmeyer, R., Beierlein, C.: Computer use and the gender gap: the issue of access, use, motivation, and performance. Comput. Hum. Behav. **23**(6), 2823–2837 (2007). https://doi.org/10.1016/j.chb.2006.05.007, https://www.sciencedirect.com/science/article/pii/S074756320600077X, including the Special Issue: Education and Pedagogy with Learning Objects and Learning Designs
7. Jeong, H.J., Jeong, I., Lee, H.J., Moon, S.M.: Computation offloading for machine learning web apps in the edge server environment. In: 2018 IEEE 38th International Conference on Distributed Computing Systems (ICDCS), pp. 1492–1499. IEEE (2018)
8. Katal, A., Dahiya, S., Choudhury, T.: Energy efficiency in cloud computing data centers: a survey on software technologies. Cluster Comput., 1–31 (2022)
9. Keegan Eamon, M.: Digital divide in computer access and use between poor and non-poor youth. J. Soc. Soc. Welfare **31**, 91 (2004)
10. Kitchens, F.: High performance computing as an educational experience well suited to developing nations. In: Fourth IEEE International Workshop on Technology for Education in Developing Countries (TEDC'06), pp. 38–43 (2006). https://doi.org/10.1109/TEDC.2006.18
11. Meuer, H.W., Strohmaier, E., Dongarra, J., Simon, H., Meuer, M.: https://www.top500.org/
12. Michalakes, J.: HPC for weather forecasting. In: Grama, A., Sameh, A.H. (eds.) Parallel Algorithms in Computational Science and Engineering. MSSET, pp. 297–323. Springer, Cham (2020). https://doi.org/10.1007/978-3-030-43736-7_10

13. M'rhaouarh, I., Okar, C., Namir, A., Chafiq, N.: Cloud computing adoption in developing countries: a systematic literature review. In: 2018 IEEE International Conference on Technology Management, Operations and Decisions (ICTMOD), pp. 73–79 (2018). https://doi.org/10.1109/ITMC.2018.8691295
14. Payton, F.C.: Rethinking the digital divide. Commun. ACM **46**(6), 89–91 (Jun 2003). https://doi.org/10.1145/777313.777318
15. Rong, H., Zhang, H., Xiao, S., Li, C., Hu, C.: Optimizing energy consumption for data centers. Renew. Sustain. Energy Rev. **58**, 674–691 (2016)
16. Van Dijk, J.: The digital divide. John Wiley & Sons (2020)
17. Wang, M., Fu, W., He, X., Hao, S., Wu, X.: A survey on large-scale machine learning. IEEE Trans. Knowl. Data Eng. (2020)
18. Zenios, S.A.: High-performance computing in finance: the last 10 years and the next. Parallel Comput. **25**(13–14), 2149–2175 (1999)

A Taxonomy of Factors Influencing Data Quality

Caihua Liu[1], Didar Zowghi[2], and Guochao Peng[1,2,3]([✉])

[1] Guilin University of Electronic Technology, Guilin 541004, Guangxi, China
[2] CSIRO's Data61, Sydney, NSW 2015, Australia
[3] Sun Yat-sen University, Guangzhou 510275, Guangdong, China
penggch@mail.sysu.edu.cn

Abstract. This paper aims at developing a taxonomy of factors influencing data quality. For this to happen, firstly, we conducted a survey of literature that has focused on examining the factors affecting data quality for the purpose of quality management and improvement in conceptual models. Secondly, referring to a well-established taxonomy development method, we distinguished 5 dimensions of the factors affecting data quality from related studies including: human, organisational, managerial, technical, and external dimensions as well as adding 11 characteristics under different dimensions that are not found in prior classifications. The proposed taxonomy was then evaluated by applying two well-known approaches: users' navigation exercises and criteria-oriented validation. The evaluation results of this study show that the proposed taxonomy can be used to categorise the factors affecting data quality. The taxonomy will benefit (a) researchers to compare differences between related studies and construct conceptual models of factors affecting data quality and (b) help practitioners improve the understanding of direct causes that improve or reduce data quality from the five dimensions and identify what are the core areas that have an impact on achieving high-quality data for enterprises and should receive more efforts to address data quality.

Keywords: Data Quality · Taxonomy Development · Taxonomy Evaluation · Literature Survey

1 Introduction

Data quality as a concept has received extensive attention in most industries, because data quality problems affect all organisations that use information systems [1] and infiltrate into all economic sectors [2]. Data quality problems are listed as one of the leading challenges enterprises face today, because poor-quality data can have negative social and economic impacts on a company, including customer satisfaction, running costs, decision-making processes, services performance, and employee job satisfaction [3]. A Gartner research paper in 2013 has reported that the cost of bad data is put at $14.2 million a year [4]. As a result, managing the increasing amount of routinely collected data and preserving the quality of this data should be put in a high priority.

In order to preserve data quality, organisations and individuals first need to know what are the areas that influence data quality. Previous studies have identified a set of factors influencing data quality and constructed their conceptual models for data quality management and improvement [5–8]. However, the comparison of differences among related studies did not receive enough attention in these studies. The knowledge and structural characteristics of conceptual models for the factors influencing data quality have not been formalised so far. A taxonomy can provide a means to organise and structure the knowledge of a field, enabling researchers to study relationships among concepts [9, 10]. Therefore, a taxonomy is a promising tool to understand and structure the factors that influence data quality from the existing literature and suggest future directions for research and practice.

This has motivated our research by focusing on classifying the factors affecting data quality and exploring the structural characteristics of the conceptual models for data quality management and improvement. Accordingly, the aim of this study is to develop a taxonomy for the factors influencing data quality based on related studies, giving insights for the future research on constructing the conceptual models of data quality management and improvement. The users of the taxonomy that we develop are researchers and practitioners of data practices in enterprises. The taxonomy of factors influencing data quality will assist in understanding direct causes that improve or reduce data quality at a high level. Additionally, the taxonomy will allow users to identify the core areas for achieving high-quality data in enterprises and to suggest potential areas for addressing data quality in the future.

The development of our taxonomy for factors affecting data quality refers to a method of taxonomy development from information systems discipline [11]. Prior studies have used the theory of Total Quality Management and Just In Time to discuss the factors influencing data quality from multiple perspectives [12]. Information products manufactured and used in the enterprise management process can be viewed as the products generated within a processing system on raw data, and thus the theory of product quality management can be also utilised to study data quality [1]. In product quality management, the factors can be divided into three groups: human, management and technology, which contribute to studying and understanding the factors that affect data quality [8]. We thus utilise this theoretical lens to develop our initial version of the taxonomy. After conceptualisation of characteristics and dimensions, we use the initial taxonomy to study and examine the factors influencing data quality identified from the literature (conceptual to empirical), and then revise the taxonomy. Referring to this taxonomy development method, we propose five dimensions of factors influencing data quality: human, organisational, managerial, technical, and external dimension, with a set of characteristics under different dimensions. Furthermore, we also take advantages of two approaches to evaluate our taxonomy: users' navigation exercises [13] and criteria-oriented validation [14].

Our study makes both academic and practical contributions. First, we include 8 factors that are not found in prior classifications, add characteristics under different dimensions and distinguish organisational and managerial factors on the taxonomy. The taxonomy developed in this study provides a means to compare prior models of factors affecting data quality and to determine the boundary of related studies and suggest potential research areas. Second, the proposed taxonomy allows practitioners to become more aware of direct causes that improve or reduce data quality from the five dimensions and identify core areas to improve data quality. Thus, the taxonomy developed in this study contributes to strategising data management priorities in enterprises.

The remainder of this paper is organised as follows: we first give definitions to the concepts used in this study and a brief summary of related studies; after that we describe our research methods; thereafter we present the proposed taxonomy and then evaluate the taxonomy using two well-known approaches; and at last we conclude this paper.

2   Definition

2.1   Data Quality

Because definitions of data quality address both "ability to satisfy needs" aspect and "fitness-for-purpose" aspect, operational definitions of data quality are context specific [15]. In the discipline of information systems, definitions of data quality are divided into dimensions [1]. For example, based on specific purposes, scholars define several dimensions of data quality such as completeness, accuracy, and consistency, which achieve context specific nature of data quality [16].

Although the literature on information quality and data quality has developed in parallel, there have been attempts to draw a distinction between the two based on the definition of data and information [17]. Researchers clearly indicated that data is objective to present a phenomenon unconcerned information systems while information is subjective to put the data into context by using information systems that users can understand. In this study, we concern the quality of the data and therefore we draw on the data quality research to investigate the factors affecting data quality.

2.2   Dimension, Characteristic and Meta-characteristic

The most important concepts used in this paper are: dimension, characteristic and meta-characteristic as summarised in Table 1. In this study, we aim at developing a taxonomy of factors influencing data quality. Taxonomy refers to both the process and the end result of grouping objects of interest by similarity, being considered as a form of classification [18]. This classification can be done either based on a single dimension or based on a number of dimensions [18]. Dimension is generally categorical data [18] and can be also called as variable in the taxonomy [11]. In this paper, we use the term dimension to describe a category of factors affecting data quality. As mentioned in Bailey's foundational book on classification techniques, characteristic is used to describe the fundamentals of the phenomenon [18]. Accordingly, we define characteristic as a specific subcategory of factors affecting data quality, being served to delineate an aspect of the dimension on the taxonomy. For meta-characteristic, as Nickerson, Varshney and Muntermann [11] notes, it is used as the basis for the choice of characteristics in the taxonomy. We define meta-characteristic as direct causes that improve or reduce data quality. In product quality management, the factors are divided into three groups: human, management and technology, and this theoretical lens also can be applied to study and understand data quality [8]. As a result, we view direct causes that improve or reduce data quality from human, managerial or technical perspective.

Table 1. Definitions of the concepts used in this study.

Concept	Definition
Dimension	a category of factors influencing data quality
Characteristic	a specific subcategory of factors affecting data quality, being served to delineate an aspect of the dimension on the taxonomy
Meta-characteristic	direct causes that improve or reduce data quality

3 Research Methods

3.1 A Survey of Related Studies

To develop a taxonomy of factor influencing data quality, we firstly conducted a survey on the literature which presents factors influencing data quality in conceptual models. This survey included three main activities: (1) identifying search keywords and databases, (2) searching initial list of studies, (3) appraising relevant studies.

Activity 1: Identifying Search Keywords and Databases. As we differentiated the definitions of data and information and our focus is on data quality, we limited the theoretical lens to the studies on data quality for search. Therefore, we adopted the term 'data quality' as a whole in our search rather than using 'information quality' and any other attributes in data quality. Additionally, we were interested in the factors influencing data quality, and we then used the term 'impact', 'influence', 'affect', and 'determinate' as synonyms for 'factor'. As mentioned in the Introduction, we intend to develop a taxonomy of factors influencing data quality based on related studies, exploring the structural characteristics of prior conceptual models for data quality management and improvement. According to [11], a convenience sample of objects of interests can be used to develop a taxonomy. To concentrate on prior models of factors influencing data quality that serve as a convenience sample for taxonomy development, we included the term 'model' and alternative terms 'framework', 'taxonomy', 'classification', 'category', 'typology', and 'ontology' in the search. As we are presenting the results from the research publications that have categorised the factors influencing data quality, not having these terms the search will increase the number of irrelevant papers by a large magnitude. Thus, we adopted the following search query for our search: (factor OR impact OR influence OR affect OR determinant) AND "data quality" AND (model OR framework OR taxonomy OR classification OR category OR typology OR ontology).

We utilised six popular databases as our initial search sources in order to cover a broad range of disciplines, including ScienceDirect, ACM Digital Library, EBSCO, IEEE Xplore, ProQuest and Google Scholar. In addition, we also screened the papers published in ICIS, AMCIS, ECIS, PACIS and HICSS proceedings.

Activity 2: Searching Initial List of Studies. With the search strings, we screened the literature from 2000 January to 2017 December in six online databases by title, abstract, and keywords to centralise our search. We customised our search with search strings in different online databases and identified the initial list of studies as shown in Table 2. We then filtered relevant studies based on our inclusion and exclusion characteristics.

Table 2. Distribution of studies in each database in our survey.

Database	Search field	Initial list of studies	Displayed studies	Relevant studies
ScienceDirect	Title, abstract, keywords	67	67	0
ACM Digital Library	Title and abstract	0	0	0
EBSCO	Title, abstract, subject terms	32	32	2
IEEE Xplore	Title, abstract, index terms	0	0	0
ProQuest	Title, abstract, subjects and indexing	359	359	0
Google Scholar	All fields	195,000	1,000	15
Total		195,458	1,458	17

Activity 3: Appraising Relevant Studies. The main objective of the last step is to filter relevant literature. The following inclusion criteria were applied: (1) studies presented are in English; (2) studies are available online from 2000 to 2017; and (3) studies have a focus on identifying and conceptualising the factors influencing data quality. For exclusion criterion, duplicate papers were once again eliminated. Although we identified another two relevant papers published in the proceedings during the manual search, the two were duplicate with the results searched by using the databases. Finally, we remained 17 relevant studies after this step.

In this study, we further select 9 papers out of surveyed 17 studies to develop the taxonomy of factors influencing data quality based on the following criteria:

- The studies have been published in book chapter, journal or proceeding (because Google Scholar includes non-published work);
- The factors identified from the studies have been empirically examined within enterprises;
- The factors derived from the literature have been conceptualised in a model.

3.2 Related Studies

Nine studies selected for our taxonomy development have made the main contributions to establish an empirical body of knowledge on identifying the factors affecting data quality. For example, Xu, Koronius and Brown [12] reported an empirical study on the identification of factors affecting data quality in accounting information systems (AIS) and grouped these factors into five categories: AIS characteristics, data quality characteristics, stakeholders' related factors, organisational factors, and external factors. This work establishes a seminal classification of factors influencing data quality in AIS, because a body of empirical studies [19–21] further the understanding of the factors affecting data quality based on Xu, Koronius and Brown [12]'s model. Using the technique of factor analysis, Xu [22] then revised the prior classification of factors influencing data quality in AIS [12], developing a more scientific conceptual model of factors influencing data quality. Similarly, a few researchers (e.g., [6–8, 23]) empirically examined the factors influencing data quality and validated their conceptual models. However, the structural characteristics of conceptual models for the factors influencing data quality have not been addressed by previous research.

The data quality domain has grown and the scope of its reference disciplines has expanded [24]. The studies related to factors influencing data quality are increasing, and new factors could emerge. Therefore, addressing the current status of the art for the factors influencing data quality and developing a new taxonomy would help us understand variance in the existing studies and ascertain possible voids of the research that potentially lead to new research directions.

3.3 Development of the Taxonomy

To develop the taxonomy of factors influencing data quality, we refer to the guidelines of the taxonomy development method [11] as depicted in Fig. 1.

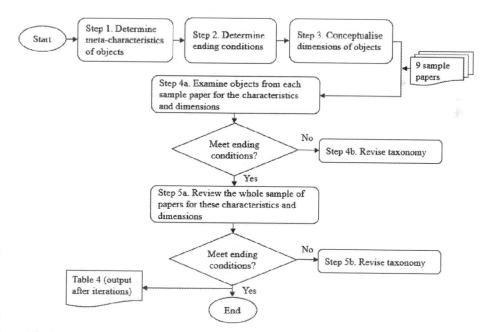

Fig. 1. The taxonomy development process of this study (adapted and revised from [11]).

Step 1: Determine Meta-characteristic of Objects. The objects of interest in our study are specific factors influencing data quality identified from related studies. We have defined the meta-characteristic as direct causes that improve or reduce data quality as presented in Table 1, and we intend to determine the characteristics of the factors affecting data quality from multiple perspectives such as human, management, and technology.

Step 2: Determine Ending Conditions. We will end the taxonomy development when both objective and subjective conditions have been met. The objective conditions indicate that each dimension in the taxonomy approaches "mutually exclusive and collectively exhaustive characteristics", while the subjective conditions concern whether a taxonomy achieves concise, robust, comprehensive, extendible, and explanatory criteria based on the researcher's viewpoints [11]. In this study, we use most objective ending conditions proposed by [11]. Since the factors influencing data quality have been identified and conceptualised in the model, these objects are not necessary to be further merged or split in the taxonomy development and a few objective ending condition related to examination or classification of objects is not applicable in this study. Additionally, we examine all five subjective conditions proposed by [11] to determine the end of the taxonomy development. See Table 3.

Table 3. Ending conditions used in our taxonomy development.

Ending conditions		Description
Definition of a taxonomy		The taxonomy includes dimensions that are with mutually exclusive characteristics
		The taxonomy includes dimensions that are with collectively exhaustive characteristics
Objective		No more factors from sample papers need to be examined
		At least one factor is classified under every characteristic of every dimension
		No new dimensions or characteristics could be added in the last iteration
		No dimensions or characteristics could be merged or split in the last iteration
		Every dimension is unique and not repeated
		Every characteristic is unique with its dimension
Subjective	Concise	The number of dimensions and characteristics for factors influencing data quality are limited
	Robust	The dimensions and characteristics to differentiate among factors influencing data quality are enough
	Comprehensive	All necessary dimensions and characteristics to classify factors influencing data quality are included
	Extendible	It is easy to include additional dimensions and characteristics
	Explanatory	It is useful to explain the characteristics of factors influencing data quality

Step 3: Conceptualise Dimensions of Objectives. As Nickerson, Varshney and Muntermann [11] notes, the taxonomy development can start from either an empirical approach or a conceptual approach. We adopt the conceptual-to-empirical approach in this study as we study and understand the factors influencing data quality from multiple perspectives (e.g., human, management, and technology). Based on the meta-characteristic, our taxonomy of factors influencing data quality developed from this conceptualisation results in five dimensions: human, organisational, managerial, technical, and external dimensions.

Step 4: Examine Objects From Each Sample Paper for the Characteristics and Dimensions and Revise the Taxonomy. We first examine the factors influencing data quality from each sample paper and determine the characteristic of these factors. We identify eleven characteristics of these factors based on the definitions given in the literature and our understanding, and then group these characteristics into five dimensions for the taxonomy development. All these factors are coded as shown in this link[1].

Step 5: Review the Whole Sample of Papers for These Characteristics and Dimensions and Revise the Taxonomy. We review the whole sample of papers and revise our taxonomy accordingly. After that, we cannot add any new characteristics and dimensions from these factors, and we have no more factors from our sample basket to examine. In addition, each dimension is unique and not repeated, and each characteristic is unique with its dimension. No dimensions or characteristics can be merged or split. At least one factor influencing data quality is classified under every characteristic of every dimension. We now meet the objective ending conditions. In terms of subjective ending conditions, we consider that our taxonomy achieves concise, extendible, comprehensive, robust and explanatory ending conditions. Thus, the taxonomy development ends.

4   A Proposed Taxonomy for Factors Influencing Data Quality

We now propose a taxonomy of factors influencing data quality, including five dimensions with 11 individual characteristics that are grouped under different dimensions. Table 4 presents our taxonomy and definitions of the dimensions and characteristics.

Table 4. A taxonomy of factors influencing data quality with definition of dimensions and characteristics.

Dimension	Definition	Characteristic	Definition
Human	individual consciousness and behavioural capability on activities related to data quality management and improvement	Individual consciousness	self-awareness of doing and of perceiving data quality management and improvement
		Individual behavioural capability	personal knowledge, skills and experience in the tasks of achieving quality data

(continued)

---

[1] https://www.dropbox.com/s/qg9i2kanb3vew81/The%20coding%20scheme%20for%20the%20factors%20that%20influence%20data%20quality%20identified%20from%20the%20sample%20papers.docx?dl=0.

Table 4. (*continued*)

Dimension	Definition	Characteristic	Definition
Organisational	organisational attributes or properties that could have an impact on achieving quality data	Organisational structure	a pattern of interrelated work activities in which it divides its labour into distinct tasks and then achieves coordination among them for the purposes of data quality
		Organisational culture	the shared beliefs and values towards data quality that guide the thinking and behavioural styles of members in an organisation
Managerial	the organisation and coordination of activities to achieve the defined goals of data quality in organisations	Recourses management	funding, human resources, and time allocation for a given task
		Business processes management	the ways of planning and monitoring the performance of business processes
Technical	information systems and development technologies to support data quality management and improvement	System quality	software and data components of an information system, with a number of attributes measured
		Supporting technology	available technical tools, methods and programs are used to support data quality initiatives
External	forces outside an organisation that have the potential to affect data quality	Physical environment	a part of the environment surrounding humans that contains only physical elements (e.g. air and water)
		Legal environment	a legal framework and regulatory for conducting business
		Competitive environment	a dynamic external system in which a business competes on a similar product or service

4.1 Human Dimension

The human factors involve personal consciousness and capability on the activities related to data quality management and improvement. This dimension entails individual consciousness and competency characteristics.

Individual consciousness is defined as self-awareness of doing and of perceiving data quality management and improvement (adapted and revised based on [25]). Individual consciousness could have an impact on achieving high-quality data. For example, the understanding of the importance of data quality and the perceived usefulness and need for data quality help organisations manage routinely collected data and preserve high-quality data [7, 8, 12]. Because high-quality data could assist in working effectively and achieving competitive advantages, decision makers are likely to support and participate in data quality initiatives. In light of this, sufficient human resource, funding, and time can be located to these initiatives, resulting in better data quality. Furthermore, if staff members satisfy their working status and career development, they are likely to play their roles in the organisation. For instance, staff members are willing to follow the rules and procedures when using information systems and to complete the routine tasks related to data management successfully [12]. As a result, the quality of the data could have the potential to preserve.

Individual behavioural capability concerns personal knowledge, skills and experience in the tasks of achieving high-quality data. Although self-awareness could drive human behaviour in data quality management and improvement, personal ability determines the extent to which the tasks related to addressing data quality can be completed. Thus, individual behavioural capability plays a vital role in achieving high-quality data.

4.2 Organisational Dimension

The organisational factors emphasise organisational attributes or properties (e.g. structure, location, size and history) that contribute to achieving high-quality data in an organisation. Two characteristics are grouped into this dimension: organisational structure and organisational culture.

Organisational structure refers to a pattern of interrelated work activities in which it divides its labour into distinct tasks and then achieves coordination among them for addressing data quality (adapted and revised based on [26]). For instance, a centralised structure in an organisation could perform better controls for data quality and further obtain high-quality data [6, 12].

Organisational culture describes the shared beliefs and values towards data quality that guide the thinking and behavioural styles of members in an organisation (adapted and revised based on Cooke and Rousseau [27]). An organisation that has a culture of focusing on data quality could have a better chance to perceive data quality, because the data quality initiatives could receive upper management group's support, sufficient resources, and staff's participation [12, 19, 20].

4.3 Managerial Dimension

The managerial factors focus on the organisation and coordination of activities to achieve the defined goals of data quality in an organisation. This dimension consists of recourses management and business processes management characteristics.

Recourses management includes funding, human resources, and time that are required to successfully complete the tasks related to data quality management and improvement. Appropriate human resources, available time and funding help guarantee effective technology being utilised in the implementation of innovative information systems and data quality initiatives [6, 23]. Without these efforts, these initiatives are unlikely to conduct.

Business processes management describes the ways of planning and monitoring the performance of business processes in achieving high-quality data, involving the information chains from data acquisition to its usage [28]. First, the amount of useful data is created and collected in the routine business process, and then this data is further used for operation, decision making and planning. At this moment, process management could regulate the business processes in creating quality data, including data creation on users' needs (e.g., user focus), data supplier quality management, data quality interventions, input controls, access controls, business-IT alignment, middle management, and audit and review [12, 19, 20]. Second, process management involves in monitoring the performance of business processes and staff participation for addressing data quality. For example, the evaluation of benefits/costs for conducting data quality initiatives helps improve the understanding of the benefits of high-quality data [12]. Thus, decision makers are likely to focus on data quality management and improvement. Meanwhile, the evaluation of staff's performance in achieving high-quality data contributes to increasing the awareness of preserving data quality in their job positions [12].

4.4 Technical Dimension

This dimension concerns information systems and development technologies to support data quality management and improvement, including systems quality and supporting technology characteristics.

Systems quality concerns software and data components of an information system, with a number of attributes measured such as ease of use, ease of learning, system features, system accuracy, flexibility, sophistication, integration, and customisation [29]. Prior literature proposed that the data derived from information systems can have a profound effect on the system initiatives, because standardised data can lead to easier data manipulation and improve data quality [6, 12, 23].

Supporting technology indicates that available technical tools, methods and programs are used to support data quality initiatives. For example, a reminder system automatically identifies incomplete records, provides a schedule about due records, and notifies the responsible personnel by an email after a certain grace period [30]. As such, the quality of the data can have a better chance to improve. Furthermore, integration technologies (e.g., data warehouse) to some degree determine the extent to which the data is aggregated from different data repositories, thus further ascertaining how good is the data delivered to users [2]. Accordingly, supporting technology also contributes to addressing data quality.

4.5 External Dimension

In this dimension, external factors influencing data quality refer to the forces outside organisations that have the potential to affect data quality, including physical, legal and competitive environment.

Physical environment: Physical working environment has the potential to influence data quality. For instance, poor air-condition environment could reduce employees' work efficiency and result in human errors in the recoding or reporting tasks. As a result, physical environment could further affect data quality [12, 22].

Legal environment: Data quality associated with the products delivered is often regulated by legal constraints or contractual obligations [7]. First, organisations must comply with relevant privacy legislation and data quality legislation that prescribe how organisations collect, secure and use the data [7]. Hence, the legal system helps determine the extent to which the data is available for different users. Second, organisations have to offer quality data to their customers within relevant contractual obligations. As a result, organisations are likely to improve their management commitment to preserving data quality [7].

Competitive environment: Competitive pressures drive organisations to improve the quality of the products and services for customers in order to stand at a competitive edge [7]. The quality-assured products and services are heavily dependent on data quality, because high-quality data enables organisations to capitalise large scale and complex data to their competitive advantages and create potential business opportunities [31]. Hence, organisations would like to make their commitment to achieving high-quality data.

5 Evaluation of the Taxonomy and Discussion

In this section, we evaluate and discuss the proposed taxonomy of factors influencing data quality using two well-known approaches: users' navigation exercises [13] and criteria-oriented validation [14].

First, users' navigation exercises allow users to allocate the content under study to a taxonomy. In this case, a taxonomy can serve as a navigation tool or visual representation of the knowledge base organised and structured in a field [13, 32]. Users apply the taxonomy to categorise the content that can be considered as a means of validation with content that is a relatively objective method to evaluate the effectiveness of the developed taxonomy [13, 32]. In this study, in order to evaluate the effectiveness of our taxonomy's construction, 7 experts in the domain of data practices and/or data quality were independently invited to take part in the navigation exercises. They were asked to categorise a given set of factors influencing data quality identified from the sample papers using the proposed taxonomy.

Second, criteria-oriented validation is a structural approach for evaluating a taxonomy based on a set of well-organised criteria [14, 32]. Lambe [14] proposed three stages in evaluating a taxonomy: structural validation, validation with people, and validation with content, together with nine essential criteria (e.g. intuitive, unambiguous, hospitable, consistent and predictable, relevant, parsimonious, meaningful, durable, and balanced). However, not all of these criteria are easy to achieve fully and can be utilised before conducting a test, because most of these criteria are subjective and supposed to be used to evaluate by experts and users [14, 32]. Three of these criteria (hospitableness, parsimoniousness, and balance) can be applied by observing the outcomes of developing a taxonomy [14]. It is also less time consuming to use these three criteria for evaluating our taxonomy. Hence, these criteria were utilised for our taxonomy evaluation in this study. Meanwhile, a structural validation for usability issues about a taxonomy can be implemented inside the research team [14]. Thus, we also included the usability criterion in the criteria-oriented validation.

5.1 Users' Navigation Exercises

In this study, 7 participants who have expertise in data practices and/or data quality were selected and independently invited to categorise the factors influencing data quality identified from the nine sample papers by using the proposed taxonomy in the navigation exercises.

Navigation Exercise Document. A navigation exercise document used in this study includes two sections: (1) an explanation of the exercises and (2) a set of factors influencing data quality (n = 42) that are needed to allocate using the taxonomy. Our navigation exercise document can be accessed using this link[2]. The first section contains the purposes and instructions of the exercise and a demographic form for the participants, while the second section (also the task section) describes the role of the participant and his/her tasks in the exercise. Furthermore, the task section entails a list of the factors that affect data quality (n = 42) identified from our sample papers. We also prepared two supplementary documents, including: (1) definition of all the factors derived from the literature; and (2) definition of dimensions and characteristics of the proposed taxonomy.

Participants and Recruitment. A total of 7 participants who have expertise in data practices and/or data quality that are colleagues of the second author were invited to participate in the exercises. We recruited all participants and distributed the navigation exercise document by email. These researchers were asked to work as coders, reviewing the definition of each characteristic and dimension of the taxonomy and allocating the factors listed in the task section to the corresponding characteristic and dimension. Finally, 6 subjects agreed to participate in our exercises. Two of the participants requested to have a face-to-face meeting with the researchers to better understand the purposes of user exercise and to clarify some points before doing the exercise. All but one participant performed their tasks on their own and completed the relevant sections. One participant requested to do the exercise in the presence of the first author to expedite the process. Table 5 lists the demographics of the participants.

Table 5. Demographics of participants in the exercise.

Characteristic	Number	Characteristic	Number
Education level		Years of Experience	
Undergraduate	1	<5 years	2
Postgraduate	5	>10 years	4
Total	6	Total	6

Most responses were collected from the respondents by email, and only one response was collected by hard copy. Furthermore, because all participants were invited to complete the exercises based on their expertise of data practices and/or data quality, few differences occur between their background and experience that need to be controlled in the analysis. We therefore focused more on the problems and comments (the last page

---

[2] https://www.dropbox.com/s/1bqil1fvb1fpyut/An%20exercise%20document%20example.docx?dl=0.

of the exercise document provided to them) presented by the participants that might be applicable to other researchers who are undertaking similar studies.

Evaluation Results. The unit of analysis was each allocation of the factors influencing data quality in the responses. We compared these responses (658 allocations for forty-two factors) with our coding scheme (546 allocations = 91 * 6 participants) prepared. Table 6 presents the numbers of prepared and actual allocations of the factors that affect data quality under five dimensions, as well as their precisions and recalls. We divided the total actual allocations from the exercises into two groups: matched allocations and additional allocations (also unmatched allocations). However, it is not necessary to say that our coding scheme established as a golden standard. We were interested in the extent to which the actual allocations deviated from the ideal allocations we prepared. Thus, precision was used to measure the extent to which matched allocations were in an agreement with total actual allocations, while recall was applied to measure the extent to which matched allocations were in an agreement with ideal allocations prepared for evaluating a taxonomy as suggested by [13]. Note that there are no specific thresholds for precision and recall and researchers could take advantages of precision and recall to explore and explain the phenomenon behind the results (e.g., [13]).

Table 6. Numbers of allocations collected and prepared in the exercise.

Dimensions of our taxonomy	No. of prepared allocations	No. of actual allocations	No. of matched allocations	No. of additional allocations	Precision	Recall
Human	15	119	42	81	35.3%	46.7%
Organisational	25	175	79	106	45.1%	52.7%
Managerial	30	171	81	101	47.4%	45.0%
Technical	7	105	23	97	21.9%	54.8%
External	14	88	39	55	44.3%	46.4%
Total	91 * 6 = 546	658	264	440		

Precision. When participants selected additional allocations, low precision occurred. As one participant did the exercise in the presence of the first author, we observed that this participant was not restricted by concepts given in the tasks and applied their own knowledge and experience to allocate the factors. Furthermore, this participant sometimes tended to figure out each factor that has impacts on the characteristics under different dimensions. For example, the participant considered that a physical working environment could have an impact on individual consciousness, and then he populated this factor under human dimension. The insufficient understanding of the tasks and definitions of the factors and the elements in the taxonomy could affect the precision of the allocations for these factors. However, all factors were successfully populated in the taxonomy without expansion based on their feedback. The lowest precision occurred for technical dimension (21.9%) as the participants grouped some managerial factors into this dimension. The highest precision for managerial dimension (47.4%) resulted from the consensus on those factors that contain the corresponding characteristics.

Recall. When participants did not select the allocations prepared, low recall occurred. As we mentioned, it was not necessary to say that our coding scheme established as a gold standard and we focused on the extent to which our classification of the factors influencing data quality was consistent with participations' perspective. Participants might partially select characteristics for each factor and not explore as many as possible characteristics for the same factor. Meanwhile, they tended to select all possible characteristics under different dimensions that could be affected by these factors, resulting in low recall in the exercises. For example, lowest recall for managerial dimension (45.0%) was partly due to confusion about the purposes of tasks in the exercise. However, the technical dimension had better recall (54.8%) because most technical factors were obvious to be allocated in this dimension that had received attention from the participants. Based on the feedback, all participants agreed with the wording and the structure of the taxonomy.

5.2 Criteria-Oriented Validation

Four criteria were selected in the study because they are less time consuming for evaluating our taxonomy and the results of the evaluation can be observed directly. The four criteria are defined as suggested by [14]. See Table 7.

Usability. As Lambe [14] notes, "usability issues in building taxonomies beyond 15 items in a level and beyond three levels in a tree" (p. 200) are needed to consider when developing a taxonomy. Our taxonomy includes two levels: dimension and characteristic. The first level of our taxonomy consists of 5 dimensions. Moreover, we add 11 characteristics in the taxonomy as the second level that are not delineated in prior classifications. These characteristics describe different aspects of the dimensions that improve the hierarchical structure of the taxonomy and help users extend the taxonomy easily and classify the factors precisely. Obviously, our taxonomy meets the recommended threshold of building a taxonomy based on the usability criterion.

Hospitableness. Hospitableness of our taxonomy was evaluated by classifying the factors influencing data quality from related studies into our taxonomy. Specifically, the factors affecting data quality from prior classifications were allocated in our taxonomy. Moreover, eight new factors from our sample papers that are not found in prior classifications were also categorised into our taxonomy. These new factors are: Perceived need for data quality, Perceived usefulness of data quality, Resources, Champion, Business-IT alignment, Extrinsic rewards, Contractual requirements, and Competitive pressure. Therefore, our taxonomy can successfully accommodate related studies.

As we mentioned, the factors influencing product quality management are divided into three groups: human, management and technology [8]. This theoretical lens can be used to study the factors influencing data quality. Furthermore, many researchers revealed that external factors have an impact on data quality [7, 12, 19, 22]. Hence, a holistic list of the factors influencing data quality contains four main groups: human, managerial,

Table 7. Criteria-oriented evaluation for our taxonomy.

Criterion	Definition	Recommended threshold	Our taxonomy
Usability	The extent to which a taxonomy can be used by specified users to achieve specified goals in a specified context of use (revised from ISO 9241-11)	≤15 items in a level	5 dimensions (1st level) 11 characteristics (2nd level)
		≤3 levels in a tree	2 levels in a tree (dimensions and characteristics make up these 2 levels)
Hospitableness	"The taxonomy will successfully accommodate probable or foreseen new content, without the need for significant expansion or restructuring" ([14], p. 199)	Not applicable	Group the factors that influence data quality from multiple perspectives Easy to extend the taxonomy by adding characteristics under dimensions
Parsimoniousness	"The taxonomy structure offers no more and no less than what is required for the content that is to be accommodated" ([14], p. 200)	Not applicable	"No characteristics are unpopulated with content" ([14], p. 200) "No characteristics are overpopulated with large amounts of undifferentiated content" ([14], p. 200)
Balance	"When the taxonomy is populated with content, there are relatively even quantities of content across the taxonomy categories" ([14], p. 200)	Not applicable	"No areas of the taxonomy are densely populated with large amounts of undifferentiated content while other areas are underpopulated" ([14], p. 200)

technical, and external factors. We include these four groups in the taxonomy, and further distinguish organisational and managerial factors. Based on this analysis, our taxonomy can be generalised from this theoretical perspective in grouping the factors that affect data quality, therefore foreseeing new content without a significant expansion or restructuring.

Parsimoniousness. It is observed in our coding scheme that every characteristic of every dimension has at least one factor that affect data quality. In addition, no characteristics are overpopulated with large amounts of undifferentiated content. Hence, our taxonomy meets the parsimoniousness criterion.

Balance. Similarly, our coding scheme shows that the quantities of the allocations for the factors affecting data quality across dimensions are relatively populated in our taxonomy. Table 6 contains the distribution of allocations in populating the factors influencing data quality under different dimensions. The most frequently used dimension is managerial dimension (n = 30), while only a few technical factors (n = 7) were included in related studies. The mean of the frequency of dimensions populated in this study is 18.2, and the standard deviation of the frequency of dimensions is 9.2.

6 Conclusion

In this paper, we have proposed a taxonomy of factors influencing data quality referring to a well-established method of taxonomy development. Our taxonomy can be divided into five dimensions with 11 individual characteristics that are grouped under different dimensions. Furthermore, we have evaluated the taxonomy by using two well-known approaches: users' navigation exercises [13] and criteria-oriented validation [14]. The evaluation results show that the taxonomy can be used to categorise the factors influencing data quality.

6.1 Contributions

The contributions of this paper are twofold. The first contribution is the taxonomy of factors influencing data quality. We add 11 characteristics under different dimensions that are not available in prior classifications, and further distinguish organisational and managerial factors for the taxonomy, thus improving the hierarchical structure of the taxonomy. This paper classifies the factors influencing data quality and proposes the taxonomy from a breadth perspective that presents the extent to which the factors affecting data quality are studied in the literature for the first time.

The empirical evaluation of the taxonomy represents our second contribution. More specifically, the results of taxonomy evaluation demonstrate that our taxonomy can help users understand the factors influencing data quality from the developed dimensions and characteristics. As mentioned in the Introduction, the users of the taxonomy include (a) researchers and (b) practitioners of data practices in enterprises. For (a), our taxonomy is a promising tool to compare differences between related studies to help researchers determine the boundary of related studies and explore potential research areas. We distil the results of the empirical evaluation into two implications for researchers who are interested in the topic of data quality.

Implication 1: Consider a breath perspective to construct the conceptual model for the factors influencing data quality. By surveying and understanding related studies, we have found that researchers included and examined the factors influencing data quality from multiple perspectives (e.g. human, managerial, and technical dimensions) in their conceptual models. Researchers tested the hypotheses for the relationships between these factors and data quality, and indicated that these factors faithfully influence data quality. Thus, when constructing a conceptual model for data quality management and improvement, human, organisational, managerial, technical, and external factors (from a breadth perspective) could be considered in the construction.

Implication 2: Consider a breadth perspective to compare differences between related studies on factors influencing data quality. Because we have developed a taxonomy by examining the factors influencing data quality from related studies, possible characteristics of these factors from the literature are captured in our taxonomy. Prior studies included different factors affecting data quality that might not have the same characteristics. Thus, our taxonomy can be used to differentiate the characteristics of related studies and ascertain the boundary of the included factors from a breadth perspective.

For (b), the developed taxonomy contributes to improving the understanding of direct causes that improve or reduce data quality from the five dimensions and helps practitioners identify (1) what are the core areas that have an impact on achieving high-quality data for enterprises and (2) which areas that have not been received sufficient attention should give more efforts to address data quality in the future. Therefore, our proposed taxonomy assists in decision making for data quality management priorities in enterprises.

6.2 Limitations and Future Study

Although this study makes significant contributions, the present work has two limitations. First, the current paper is developed based on a limited number of empirical studies for taxonomy development, and therefore, it may underestimate the current state of the art of factors influencing data quality. Researchers therefore are suggested to conduct (1) a systematic review of the literature on data quality and attributes of data quality (e.g., completeness and accuracy) or (2) an empirical study to collect the factors influencing data quality from industries to see whether the taxonomy can be expanded. Second, this study focuses on the taxonomy development and evaluation for the factors influencing data quality, and thus we did not demonstrate the application of our proposed taxonomy in enterprises. A topic of interest in the future is to investigate how practitioners use the taxonomy to determine which areas should receive more attention to address data quality in enterprises.

Acknowledgement. This research was supported and funded by the Humanities and Social Sciences Youth Foundation, Ministry of Education of the People's Republic of China (Grant No. 21YJC870009).

References

1. Wang, R.Y., Strong, D.M.: Beyond accuracy: what data quality means to data consumers. J. Manag. Inf. Sys. **12**(4), 5–33 (1996)
2. Cappiello, C., Francalanci, C., Pernici, B.: Time-related factors of data quality in multichannel information systems. J. Manag. Inf. Sys. **20**(3), 71–92 (2003)
3. Haug, A., Zachariassen, F., Van Liempd, D.: The costs of poor data quality. J. Ind. Eng. Manag. **4**(2), 168–193 (2011)

4. Friedman, T., Judah, S.: The state of data quality: current practices and evolving trends (2013). https://www.gartner.com/doc/2636315/state-data-quality-current-practices

5. Al-Hiyari, A., AL-Mashre, M.H.H., Mat, N.K.N.: Factors that affect accounting information system implementation and accounting information quality: a survey in University Utara Malaysia. Am. J. Econ. **3**(1), 27–31 (2013)

6. Kokemueller, J.: An empirical investigation of factors influencing data quality improvement success. Paper Presented at the 17th AMCIS, Detroit, Michigan, August 2011

7. Tee, S.W., Bowen, P.L., Doyle, P., Rohde, F.H.: Factors influencing organizations to improve data quality in their information systems. Account. Finance **47**(2), 335–355 (2007)

8. Xiao, J.-h., Xie, K., Wan, X.-w.: Factors influencing enterprise to improve data quality in information systems application - an empirical research on 185 enterprises through field study. Paper presented at the 16th International Conference on Management Science and Engineering, Moscow, Russia, September 2009

9. Glass, R.L., Vessey, I.: Contemporary application-domain taxonomies. IEEE Softw. **12**(4), 63–76 (1995)

10. McKnight, D.H., Chervany, N.L.: What trust means in e-commerce customer relationships: an interdisciplinary conceptual typology. Int. J. Electron. Commun. **6**(2), 35–59 (2001)

11. Nickerson, R.C., Varshney, U., Muntermann, J.: A method for taxonomy development and its application in information systems. Eur. J. Inf. Syst. **22**(3), 336–359 (2013)

12. Xu, H., Koronius, A., Brown, N.: Managing data quality in accounting information systems. In: Joia, L.A. (ed.) IT-Based Management: Challenges and Solutions, pp. 277–299. Idea Group Publishing, Hershey and London (2002)

13. Wang, Z., Khoo, C.S., Chaudhry, A.S.: Evaluation of the navigation effectiveness of an organizational taxonomy built on a general classification scheme and domain thesauri. J. Assoc. Inf. Sci. Technol. **65**(5), 948–963 (2014)

14. Lambe, P.: Organising Knowledge: Taxonomies, Knowledge and Organisational Effectiveness. Chandos Publishing Limited, Oxford (2007)

15. Fehrenbacher, D.D., Helfert, M.: Contextual factors influencing perceived importance and trade-offs of information quality. Commun. Assoc. Inf. Syst. **30**(1), 111–126 (2012)

16. Ji-fan Ren, S., Fosso Wamba, S., Akter, S., Dubey, R., Childe, S.J.: Modelling quality dynamics, business value and firm performance in a big data analytics environment. Int. J. Prod. Res. **55**(17), 5011–5026 (2017)

17. Tilly, R., Posegga, O., Fischbach, K., Schoder, D.: Towards a conceptualization of data and information quality in social information systems. Bus. Inf. Syst. Eng. **59**(1), 3–21 (2017)

18. Bailey, K.D.: Typologies and Taxonomies: An Introduction to Classification Techniques. Sage Publications, Thousand Oaks (1994)

19. Nord, G.D., Nord, J.H., Xu, H.: An investigation of the impact of organization size on data quality issues. J. Database Manag. **16**(3), 58–71 (2005)

20. Xu, H.: Data quality issues for accounting information systems' implementation: systems, stakeholders, and organizational factors. J. Technol. Res. **1**, 1–11 (2009)

21. Xu, H., Lu, D.: The critical success factors for data quality in accounting information system different industries' perspective. Issues in Inf. Syst. **4**, 762–768 (2003)

22. Xu, H.: Factor analysis of critical success factors for data quality. Paper Presented at the 19th AMCIS, Chicago, Illinois, August 2013

23. Wixom, B.H., Watson, H.J.: An empirical investigation of the factors affecting data warehousing success. MIS Q., 17–41 (2001)

24. Sadiq, S., Yeganeh, N.K., Indulska, M.: 20 years of data quality research: themes, trends and synergies. In: Proceedings of the 22nd Australasian Database Conference, vol. 115, pp. 153–162 (2011)

25. Fenigstein, A., Scheier, M.F., Buss, A.H.: Public and private self-consciousness: assessment and theory. J. Consult. Psychol. **43**(4), 522–527 (1975)

26. Maguire, E.R.: Organizational Structure in American Police Agencies: Context, Complexity, and Control. State University of New York Press, New York (2003)
27. Cooke, R.A., Rousseau, D.M.: Behavioral norms and expectations: a quantitative approach to the assessment of organizational culture. Group Organ. Stud. **13**(3), 245–273 (1988)
28. Juran, J., Godfrey, A.B.: Juran's Quality Handbook, 5th edn. McGraw-Hill, New York (1999)
29. Gorla, N., Somers, T.M., Wong, B.: Organizational impact of system quality, information quality, and service quality. J. Strateg. Inf. Syst. **19**(3), 207–228 (2010)
30. Herzberg, S., Rahbar, K., Stegger, L., Schäfers, M., Dugas, M.: Concept and implementation of a computer-based reminder system to increase completeness in clinical documentation. Int. J. Med. Inform. **80**(5), 351–358 (2011)
31. Kwon, O., Lee, N., Shin, B.: Data quality management, data usage experience and acquisition intention of big data analytics. Int. J. Inf. Manag. **34**(3), 387–394 (2014)
32. Wu, Y., Yang, L.: Construction and evaluation of an oil spill semantic relation taxonomy for supporting knowledge discovery. Knowl. Organ. **42**(4), 222–231 (2015)

Designing a Smart Standards Information Service: A Research Framework

Jie Liu and Guochao Peng[✉]

Sun Yat-sen University, Guangzhou 510006, China
penggch@mail.sysu.edu.cn

Abstract. As an importance science and technology information resource, standards information plays a significant role in the social and economic development. However, enterprises users' need of standards information could hardly be fulfilled by current standards information services due to various reasons. Moreover, limited researches are done in the understanding of customer needs of standards information and the improvement of standards information services. This research analyzed the problems of current standards information services and pointed out the significance of improving them. An introduction of related theories about understanding users' needs and designing services is then presented. In the end, a research framework integrating KANO, QFD and TRIZ is presented to seek a user-based solution for smart standards information service design.

Keywords: standards information · smart standards information service · KANO · QFD · TRIZ · service design

1 Introduction

Standards information generally refers to the relevant information generated by all standardization activities, including standard documents, news, reports, laws and regulations related to standardization activities. Standards information service refers to the collection, release, sorting, and processing of standard information [1], which is an important part of scientific and technological information service [2, 3]. As "a formula that describes the best way of doing something" [4] that developed based on the achievements of science, technology and experience [5], the standard is a bridge between enterprises and users, and one of the important foundations to promote economic growth and technological innovation. How to make full use of standard information and serve national development, scientific and technological innovation and the public is the core issue of standard information service.

Nevertheless, limited literatures could be found about standards information service. Furthermore, the major theme of the limited literatures is about how to collect standards and provide standards for customers. Phillips [6] introduced a brief history of the development of standard collections in university libraries, and pointed out that the collection of standards is faced with high costs, separate ICS classification index, cataloging difficulties, and high real-time requirements. In particular, developing countries are limited in their ability to purchase standard libraries due to financial constraints [7]. With the emergence of the Internet and the interconnection of network resources, this problem has been solved to a certain extent. Jennifer [7] pointed out that standard electronic resources and databases are a good way for libraries in developing countries to obtain collections with limited financial resources. In the digital age, scholars began to explore how to use network and electronic resources to solve the pain of difficult purchases and high prices of the standards [8], and how to deal with the rising demand for standards [9]. Some researchers realized that standards service has emphasized too much on literature service [10]. Knowledge service and intelligence service based on standards information are underdeveloped [10–12]. One of the reasons that cause the development dilemma of standards information service is insufficient understanding of users' needs [10].

For a long time, although a consensus has been reached that standards information services should focus on users' needs [13], the researches on users' needs only focus on the literature services. For example, Zhao and Cai [14] conducted a survey on the satisfaction of enterprise users with the standards literature service to find that 24% of users' needs are fulfilled, 53% basically fulfilled, and 24% not satisfied. They also pointed out that enterprise users' needs more timely, comprehensive, in-depth standards service. Nonetheless, the current resource-oriented service mode could hardly satisfy the users' needs. Both scholars and practitioners are exploring this new form of service, yet the solutions are provided based more on experience than rigorous scientific research. As Liu and Peng pointed out, the standards information service has entered a new stage of smart service development [15]. More thoughts should be put into the promotion of the service based on users' needs.

This research strives to provide a research framework on designing a smart standards information service based on customer requirements. KANO model is applied to collect users' needs, QFD is conducted to deploy the functions of standards information service and TRIZ is used to find innovative solutions for the contradictions found.

The next section briefly introduces standards information service at present, and pointed out the problems through a comparative analysis. Then a literature review is presented from the perspectives of understanding users' needs and service design. The proposed research framework is explained and illustrated in Sect. 4. Conclusions are presented in the end.

2   Standards Information Service at Present

In the age of globalization, standards have played a more and more important role in international trade and quality management in all fields. The significance of standards is becoming more prominent, not only for enterprises and government, but also for individuals. Standards information are required by practitioners in their work, by students in their preparation for careers, and by researchers in scientific research. For different purposes, the providers of standards information services could be generally divided into 3 types: standardization organizations, libraries, and third-party databases.

2.1 Standardization Organizations

Standardization organizations are developers of standards and producers of standards information, such as international organizations like International Standardization Organization (ISO), International Electrical Commission (IEC), and International Telecommunication Union (ITU), and national organizations like American National Standards Institute (ANSI), British Standards Institution (BSI) and Standardization Administration Commission of China (SAC).

These standardization organizations not only develop and publish standards, but also provide standards information services like standards, standards catalogue information, standardization process information and documentation, etc. Based on their "fresh" data and information resources, more in-depth services like standards development, standards consultation, standards database construction, etc. are also provided. Take ISO as an example, all the paper copies (some are digital versions) of ISO standards could be purchased online, the catalogue information and development records of all standards are also provided. In USA, National Standards Information Services was found in 1965 [16] to provide various forms of standards information resources, including standards, technical reference books, reports, etc. Identifying sources of standards and directing requirements were also conducted with the assistance of Key-Word-In-Context (KWIC) indexes. To provide better standards information service, ANSI built a web-based search engine in the early 20th century [17]. In China, standardization research institutes are set under the management of SAC which serves to provide more in-depth services of standards research, standards development and standards consultation.

2.2 Libraries

Many types of libraries collect standards, including public, corporate, and academic libraries. Academic Engineering Libraries, in particular, are the main standards information providers for students and teachers for the purpose of standardization education and research. It is important and necessary to cultivate students' notion of the importance of standards, and the ability to read and implement them in practice in order to prepare for their career [18]. In order to support education and research, university libraries should not only collect and manage standards collections, but also find ways to provide good standards information services for students and teachers. Despite the challenges in the standards collections including lack of a comprehensive index, inconsistent index, difficulties in cataloging, and high cost [6], libraries still need to improve their standards information services for the future. Dunn and Xie [19] introduce 6 recommendations about standards collection development and management, including reviewing the standards collections policy, updating and evaluating standards, ensuring easy access to standards, maintaining online library guides, looking for fundings to purchase standards, and considering alternative subscription or purchase mode [20]. In China, standards libraries are founded to provide standards information services for local government, enterprises, colleges, research institutes and social organizations, including information retrieval, original text transmission, novelty and validity verification, etc. [21]. Standards libraries also provide knowledge services like online standards consultation, and strategic consultation [22].

2.3 Third-Party Database

The third-party databases aggregate various standards information resources and could provide customized solutions for the requirements of standards database construction, such as IHS Markit Standards Store and TechStreet Store. Standards from various publishers could be found, like IEC, IPC, CSA, etc. The main business of these databases is to sale standards. Other standards information like standardization polices, latest progress of standards development would not be provided. The advantages of the third-party standards information services are simplified access to standards from different organizations, instantaneous access to the standards resources and customized subscription [6]. Yet the disadvantage is their higher price compared with subscription directly to publishers of standards.

2.4 Problems of Current Standards Information Service

The 3 types of providers of standards information service have their own characteristics. The standardization organizations and institutes only provide their own standards. Yet they are the authority of the standards they publish, and could provide more detailed information about their standards references, development process, and reliable explanations. Libraries usually provide services to certain groups of users, and could provide more in-depth services like strategic consultation. However, they usually lack of fund to purchase a large number of standards and keep them updated in time. The third-party database could provide aggregated standards resources and easy access at the price of a higher cost.

Table 1. Comparison of standards information service from different providers

	Standardization organizations	Libraries	Third-party database
Advantages	Authority; more details about standards; reliable explanation of the standards; most up to date information	More in-depth services; targeted user service	Aggregated standards resources; easy access
Disadvantages	Single source of standards	lack of fund; limited collection of standards; information lag	High cost; less in-depth services

In sum, the most common standards information service is still document service and information transport. Although standardization organizations and institutes and libraries provide more in-depth services, they are either based on limited standards information or facing certain groups of users.

For enterprise users, their main purposes for accessing standards information resources are to support technology development, product design and marketing strategy.

The current standards information services could hardly fully satisfy their needs. The enterprise users have to devote a lot of time, money and people to possess and analyze related standards information.

To change the situation and upgrade the standards information services, smart standards information services based on users' needs could be the solution. The core of smart standards services is to listen to the users' voices and provide innovative services. Therefore, the research framework for designing such a service should both support a better understanding of users' needs and provide an innovative design of service.

3 Literature Review

3.1 Understanding Users' Need

Understanding users' needs is becoming more prominent than before. Under the current intense global market competition, it is recognized by enterprises that to survive or maintain growth in market competition, they should devote more to understanding customers' requirements and achieving customer satisfaction rather than relying simply on low-cost and high-volume production [23]. For standards information services, the vitality lies in the users' satisfaction as well. The users' needs and satisfaction push forward the advancement of standards information services.

KANO Model. To help understand customers' requirements, various tools and methods have been developed. Kano model is a widely used tool among them. Kano model is a tool for classifying and prioritizing user needs proposed by Professor N. Kano of Tokyo Institute of technology in 1979 inspired by the two-factor theory [24]. Through a positive and negative survey of each attribute, the model divides users' requirements into 6 categories: Must-be quality, One-dimensional quality, Attractive quality, Indifferent quality, Reverse quality and Questionable quality. Their differences are:

Must-Be Quality (M). Users take this quality for granted. Fulfillment of this kind of requirement will not significantly improve user satisfaction. However, failure to fulfill this requirement will greatly reduce users' satisfaction (Fig. 1).

One-Dimensional Quality (O). If users' requirements of this category are met, satisfaction could be proportionally improved. Otherwise, the satisfaction will be decreased dramatically. The better the requirements are fulfilled, the higher the satisfaction is.

Attractive Quality (A). Requirements in this category are usually not expressed explicitly. Fulfilling these requirements can bring satisfaction unproportionally. If they are not met, there will not be much decrease in satisfaction.

Indifferent Quality (I). Whether fulfillment or not, this category does not influence much on users' satisfaction.

Reverse Quality (R). Users dislike this quality. If these qualities are met, satisfaction will reduce. On the contrary, if they are not met, users are more satisfied.

Questionable Quality (Q). If the category indicates either the questions are unreasonable or the answer of the user is illogical.

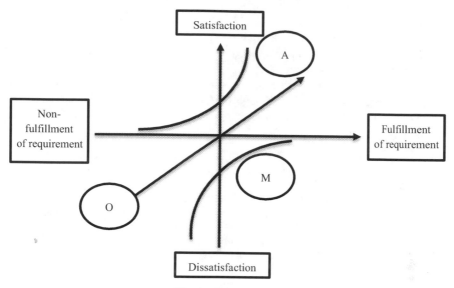

Fig. 1. KANO model

By classifying customer needs into different categories, KANO model contributes to identifying the different relationships between the fulfillment of customer needs and customer satisfaction [25, 26]. Nevertheless, the traditional KANO model is limited to qualitative analysis of the relationships, and could not describe the extent to which the customers are satisfied [27]. In order to fill the gap, Berger proposed Customer Satisfaction (CS) coefficient (or Better Coefficient) and Dissatisfaction (DS) coefficient (or Worse Coefficient), which indicates the percentage of customers that are satisfied and dissatisfied once certain attributes/customer need is fulfilled or not respectively[27].

$$CS = \frac{A+O}{A+O+M+I} \tag{1}$$

$$DS = -\frac{O+M}{A+O+M+I} \tag{2}$$

Based on Berger's CS coefficient, Clegg and Wang [23] proposed S-CR relationship functions, which could identify the relationship between the customer satisfaction and customer requirement fulfillment. Starting with the calculation of Berger's CS coefficient, [23] proposed that the degree of customer satisfaction S could be quantified by an function involving the degree of customer satisfaction x, CS and DS coefficient and adjustment parameters a and b, which are differentiated by KANO categories. This finding contributes to the integration of KANO model with other mathematical models.

$$S = af(x) + b \tag{3}$$

Nonetheless, [23] only considers 3 KANO categories, which are A, M, O. Considering the dynamic nature of KANO categories, indifferent attributes may also become valuable if they turn into attractive ones [28, 29]. In this consideration, [30] proposed S-CR+ which extends original S-CR analysis to 4 KANO categories of A, M, O and I.

KANO model has been widely applied in the analysis of customer needs and satisfaction in order to achieve better design of products and services in many industries, such as e-learning services, website design, car design, health information service and logistic services [25, 29, 31–33]. Although KANO model highlights the main customer requirements to be satisfied, it does not provide a solution about how these requirements could be satisfied [34].

3.2 Service Design

Service design is a whole process of innovation and standardization to promote the satisfaction and efficiency of services [35, 36]. QFD and TRIZ are both methods of product and service design.

Quality Function Deployment. Quality Function Deployment (QFD) is a methodology developed in Japan in the late 1960s to translate customer needs into design requirements of products [37–39]. QFD proposed a useful tool of House of Quality (HOQ), which includes 4 phases of matrices: customer requirements (WHATs), functional characteristics or technical specifications (HOWs), the correlation between design requirements, and the relationship matrix.

QFD starts with the understanding of customer needs, which is usually collected through personal interviews and/or focus groups. After that, a quantitative marketing research about the competitive position of the product is conducted and the customers are asked to mark the importance to each requirement. The competitive analysis serves to the setting of target customer satisfaction for each requirement. Then the improvement ratio (IR), the weight of each customer requirement (W_C), and the relative weight of each customer requirements (RW_C) are calculated in sequences.

$$W_{Ci} = IR_i \times w_i \tag{4}$$

where

W_{Ci} absolute weight of CR_i
IR improvement ratio
w_i customer-stated satisfaction (weight) of CRi
Relative weight of a CR

$$RW_{Ci} = \frac{W_{Ci}}{\sum_{i=1}^{n} W_{Ci}} \tag{5}$$

Based on customer requirements, the functional characteristics are determined. Then the relationship between customer requirements and functional characteristics are evaluated usually by invited experienced experts in the industry. The relationships are usually marked as "strong", "moderate", "weak", or "none" by different symbols or by direct ratings of 9, 3, 1 and 0 respectively [40]. Then, the absolute importance weight and relative importance weight of each functional characteristic is calculated based on the relationship and customer requirements. A competitive analysis is then conducted between the designed/improved products and its competitors. Thereafter, the process specifications, quality control specifications and material requirements are determined by conducting other matrices.

$$W_{Fj} = \sum_{i=1}^{n} W_{Ci}R_{ij} \qquad (6)$$

where

W_{Fj} absolute weight of FC_j
W_{Ci} relative weight of CR_i
R_{ij} relationship rating representing the strength between CR_i and FC_j
$i = 1, 2, \ldots, n$, where n is the total number of CRs.
$j = 1, 2, \ldots, m$, where m is the total number of FCs.
Relative weight of a FC

$$RW_{Fj} = \frac{W_{Fj}}{\sum_{j=1}^{m} W_{Fj}} \qquad (7)$$

QFD has been widely applied to product development, quality management, and customer need analysis, and expanded to service improvement, product design, planning, engineering, decision-making, management and other areas [41–43] (Fig. 2).

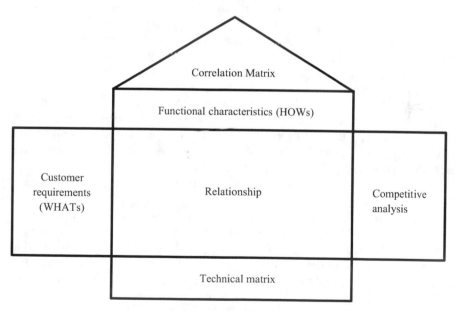

Fig. 2. House of Quality

Nevertheless, the traditional QFD requires the involvement of customers that have experience with the product or service, and are capable to evaluate the importance and satisfaction with the product's requirements, while the voice of customers is still qualitative, which is vague, subjective and difficult to represent the customer needs [44–47].

Besides, it assumes that customer-stated importance and satisfaction have a linear and independent relationship [48], which is not always true [49, 50]. Moreover, the traditional QFD matrix is too large [51, 52], and the framework is no longer suitable for the product design and development requirements [41, 53, 54]. Under these circumstances, the innovative integrations of QFD and other models are explored [34, 42, 45].

TRIZ. In 1946, after analyzing more than 2 million patents, Genrich Altshullerand his colleagues [55] found that various engineering systems and technologies showed a common evolutionary model, and some rules could be followed when solving problems [56]. Thus, they put forward a set of innovative problem-solving theories with highly structured innovative thinking methods, namely, the theory of invention problem solving, which is also called "TRIZ" theory (based on the abbreviation in Russian, meaning "the theory of solving tasks related to invention"). TRIZ technology is a modeling method used in the conceptual stage of product, process and service design. Through the creative problem-solving process, combined with other methods, it can effectively improve the efficiency of the project team [57].

Compared with traditional methods to support innovation, TRIZ has the following advantages: (1) improve innovation productivity; (2) Accelerate the search for creative and innovative solutions; (3) It provides a systematic tool for predicting the evolution of technical systems, products and processes. The benefits of TRIZ can be divided into the following categories: problem-solving methods, creative generation, innovation and new solutions, speed, outlook on the future, teamwork and patent deconstruction [58, 59]. Compared with traditional concept generation methods such as brainstorming, synthesis, horizontal thinking, morphological analysis and mind mapping, Savansky [55] believes that only TRIZ can help solve most difficult problems, which are divided into types of unknown causes and unknown exploration directions.

Through years of experience analysis by Altshulle and others, different tools/technologies have been developed to promote creative or creative thinking [60]. Ilevbare, Probert and Phal [58] summarized the main tools and technologies in TRIZ, such as 40 principles of invention, 76 standard solutions, Contradiction matrix, Ideal Final Result (IFR) and Ideality, etc.

The typical TRIZ problem-solving process includes three stages: problem definition, problem-solving and solution evaluation. The problem is defined by referring to similar problems and compiling the references into 39 engineering parameters (Table 1). This leads to 39 × 39 the contradiction matrix of engineering parameters is used to determine the contradiction points, that is, to construct the contradiction matrix. TRIZ contradiction matrix is the most commonly used method to solve innovation problems, because problems often mean conflicts (that is, another problem arises while solving another problem), which is called "contradictions". Subsequently, these parameters can be matched with 40 innovation principles (Table 2) to determine a satisfactory invention idea or innovation concept, so as to develop a possible problem-solving plan [61] (Table 3).

TRIZ's application fields are mostly technology oriented, such as manufacturing and product-related fields [62]. However, in addition to traditional application fields, TRIZ is also effectively used in medicine, biomedical research, computer programming and business management [63]. Nowadays, more and more studies apply TRIZ in structural

Table 2. 39 Engineering Parameters

No.	Engineering parameters	No.	Engineering parameters
1	Weight of moving object	21	Power
2	Weight of stationary objects	22	Energy loss
3	Length of moving object	23	Material loss
4	Length of stationary object	24	Loss of information
5	Area of moving object	25	Waste of time
6	Area of a stationary object	26	Quantity of substance
7	Volume of moving object	27	Reliability
8	Volume of a stationary object	28	Measurement accuracy
9	Speed	29	Manufacturing accuracy
10	Power	30	Sensitivity of external factors of objects
11	Pressure or tension	31	Harmful factors generated by objects
12	Appearance	32	Processability
13	Stability of structure	33	Comfort of use
14	Strength	34	Comfort of maintenance
15	Action time of moving object	35	Adaptability
16	Action time of stationary object	36	Complexity of the system
17	Temperature	37	Complexity of monitoring and testing
18	Brightness	38	Degree of automation
19	Energy of moving objects	39	Productivity
20	Energy of stationary objects		

service innovation methods and service quality product service system driving methods [64–66]. Scholars are also committed to studying parameters and invention principles applicable to management, service and other fields. For example, Mann and Domb [67] proposed 40 principles of invention for management. Zhang, Cai and Tan [68] proposed 40 principles of invention for service operation management.

3.3 Integrated Methods

KANO+QFD. Understanding customer needs is the basic foundation of QFD application. KANO model can help identify and quantify customer needs by classifying product attributes from the customer perceptions and the relationship between product attributes and customer satisfaction [69]. Considering this, some researchers incorporated KANO model into QFD to improve the accuracy, efficiency and objectiveness of the interpreting of customer needs [70]. [71] introduces that CS coefficient can be a supplementary tool in QFD analysis. Yet it did not specify the process of the integration. Tan and Shen [43] proposed a method to adjust the QFD improvement ratio by using an adjustment factor

Table 3. 40 Principles of Invention

No.	Principle of Invention	No.	Principle of Invention
1	Division	21	Emergency action
2	Extract	22	Turn harmful into beneficial extraction
3	Local mass	23	Feedback
4	Asymmetry	24	Intermediary
5	Merge	25	Self service
6	Versatility	26	Copy
7	Nesting	27	Replace expensive and durable objects with low-cost and short-lived objects
8	Quality compensation	28	Substitution of mechanical systems
9	Pre reaction force	29	Pneumatic and hydraulic structure
10	Pre operation	30	Flexible shell or membrane
11	Precompensation	31	Porous material
12	Equipotentiality	32	Change color
13	Reverse	33	Homogenization
14	Camber	34	Abandonment and repair
15	Dynamic	35	Parameter change
16	Does not meet or exceed the function	36	State change
17	Dimensional change	37	Thermal expansion
18	Vibration	38	Accelerated strong oxidation
19	Periodic action	39	Inert atmosphere
20	Continuity of effective action	40	Compound material

"k", the value of which is determined by KANO category. The equation of the adjusted improvement ratio is shown in Eq. 4:

$$IR_{adj} = (IR)^{1/k} \tag{8}$$

Tontini [48] proposed to use CS coefficient directly in QFD matrix, arguing that both traditional importance rating or assigning certain value to KANO category as an adjusted factor may either underestimate the weight of basic requirements or overestimate the attractive values. He proposed to use the higher absolute value of CS and DS as shown in the following equation:

$$k = Max(|CS|, |DS|) \tag{9}$$

However, this method may not be able to differentiate the weight of different KANO categories. For example, (0.75, 0.25) and (0.25, 0.75) may get the same adjustment factor although they may be in different categories. Chaudha [29] proposed a new equation of

IR to solve the problem:

$$IR_{adj} = (1 + m)^k \times IR \tag{10}$$

where m = Max (|CS|, |DS|), and k is determined according to KANO category as 0, 0.5, 1 and 1.5 for I, M, O, and A respectively.

Table 4 illustrates some researches integrating KANO model and QFD analysis.

Table 4. Part of the researches integrating KANO model and QFD

Applied field	Methods	Contribution	Comments	Reference
Service development	SERVQUAL+KANO+QFD	Assign 4, 2, 1 to KANO categories (A, O, M) to calculate adjusted customer importance	The proposal increases the weight of requirements of M while decrease that of A	[43]
New product design	KANO+QFD	Use the higher absolute value of CS and DS as adjusted factor	The same weights may be assigned to different KANO categories	[48]
Website design	KANO+QFD	Propose a new adjustment factor for IR calculation; 0, 0.5, 1 and 1.5 are assigned to I, M, O, and A	Provide more appropriate weights to different categories than previous methods	[29]
Classification of aesthetic attributes of SUV car profile	QFD+Fuzzy KANO	Expand Chaudha's equation to 5 KANO categories by assigning −1, 0, 0.5, 1, 1.5 to R, I, M, I, and A categories as k factor used in adjusted IR calculation	Expand Chaudha's equation to R category	[72]

Researchers have made great efforts on improving the integration of KANO and QFD. It is also obvious that the focus of the integration lies on the determination of adjustment factors in the calculation of IR.

QFD+TRIZ. QFD method can improve the efficiency of the production process and reduce unnecessary discussion. In addition, QFD helps to identify problems in service design and the relationship between service product attributes [73]. However, this method still has shortcomings. Since this model relies heavily on experience, creativity is limited [74]. Therefore, it is necessary to apply multiple theories to fully support the definition of the problem. In addition, QFD mainly solves the problem of "what to do", rather than the problem of "how to do". As an innovative problem-solving theory, TRIZ mainly solves the problem of "how to do", which makes up for the defects of QFD in these two aspects.

Many scholars have explored the mixed method of QFD and TRIZ. Kim and Yoon [75] showed the method of using QFD and TRIZ to design a product service system. Zhang, Yang and Liu [76] used the integrated method of QFD and TRIZ to conduct innovative design and evaluation of ergonomic products. In addition, Yamashina, Ito and Kawada [77] demonstrated a hybrid approach when designing new products. Su and Lin [78] used QFD and TRIZ at the same time to improve the quality of e-commerce services. Although previous studies combined the concepts of QFD and TRIZ in service design, they also lacked empirical studies and application analysis. Yu Hui Wang et al. [74] integrated TRIZ and QFD into the service design blueprint method and applied them to the design of the meal ordering system. It can be seen that this hybrid approach is not only applied to product design, but also applicable to service design.

At present, the integration research of QFD and TRIZ first uses QFD to analyze user requirements, and generates service or product design requirements based on user requirements, so as to build the first House of Quality. Then the service/product design requirements are introduced into the contradiction matrix to find solutions. Then the second house of quality is constructed according to the solution to generate quality and function elements. Finally, the method outputs service specifications and quality standards, or conducts the next round of construction of the House of Quality [74, 79].

4   The Proposed Research Framework

As mentioned above, to design a smart standards information service, the core is to understand users' needs followed by an innovative solution. Therefore, this research proposed to use KANO+QFD+TRIZ method for the following reasons:

1. KANO could overcome the vague expression by users in interviews, and therefore contributes to a better understanding of users' needs;
2. QFD could help to transform users' needs to design requirements of the standards service by systematic analysis and constructions of HoQs;
3. TRIZ contributes to the identification of contradictions between users' needs and design requirements, and help to find innovative solutions to problems.

In this way, the KANO, QFD and TRIZ could compensate for each other's shortages and provide an innovative solution based on the users' needs. The proposed research framework consists of three phases: users' needs recognition, service function identification, and solutions (as shown in Fig. 3).

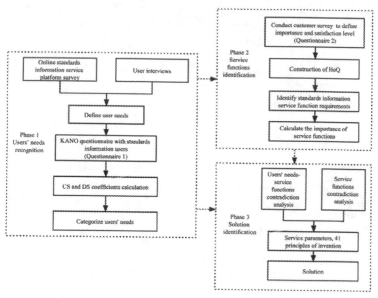

Fig. 3. The proposed research framework

In the first phase, a web-site survey, interviews and questionnaire are used to help recognize users' needs. Through online standards information service platform survey, the standards information services are collected as a reference for the design of user interviews. The face-to-face interview help to recognize users' needs. Then a KANO questionnaire is conducted aiming at a better understanding of users' needs. In the second phase, the second questionnaire about users' rating of importance and satisfaction of the identified users' needs. Then, a HoQ is constructed to deploy the service functions according to the users' needs. The output of the second phase is the importance of the identified service functions. In the third phase, the contradiction matrixes of the users' needs and service functions, and of the service functions themselves are analyzed. The service parameters adapted from the 39 engineering parameters and the 41principles of inventions are applied to find innovative solutions.

5 Conclusion

To find a better solution for the enterprise users' standards information needs, this research proposed a research framework integrating KANO, QFD and TRIZ to design a smart standards information service. Interviews and questionnaires are conducted to collect users' needs, followed by KANO analysis to better understand users' needs by categorization of users' needs and calculation of the adjusted factors. A further question-naire is conducted to assist the construction of HoQ for the purpose of identification of service functions. Then contradiction matrixes analyses are conducted to find the solution. Through this method, a smart standards information service design is completed based on the users' needs.

This paper only presents the formation process of the research framework. In the future, the interviews and questionnaires will be conducted accordingly. More complete research will be presented based on this research framework.

Acknowledgement. This research was supported by a grant funded by the National Natural Science Foundation of China (No.: 71974215).

References

1. Chen, Y.: Research on the Architecture of Jiangsu Standards Information Service Sharing Platform. Nanjing University of Science and Technology (2011)
2. Liu, J.: Standard literature and its intelligence value. Libr. Inf. (Z1), 166–168 (1987)
3. Xiaoping, F.: Enterprises should strengthen the management and research of standard information. China Pet. Chem. Stand. Qual. **06**, 26–27 (1990)
4. ISO. https://www.iso.org/standards.html. Accessed 30 Dec 2022
5. National Technical Committee for Standardization of Principles and Methods of Standardization, Guidlines for Standardization-Part 1: Standardization and related acitivties–General vocabularies (2014)
6. Phillips, M.: Standards collections: considerations for the future. Collect. Manag. **44**(2–4), 334–347 (2019)
7. Papin-Ramcharan, J., Dolland, A., Dawe, R.A.: Making engineering standards available at the university of the West Indies: perspectives of a developing country. Collect. Build. **30**(2), 86–93 (2011)
8. Schlembach, M.C.: Access to standards over the Web. Sci. Technol. Libr. **19**(2), 53–74 (2000)
9. Wainscott, S.B., Zwiercan, R.J.: Improving access to standards. In: 2020 ASEE Virtual Annual Conference Content Access, pp. 1–14 (2020)
10. Peng, G., Liu, J., Zhang, B.: Research on the classification and development status of China's standards information service. Inf. Sci., 1–22 (2022)
11. Chen, Y., Wang, X., Gao, Y., et al.: Research on service model of standards information reporting based on standards life cycle. Stand. Sci. (12) 6–8+24 (2015)
12. Chen, Y.: Research on the Measurement and Analysis Method of Standards and its Agricultural Applications. Chinese Academy of Agricultural Sciences (2016)
13. Lu, L.: Taking customer demand as the center to promote standard information service – on the role of customer relationship management system to standard information service. Qual. Stand. (02), 3+14–18 (2006)
14. Zhao, Q., Cai, Y.: Research on standard document information service for world top 500 enterpriese. China Stand. (22), 271–272+275 (2019)
15. Liu, J., Peng, G.: The development and evolution of standards information service in China. J. Intell. **40**(04), 119–125+162 (2021)
16. Slattery, W.J.: Standards information service of the national bureau of standards. J. Qual. Technol. **8**(4), 232–234 (2018)
17. Dowell, N.J.: ANSI standards: creating a local, searchable database. Collect. Build. **24**(1), 29–34 (2005)
18. Katusic, D., et al.: Hands-on education about standardization: is that what industry expects? IEEE Commun. Mag. **55**(5), 133–144 (2017)

19. Dunn, L.K., Xie, S.: Standards collection development and management in an academic library: a case study at the university of Western Ontario libraries. Issues Sci. Technol. Librariansh. **87** (2017)
20. Levine-Clark, M.: Imagining the future academic library collection. Collect. Manag. **44**(2–4), 87–94 (2019)
21. Gang, Y., Wei, Z., Qi, Z., et al.: Research on present situation and countermeasure of information service of provincial standard. China Qual. Stand. Rev. **07**, 34–36 (2019)
22. Shurui, Y., Zhiqiang, W.: Study on status and countermeasures in the construction of local libraries of standards based on knowledge service. Stand. Sci. **03**, 88–91 (2019)
23. Wang, T., Clegg, B., Ji, P.: Understanding customer needs through quantitative analysis of Kano's model. Int. J. Qual. Reliab. Manag. **27**(2), 173–184 (2010)
24. Kano, N., Seraku, N., Takahashi, F., et al.: Attractive quality and must-be quality. J. Jpn. Soc. Qual. Control **14**(2), 147–156 (1984)
25. Chen, L.-H., Kuo, Y.-F.: Understanding e-learning service quality of a commercial bank by using Kano's model. Total Qual. Manag. Bus. Excell. **22**(1), 99–116 (2011)
26. Shen, X.X., Tan, K.C., Xie, M.: An integrated approach to innovative product development using Kano's model and QFD. Eur. J. Innov. Manag. **3**(2), 91–99 (2000)
27. Berger, C., Blauth, R.E., Boger, D.: Kanos methods for understanding customer-defined quality. Qual. Manag. J. **2**(4) (1993)
28. Kano, N.: Life cycle and creation of attractive quality. In: The 4th International Quality Management and Organisational Development Conference, Linköping (2001)
29. Chaudha, A., Jain, R., Singh, A.R., et al.: Integration of Kano's model into quality function deployment (QFD). Int. J. Adv. Manuf. Technol. **53**(5–8), 689–698 (2011)
30. Kirgizov, U.A., Kwak, C.: How can a quantitative analysis of Kano's model be improved further for better understanding of customer needs? Total Qual. Manag. Bus. Excell., 1–20 (2021)
31. Ilbahar, E., Cebi, S.: Classification of design parameters for E-commerce websites: a novel fuzzy Kano approach. Telemat. Inform. **34**(8), 1814–1825 (2017)
32. Chen, M.-C., Hsu, C.-L., Lee, L.-H.: Investigating pharmaceutical logistics service quality with refined Kano's model. J. Retail. Consum. Serv. **57** (2020)
33. Meng, Y., et al.: An analysis of university students' health information service needs from academic library in the post-COVID-19 age through Kano model. Libr. Hi Tech **39**(3), 711–721 (2021)
34. Baki, B., et al.: An application of integrating SERVQUAL and Kano's model into QFD for logistics services. Asia Pac. J. Mark. Logist. **21**(1), 106–126 (2009)
35. Zeithaml, V.A.: consumer perceptions of price, quality, and value: a means-end model and synthesis of evidence. J. Mark. **52**(3), 2–22 (2018)
36. Luo, S., Zhu, S.: Service Design. China Machine Press, Beijing (2011)
37. Terninko, J.: Step-by-Step QFD: Customer-Driven Product Design. Routledge (2018)
38. Akao, Y.: Quality function deployment: integrating customer requirements into product design (1990)
39. Sullivan, L.P.: Quality function deployment. Qual. Prog. **19**(6), 39–50 (1986)
40. Sireli, Y., Kauffmann, P., Ozan, E.: Integration of Kano's model into QFD for multiple product design. IEEE Trans. Eng. Manag. **54**(2), 380–390 (2007)
41. Chan, L.-K., Wu, M.-L.: Quality function deployment a literature review. Eur. J. Oper. Res. **143**, 463–497 (2002)
42. Lizarelli, F.L., Osiro, L., Ganga, G.M.D., et al.: Integration of SERVQUAL, analytical Kano, and QFD using fuzzy approaches to support improvement decisions in an entrepreneurial education service. Appl. Soft Comput. **112** (2021)
43. Tan, K.C., Pawitra, T.A.: Integrating SERVQUAL and Kano's model into QFD for service excellence development. Manag. Serv. Qual. **11**(6), 418–430 (2001)

44. Law, H.-W., Hua, M.: Using quality function deployment in singulation process analysis. Recent Adv. Eng. Comput. Sci. **62**, 189–193 (2007)
45. Ming, Z.: Fuzzy logic and optimization models for implementing QFD. In: 23rd International Conference on Computers and Industrial Engineering, pp. 237–240 (1998)
46. Kim, K.-J., Herbert, M., Dhingra, A., et al.: Fuzzy multicriteria models for quality function deployment. Eur. J. Oper. Res. **121**, 504–518 (2000)
47. Fung, R.Y.K., et al.: A fuzzy expected value-based goal programing model for product planning using quality function deployment. Eng. Optim. **37**(6), 633–645 (2005)
48. Tontini, G.: Integrating the Kano model and QFD for designing new products. Total Qual. Manag. Bus. Excell. **18**(6), 599–612 (2007)
49. Anderson, E.W., Mittal, V.: Strengthening the satisfaction-profit chain. J. Serv. Res. **3**(2), 107–120 (2016)
50. Ting, S.-C., Chen, C.-N.: The asymmetrical and non-linear effects of store quality attributes on customer satisfaction. Total Qual. Manag. **13**(4), 547–569 (2002)
51. Prasad, B., et al.: Review of QFD and related deployment techniques. J. Manuf. Syst. **17**(3), 221–234 (1998)
52. Kao, H.-P., Su, E., Wang, B.: I2QFD: a blackboard-based multiagent system for supporting concurrent engineering projects. Int. J. Prod. Res. **40**(5), 1235–1262 (2002)
53. Akao, Y., Mazur, G.H.: The leading edge in QFD: past, present and future. Int. J. Qual. Reliab. Manag. **20**(1), 20–35 (2003)
54. Brad, S.: Complex system design technique. Int. J. Prod. Res. **46**(21), 5979–6008 (2008)
55. Savransky, S.D.: Engineering of Creativity: Introduction to TRIZ Methodology of Inventive Problem Solving. CRC Press, Florida (2000)
56. Domb, E., Kowalick, J.: Applying TRIZ to develop new designs for the future of the airbag. In: SAE Technical Paper 980647, International Congress and Exposition (1998)
57. Chechurin, L., Borgianni, Y.: Understanding TRIZ through the review of top cited publications. Comput. Ind. **82**, 119–134 (2016)
58. Ilevbare, I.M., Probert, D., Phaal, R.: A review of TRIZ, and its benefits and challenges in practice. Technovation **33**(2–3), 30–37 (2013)
59. Sheu, D.D., Chiu, M.-C., Cayard, D.: The 7 pillars of TRIZ philosophies. Comput. Ind. Eng. **146** (2020)
60. Koswatte, K.R.C., et al.: Innovative product design using metaontology with semantic TRIZ. Int. J. Inf. Retr. Res. **5**(2), 43–65 (2015)
61. Chen, H.-M., Wu, H.-Y., Chen, P.-S.: Innovative service model of information services based on the sustainability balanced scorecard: applied integration of the fuzzy Delphi method, Kano model, and TRIZ. Expert Syst. Appl. **205** (2022)
62. Ko, Y.-T.: Modeling a hybrid-compact design matrix for new product innovation. Comput. Ind. Eng. **107**, 345–359 (2017)
63. Govindarajan, U.H., Sheu, D.D., Mann, D.: Review of systematic software innovation using TRIZ. Syst. Innov. **5**(3), 72–90 (2019)
64. Lee, C.-H., et al.: Customized and knowledge-centric service design model integrating case-based reasoning and TRIZ. Expert Syst. Appl. **143** (2020)
65. Lee, C.-H., Chen, C.-H., Trappey, A.J.C.: A structural service innovation approach for designing smart product service systems: case study of smart beauty service. Adv. Eng. Inform. **40**, 154–167 (2019)
66. Lee, C.-H., Zhao, X., Lee, Y.-C.: Service quality driven approach for innovative retail service system design and evaluation: a case study. Comput. Ind. Eng. **135**, 275–285 (2019)
67. Mann, D.L., Domb, E.: 40 inventive (business) principles with examples **9**, 67–83 (1999)
68. Zhang, J., Chai, K.-H., Tan, K.: 40 inventive principles with applications in service operations management. TRIZ J. **8**(12), 1–16 (2003)

69. Yeh, C.H., Huang, J.C.Y., Yu, C.K.: Integration of four-phase QFD and TRIZ in product R&D: a notebook case study. Res. Eng. Design **22**(3), 125–141 (2011)
70. Ginting, R., Hidayati, J., Siregar, I.: Integrating Kano's model into quality function deployment for product design - a comprehensive review **319**(1), 1–9 (2018)
71. Matzler, K., Hinterhuber, H.H.: How to make product development projects more successful by integrating Kano's model of customer satisfaction into quality function deployment. Technovation **18**(1), 25–38 (1998)
72. Avikal, S., Singh, R., Rashmi, R.: QFD and fuzzy Kano model based approach for classification of aesthetic attributes of SUV car profile. J. Intell. Manuf. **31**(2), 271–284 (2018). https://doi.org/10.1007/s10845-018-1444-5
73. Rovira, N.L., Aguayo, H.: A new model of the conceptual design process using QFD/FA/TRIZ. In: Proceedings of the 10th Annual Quality Function Deployment Symposium, pp. 1–10 (1998)
74. Wang, Y.-H., Lee, C.-H., Trappey, A.J.C.: Service design blueprint approach incorporating TRIZ and service QFD for a meal ordering system: a case study. Comput. Ind. Eng. **107**, 388–400 (2017)
75. Kim, S., Yoon, B.: Developing a process of concept generation for new product-service systems: a QFD and TRIZ-based approach. Serv. Bus. **6**(3), 323–348 (2012)
76. Zhang, F., Yang, M., Liu, W.: Using integrated quality function deployment and theory of innovation problem solving approach for ergonomic product design. Comput. Ind. Eng. **76**, 60–74 (2014)
77. Yamashina, H., Ito, T., Kawada, H.: Innovative product development process by integrating QFD and TRIZ. Int. J. Prod. Res. **40**(5), 1031–1050 (2002)
78. Su, C.-T., Lin, C.-S.: A case study on the application of Fuzzy QFD in TRIZ for service quality improvement. Qual. Quant. **42**(5), 563–578 (2007)
79. Tseng, F.-M., et al.: Integrating service QFD and TRIZ for a lucky draw system design: the case study. In: 2017 IEEE 7th International Symposium on Cloud and Service Computing (SC2), Kanazawa (2017)

Estimation of Water Consumption in a Family Home Using IOT Systems

Humberto López[1]([✉]), Leopoldo Laborde[1], Carlos Barros[1], Rubén Guerra[1], and Javier Ramirez[2]

[1] Institución Universitaria de Barranquilla, 45 Street #48-31, Barranquilla, Colombia
hlopez@unibarranquilla.edu.co
[2] Corporación Universitaria, Taller Cinco, Km 19, Chía, Colombia

Abstract. Part of the percentage of water consumption in the domestic sector is linked to inadequate management of the resource in homes where 60% of total water consumption in the home is used for bathing and going to the toilet. The efficient use of water is an issue that has captured the attention of scientists, technicians, politicians and the community in general. The sustainability of water resources has been threatened by the current imbalance between water supply and demand. Thanks to new technologies, intelligent consumption of water in the home could balance the balance and reduce household expenses. The present work aims to estimate the water consumption of a family home with the help of a residential water consumption monitoring system using the Internet of Things. With the implementation of this system, it was possible to identify in real time the water consumption habits per user in a home, allowing to understand the dynamics or behavior within a family unit and validate with respect to the average value stipulated by the World Health Organization (WHO). It was also possible to determine consumption patterns, times of higher and lower demand and behavioral habits within the home that can generate future strategies for saving water. Based on the data obtained, it was possible to estimate the general consumption of the household and the behavior patterns of the members of the family unit. In addition, the project will allow the user who owns the system to employ preventive and corrective actions that optimize their water consumption.

Keywords: Water consumption · Home economy · Reduce expenses · Water service · Intelligent consumption

1 Introduction

The world is currently in a great paradigmatic change, where the importance of natural resources for the subsistence of humanity and future generations is increasingly recognized; where the so-called sustainability makes a great presence in all areas such as educational, organizational, industrial [1, 2], among others. This leads to locate and emphasize the problems associated with the consumption and contamination of these natural sources [3].

© The Author(s), under exclusive license to Springer Nature Switzerland AG 2023
N. A. Streitz and S. Konomi (Eds.): HCII 2023, LNCS 14036, pp. 366–377, 2023.
https://doi.org/10.1007/978-3-031-34668-2_24

In this sense, it is mentioned that 70% of the Earth's surface is covered by water and only 30% of it is land. Even so, it can be affirmed that water is a limited natural resource considering that, according to National Geographic: "less than 1% of water is available to about 7 billion people and a multitude of freshwater ecosystems" [4]. Additionally, Manco, Guerrero and Ocampo [5] indicate that the relationship between the availability and demand of water has been unbalanced by factors such as urban development, climate change, population growth, water pollution and changes in the patterns of consumption.

The Colombian Ministry of the Environment indicates that, according to IDEAM estimates, "the total demand for water in Colombia in 2010 was 35,877 Mm3/year, corresponding to the use of water in the following sectors: Domestic 7.3%, Agricultural 54%, Energy 19.4%, Aquaculture 7.2%, Livestock 6.2%, Industry 4.4% and Services 1.5%" [6]. From the above statement it can be deduced that the domestic sector has the greatest demand for water, after the agricultural and energy sectors. However, part of the percentage of water consumption in the domestic sector is linked to the inadequate management of the resource in homes.

As a result, there is a waste of water that affects the economy of the inhabitants of the property. It is worth saying that if this situation continues, not only will the user who pays a higher cost for unnecessary water consumption be affected, but the availability of the resource will also decrease to a greater extent and the deterioration of the ecosystems that depend on the water will be contributed to fresh water [7]. This situation allows us to reveal a great problem related to the depletion of non-renewable resources; which promotes the generation of studies that can be presented as a solution to those previously exposed, with a direct repercussion on the use of domestic water, since it has a high level of impact and, in turn, is very close to the daily life of people in their homes.

From this, it can be highlighted how new technologies allow a practical and effective development of new solutions related to the problems of the Society. The so-called industry 4.0 technologies such as IOT, machine learning or blockchain are applied as catalytic elements of the Society for the achievement of sustainability as a goal and a policy of a social nature [8, 9]. In accordance with the above, the design of a water consumption monitoring system consisting of: flow, temperature and humidity sensors; an information processing unit with Wi-fi connection and open platform for IoT.

Various studies have addressed this issue, such as in 2007, when Jiménez and Marín [10] designed a program for the efficient use and saving of water for the "Asamun" aqueduct in the Mundo Nuevo village of the city of Pereira. In the project, water consumption habits were identified in a sample of 20 users of the aqueduct and three strategies aimed at the efficient use and saving of water were applied. The strategies were: (1) installation of low consumption technologies; (2) detection and elimination of leaks and drips and (3) environmental education. Each alternative was evaluated during a period of 30 days, highlighting the installation of low consumption technologies with a saving percentage of 49.1%.

It should be noted that the diagnosis was based on the record of water consumption by activity and dwelling. An electronic water flow meter (Contazara, model CZ2000-3MQ) was used and the reading of the meter was recorded every 5 min for 24 h; Likewise, the domestic activity carried out in that period of time was recorded. In addition, the intervention of an aqueduct plumber was necessary to remove the residential meter and connect the electronic meter in each sampled house.

In 2012, Garmabdari, Shafie and Mohd Isa [11] published the article Sensory System for the Electronic Water Meter. There, the design of an electronic circuit based on the Hall Effect sensor for measuring water consumption is described. The authors clarify that there are a variety of technologies in this area (ultrasonic sensors, electromagnetic sensors, mechanical elements, etc.), although they also indicate that these have many restrictions such as accuracy, power supply and the cost of implementing the instrument. In the circuit, a new technique was applied to remove signal distortion effects, derived from strong electromagnetic fields or temperatures. Similarly, CMOS technology was used to reduce energy consumption.

In 2015, Suh, H. Kim and J. Kim [12] published the article Estimation of Water Demand in Residential Building using Machine Learning Approach. The paper shows an estimation model for residential water consumption using approximate machine learning in Korea. To design the model, distinctive factors (impact of price, income, population, climate, among others) related to the use of water in apartment buildings were explored. According to the authors, the proposed model could offer a reliable supply that meets the useful needs of customers and facilitates efficient water consumption.

In the same way, Fuentes and Mauricio presented the research "Smart water consumption measurement system for houses using IoT and cloud computing" with the aim of showing the application of a water monitoring system in homes based on the IOT and information in the cloud. This system made it possible to recognize the context and location of the home to cover 10 water consumption scenarios. This data is sent to the cloud so that, through algorithms, leaks can be located within the home's water system. Said system presented positive results and an effectiveness of 100% [13].

Finally, the authors Arsene, et al. carried out the study "Advanced Strategies for Monitoring Water Consumption Patterns in Households Based on IoT and Machine Learning" in which an IOT-based model is presented to predict water consumption in homes through various separate sensors to be able to apply various techniques in the information gathering process. It is important to mention that as a limitation and added value of this study is the use of sensors in specific places in the home; requiring multiple facilities for each sector and in turn not obtaining the real value of the total consumption of the home where the pilot test is applied by having more sources of water consumption [14].

2 Materials and Method

For the development of the project, the architecture shown in Fig. 1 was established, which is composed of 3 MCU nodes and a data reception, recording and visualization station. The first node corresponding to flow measurement was located in the bathroom, the other two nodes corresponding to temperature and humidity were located inside and outside the residential unit in order to determine if there is a relationship between water consumption and home temperature.

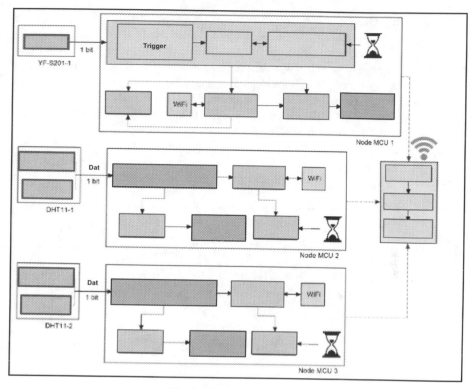

Fig. 1. System Architecture

Likewise, with the help of the ThingSpeak application, it was possible to assemble the IoT infrastructure using its included channels and applications (MATLAB Analysis, MATLAB Visualizations and TimeControl), in order to carry out the processes of the flow chart in Fig. 2. The color blocks red are processes that interact with the hardware of the built system, to store the measured data. The purple blocks are processes that work with the data acquired by the red blocks and analysis data generated within the platform.

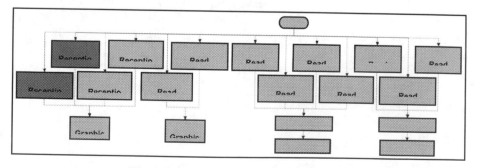

Fig. 2. Process flow diagram in IoT platform

In Fig. 3 the schematics corresponding to the MCU Nodes used for data collection in the project are shown. The design and construction of the PCBs were developed, as well as their calibration verification and commissioning. With its subsequent calibration in which the number of output pulses of the flow sensor, caused by the circulation of a certain volume of water through the device, was detected, counted and displayed (by serial monitor). This volume of water was contained in a graduated container, obtaining its value in milliliters (mL). The process was carried out 5 times with water volumes of 500 to 600 mL and 5 times with water volumes of 1000 to 1100 mL. On each occasion, the value obtained (measurement) was recorded, associating it vertically with the volume measured with the graduated container and horizontally with the measurement number, as shown in Table 1.

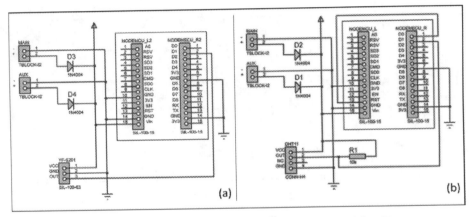

Fig. 3. Schematic flow circuit (a) temperature and humidity (b)

4 measurements were recorded with 500 mL of water, 1 measurement with 600 mL of water, 4 measurements with 1000 mL of water, and 1 measurement with 1050 mL of water, for a total of 10 measurements. The blank space indicates that the measurement was carried out with a volume of water different from that associated vertically (for example: measurement N°1 with water volumes of 500 to 600 mL, was carried out with 600 mL, not with 500 mL; the measurement No. 1 with water volumes of 1000 to 1100 mL, was carried out with 1000 mL, not with 1050 mL). With the data, an approximate average of 422 pulses per liter was calculated, used in the source code implemented in the Water Volume Unit.

In Fig. 4 can be seen the behavior curve of the average temperature and humidity around a specific time of the day, captured by both indoor and outdoor MCU nodes and which were recorded and graphed on the ThingSpeak platform.

3 Results

In Fig. 5 and Fig. 6 the temperature and humidity averages are plotted respectively. At various points in both graphs it can be seen that the indoor area variable follows the behavior of the outdoor area variable. This means that if the temperature or humidity

Table 1. Calibration test

mL N°	500	600	1000	1050
1		255	411	
2	207			439
3	223		408	
4	212		411	
5	229		407	
Pulses per volume	217,75	255	409,25	439
Pulses per liter	435,5	425	409,25	418,095238
Average pulses per liter				421,96131

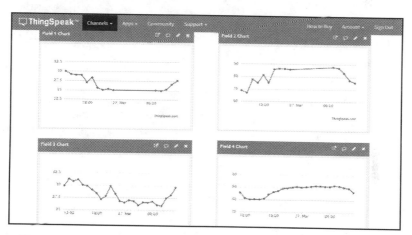

Fig. 4. Channel averages and totals per hour - Residential H2O consumption

of the environment increases, it is most likely that the temperature and humidity of the study room will also increase.

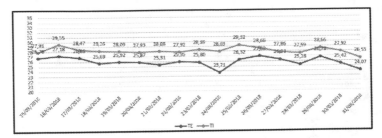

Fig. 5. Average outdoor and indoor temperature on days of data collection

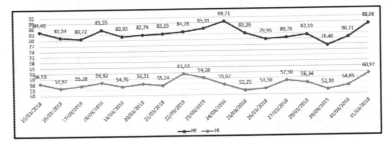

Fig. 6. Average outdoor and indoor humidity on days of data collection

In the graph of Fig. 7, the temperature (°C) was located on the abscissa axis and the consumption (Liters) on the ordinate axis. In the graph of Fig. 8, the relative humidity (%) was located on the abscissa axis and consumption (Liters) on the ordinate axis.

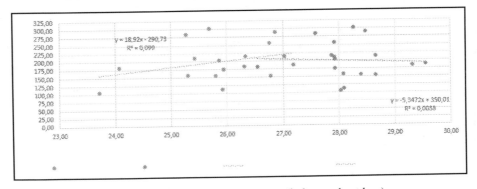

Fig. 7. Consumption Vs. Temperature (indoor and outdoor)

In each graph two data series appear, since temperature and humidity were measured in two different areas. The purpose is to find the incidence that both variables and both areas could have on water consumption. Values were plotted without relationship or date specification. The relationship between two quantitative variables (consumption - TO; consumption - TI; consumption - HO; consumption - HI) is represented by the line of

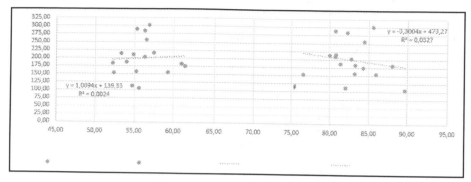

Fig. 8. Consumption Vs. Humidity (indoor and outdoor)

best fit (line drawn from the cloud of points). Regarding the cloud of points of each of the 4 data series, represented in Fig. 7 and Fig. 8, it can be stated that:

- The strength of the point cloud is weak, because its shape is not narrow and elongated. The 2 clouds in Fig. 7 have an elliptical trend, while the 2 clouds in Fig. 8 have a circular trend.
- The cloud of points does not make sense, because there is no variation of the consumption values with respect to the values of temperature or humidity. The point cloud does not form a slope or inclination that allows identifying a direct or inverse relationship between the data. Of the 4 point clouds, the one that perhaps makes a slight sense is the relationship: TO – consumption. In this case, it would be said that the consumption of water in the dwelling subject to test may increase if the temperature of the environment (TO) increases, because the variables are directly related.
- The cloud points are scattered making it difficult to establish the line type of best fit.

A linear regression analysis was performed with Excel, obtaining the 4 equations and the 4 determination coefficients that are observed in Fig. 7 and Fig. 8. However, the values of the determination coefficients are low (very close to zero).). For this reason, the models obtained with linear regression are not reliable and are not the most suitable for establishing a relationship between consumption, temperature and humidity. It can only be stated that there is no linear relationship between consumption and the other variables (TO, TI, HO, HI) registered by the system.

To examine characteristics in detail, 5 graphs were made, ranging from Fig. 9 to Fig. 13. In each graph, the time variable was located on the abscissa axis and a system variable (TO, TI, HO, HI, volume) on the ordinate axis. It is necessary to clarify that the time has a range of 24 h (1 day, from 0:00:00 to 23:59:59 h). This is why the data for each test day belongs to different series (17 test days = 17 data series) that are superimposed on each other on the same graph.

In Fig. 9 a monomodal temperature regime in the environment can be seen. ET has a well-defined maximum of 30 to 33 °C, present between 11:30 a.m. and 3:00 p.m. The temperature rises gradually from 7:00:00 to its maximum peak. Then it gradually descends to its minimum that oscillates between 23 and 25 °C. The lowest temperature goes from 20:00:00 to 7:00:00 the next day, approximately.

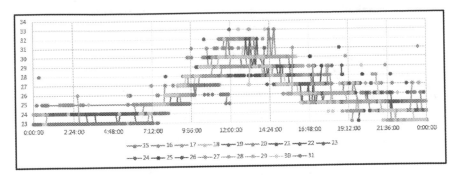

Fig. 9. 24-h record of outdoor temperature on test days (March 15 – March 31)

In Fig. 10 a repetitive behavior can be seen at the temperature of the study room, although the data of some series are far from the majority of the series. The TO sequence is clearer and more marked than the TI sequence. IT has a maximum of 30 to 35 °C, present between 12:00:00 and 17:00:00 h; except on March 24, 25, 26 and 30, which registered temperature peaks outside these hours and some with higher temperature values (up to 41 °C). In general, the temperature drops gradually from 9:00:00 am to its maximum peak. Then it gradually descends to its minimum that oscillates between 25 and 27 °C. The lowest temperature can occur from 9:00 p.m. to 8:00 a.m. the next day, approximately.

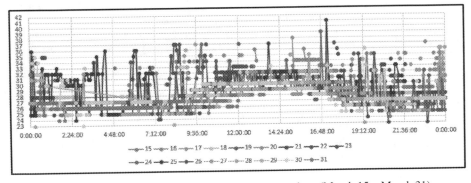

Fig. 10. 24-h record of indoor temperature on test days (March 15 – March 31)

In Fig. 11 a monomodal humidity regime in the environment can be seen. HO has a well-defined maximum of 88 to 93%, present between 7:30 p.m. and 7:00 a.m. the next day. Humidity gradually drops from 7:00:00 a.m. to its minimum peak, which oscillates between 60 and 67%. It then gradually rises to its maximum. The lowest humidity goes from 11:30 a.m. to 2:30 p.m., approximately. It is evident that the lowest HO occurs when the TO is the highest.

In Fig. 12 a monomodal humidity regime can be seen in the study room. HI has a maximum of 58 to 70%, present between 5:30 p.m. and 7:00 a.m. the next day. Humidity gradually drops from 7:00:00 a.m. to its minimum peak, which oscillates between 37 and

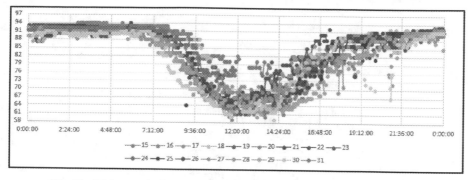

Fig. 11. 24-h record of outdoor humidity on test days (March 15 – March 31)

46% (although on March 16 it decreased to 30%). It then gradually rises to its maximum. The lowest humidity is recorded between 11:30 a.m. to 5:00 p.m., approximately. It is evident that the lowest HI occurs when the overall TI is the highest.

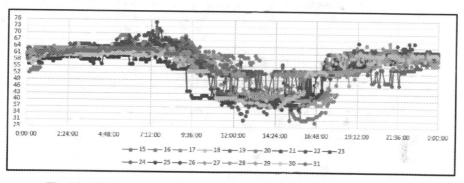

Fig. 12. 24-h record of indoor humidity on test days (March 15 – March 31)

In Fig. 12 a pattern can be seen in the volume of water consumed in the shower. In general, water consumption originates in two intervals of the day: 5:00:00 a.m. to 12:00:00 p.m. and 8:30:00 p.m. to 11:00 p.m. It is highlighted that the highest water consumption occurs in the morning. It can be asserted that at night: (1) the inhabitants use less water in their bathing routine and/or (2) some inhabitants do not take a shower. In fact, there were days (although few) in which no water consumption was recorded at night.

Looking at Fig. 7, Fig. 8, Fig. 9, Fig. 10, Fig. 11 and Fig. 12, as a whole, it is noted that there is usually no water consumption at the most critical instants of thermal sensation. These moments refer to the time of day, in which TO and TI combined with HO and HI, respectively, reach the highest values of thermal sensation. Consequently, it is considered that the measured water consumption, in the shower of the dwelling subject to test, is more influenced by the customs or occupations of its inhabitants than by climatic factors.

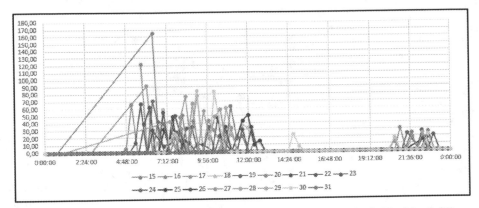

Fig. 13. 24-h record of volume of water consumed on test days (March 15 – March 31)

On the other hand, no fault was detected in the stopcock or valve at the water intake point of the shower. The foregoing is supported, given that a remaining or residual consumption value was not recorded, in the spaces where there was no consumption. For long periods, if there was no consumption, the value recorded by the system was 0 L.

4   Conclusions

The proposed objective was met by designing an online monitoring system for residential water consumption using IoT. The programming of the NodeMcu focuses on the flow reading, the determination of the water consumption and the visualization of the obtained data. However, the measurement of temperature and humidity was added because, according to the literature studied, water consumption varies depending on these variables. Thus, the user can observe this pattern of behavior in their water consumption and take corrective measures.

As future work, the capabilities of the system in ThingSpeak would be extended. Apart from the analyzes with Matlab codes, new codes would be created to calculate maximums, minimums and costs, saving effort and analysis time in Excel. Also, the reaction applications offered by ThingSpeak would be used, such as alerts or notices on Twitter (using ThingTweet) and device controls (using TalkBack, TweetControl and/or ThingHTTP). Considering the controls, the system would be strengthened with actuators that respond to control orders.

Acknowledgments. The authors thank Ministerio de Ciencia, Tecnología e Innovación from Colombia and the Institución Universitaria de Barranquilla for funding this product under the project "FORTALECIMIENTO DE LAS CAPACIDADES DE INVESTIGACIÓN, INNOVACIÓN Y DESARROLLO DE TECNOLOGÍAS EN LA INSTITUCIÓN UNIVERSITARIA ITSA, A TRAVÉS DE LA DOTACIÓN DEL LABORATORIO DE PRODUCTIVIDAD EN EL DEPARTAMENTO DEL ATLÁNTICO" BPIN: 2020000100316.

References

1. Khan, I.S., Ahmad, M.O., Majava, J.: Industry 4.0 and sustainable development: a systematic mapping of triple bottom line, circular economy and sustainable business models perspectives. J. Clean. Prod. **297**, 126655 (2021)
2. Garcia-Samper, M., Manotas, E.N., Ramírez, J., Hernández-Burgos, R.: Cultura organizacional verde: análisis desde las dimensiones de sostenibilidad corporativa. Información Tecnológica **33**(2), 99–106 (2022)
3. Liu, Y., et al.: Water resource conservation promotes synergy between economy and environment in China's northern drylands. Front. Environ. Sci. Eng. **16**(3), 1–12 (2021). https://doi.org/10.1007/s11783-021-1462-y
4. National Geographic: Cómo ahorrar agua. [En línea]. http://www.nationalgeographic.es/medio-ambiente/aguas-dulces/agua-ahorro. Consultado 17 de Abril del 2016
5. Manco, D., Guerrero, J., Ocampo, A.: Eficiencia en el consumo de agua de uso residencial. In: Revista Ingenierías Universidad de Medellín. Julio–Diciembre, vol. 11, no. 21, pp. 23–38 (2012)
6. Colombia. Ministerio de ambiente. Uso eficiente y ahorro del agua [En línea]. https://www.minambiente.gov.co/index.php/component/content/article?id=1449:plantilla-gestion-integral-del-recurso-hidrico-34. Consultado 17 de abril del 2016
7. Castro Pacheco, M.C., López López, J.: Estrategias pedagógicas y tecnológicas para promover el ahorro y uso eficiente del agua en las instituciones educativas del municipio de Valledupar (Colombia). Revista Espacios, **40**, 29–30 (2019)
8. Samper, M.G., Florez, D.G., Borre, J.R., Ramirez, J.: Industry 4.0 for sustainable supply chain management: drivers and barriers. Procedia Comput. Sci. **203**, 644–650 (2022)
9. Dixit, A., Jakhar, S.K., Kumar, P.: Does lean and sustainable manufacturing lead to Industry 4.0 adoption: the mediating role of ambidextrous innovation capabilities. Technol. Forecast. Soc. Change **175**, 121328 (2022)
10. Jiménez, A., Marín, M.: Diseño de un programa de uso eficiente y ahorro de agua para el acueducto "Asamun" de la vereda Mundo Nuevo de la ciudad de Pereira. Tesis de grado en Administrador del Medio Ambiente. Pereira: Universidad Tecnológica de Pereira, 105 p. (2007)
11. Garmabdari, R., Shafie, S., Mohd Isa, M.: Maryam. sensory system for the electronic water meter. Selangor (2012). ISBN 978-1-4673-3119-7
12. Suh, D., Kim, H., Kim, J.: Estimation of water demand in residential building using machine learning approach. Korea (2015). ISBN 978-1-4673-6537-6
13. Fuentes, H., Mauricio, D.: Smart water consumption measurement system for houses using IoT and cloud computing. Environ. Monit. Assess. **192**(9), 1–16 (2020). https://doi.org/10.1007/s10661-020-08535-4
14. Arsene, D., Predescu, A., Pahonţu, B., Chiru, C.G., Apostol, E.S., Truică, C.O.: Advanced strategies for monitoring water consumption patterns in households based on IoT and machine learning. Water **14**(14), 2187 (2022)

Development of Large-Scale Scientific Cyberinfrastructure and the Growing Opportunity to Democratize Access to Platforms and Data

Jakob Luettgau[1]([envelope]) [ID], Giorgio Scorzelli[2], Valerio Pascucci[2] [ID], and Michela Taufer[1] [ID]

[1] University of Tennessee, Knoxville, TN, USA
{luettgauj,taufer}@acm.org
[2] University of Utah, Salt Lake City, UT, USA
valerio.pascucci@utah.edu

Abstract. As researchers across scientific domains rapidly adopt advanced scientific computing methodologies, access to advanced cyberinfrastructure (CI) becomes a critical requirement in scientific discovery. Lowering the entry barriers to CI is a crucial challenge in interdisciplinary sciences requiring frictionless software integration, data sharing from many distributed sites, and access to heterogeneous computing platforms. In this paper, we explore how the challenge is not merely a factor of availability and affordability of computing, network, and storage technologies but rather the result of insufficient interfaces with an increasingly heterogeneous mix of computing technologies and data sources. With more distributed computation and data, scientists, educators, and students must invest their time and effort in coordinating data access and movements, often penalizing their scientific research. Investments in the interfaces' software stack are necessary to help scientists, educators, and students across domains take advantage of advanced computational methods. To this end, we propose developing a science data fabric as the standard scientific discovery interface that seamlessly manages data dependencies within scientific workflows and CI.

Keywords: Scientific data · Cyberinfrastructure · National Science Data Fabric

1 Introduction

Computational sciences in the last decade experienced rapid adoption throughout a wide range of domain sciences. Many computational methods that only a few decades ago required supercomputers evolved and matured into tools available to the research community and the general public. Two trends, in particular, are contributing to the adoption. First, miniaturization, innovation, and economies-of-scale make vast amounts of computational power available both

© The Author(s), under exclusive license to Springer Nature Switzerland AG 2023
N. A. Streitz and S. Konomi (Eds.): HCII 2023, LNCS 14036, pp. 378–389, 2023.
https://doi.org/10.1007/978-3-031-34668-2_25

in small form factors and at an affordable price. Second, ubiquitous access to fast internet and wireless/cellular services allows sharing of remote computational resources, offering opportunities for better utilization and enabling new usage models such as near real-time integration of supercomputing into fieldwork. Miniaturization, innovation, and economies-of-scale allowed transferring methodologies that used to require supercomputers and applying them to new problems outside the data center and at affordable costs. What used to be a supercomputer 40 years ago is routinely carried in our pockets as a smartphone. However, miniaturized computing platforms can not overcome all constraints to actual problem size, time to solution, or energy requirements. These constraints are largely lifted by ubiquitous access to fast internet that allows using of custom context as data input and returns the results of computations performed in the cloud or at an HPC site.

The technologies to democratize **access to platforms** exist today, but their adoption is progressing at different paces for different communities and regions. Access to compute and networking infrastructure alone is not sufficient; overcoming barriers to **access to data** and to the use of distributed systems are similarly crucial. While students today can reproduce many computations that made history, it can be not easy to find existing datasets [18, 25] and be able to process the retrieved data to answer scientific questions.

We argue that both finding data and using advanced computational methods, while associated with many technical challenges, today is also a challenge in making the proper application programming interfaces (API) available to the scientific community. A workflow to answer a seemingly simple research question may contain numerous tasks and process large amounts of data requiring a long time for the execution on a single computer. Modern data science libraries allow for hiding a lot of the complexity of scaling to additional resources. Still, the scientist must be comfortable navigating a fragmented landscape of computing providers, best practices, and technical jargon [19, 21, 22]. The navigation process can be a significant barrier for users whose priority is scientific discovery.

In this paper, we systematically analyze the development of two large-scale cyberinfrastructures (i.e., computing facilities and network infrastructure) and how the roll-out of network technologies, public clouds, and new models of providing access to compute resources allow a broader audience to leverage technologies that originated in HPC.

The contributions of this paper are:

- An analysis of compute capabilities over time about the capabilities in modern devices widely available today to understand the constraints for applications with and without remote compute capabilities.
- An analysis of the roll-out of different networking infrastructures with a special focus on the distribution and capabilities of research networks.
- A discussion of the combined perspective to better understand where efforts to improve the software ecosystem and aspects of human-computer interaction (HCI) provide an opportunity to help democratize access to platforms and data.

The remainder of this document is structured as follows: In Sect. 4, we discuss related work that also develops an overview of networking and computing research infrastructure. In Sect. 2, we consider the development and distribution of compute capabilities and relate them to applications and capabilities possible on current consumer electronics. In Sect. 3, we consider the development and distribution of national and education networks (NRENs) and other connecting nations, organizations, and individuals. We discuss and summarize the study's results in Sect. 5.

2 Development and Distribution of Compute Capabilities

We analyze the development and the geographic distribution of computing capabilities and break our analysis into two focus areas:

- The history of supercomputing and equivalent of computational power in different modern devices through seven eras characterized by the FLOPS ceiling Sect. 2.1 to understand the development of computational power in different platforms over time.
- The geographic distribution of computing and data resources to understand which regions have direct access and where centers of advanced computing innovation are located in Sect. 2.2.

2.1 Milestones and Eras of Computational Power

Computing power increased many orders of magnitude from hundreds of floating-point operations per second (FLOPS) available in the first computers to exaFLOPS (10^{18} FLOPS) in 2022 [10, 27]. Table 1 lists seven milestones or eras of computing in terms of FLOPS, each characterized by a three-order of magnitude increase in computing power. The table presents the first computer of a given era, the year the milestone was reached, and a modern-day equivalent that provides the same computing power where appropriate.

Miniaturization enabled by Moore's Law and Dennard Scaling [8] allows even standard consumer electronics to out-compete supercomputers from only a few decades ago. To put this into perspective, a low-cost microcontroller available since 2003 used by millions of hobbyists (e.g., Arduino Uno) routinely outperforms the leading supercomputer of 1954, just 49 years after it became the first computer of the kiloFLOPS era [15]. A high-end smartphone CPU from 2015 (e.g., Qualcomm Snapdragon 617) achieves 228.4 MFLOPS in LINPACK for Android just 39 years after supercomputers entered the 100+ MFLOP era. A Raspberry Pi 2 from 2015 is as powerful as a Cray2 that unlocked the GFLOPS era in 1985 [28]. A modern gaming console (e.g., the PlayStation 4), of which over a hundred million units were sold, through their graphic card features enough processing power to rival a supercomputer from the 1+ TFLOPS era [24]. Finally, modern Graphical Processing Units (GPUs) are beginning to rival systems in the 100+ TFLOPS era for single-precision workloads and even over 1+ PF in Tensor Performance (e.g., GeForce RTX 4090 with up to 82 TFLOPS) [20].

Table 1. History of computing systems passing significant milestones concerning the FLOPS achieved by supercomputers compared to modern devices integrating the same computational capabilities in a single device/package. The two modern systems marked with "*" denote that these devices surpass the TFLOPS and PFLOPS barriers for a more specialized operation only. This table is an adaption of [10] that was augmented with modern devices performance information from [15, 20, 24, 28].

FLOPS	Machine	Year	Speed	Same performance available in a ...
	ENIAC	1946	385 FLOPS	
kilo	IBM 704	1954	12 KFLOPS	2003 Low-Cost Microcontroller [15]
mega	IBM 360	1964	1 MFLOPS	
	CDC Cray-1	1976	160 MFLOPS	2015 Smartphone CPU [28]
giga	CDC Cray2	1985	1.9 GFLOPS	2015 Raspberry Pi 2 [28]
	Num. Wind Tunnel	1993	124.0 GFLOPS	2010 GPU (double-precision)
tera	ASCI Red	1997	1.1 TFLOPS	2013 Gaming Console (double-precision) [24]
	IBM Blue Gene/L	2006	136.8 TFLOPS	*2022 GPU (single-precision) [20]
peta	Roadrunner	2008	1.0 PFLOPS	*2022 GPU (tensor-performance) [20]
	Tienhe-2	2013	33.9 PFLOPS	–
	IBM Summit	2018	122.3 PFLOPS	–
	Fujitsu Fugaku	2020	442.0 PFLOPS	–
exa	ORNL Frontier	2022	1.102 EFLOPS	–

As these devices become more powerful and affordable, computing finds its way into more and more aspects of our daily lives for professional and recreational purposes. We now take many once-demanding computational applications, such as route planning, panorama stitching, or speech recognition, for granted to be available on a smartphone. At the same time, applications such as search services or speech recognition are often still augmented by network requests to cloud services for more sophisticated functionality. Notably, billions of people use these technologies without noticing the complex systems making this possible because many insights from human-computer interaction (HCI) are employed to make them as easy to use as possible and for non-technical users. *A consequential question is how can we help researchers, educators, and students to take advantage of this relative wealth of processing power for their research?*

2.2   Geographic Distribution of Supercomputers

Learning to use advanced computing systems requires practice and exposure to actual systems. For decades this required in-person access to a computing facility operated by the university or research institution. Today, most users of cloud and HPC systems never set foot anywhere near the facilities they are running their calculations. While geographic access has become less important to users due to high-speed internet from the direct user perspective, they remain relevant for research both from an operational and educational perspective. For operations, many tasks and processes triggered by users, such as data transfers, are constrained by the underlying physical network topology and geographic

(a) November 1993 - 100+ GFLOPS   (b) November 1997 - 1+ TFLOPS

(c) November 2006 - 100+ TFLOPS   (d) November 2008 - 1+ PFLOPS

(e) November 2018 - 100+ PFLOPS   (f) November 2022 - 1+ EFLOPS

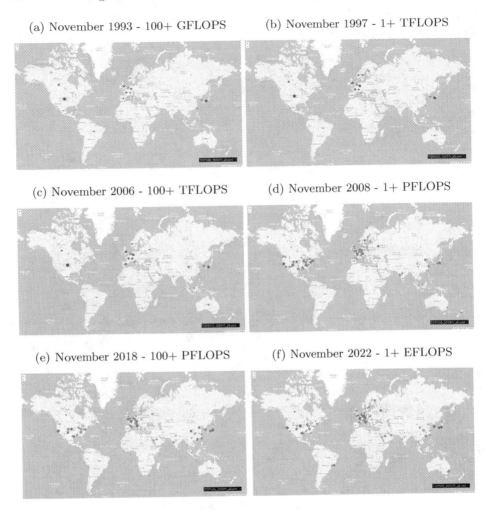

Fig. 1. Top500 Supercomputers plotted on the world map at the end of every year in which the fastest system surpassed one of the milestones denoting a new era: 100+ GFLOPS, 1+ TFLOPS, 100+ TFLOPS, 1+ PFLOPS, 100+ PFLOPS, 1+ EFLOPS. Figures: [17]

distribution. Similarly, research into improving these operations through better system architectures, scheduling, and data management is usually driven by exposure to an operational problem which appears to be also reflected in the authorship of publications related to such improvements.

For this reason, we want to understand the geographic distribution of super-computing resources better. Figure 1 plots the geographic distribution of the Top500 supercomputers over time for every year in which the fasted system on the list surpassed a critical milestone entering a new era between 1993 and 2022: 100+ GFLOPS, 1+ TFLOPS, 100+ TFLOPS, 1+ PFLOPS, 100+ PFLOPS, 1+

EFLOPS. The Top500 does not include all operating HPC systems but only lists the 500 fastest systems for which benchmark results were submitted. Interestingly, supercomputer adoption is spreading only relatively slowly to new regions. In the 1990s, most supercomputers were located in the US, Europe, and Japan, but in 1993 there were systems also in Brazil and Australia. In the 2000s, China and India start deploying more supercomputers. From 2007 going forward, the Top500 began to record city and country for most sites, with only some opting to remain anonymous. At the end of 2018 and 2022, 45.4% and 32.4%, respectively, of all the supercomputers were deployed in China, many of the systems were not resolved to a city. In Africa, only South Africa and Morocco ever appear on the list.

3   Development and Distribution of Networking Infrastructure

One of the enabling technologies to make advanced computing techniques available to off-site collaborators or research institutions is communication networks. We analyze how networking infrastructure's performance and geographic distribution evolved, how the increased connectivity provides opportunities for new supercomputing applications, and the democratization of access to platforms and data. Our analysis focuses on the following:

- An assessment of network topologies and capacities of different research and educational networks in the US (i.e., ESnet6, Internet2, and regional NRENs) and the state of high-speed internet coverage through broadband and mobile networks within the US.
- The comparison of the US-based network topologies and capacities to similar efforts in other regions (i.e., Africa, Asia, Europe, and South America).

Many networks report their link capacity in gigabits per second (Gbps) or short just G. We adopt the same convention and will use the shorthand unless it is ambiguous. Some networks do not explicitly report the link capacity but denote that two nodes are connected via "fiber." These links deploy so-called open-line fibers for which capacity is primarily constrained by the optical transmitter and receiver technologies, which can be continuously upgraded as better technologies or funding becomes available while not needing to change the fiber connecting two sites.

3.1   High-Speed Research and Education Networks in the US

ESNet. The Energy Sciences Network (ESnet) is among the world's fastest research networks. It was officially formed in 1986. Today ESnet6 connects most Department of Energy (DOE) facilities and other national and international research institutions (e.g., NASA, CERN). Figure 2b shows a topology including link capacities forming ESnet6. Most of the links in ESnet6 are equipped to provide 800G+ network capacity.

(a) Internet2 [16]   (b) ESnet6 [6]

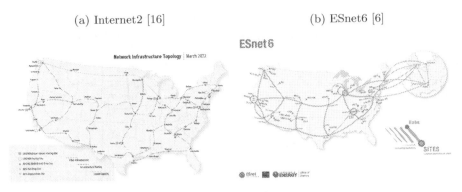

(c) Regional NRENs [1]

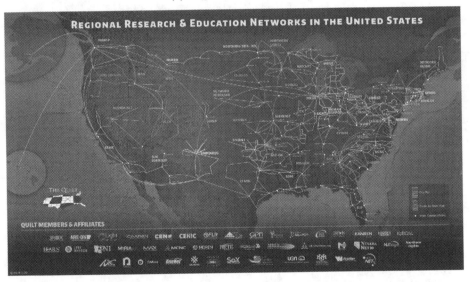

(d) Fixed Broadband [11]   (e) Mobile Internet [11]

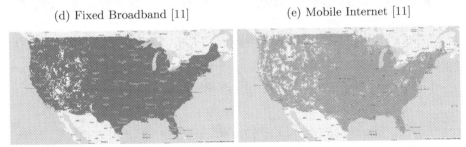

Fig. 2. Snapshot of topologies and coverage for different network and internet infrastructure in the US.

Internet2. Research and education communities, industry, and government members jointly lead the Internet2 non-profit networking consortium. First established in 1996, the project achieved 10 Gbit/s connectivity between over 230 member institutions in early 2004. Shortly after, the network was upgraded to 100 Gbit/s and today largely features a fiber network as illustrated in Fig. 2a showing the internet's topology, including the underlying link technologies.

Regional NRENs in the US. At the regional level, many states and universities in the US are invested in their own educational and research networks (NREN). Today most of these networks are part of the coalition for Advanced Regional Networking in Support of Research and Education (Quilt) [1]. Quilt currently lists 43 networks that connect over 900 universities as well as tens of thousands of other educational and community anchor institutions. Figure 2c shows the mesh of connections that span the US through regional NRENs. Unfortunately, the maps do only cover connectivity but not link capacities. Many of these NRENs are connected to Internet2, allowing them to accelerate long-distance transfers vastly.

Broadband and Mobile Networks. The widespread availability of high-speed broadband and mobile internet is also essential for field applications that integrate advanced computing. Figure 2d and Fig. 2e show the coverage for fixed broadband internet and mobile internet, respectively, as collected by the Federal Communications Commission (FCC) [11]. The coverage maps show that high-speed internet is widely available across the US via fixed broadband and cellular networks. This allows considering access to advanced computing methodologies not only for users with fixed internet connection but also enables many mobile applications. Examples of mobile applications that use supercomputing resources include integrating wildfire simulations into team-awareness tools available to firefighters [14].

3.2 GÉANT and Other International and Regional NRENs

Investments in networking infrastructure to connect advanced computing infrastructure and institutions are not limited to the US. Figure 3 shows the network topologies of similar efforts in other regions such as Europe, South-East Asia, South America, and Africa. The GEANT project, in succession to various earlier European efforts (EARN, EUNET, EuropaNET, TEN-34, TEN-155) to connect research institutions dating back to 1983, began in 2000 to build the Gigabit European Academic Network. In its current iteration, GEANT connects 44 national NRENs in Europe [12]. GEANT is connected to ESnet and Internet2, as well as many other regional NREN coalitions. Beginning in 2003, the RedCLARA network connects 15 countries in Latin America with direct connections to Internet2 [23]. Established in 2004, The Trans-Eurasia Information Network (TEIN) connects various institutions across 21 countries in Asia and is also connected to GEANT and Internet2 [26]. In Africa, multiple NREN coalitions coexist: The

(a) GÉANT in Europe [12]   (b) TEIN in Asia [26]

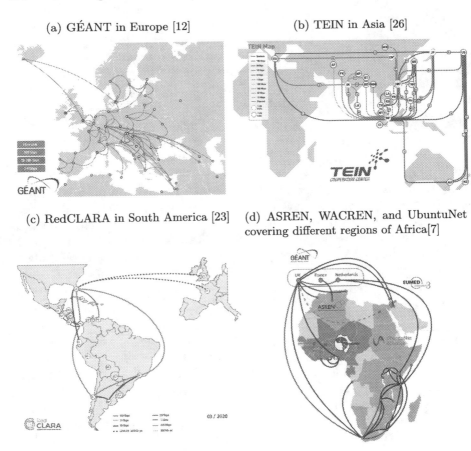

(c) RedCLARA in South America [23]   (d) ASREN, WACREN, and UbuntuNet covering different regions of Africa[7]

Fig. 3. Network topology of different NRENs or coalitions of NRENs in Africa, Asia, Europe, and South America. Figures are modifications of the originals to fit space and enhance contrast [7,12,23,26].

Arab States Research and Education Network (ASREN) connects 22 countries in Asia and North Africa. The West and Central African Research and Education Network (WACREN) connects 14 West and Central African countries. The UbuntuNet Alliance for Research and Education Networking (UbuntuNet) connects 17 countries in Eastern and Southern Africa. Each of the three networks is also connected to GEANT.

4   Related Work

Development and the assessment of access to computational resources and connectivity of research organizations have been subjected to extensive research and surveying activities [1,9,27] and annual assessments of, for example, funding agencies [2–5,13]. In the context of HPC, the Top500 list[1] started tracking the 500 fastest supercomputers since 1993 on a bi-yearly basis [27]. We take a closer look at the data provided by the Top500 but add the geographic perspective in Sect. 2.2 and analyze the development over time. For advanced communication and network infrastructure, most network providers and alliances provide current topology maps, including capacity information [1,6,12,16], but not in a standardized or machine-friendly format. For regional NRENs in the US, the Quilt[2] [1] is a coalition representing 43 educational networks across the United States. This effort also includes publishing up-to-date maps to visualize where research and education networks are deployed see Fig. 2c. While these efforts focus on specific categories of cyberinfrastructure, our work performs a combined analysis. It relates it to new opportunities in democratizing access to platforms and data and the role of human-computer interaction therein.

5   Lessons Learned

We analyzed the development of two important cyberinfrastructure (i.e., computing facilities and network infrastructure). We analyzed the computing capabilities of supercomputers over 7 decades and the geographic distribution of the Top500 over the last 3 decades. We also related the computing capability of past supercomputers to modern devices and consumer electronics ubiquitous today. The analysis shows that while we may have a relative wealth of computing power in comparison to previous decades, direct geographical access to supercomputing only slowly evolves and most new supercomputers replace already existing ones.

In a second analysis, we considered the network infrastructure connecting researchers worldwide. We observe that a hierarchy of networks connects research and education networks globally. While the US and the EU networks are accommodating more participants at high link speeds, research networks in Asia, South America, and Africa rapidly connected countries and institutes in the last 20 years. In the US the largest network capacity for research transfers is found in ESnet at 800+G which connects the DOE national labs and other large research facilities. At the regional level universities and states invested in local networking infrastructure. This mesh of regional research and education networks already ensures connectivity across institutions and universities but at potentially high latency and low bandwidth. Here cross-regional efforts such as Internet2 connect even geographically distant NRENs with low latency while reducing contention in local networks. Finally, we also considered the availability of broadband and mobile internet in the US. The analysis using FCC data suggests that internet coverage is available except for remote areas such as the mountains.

This analysis suggests that many of the technologies to democratize access to platforms and data are in place. Yet, our experience working with institutions, universities, domain scientists, and students tells us that adopting these technologies remains challenging for many. Continued investments into expanding

---

[1] https://www.top500.org/.
[2] https://www.thequilt.net/.

the physical infrastructure remain important, but if we want to empower more researchers to leverage advanced computing methodologies, it is absolutely necessary to also invest in the software stack so research can turn to a standard API to define their data dependencies allowing researchers to reclaim time spent on research while also giving cyberinfrastructure providers mechanisms to optimize.

Acknowledgment. This research was supported by the National Science Foundation (NSF) under grant numbers #1841758, #2028923, #2103845, and #2138811; the Advanced Cyberinfrastructure Coordination Ecosystem: Services and Support (ACCESS) program, under allocation TG-CIS210128; Chameleon Cloud under allocation CHI-210923; and IBM through a Shared University Research Award.

References

1. The Quilt - Advanced Regional Networking in Support of Research and Education. https://www.thequilt.net/
2. Scientific and Engineering Research Facilities: 1999. https://wayback.archive-it.org/5902/20150628160048/http://www.nsf.gov/statistics/nsf04334/pdfstart.htm
3. Scientific and Engineering Research Facilities: 2001. https://wayback.archive-it.org/5902/20150629121928/http://www.nsf.gov/statistics/nsf02307/sectb.htm
4. Scientific and Engineering Research Facilities at Colleges and Universities: 1998. https://wayback.archive-it.org/5902/20150627201815/http://www.nsf.gov/statistics/nsf01301/
5. Scientific and Engineering Research Facilities at Colleges and Universities: 1998 - Appendix E. https://wayback.archive-it.org/5902/20150629135427/http://www.nsf.gov/statistics/nsf01301/appe.htm
6. ESnet6 Maps (2022). https://www.es.net/welcome-esnet6/esnet6-maps/
7. Banda, T.: Research and Education Networks in Africa, August 2020
8. Bohr, M.: A 30 Year retrospective on Dennard's MOSFET scaling paper. IEEE Solid-State Circuits Soc. Newslett. **12**(1), 11–13 (2007). https://doi.org/10.1109/N-SSC.2007.4785534
9. Chalker, A., Hillegas, C.W., Sill, A., Broude Geva, S., Stewart, C.A.: Cloud and on-premises data center usage, expenditures, and approaches to return on investment: a survey of academic research computing organizations. In: Practice and Experience in Advanced Research Computing, pp. 26–33. ACM, Portland OR USA, July 2020. https://doi.org/10.1145/3311790.3396642
10. Chen, J., Ghafoor, S., Impagliazzo, J.: Producing competent HPC graduates. Commun. ACM **65**(12), 56–65 (2022). https://doi.org/10.1145/3538878
11. FCC: FCC National Broadband Map (2023). https://broadbandmap.fcc.gov/home
12. GEANT: GÉANT Connectivity Map (2023). https://map.geant.org/
13. Gibbons, M.: Computing and Networking Capacity Increases at Academic Research Institutions (2013)
14. Holland, T.M.: ATAK Improves Situational Awareness for California Fire Department. https://insights.samsung.com/2019/10/16/atak-improves-situational-awareness-for-california-fire-department/, October 2019
15. Ian: Answer to "How computationally powerful is an Arduino Uno board?", November 2012. https://robotics.stackexchange.com/a/538
16. Internet2: Operations and Support (2023). https://internet2.edu/network/operations-and-support/

17. Luettgau, J.: Maps of the Top500 Supercomputers over Time, November 2022. https://doi.org/10.5281/zenodo.7606369
18. Luettgau, J., Kirkpatrick, C.R., Scorzelli, G., Pascucci, V., Tarcea, G., Taufer, M.: NSDF-catalog: lightweight indexing service for democratizing data delivering. In: IEEE ACM International Conference on Utility and Cloud Computing (UCC2022) (2022)
19. Luettgau, J., Olaya, P., Zhou, N., Scorzelli, G., Pascucci, V., Taufer, M.: NSDF-Cloud: enabling ad-hoc compute clusters across academic and commercial clouds. In: Proceedings of the 31st International Symposium on High-Performance Parallel and Distributed Computing, pp. 279–280. ACM, Minneapolis MN USA, June 2022. https://doi.org/10.1145/3502181.3533710
20. NVIDIA: ADA GPU Architecture V1.01 (2022). https://images.nvidia.com/aem-dam/Solutions/geforce/ada/nvidia-ada-gpu-architecture.pdf
21. Olaya, P., et al.: Building trust in earth science findings through data traceability and results explainability. IEEE Trans. Parallel Distrib. Syst. **34**(2), 704–717 (2023). https://doi.org/10.1109/TPDS.2022.3220539
22. Olaya, P., et al.: NSDF-FUSE: a testbed for studying object storage via FUSE file systems. In: Proceedings of the 31st International Symposium on High-Performance Parallel and Distributed Computing, pp. 277–278. ACM, Minneapolis MN USA, Jun 2022. https://doi.org/10.1145/3502181.3533709
23. RedCLARA: Network Maps, Mar 2020. https://www.redclara.net/index.php/en/recursos/publicaciones-para-difusion/mapas-de-la-red
24. Sony Entertainment: Announcement of the Playstation 4, April 2013. https://web.archive.org/web/20130424075309/http://scei.co.jp/corporate/release/130221a_e.html
25. Tarcea, G., et al.: The materials commons data repository. In: 2022 IEEE 18th International Conference on E-Science (e-Science), Salt Lake City, UT, USA, pp. 405–406. IEEE, October 2022. https://doi.org/10.1109/eScience55777.2022.00060
26. TEIN: Network Maps (2020). https://www.tein.asia/sub/?mc=2030
27. Top500: Top500 Supercomputing Sites (2019). http://www.top500.org/
28. Vince Weaver: The GFLOPS/W of the various machines in the VMW Research Group (2023). https://web.eece.maine.edu/vweaver/group/green_machines.html

Understanding Regional Characteristics Through EC Data Analysis

Kohei Yamaguchi[1]([✉]), Kazuyuki Shoji[1], Naoki Tamura[1], Namiki Sakakura[1],
Yuki Matsukura[2], Yu Hiranaga[2], Kohei Shimomura[2], Kenta Urano[1][ID],
Takuro Yonezawa[1][ID], and Nobuo Kawaguchi[1,3][ID]

[1] Nagoya University, Furo-cho Chikusa-ku Nagoya 464-8601, Japan
kohei@ucl.nuee.nagoya-u.ac.jp
[2] Minedia, Inc., Tokyo, Japan
[3] Institutes of Innovation for Future Society, Nagoya University, Nagoya, Japan
https://corporate.minedia.com/en

Abstract. The COVID-19 pandemic, which began in 2020, has changed people's lives, and people are shopping more online. While the analysis of online shopping is becoming increasingly important, regional differences in consumption trends exist. This study proposes a data-driven regional modeling method based on EC purchase data to examine the regional characteristics of online shopping purchase trends. Using the proposed method, we quantified and visualized the degree of similarity of consumption trends among regions and the degree of dispersion of consumption trends within regions using approximately 300,000 lines of online shopping history for 3 years in Japan. As a result, we found that there was some disruption in the early stages of e-commerce for food products by region, while there was little difference in consumption trends among regions for daily necessities. In addition, for consumer durables and clothing, regional differences in consumption trends were confirmed in terms of the number of cars owned per capita, urbanization status, and other regional characteristics.

Keywords: EC data · COVID-19 · regional purchasing characteristics

1 Introduction

The COVID-19 pandemic, which has been ongoing since 2020, has placed significant restrictions on people's behavior, forcing them to live differently than before. Behavioral changes, such as avoiding crowds and refraining from going out, wearing masks, and not staying in enclosed spaces, have affected economic activity, with unemployment, consumer spending, and business inventories in 2020 affected more severely than the global financial crisis [6]. Economic uncertainty on par with the Great Depression has also been reported [2]. On the other hand, online shopping was one of the marketing areas that developed during the COVID-19 pandemic. The volume of online shopping transactions has increased over the years, with a particularly marked increase observed in the COVID-19 pandemic [9]. This is due to people avoiding face-to-face encounters with an indefinite number of people. Although online shopping is not replacing all retailing at the moment, the increasing share of e-commerce to all shopping is making an irreversible change in society. E-Commerce markets are becoming increasingly important in marketing strategies.

On e-commerce sites, users can browse all products regardless of geographic conditions, but there are global differences in users' propensity to purchase products by geographic location. For example, geographic characteristics such as access to physical stores, nearby traffic, distance from urban centers [3], and residential density [4] affect the amount of online shopping and the types of products purchased. There are also various seasonal factors such as season and weather, as well as changes in EC purchasing behavior due to the spread of infectious diseases and economic difficulties, as seen in COVID-19. Age and occupational status affect trends in EC use [13], and it has also been suggested that the COVID-19 pandemic may have led to new acceptance of online shopping [5].

Thus, efficient marketing and support can be provided to regions with different purchasing trends if promotions can be tailored to those regions and if responses can be tailored to local reactions to events such as infectious diseases, disasters, snowfall, and sales. For example, when advertising products on the web, it would be possible to improve marketing efficiency by targeting advertisements to areas where there are many residents who are more likely to purchase the products. In this context, we have developed a system to detect the regional purchasing trends. Therefore, in order to understand reginal purchasing trends, the objective of this study is to verify whether there are regional differences in purchasing trends for each genre of products.

Modeling of regional purchasing trends require a data-driven approach that does not use a priori decision-making or other modeling to reflect purchasing behavior that shifts from day to day. To achieve this, this paper proposes Area2Vec based on Shopping Data (Area2Vec-bSD). Area2Vec-bSD is a method that uses the structure of Word2Vec in natural language processing, and through learning, obtains distributed representations that embed information on purchases made in each area. Using the distributed representations obtained by the proposed method, we calculate the similarity of purchasing trends at the region level and analyze the variation of distributed representations within a region. In this study, the target region is Japan, and we capture regional online shopping purchasing trends in product genres such as foods and durable consumer goods. The results confirm that while purchasing trends for daily necessities were similar across the country before and after the COVID-19 pandemic, purchasing trends for food and clothing varied across regions. For durable consumer goods and clothing, some regions had similar purchasing trends within regions while others did not, i.e., some regions had strong and others had weak regional purchasing trends. The contributions of this study are as follows.

– A data-driven area characterization method using purchase information is proposed.

- Regional online shopping trends in Japan is revealed.
- We quantified the diversity of state-wide purchasing trends across product genres.

2   Related Works

2.1   Spatial Distribution Analysis of EC

The relationship between online shopping and real-space purchasing has been discussed since the early 2000s [1]. In the early days, two hypotheses were proposed: the diffusion of innovation hypothesis and the efficiency hypothesis. The former hypothesis explains the diffusion of innovation mainly in urban areas, where fashion-conscious residents spontaneously use innovative technologies. The latter hypothesis, on the other hand, explains the diffusion of technology away from urban areas as a result of the search for efficiency. These hypotheses have been tested with the spread of the Internet and online shopping [3,4]. Even now that online shopping has become widespread, the innovation diffusion hypothesis is still supported by the fact that more online purchases of clothing are made in urban centers [7]. However, these results are based on urban-rural land divisions, and no comparison of purchase trends or discovery of similar regions has been made.

2.2   Temporal Changes in EC

Temporal changes in EC are mentioned in the context of forecasting sales and improving the efficiency of delivery arrangements. Examples of those dealing with temporal variation include those that investigated purchasing decisions during major online sales [12] and those that proposed models that take into account changes in the number of orders due to weather conditions [11]. These model the impact of the above factors on people's everyday online shopping decisions. On the other hand, there has also been a lot of analysis of the impact of the propagation of COVID-19, in which all behaviors, including purchasing, have changed. Households in areas where regular delivery services were available and with sufficient income were more likely to use online shopping after the pandemic, while households that had used it several times a month before were predicted to return to their original levels after the pandemic [13]. As described above, while there has been some analysis of changes in online shopping over time, particularly during the COVID-19 pandemic, few consider geographic factors and none discuss the regional nature of purchasing trends.

2.3   Word2Vec-Based Area Modeling

On the other hand, there are studies that represent areas as vectors and model them in a form that is easy to interpret. Most of them mainly use movement trajectories. Examples of studies based on the Word2Vec structure include: modeling an area in terms of the way it is used, using GPS data to obtain stay information such as the time when the stay started and the time spent in the area

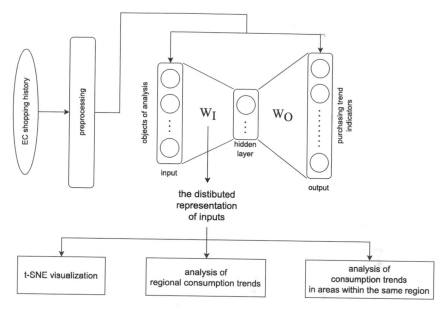

Fig. 1. The overview of proposed model.

[10]; estimating land use using the trajectory of taxi location information [14]; and geographically and semantically modeling the relationship between various POIs (Point of Interest) [15]. The advantages of using the Word2Vec structure are that it can be embedded in a lower dimension while maintaining the information that the data has, such as POI information, stay information, or movement transitions, and that it is possible to calculate similarity and perform operations between distributed representations. On the other hand, these mainly use only location data, and there are none that handle purchasing information.

3   Methodology

3.1   Overview

We propose Area2Vec based on Shopping Data (Area2Vec-bSD), a method for modeling purchasing trends based on consumption trends. Area2Vec-bSD uses the structure of Word2Vec, a vector embedding method for words in natural language processing, to represent regions as distributed representations. Figure 1 is an overall view of proposed method. The input to the network is the target to be analyzed, often a geographic feature, and the output is an index representing purchasing behavior. After training the network, each row of weights in the first layer of the network becomes a distributed representation of the purchasing behavior of the analyzed target. The resulting distributed representations are visualized in t-SNE. The distributed representations of regions are calculated from the distributed representations of the areas that constitute each region, and the similarity of purchasing tendencies for each region is quantified and analyzed as cosine similarity. The variance of the distributed representation is also defined and analyzed for areas within the same region in order to quantify the differences in their purchasing propensities.

3.2   Area2Vec-bSD

Area2Vec-bSD is a method for modeling local consumption trends based on location-linked purchase information. A schematic diagram of the model is shown in the upper part of Fig. 1. The proposed method was inspired by Area2Vec [10], a method proposed by Shoji et al. for modeling local usage based on users' stay information. Area2Vec is a method that uses the structure of Word2Vec, one of the word embedding methods in natural language processing. In Area2Vec, instead of one-hot vectors of words, one-hot vectors corresponding to area IDs are used on the input side and discretized stay information processed into one-hot vectors is used on the output side. In contrast, the proposed method uses a one-hot vector corresponding to the ID of the area where the purchase was made as an input, and a one-hot vector indicating the purchase information processed according to the task as an output. When modeling the time at which purchases occur, the time information should be included in the one-hot vector on the output side, and when modeling by purchase trends of product genres, the genre information should be included in the one-hot vector on the output side. Learning is performed as in the skip-gram method, which is one of the architectures of Word2Vec. After learning, the weights of each row of the embedding layer on the input side become distributed representations according to the area. The definition of an area is defined by the spatial granularity of the data. In the experiments described in Chap. 4 of this paper, the unit of area is the largest administrative division in Japan, but it is also possible to analyze more detailed areas. One advantage of this method is that areas can be represented as vectors that take their characteristics into account. The information can be embedded in a low-dimensional vector while preserving the information, and it is easy to calculate similarities and distributed representations.

3.3   Methods for Analyzing Regional Differences

A region is defined as a group of geographically or culturally similar areas composed of one or more. Similar to the way Word2Vec represents a sentence as a distributed representation by the average of words, we define the distributed representation of a region as the average of the those of the areas that constitute the region. Based on the hypothesis that the more similar the distributed representations between regions are, the more similar the purchasing tendencies of the regions are, we analyze the similarity of purchasing tendencies between regions. Furthermore, we will focus on the purchasing tendencies among the areas that constitute a region. Let the distributed representation of an area be an N-dimensional vector

$$\boldsymbol{v} = \{v_1, ..., v_N\} \in \mathbb{R}^N,$$

Table 1. Columns of the dataset.

column names	detail
DATE	purchased date (YYYY-MM-DD)
EC SITE CODE	the EC site used
STATE	the user's prefecture of residence
JICFS CATEGORY CODE PREFIX	the large categories of products
GENDER	user's gender
GENERATION	user's generation
COUNT NUMBER OF ITEMS	the number of items purchased
SUM PRICE ITEMS AMOUNT	purchase price
PRICE CURRENCY	the currency used

and let $D = \{v_1, ..., v_m\}$ be the set of distributed representations of the areas that make up the region. Sum of variances in each dimension

$$var = \sum_{i \in N} \left(\frac{1}{m} \sum_{v_j \in D} (v_j - \mu_i)^2 \right)$$

be the variance of the distributed representations, where mu_i is the average in dimension i. The greater the value of the variance of this distributed representations, the less similar the purchasing tendencies are, and thus quantifies the differences in purchasing tendencies among areas. This is equal to $tr(\Sigma)$ when the variance-covariance matrix is Σ, and is called the total variance.

4   Experiment

4.1   Dataset

The data consisted of three years and 292,344 lines of Japanese online shopping history obtained by mail scraping. Four Japanese e-commerce sites were targeted. The columns are as shown in Table 1. Each row records the attributes of the user and the genre of the purchased product, but no personally identifiable information, such as the user's ID, is assigned to protect personal information. In addition, information on the user's prefecture of residence (the largest administrative division in Japan) is also recorded as location information. The JICFS CATEGORY CODE PREFIX in Table 1 is the upper two digits of the classification code of the product in Japan. Table 2 shows the details.

Data Collecting. The scraping targets are users of Pint (https://lp.pint-app.com/), a service provided by minedia, Inc. This is a service that collects data in exchange for incentives in the form of point rewards for online shopping. The target e-commerce sites are Rakuten Ichiba, Yahoo! Shopping, LOHACO, and ZOZOTOWN, which are major e-commerce sites in Japan. As a preprocessing step, purchase histories with unknown prefecture or JICFS code are excluded.

Table 2. List of the first two digits of the JICFS category code.

the large categories		the medium categories	
1	foods	1	processed foods
		2	perishable foods
		3	confectionery
		4	beverages and liquors
		9	other foods
2	daily necessities	1	miscellaneous daily necessities
		2	OTC medicines
		3	cosmetics
		4	housewares
		5	DIY products
		6	pet supplies
		9	other daily necessities
3	cultural products	1	stationery & office supplies
		2	toys
		3	books
		4	musical instruments & audio software
		6	information devices & softwares
		9	other cultural products
4	durable consumer goods	2	furniture
		3	vehicle supplies
		4	watches & glasses
		5	optical & photographic products
		6	consumer electronics
		9	other durable consumer goods
5	clothing	1	clothing
		3	bedding
		4	personal effects
		5	shoes & footwear
		6	sporting goods
9	other products	9	other products

The data period is 2019, 2020, and 2021, with approximately 300,000 lines, 4 million total purchases, and 10 billion yen in total purchases. Of this total, 3.2 million items were purchased by Rakuten Ichiba and the total purchase amount was 9 billion yen, so the data set is heavily influenced by Rakuten Ichiba. Table 3 shows the number of items purchased and the value of purchases for each category and their percentage of the total.

4.2   Experimental Method

To verify whether there are regional differences in purchase tendencies for each genre of products, the proposed method is used to learn distributed representations of areas. In view of the amount of data in Table 3, the genres targeted in

Table 3. The number of purchases/purchase amount of each JICFS genre.

JICFS genre	the number of purchases	purchase amount [yen]
1x: foods	1,490,461	3,137,672,898
2x: daily necessities	1,625,891	3,217,824,114
3x: cultural products	86,395	297,684,494
4x: durable consumer goods	449,519	2,639,695,744
5x: clothing	438,159	1,095,618,044
9x: other products	157,277	294,409,552

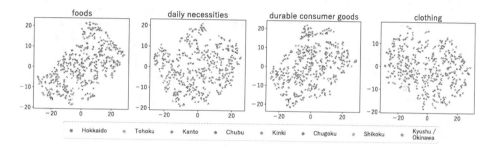

Fig. 2. T-SNE visualization of distributed representations.

the experiment were food, daily necessities, durable consumer goods, and cloth-ing. The Area2Vec-bSD input is the prefectures in Japan, considering the spatial granularity of the dataset, with three seasonal indices (winter, spring, and sum-mer) for one prefecture in each year. That is, each prefecture has 9 distributed representations, such as winter 2019, spring 2020, and summer 2021. The output is the medium categories in Table 2, and The distributed representation is trained for each genre. The one-hot vector described above was generated for each row of the dataset, and the input-output pairs were added to the training data for the number of purchases. Hence, the distributed representations obtained from this training are expected to be embedded with information on the purchase tenden-cies of the JICFS middle category and the quantity of products purchased in a given prefecture, season, and year. The dimension of the hidden layer was set to 4 dimensions. Therefore, the dimension of the distributed representation is also 4-dimensional. Adam was used as the optimizer, and the learning rate was set to 0.001, beta to 0.9 and 0.999. The number of learning epochs was set to 200.

4.3 Result

The obtained distributed representation was visualized for each genre using t-SNE [8], which is a method of dimensionality reduction keeping point maldis-tribution and is used for the visualization. The results are shown in Fig. 2, with each region colored. Note that each region consists of one or more prefectures, and that a prefecture has a total of nine distributed representations, three years and three seasonal divisions.

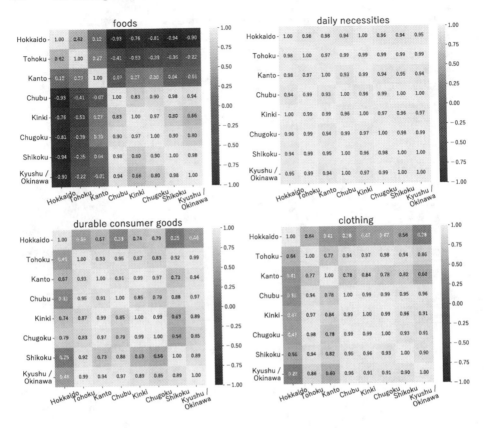

Fig. 3. Cosine similarity between regions.

Similarity Between Regions. We present results on the similarity of purchasing propensities among regions. For the regions, we used the eight regional divisions, which are often viewed as geographically and administratively homogeneous. The sum of all distributed representations for the prefectures that constitute a region was used as the distributed representation for the region, and the results of calculating the cosine similarity between the regions are shown in Fig. 3. Foods were identified in the Hokkaido-Tohoku, Kanto, and the rest of the groups. The Hokkaido-Tohoku group, especially pronounced for these two regions, both of which are located in the north, showed a completely different consumption trend from the other regions, as the cosine similarity with the other areas was negative. Daily necessities, on the other hand, were similar in all regions, with a cosine similarity of no less than 0.9. This means that the purchase trend is uniform regardless of the region. Durable consumer goods differed significantly between Hokkaido and Shikoku. Clothing was categorized into Hokkaido, Kanto, and other regions. Kyushu/Okinawa, which is located in the southern part of Japan, showed relatively low similarity to other regions.

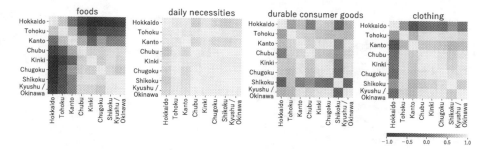

Fig. 4. Cosine similarity between regions in 2019.

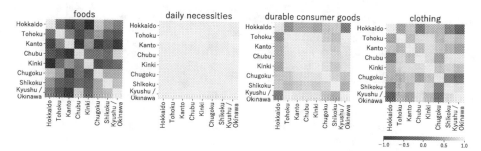

Fig. 5. Cosine similarity between regions in 2020.

In order to visualize the impact of the COVID-19 pandemic, we also analyze the distributed representation of regions in 2019 and 2020. Figure 4 shows the results in 2019 and Fig. 5 shows the results in 2020. Foods in 2019 are divided into Hokkaido-Tohoku, Tohoku-Kanto, and other groups. The Tohoku region is somewhat similar to both Hokkaido and Kanto, while the Hokkaido-Kanto region is less similar. On the other hand, food in 2020 is not very similar in all regions, with only Hokkaido-Chugoku and Chubu-Kyushu/Okinawa being above 0.75. Daily necessities were similar in all regions in both 2019 and 2020, but some areas were less similar to other regions in 2019. In 2019, Hokkaido and Shikoku had low similarity in durable consumer goods, while Kanto - Kinki - Chugoku - Kyushu/Okinawa had very high similarity. Similarity between Hokkaido and other regions was low in 2020 as well. For clothing in 2019, Hokkaido had low similarity to other regions, and Kanto and Shikoku also had relatively low similarity. Conversely, the similarity between Hokkaido and other regions was high. In 2020, Hokkaido and Chugoku had low similarity, while the Chubu-Shikoku-Kyushu/Okinawa region had a high similarity. As described above, the distributed representation of regions allowed us to confirm the similarity of purchasing trends among regions.

Dispersion Within a Region. Next, we investigate the distribution of distributed representation for the prefectures. Here, as shown in Fig. 6, we observed that the norm of distributed representation tended to be larger as the number of purchases was smaller. Since the variance of the distributed representation is

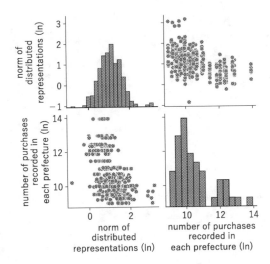

Fig. 6. Figure showing the relationship between the norm of the distributed representations and the number of purchases recorded in each prefecture. The upper left and the lower right are histograms of the norm and the number of purchases, respectively; the others are scatter plots with two variables.

calculated using Euclidean distance, distributed representations with disparate magnitude may not accurately capture the variation in purchasing trends. Therefore, from now on, the distributed representation is normalized so that its norm is 1. Figure 7 visualizes the distributed representations of each of the prefectures studied in terms of their propensity to purchase durable consumer goods, using t-SNE. Some regions, such as Shikoku, were skewed to the right, while others, such as Chubu, were found to be clustered in several groups. Thus, it was confirmed that the variation in distributed representations, and therefore the variation in purchase propensity, differed by region.

The variance of distributed representations by genre is shown in Fig. 8. Distributed representations for all prefectures within a region were used, regardless of year or season. The dispersion of food was very high in all regions except Hokkaido, suggesting that the purchasing trends were very different even within the same region. Conversely, the dispersion of daily necessities was low in all regions. This is supported by the high degree of similarity among regions. The dispersion of durable consumer goods and clothing was different among the regions. This implies that there are regions with strong and weak purchasing tendencies.

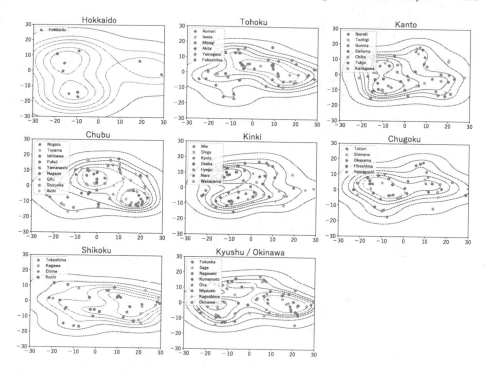

Fig. 7. T-SNE visualization of distributed representations of durable consumer goods in each region with kernel density estimation.

5   Discussion

5.1   Similarity Between Regions

In Fig. 3, Hokkaido had low similarity to other regions in many genres. This is partly due to the fact that Hokkaido is located at the northern part of Japan and is separated from the other regions by the sea. On the other hand, food and clothing products were relatively similar to those of Tohoku, which is geographically close to Hokkaido. The geographic proximity may have resulted in similar temperatures, climates, and delivery costs, which may have led to similar purchasing patterns. Kanto also had low similarity in foods and clothing. Kanto is a region with a huge metropolitan area, well-developed transportation networks, and can access to the sea, which means that Kanto is a region with a wide variety of food products. In terms of clothing, more people in urban areas purchase clothing online, and given that online shopping for clothing is still in a transitional stage, we conclude that the purchasing trends in the Kanto, with its large population, differ from those in the other regions.

Figs. 4 and 5 show that food and clothing were less similar in 2020 than in 2019, indicating that there was some confusion in online shopping. While food is a genre that has seen slow progress in e-commerce due to factors such as not

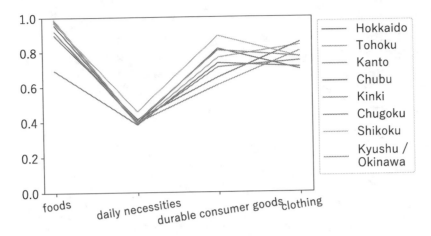

Fig. 8. Dispersion by region in each product category.

being able to see the actual product on e-commerce and the already existing supermarkets playing a sufficient role, the COVID-19 pandemic has also led to a gradual shift to food e-commerce as a result of people avoiding trips to nearby stores [9]. Since the impact of the COVID-19 pandemic varies by area, it is likely that the use of EC to buy food and clothing, which are often actually picked up and examined, will vary by area. In other words, these are the genres in which regional differences in changes in purchasing trends were observed.

Note that in this experiment, the distributed representation of a region is the average of the distributed representations of the prefectures constituting the region, but this is debatable. As shown in Fig. 6, the norm of the distributed representation varies with the amount of data, and may not accurately represent the distributed representation of a region. Other methods other than the average include a weighted average using the percentage of purchases within a region as a weight, taking the average of angles with the norm fixed at 1, or adding indexes of regions and learning the distributed representation in the same way as for that of areas. Verification of these methods will be the subject of future work.

5.2   Dispersion Within a Region

Fig. 8 shows that the dispersion of foods was large in all regions. As mentioned earlier, foods are a genre that is in the transitional stage of EC, and the COVID-19 pandemic may have resulted in areas where EC was promoted and areas where it was not promoted as much, leading to a large dispersion even within a region. On the other hand, when the similarity of daily necessities by region (Fig. 3) is taken into account, it is clear that the same purchasing trends are observed in all prefectures. This indicates that the purchase trend is uniform regardless of area, even for new EC users. Durable consumer goods and clothing were the two genres for which purchase trends varied by region. As for durable consumer goods, those without cars are likely to have to rely on online shopping for furniture and electronics in many cases. Clothing was another genre that varied within regions, depending on the impact of the COVID-19 pandemic and the degree of popularity of online shopping. In other words, the two genres are genres in which purchasing trends varied by area, and we believe that this affected the degree of variation in the size of the dispersion.

6   Conclusion

Online shopping is one of the industries currently gaining strength and is becoming increasingly important through the COVID-19 pandemic that will continue in 2020. Therefore, analysis of online consumption trends is essential; however, regional differences in online shopping exist. In this paper, we propose a data-driven area characterization method using purchase information to reveal area differences in online consumption trends. The proposed method is based on the Word2Vec structure used in natural language processing, and represents an area as a distributed representation embedded with the purchasing trends made there. The proposed method reveals regional differences in EC usage tendencies in Japan. While purchase tendencies for daily necessities were similar in all areas, regional differences in purchase tendencies for durable consumer goods and clothing were observed depending on the characteristics of the area, suggesting that simple geographical proximity may not affect purchase tendencies. In addition, the increase in the volume of e-commerce of foods due to the COVID-19 pandemic changed purchasing patterns in many areas.

On the other hand, there is still room for discussion in this study, including the definition of a distributed representation of a region, the validation of a measure of the variability of distributed representation, the bias of the data set, and the impact of a sale. Moreover, although this study used only purchase information tied to location information to characterize areas, we expect that more valuable modeling can be achieved by considering information on purchasing behavior in real space, consumer decision making, and interactions at e-commerce sites. Comparison of the results obtained in this study with actual changes is also an issue to be addressed in the future.

Acknowledge. This research is partially supported by JST CREST(JPMJCR1882, JPMJCR22M4), and NICT(222C0101).

References

1. Anderson, W.P., Chatterjee, L.R., Lakshmanan, T.R.: E-commerce, transportation, and economic geography. Growth Chang. **34**, 415–432 (2003)
2. Baker, S.R., Bloom, N., Davis, S.J., Terry, S.J.: Covid-induced economic uncertainty. Macroeconomics eJournal, Econometric Modeling (2020)
3. Cao, X.J., Chen, Q., Choo, S.: Geographic distribution of e-shopping: Application of structural equation models in the twin cities of minnesota. Transp. Res. Rec. **2383**(1), 18–26 (2013). https://doi.org/10.3141/2383-03

4. Farag, S., Weltevreden, J.W.J., van Rietbergen, T., Dijst, M., van Oort, F.G.: E-shopping in the netherlands: Does geography matter? Environ. Plann. B. Plann. Des. **33**, 59–74 (2006)

5. Jain, A.V.: "covid-19 & consumers: An empirical study on the impact of covid-19 pandemic on consumer's buying behavior towards online shopping in rajasthan -permanent or transient?" (2021)

6. Li, Z., Farmanesh, P., Kırıkkaleli, D., Itani, R.: A comparative analysis of covid-19 and global financial crises: evidence from us economy. Economic Research-Ekonomska Istraživanja **35**, 2427–2441 (2021)

7. Maat, K., Konings, R.: Accessibility or innovation? Store shopping trips versus online shopping. Transp. Res. Rec. **2672**, 1–10 (2018)

8. van der Maaten, L., Hinton, G.E.: Visualizing data using t-sne. J. Mach. Learn. Res. **9**, 2579–2605 (2008)

9. Ministry of Economy, Trade and Industry: Results of fy2021 e-commerce market survey compiled, August 2022. https://www.meti.go.jp/english/press/2022/0812_002.html

10. Shoji, K., Aoki, S., Yonezawa, T., Kawaguchi, N.: Area modeling using stay information for large-scale users and analysis for influence of covid-19. IPSJ J. **62**(10), 1644–1657 (2021)

11. Steinker, S., Hoberg, K., Thonemann, U.W.: The value of weather information for e-commerce operations. Prod. Oper. Manag. **26**, 1854–1874 (2017)

12. Swilley, E., Goldsmith, R.E.: Black Friday and cyber Monday: understanding consumer intentions on two major shopping days. J. Retail. Consum. Serv. **20**, 43–50 (2013)

13. Unnikrishnan, A., Figliozzi, M.A.: Exploratory analysis of factors affecting levels of home deliveries before, during, and post- covid-19. Transp. Res. Interdiscipl. Perspect. **10**, 100402–100402 (2021)

14. Yao, Z., Fu, Y., Liu, B., Hu, W., Xiong, H.: Representing urban functions through zone embedding with human mobility patterns. In: Proceedings of the Twenty-Seventh International Joint Conference on Artificial Intelligence, IJCAI-18, pp. 3919–3925. International Joint Conferences on Artificial Intelligence Organization, July 2018. https://doi.org/10.24963/ijcai.2018/545

15. Yuan, J., Zheng, Y., Xie, X.: Discovering regions of different functions in a city using human mobility and pois. In: Proceedings of the 18th ACM SIGKDD International Conference on Knowledge Discovery and Data Mining, KDD 2012, New York, NY, USA, pp. 186–194. Association for Computing Machinery (2012). https://doi.org/10.1145/2339530.2339561

Author Index

N. A. Streitz and S. Konomi (Eds.): HCII 2023, LNCS 14036, pp. 405–407, 2023.
https://doi.org/10.1007/978-3-031-34668-2